J. S. MAYR

Father
of
19th century Italian Music

Johann Simon Mayr (1763 - 1845)

J. S. MAYR

Father
of
19th century Italian Music

by
John Stewart Allitt

ELEMENT BOOKS

First published in 1989 by
Element Books Limited
Longmead, Shaftesbury, Dorset

Typeset in 10/11 pt Times
Printed and bound in Germany
Designed by Siemens-Druckerei, Munich
Cover design by Siemens-Druckerei, Munich
Cover illustration: The Mayr + Donizetti Collaboration.

British Library Cataloguing in Publication Data

Allitt, John Stewart
  J. S. Mayr: father of 19th Italian century music.
  1. Opera in Italian. Mayr, Johannes Simon 1736-1845
  I. Title
  782.1'092'4

ISBN 1-85230-126-0

This book was published with the kind assistance of Siemens AG,
Berlin and Munich.

Musicam docet Amor.

(The Symposium - Plato)

Ritrovatore di soavi numeri.

(From the inscription for Mayr's
funeral, 1845, on the South door of
S. Maria Maggiore, Bergamo.)

Confess that wise ignorance which
when it exists has true science as
its fruit.

(The Notebooks - Mayr.)

Contemplare et contemplata aliis tradere.

(St Dominic)

This study is dedicated
to all those who find joy and strength
in Mayr's music and thought.

My aim is to evoke Mayr's life,
work and significance. Since there
remains so much work to be done in dis-
covering, editing and reviving Mayr's
work, I see my efforts rather like scaf-
folding which one day, soon I hope, will
be cast down for Mayr to stand in his
own right. I have sought to convey an
overall grasp rather than be caught by
details. (Also I am reluctant to write
about music I have not heard.)

J. S. A.

Contents

The Proper of the Mass

The Common of the Mass

Vespers

Requiem Mass

Preface

Long before there was a revival of interest in Donizetti, the sounds from a few battered and scratchy 78 rpm discs deeply moved me. I knew only *Lucia di Lammermoor, Don Pasquale*, extracts from *La favorite* and *L'elisir d'amore*, odd arias and scenes, and a beautiful string quartet on a German HMV Label. These records were a source of joy; they convinced me of beauty as a property which could be experienced within the beholder. Sometime after 1948 my father gave me Zavadini's fundamental volume and Barblan's committed re-appraisal of Donizetti. One realized just how much was yet to be known. My knowledge of Italian was given a boost, struggling with Barblan's prose, Donizetti's letters and the verses of librettos.

There came a time when it was not enough to listen to records - the question was asked: "Why, why does this apparently simple music move me as much as that of Bach, Mozart or Beethoven?" "Why does this music convey an appreciation of Beauty?" "Why does it carry with it what can only be termed a spiritual force?" Of course, I was soon to learn that few people appreciated Donizetti and even those who did so, for the greater part, seemed to know and hear a different composer than the one I loved. My questioning led to a thorough reading of Donizetti's letters. The task revealed the quality of those written to his teacher, Simon Mayr. These displayed genuine affectionate and thankful love for the man to whom he owed not only his career, but, more important, his knowledge of music. Donizetti's letters to Mayr may be argued to be his finest. It is to be regretted that the master's letters to his pupil have been lost except for those published by Zavadini. If the music of Donizetti was hardly known in those days that of Mayr was totally unknown.

But it became clear that the answers to my questions lay in this shadowy German composer who had formed a charity school for paupers. The beauty known in Donizetti's art had to have its roots in this man to whom the pupil said he was "eternally grateful". There was something more than just the music; it was clear that the Bergamasque composer owed a lion's share to his schooling.

Certain stained glass windows in Chartres Cathedral show the Apostles carried on the shoulders of the Prophets, indicating the bond that exists in true creativity between the old and the new. There was no doubt in my mind. Donizetti too was carried shoulder high by Mayr. Judging by the letters, he would have been the first to say so, adding that he had never surpassed Mayr's *Medea in Corinto* and that Mayr was to him a second father.[1]

Any student of Donizetti will know the role played by fate and destiny in the stories of tragic operas. There was a strange twist in the game of my own life when a Bergamasque

---

1   Z.31, see Zavadini, - *vita, musiche, epistolario*, Bergamo 1948

priest, Don Luigi Cortese in, I think, 1972, asked me to revive Mayr's opera, *L'amor con-iugale*. At the time, I thought he was joking because I had no knowledge of music. Musical annotation was an enigma to me. What can one say to a smiling priest in a soutane and appropriate hat holding out a pile of printed full scores for the taking, insisting it was all part of one's destiny!

Thus it was that I came to know Mayr. Now is the time to set down on paper a few gleanings reaped, with the hope that others will take up the cause of Johann Simon Mayr and enable his music and thought to be better known.

The gleanings are few. I cannot claim that the music is here fully catalogued; it is an on-going task; furthermore, the sheer volume of his writings poses an immense task, and certainly I have not traced all his letters. Perhaps more important, at least another half dozen operas need to be revived, together with a substantial amount of Mayr's religious music - also, it is not enough that the outward ears are stimulated by "one off" revivals. A number of performances are necessary in order that the "ear" by which the ears hear is moved to recognize a music's true qualities and nuances. Above all, patience is required. For example, the Donizetti revival began in 1948 thanks to Maestro Gavazzeni and Maestro Missiroli, but it was not until the seventies that it reached its zenith. Even now Donizetti is *still* to be understood and better known, and I hope what follows is a contribution towards his reassessment, as well as that of Rossini and Bellini.

To settle and attempt to write a book on Mayr, is to accept the fact that it is impossible to bring into true focus all the facets of this remarkable man. His learning was encyclopaedic as well as creative, and the music revived to date represents only the first stirrings of interest and curiosity. Authenticity of performance, whatever is meant by that term, is still a long way off, for each interested party will argue its case. Perhaps sincerity of performance is just as important as "authenticity". One can but prepare performing material and do one's best under the circumstances.

To study Mayr implies not only working at his numerous operas, oratorios, cantatas and vast catalogue of religious music, but also his writings, attempting to understand his teaching and intentions as a man. There is also the historical background, the tradition and customs he was content to identify himself with in the small northern Italian city of Bergamo, *La Patria*, as he refers to it, time and time again.

At first one is encouraged by the composer's own autobiographical notes and early pamphlets commemorating his life. Mayr's biography should be a simple task. It is quite the contrary. He draws a veil over his most important formative years, from approximately 1773 to 1789, that is, from about the age of ten to twenty-six, in other words, from the closure of the Jesuit College in Ingolstadt to his arrival in Bergamo. Something has to be said about these "missing years", for they place the young Mayr in the *Sturm und Drang* movement, the teachings of Herder and Goethe, and more important, though obscure, the ethos of the Bavarian Illuminati. Adam Weishaupt, the founder of the Illuminati, must have been his lecturer in canon law at Ingolstadt University, whilst his patron was a pillar of the Illuminati Order, Baron Tomaso v. Bassus. Was Mayr, a protégé of the Illuminati, sent to Italy to succeed where v. Bassus had failed, commissioned to promote the Order's ideals through the theatre and through teaching very much in the example left in Goethe's *Wilhelm Meister*? I doubt if the question will ever be answered.

Mayr is silent with the silence of a true initiate. Yet his music with patient study ought to be as transparent as any work resulting from an encounter with *gnosis*, the knowledge of the self.

Historically, he had to be silent; the Masons and the Illuminati were not *personae gratae* in Catholic Italy. Weishaupt nicknamed himself "Spartacus", v. Bassus was known as "Hannibal", names which make their intentions clear. And Mayr? We know he indentified himself with Aristotle, but more we cannot say. If the historical Spartacus and Hannibal had been political enemies of Rome, Aristotle certainly was not, except as an opponent to false learning and weak philosophy.

The closer we approach Mayr, the more we encounter problems. Can we really believe his assertion that he was a self-taught composer? At the most, on his own trust, he says he learnt little from Bertoni[2] and less from Lenzi[3]. The only other information we have is that his father taught him the rudiments of music and that he must have been a child protégé known for his singing and playing of the piano and organ. He also tells us that in Ingolstadt he taught himself all the instruments of the orchestra and had published in 1786 a collection of songs at Regensburg. That is all. The next thing we know is that he emerges in Venice about 1790 and composes by 1794, a block-buster of an opera, *Saffo*, as well as his fourth oratorio within a few years, *La Passione*. From the evidence of *La Passione*, revived in London in 1974, we can conclude that he was already a reasonably mature composer who had digested Galuppi, Cimarosa and Paisiello, a German who was bringing the drama of Gluck, the insights of Mozart and especially of Haydn to bear on Italian music. By 1801 he had taken over Cimarosa's crown which he held until the rise of Rossini - a composer who freely used Mayr's ideas and music. By 1813, it is usual to comment that Mayr had said with *La rosa bianca e la rosa rossa* and *Medea in Corinto* all that he wished to say, in operatic terms. It is true that the essence of his "reform" had been accomplished, but his real genius is to be discovered in late dramatic works like *Fedra* (1820) and *San Luigi Gonzaga* (1822), together with his religious music. On hearing, it is the sheer variety and scope of his music which astounds his listener. The century would follow in his wake as he increasingly turned his attention away from the cabals of the theatre to the composition of religious music, his school and the compilation of his *Notebooks*.

Mayr's contemporaries were either fascinated by his music, or like Stendhal, were against it. His opponents were patronising "Papa Mayr"; his supporters were more discerning and

---

2   Ferdinando Bertoni, 1725 - 1813.

3   Carlo Lenzi, 1735 - 1805

likened the profundity of his art to the genius of Dante or Poussin. Vincenzo Bellini referred to himself as a follower of Mayr rather than of Zingarelli. All, even Stendhal, noted his operatic innovations, qualities which made him distinct. His musical voice was personal, clear and easily recognizable. The ingredients of his operas became the stuff of 19th century Italian operatic music.

But his contemporaries noted another quality which we today may easily overlook. Mayr was a German composing fluent Italian music, music rich enough to "reform" the direction of Italian opera. The writer of the *Elogio*[4] emphasises that Mayr considered himself to be an *Italian* composer. The *Elogio* compares Mayr to Mozart and concludes that Mozart remains, even at his most Italianate, a German composer, whereas Mayr is unquestionably Italian. He asks the rhetorical question: what would Mayr have contributed if he had come to Italy and composed from an earlier age? The writings, especially the *Memoria*[5], show the extent to which Mayr consciously identified himself with the Italian tradition.

It is important to note, that besides all the dramatic and orchestral innovations of his operas noted by musicologists, Mayr could write pure melody and melodies which through a few bars of harmonic progression could turn lyricism into poignant drama. It was a lesson that was not lost on Rossini. Donizetti learnt it to greater effect and passed on his master's insight to the young Verdi.

Mayr is remembered as an operatic composer; however, he freely acknowledged that his greatest interest lay in liturgical music through which he could express *"tutta la potenza, il vero ingegnio, tutta la immaginazione sua"*[6] ("all the power, real ingenuity, all his imagination"). Religious music freed him from the glare of publicity and theatrical conventions. This love he passed on to Donizetti, who, in the *Requiem for Bellini* and the two closely related settings of the *Miserere* found a clarity, a freedom and a transparent sincerity exceeding his theatrical works.

Here is another paradox. Mayr, the young man orientated to political reform at the hands of the Illuminati, displays little interest in politics. On the other hand, the *Notebooks* show a concern for his century's loss of tradition in favour of shallow innovations. He was a totally committed catholic, a man who knew the way of prayer, and yet he was concerned for ecclesiastical reforms, reforms which today have been accepted as a natural consequence of the passing time. He was political in the deepest sense, having little time for political "banner waving".

In keeping with the teachings of the Illuminati, Mayr shows a desire for the Church to return to the simplicity of intention of the early Christians, but this is paralleled by a deep

---

4   Written by Gerolamo Calvi, perhaps the most discerning contemporary writer on Mayr's work and its worth.

5   See the selections from Mayr's writings.

6   Mayr's own annotation added to the text of the *Elogio*.

love of liturgy and an intellect immersed in Pythagorian, Platonic and Aristotelian philosophy. However, in Mayr there is no taint of the dualism which is so often to be found in classical philosophy. By the evidence of his own life, his devotional discipline was centred in the conviction of the creation as sacrament - that under the veil of nature and life, the Divine was to be found. The hallmark of his teaching was emancipation from the arrogance of the self; he was convinced that forgiveness was the Christian secret. This may also be traced in Donizetti's letters to Mayr[7].

Those who study Mayr for signs of political revolution will, as with Donizetti, remain disappointed. Nowhere is there to be found a rose-water socialism. In its place will be discovered an understanding of Catholicism as an orthodox tradition in which the exoteric and the esoteric are made known in a way of life. Whatever is studied, the music, the letters, the writings, the result is the same; we meet a thoroughly integrated person.

The *Notebooks* reveal a man totally aware of the musical world of his period. He accepted change as a sign of the times but was critical of Romanticism - the very movement he had helped to evolve[8]. But Mayr's romanticism is that of Goethe. The passions may be expressed in order to be understood and to be healed as required - never must passion be allowed to destroy form. His world is akin to that of Renaissance humanism at its best - the arts must be tempered by classicism, a classicism softened by a benevolent humanism emanating from the Christian revelation. Like Ficino or Pico, his musical interests could move from the disciplines of one tradition to another, providing they were reflections of a truth[9].

The reforms which Mayr anticipated resulted from the consequences of the Revolution - those deep and radical changes taking place in the society of his times. He considered that it was folly for the Church to ignore what was happening, for it would result in the eventual loss of its people owing to a lack of a sympathetic understanding of what he termed the *popular arts*. Even more serious would be the people's forgetting of those precious insights gained over the centuries, generally called Tradition. Mayr foresaw the possible break-up of the Western Civilization.

The reforms eventually came with the Second Vatican Council. However, reform had been already under way during Mayr's generation. Unfortunately, it was shelved after his death due to the activities of political hotheads and Pio Nono retiring within the safe enclave of the Vatican. Sentimental conservatism was to become the order of the day.

---

7   See for example Z.25. A quotation in keeping with the teaching of the Illuminati.

8   For example, the extracts in translation from the *Notebooks*.

9   For example, his remarks on Chinese classical music.

The course of events has resulted in the demise of the liturgical order which Mayr loved and for which he composed so much of his music. There has also been a vanishing of the sense of the sacred from most sanctuaries, and the rift between the language of Tradition and the *popular arts*. The old wisdom has been replaced by psychology, which, by definition is concerned with psychic residues rather than spirituality - that binding of the inner and the outer worlds in a sacramental embrace. More serious, in modern times a grasping materialism of both body and soul threatens to sweep aside Nature's laws with the result that both environment and the promise of life are now threatened. Thus it is that the intellect is left to play self-deluding games, building up ever more labyrinthine systems which are increasingly removed from an understanding of the gnosis to which Mayr dedicated his life and work.

Acknowledgements

My book would not have been written except for the encouragement of the late Don Luigi Cortesi and the late Prof. Guglielmo Barblan. Gratitude must be expressed to the full collaboration of the *Biblioteca Civica*, Bergamo, especially the late Signorina Dora Coggiola and Dr. Orazio Bravi; Professoressa Giuliana Donati-Petténi, the late Gianni Brivio, Dr. Eugenio Cattaneo, the Conservatorio Gaetano Donizetti, Bergamo, especially Prof. Valeriano Sacchiero, Prof. Luigi Tironi and Sig. Fabrizio Capitanio, Don Giuseppe Pedemonti, Dr. and Mrs. Giuseppe Paravicini Bagliani and Prof. Giuseppe Angeloni. I am very grateful to *all* my Bergamasque friends.

Special mention must be made of the assistance of Don White and Patric Schmid of *Opera Rara* and the many librarians who sent lists and answered my questions. Dr. Heinrich Bauer (whose recent death has robbed the revaluation of Mayr's music of one of its main protagonists) and Newell Jenkins helped me with musical examples, libretti and recordings. I am also very grateful to Dr Kathleen Raine, Paul Goldman, Dr Hannelore Bauer-Ehnes and Dr Cecilia Powell for reading my manuscript and for their corrections and comments. Every student of Mayr is indebted to Ludwig Schiedermair's basic study of the operas (1907) and Arrigo Gazzaniga's catalogue of the *Fondo Mayr*, Bergamo (1963). Special gratitude must be extended to the musicians who helped revive the works of Mayr in London over a decade ago, especially the memorable singing of Lois McDonall in the role of Zeliska in *L'amor coniugale* and Wendy Eathorne as St Mary in *La Passione*; Tom Vernon for trusting Mayr and for arranging broadcasts on BBC Radio London; and the support of *Opera Viva* and the *Donizetti Society* for promoting the concerts; Gill Mallinson and Leanne Fjetland for typing from my manuscript.

In recent years, I am most indebted to Mr. Ian Caddy, whose collaboration and friendship has sustained my work and revitalized my interest in Mayr. Without his encouragement and dedication to reviving the music of Mayr and Donizetti, this book may well never have been written.

The book would not have been published without the generosity of Dr. Rüdiger v. Canal, to whom I am especially grateful. Dr. v. Canal was the friend of the late Dr. Heinrich Bauer who dedicated his life to reviving Mayr's music; therefore, I am more than pleased to dedicate my work to his memory.

Finally, I must thank my family, especially my wife, Eleanor, for their patience and support.

John Stewart Allitt
Thickthorn Cottage
1987

1
Johann Simon Mayr:
his life and work

Mayr's life may be ordered for convenience into five phases:

I   1763 - 1789   From his birth to his arrival in Italy.

II 1789 - 1802   The Venetian years to his appointment as Kapellmeister to *S. Maria Maggiore*, Bergamo.

III 1802 - 1813   The important Bergamo years, a period of maximum activity, the founding of his school. 1813 is the year of his two famous operas *La Rosa Rossa e la Rosa Bianca* and *Medea in Corinto*.

IV 1813 - 1824   Years in which Mayr dedicates his life increasingly to teaching and the composition of church music. 1824 is the year of his last opera, *Demetrio*.

V   1824 - 1845   The elder statesman years towards the end of which writing becomes increasingly difficult due to cataracts on his eyes. These were unsuccessfully operated on, and, for all intents and purposes, Mayr is blind in his last years. It is a period of composition (Church music), writing treatises and essays, and his participation in the Catholic revival with the hymn book, the *Melodie Sacre*.

I   1763 - 1789

1   The Beginnings

Johann Simon Mayr was born on 14 June 1763 at Mendorf, a small Bavarian village in the region of the Upper Danube between Ingolstadt and Regensburg. His father Joseph Mayr, the village organist, came from a family of organists. He married Maria Anna Prantmayer of Friedberg near Augsburg on 30 September 1761. Five children grew to maturity; Maria Viktoria, born 13 June 1762; Johann Simon; Joseph, born 6 May 1765; Johannes Petrus, 7 June 1767 and Maria Anna, 7 May 1770. When Mayr returned on a brief visit to his native land in the summer of 1838, after an absence of 51 years, he found only one of his sisters to be alive.

The typical Bavarian parish church of Mendorf with its baroque furnishings, painted ceiling and small organ where Mayr received his first lessons is still to be seen, likewise the house where he was born, though it has been made rather tastelessly into a modern butcher's shop.

Joseph Mayr taught his eldest son the rudiments of music. His example of dedication, Mayr tells us in his autobiographical notes, was to influence him throughout his life. By seven and a half he could sight read ecclesiastical compositions such as those of Johann Anton Bernard Kobrich (an organist and composer active in the second half of the 18th century in Bavaria whose church compositions were once admired) and Ignaz Franz Xavier Kürzinger (a composer in the service of the Mergentheim court in Württemberg).

A year's piano studies drew attention to the young Mayr's gifts. Soon he could play the none too easy works of composers of the period like Johann Schobert (c1740-1767) (who is said to have stylistically influenced Mozart) and the French composer-soloist, Jean Erard. Mayr remembered that, already at seven, he was attempting to jot down his first attempts at composition.

His talent for the keyboard and the gift of a good soprano voice did not go unheeded. A well-known person (Mayr does not supply us with his name) wished to take the boy to Vienna, the "home of German music", in order to expose him to a more cultured life than that of a Bavarian village, thus enabling him to perfect his musical studies. His father declined the offer on the pretext that his son was still too young to be removed from home to the "noise and whirl" of city life.

About 1772 or 73, Mayr was granted a free place, on the basis of his vocal gifts, at the Jesuit Seminary in Ingolstadt, not long before the suppression of the Jesuit Order. Mayr would have been about 10 or 11 when this first crisis came in his troubled education; it must be presumed that somehow his secondary education continued. Indeed, Mayr informs his reader that the college taught him Grammar, Rhetoric, Logic and Physics and that he left to attend Ingolstadt University to study Law. More precisely he signed on for further studies on 23 September 1781 at the cost of 30 Kreuzer to study Theology and Canon Law.

So we have a Mayr by the age of 18 who seems more destined to the cloth than to music. However, the autobiographical notes tell us that the "love of music" was not extinguished. The lack of teachers, failure to continue his keyboard studies and the loss of his voice encouraged him to study for himself the stringed (later he nicknamed himself *Il vecchio suonatore di viola,* "the old viola player") and wind instruments of the orchestra. He paid for his keep by playing the organ at the Church of St. Moritz and for the Augustian Fathers. He notes that he had no instruction in composition in Germany, that he only heard three or four *singspiel* operas of Johann Adam Hiller (1728 - 1804) at the theatre in Ingolstadt, that he only heard music in an "Academy" briefly, on a flying visit to Munich (on his way to Italy?).

The next fact the notes present us with is 1787 when Baron Tommaso v. Bassus took him to Poschiavo in the Grisons and Tirano in the Valtellina (the valley that runs eastwards from the north point of Lake Como). Mayr was then 23 or 24 years old. We have one more fact: in 1786 he published his first collection of songs, at Regensburg, *Lieder beim Klavier zu singen.*

In other words, Mayr leaves us in the dark as to what his education was about, other than that he was officially studying Theology and Canon Law and unofficially studying all the instruments of the orchestra, making a living playing the organ and trying his hand at his first compositions. The formative years from 11 to 24 (1774 - 1787) are only discretely referred to. Why? There seems little doubt that Mayr became actively involved with the Bavarian Illuminati, a secret order that had fallen into disrespect by the time Mayr wrote his autobiographical notes. His patron to be, v. Bassus, was an ex-student of Weishaupt, intimately involved with the activities of the Order, especially in Italy and may be described along with Weishaupt and Adolf v. Knigge as the "trinity" upon which the Illuminati drew inspiration.

There are two courses open to the student of Mayr. One either follows Mayr's example and draws a veil of secrecy over these years or one attempts to recreate the *salient* points which must have contributed to his intellectual and emotional formation, especially in the light of his career and Notebooks.

2   Mayr's attitude to the Church and Religion

This is crucial to any interpretation of Mayr - a child protégé, destined to music, born in Catholic Bavaria, who received initially a Jesuit education, studying perhaps for the Church, and who was caught up with the most anti-Jesuitical of men - Adam Weishaupt. Freemasons write of Weishaupt as insidious; traditionalists, as an arch-heretic and the founder of a pre-marxist revolutionary organisation, whilst the Marxists consider him a "materialist atheist"; an "enlightened" figure in the age of revolutions.

It would appear that all three of these views are extreme and unbalanced.

Mayr remained throughout his life a devout son of the Church. His Notebooks show him to be a genuine Catholic and an illuminatus, that is, a person grounded in the gnosis, an approach to wisdom which in every age is handed on orally, and which is not to be confused with modern theosophy. His religious music shows that his theological training was never lost, his hymn book and oratorio *Samuele* indicate that his religious views were enlightened, amazingly in keeping with the ethos we associate with Pope John XXIII, a product of Bergamo's seminary, to the halls of which Mayr was no stranger.

If Weishaupt was the devil incarnate to all his enemies, it should be pointed out that he had no negative influence over Mayr the Christian, the Catholic, except to encourage in his young student a view that valued the practice of the moral life, a simplicity of values in keeping with early Christianity, and to strive to free himself from prejudice. Mayr could not tolerate, for example, corruption such as the practice of castration in order to preserve soprano voices. He later founded a school to provide choir boys in the modern sense, who received a good education ensuring them of employment. He studied and valued the beauty of liturgy, composing music for every aspect of the Church's year. He preferred, as we shall see, composing religious music, to the artificial world of opera. He was deeply involved with the interpretation of the "Mysteries", the profound inner implications of religion, which society for the greater part ignores or renders into a frivolity. His friends, besides musicians and intellectuals from all works of life, included many priests who clearly viewed him as a holy man; evidence of this being the sermon preached at his funeral by Canon Finazzi.

The abiding values of religious thougt permeate Mayr's Notebooks. He was, in many ways, what may be described as a "Christian platonist", though he himself would have considered his "platonism" as a natural ingredient of the world view of his times.

Mayr became increasingly concerned for the future of Western civilisation. Like Goethe, he considered the excesses of romanticism to be a mental sickness. The free and unrestrained display of the emotions over the intellectual and imaginative life could only lead to the disintegration of the west's tradition, and ultimately cause social chaos.

Without a doubt, Mayr considered religion, in its true sense, as the binding and re-binding path which linked humanity with the order of the universe and human being to human being. Religion in one sense was a fundamental pattern giving meaning and purpose to life; it was also, as a Christian, the fulcrum through which the Divine revealed himself as the formative Idea through which humanity might grow to its true status and level of consciousness. As a Catholic, the masculine and feminine mysteries were hidden in the figures of Christ and Mary, God and the Church, Jesus and the individual soul. Mayr was first and foremost a Christian with his roots in the Catholic Church. However, like any real person, he carried within himself the contradictions of his times, those elements which go to make the Job argue within men of faith in every age.

Before considering Mayr's secretive years, this has to be said in order, to ensure that he is not misrepresented due to his "masonic" background.

3   The Bavarian Illuminati

Germany was rife with secret societies and freemasonry during Mayr's formative years; Italy was in increasing ferment during his Italian years, fundamental years which led up to the Risorgimento and the final unification of the Peninsular states. Secret societies and freemasonry were at every turning of the street, at their best, responding to the laudable aspects of the Enlightenment, and at their worst, encouraging anarchy, even murder.

Two examples of the late 18th century are the lodge *Les Neufs Soeurs* and the Illuminati, both coming into existence in 1776, when Mayr was 13. *Les Neufs Soeurs* boasted in its ranks Lalande, Franklin, D'Alembert, Voltaire, Pestalozzi, the Tuscan reformer Giovanni Fabbroni, Francesco Pignatelli, an intimate of Neapolitan masonry, Giorgio Santi, the geologist of the enlightened Leopold, Grandduke of Tuscany, who Mayr admired, and the composer Niccolò Piccinni, who was to influence Mayr at a turning point in his career. Both *the Neufs Soeurs* and Weishaupt's followers were reactions to the occult world of "Rosicrucianism", freemasonry and the power of the Jesuits.

Like Mayr, Adam Weishaupt was the product of Jesuit education and this fact coloured the organisation of his Order, formed with the express intention" of using to good end the means which the Jesuit order had employed for bad". Weishaupt demanded unconditional obedience, far reaching mutual surveillance among members, and an auricular confession each inferior had to make to his superior. (In Mayr's case, it would appear to have been ultimately v. Bassus).

The idea of a society came to Weishaupt when he noticed the effect of Rosicrucianism over his students. In order to free his young followers from alchemy, spiritism, dabbling in black and white magic, he formed, with their collaboration, a *Society of Perfectibilists* (later renamed, the *Order of the Illuminati*) expressly for "combating moral evil, for improving the morals of the members, and for the higher instruction of humanity". This is confirmed by v. Bassus writing in 1787 "an Order which preached nothing more than a rigorous morality, golden temperance and an undisputed application to study". Also it is quite likely that the Society was initially a kind of self-protection against the influence of the Jesuits, who even after their fall from favour held positions of power. Bavaria was one of their vigorous strongholds.

Thus Weishaupt's struggle was against ecclesiastical power and prejudice, the privileges of the aristocracy, obscurantism, superstition and prejudice. He called it "a league against the enemies of Reason and Humanity". His sources were basically Diderot, Mably and Rousseau.

The Order came into being on 1 May 1776. Initiates took on nicknames, *noms de guerre*; Weishaupt - *Spartacus*; v. Bassus - *Hannibal*; v. Knigge - *Philo*; Goethe - *Abaris*; Pestalozzi - *Alfred*; Mayr - ? *Aristotle*. Other essential names linked to the Illuminati are v. Born, Mozart, Herder, Schiller and Beethoven. There were three grades: novice, minerval, minerval illuminatus. These were, regardless of the ceremonial associated with secret societies, essentially teaching grades since Weishaupt professed that it was useless to have a political outlook without first learning the good life. Morality was the basis for growth, for without it society would end up a community of swindlers and knaves. Also it was first necessary to free initiates from a narrow and prejudiced education. Step by step the ideal was to lead adepts to the communual values of the early Christians.

The study programme read the stoic philosophy of Seneca, Epittetus, Plutarch and Sallust, then Robinet's *De la nature*, Mirabeau, Boulanger, Holbach and Helvétius. "Morality must be the object of all our teaching". Thus it was that each member had to "confess" to his superior:

1.   What he considered to be examples of prejudice.
2.   Who were the people in whom he had met such prejudices.
3.   What are the prejudices that he had found in his own self.
4.   Which and how many predominated in him.
5.   Which of these prejudices he had been able to weaken or to overcome.

The reason for the "confession" was for the adepts to conclude for themselves the essential teachings of the order without their being taught, thus becoming realities rather than ideas. By removing false concepts and the effects of bad education, Weishaupt believed it was possible to expose the goodness of heart latent in every person. He taught: ". . . there is no truth to be discovered which has not been already discovered and stated, the world is still that which it has always been, simply because the mischief makers oppose all the efforts of the wise, the just and the good, who are always a minority in regards to others. . . I have always felt an uncontrollable hatred of all debasement and every form of oppression, and very soon I understood how weak is man in isolation and how strong instead he could be once united to similar minds."

Morality was one side of the coin; the other was understanding and wisdom, the traditional teachings of esoteric schools. In his own words, Weishaupt's ideal was "the victory of virtue and wisdom over foolishness and malice. What must we do then, oppose violence with violence? Tyranny with tyranny? What progress can come from disorder opposing disorder, from injustice which encourages iniquity, from crime which pretends to punish crime? The true way of salvation is not that of vain words, nor of vain repression. It consists in protecting, favouring and recompensing wisdom. It must also be by constituting and maintaining secret of arms which are the quiet and charitable defenders of freedom, love, and peace, for such was the pure and genuine source of the Christian religion. One needs to return to such a religion, enlisting a legion of unwearying men, pledged to the good of their neighbours. This does not relate to any external manifestation, rather it is a silent, inward transformation, permanent and hidden from others."

Members had to keep detailed diaries in which they noted the conduct of persons around them and salient events. These were passed on to their superiors and analysed, taking note of social changes. Such an early discipline helps to appreciate the impetus behind Mayr's Notebooks, compiled later in life, which may record his thoughts or jot down something that has caught his attention when reading. It is often hard when consulting the Notebooks to separate what is Mayr and what comes from another source. He noted musical activities taking place as far away as Prague or York, or incidents which left a lasting impression on him, like watching Beethoven play the piano (presumably in 1803 when Mayr was in Vienna for the première of his opera *Ercole in Lidia*) or noting the content of an engraving by Hogarth (*The Enraged Musician*), or a poem by Salvator Rosa. His writings are a testimony to the breadth and balance of his learning.

The custom of adepts keeping Notebooks was one of the misunderstood practices of the Illuminati owing to Weishaupt's dramatic "ex-Jesuit" overstatements: "This spying out is a constant and assiduous duty of every initiated member. It will be doubly useful, first to the Order and its superiors, then to the adept himself. He will twice a month give a detailed report on his daily observances . . . The Order will in this way be informed on those who are in need in both the cities and the villages, offering them help and protection, finding a way to their sympathy and at the same time enabling us to be aware of the hostile".

Adolf v. Knigge with v. Bassus developed the structure of the Illuminati. By January 1782 (Mayr was at university and 19 years old) the inner world of the Illuminati was as follows:

1.	The Nursery	Novice
		Minerval
		Minerval Illuminatus
2.	Symbolic Masonry	Apprentice
		Companion
		Master
		Scottish Novice
		Scottish Knight
3.	Lesser Mysteries	Priest
		Prince Regent

Greater Mysteries	Magus
	Man-King

Every aspect of knowledge was classified with "Priests" responsible for their promulgation and teaching. For example:

1. Physics (Optics, hydraulics, hydrostatics, electricity, gravity, magnetism, attraction, flight etc.)

2. Medicine (Anatomy, research into sickness and medicines, semiotics, obstetrics, surgery, chemistry etc.)

3. Mathematics (Calculus, algebra, pure maths, military and civil architecture, boat-building, nature of the planets, astronomy etc.)

4. Natural History (Agriculture, gardening, domestic ecology, zoology in the widest sense, geology, metallurgy, phenomenology of unexplained forces, the influence of the stars etc.)

5. Political Science (History, geography, the lives of wise men, ancient institutions, diplomacy etc.)

6. The Arts and Crafts (Painting, sculpture, music, dance, elocution, poetry, languages, plus Latin and Greek, literature etc.)

7. The Hermetic Sciences (Oriental languages, study of ancient texts, hieroglyphs, symbolism, gnosis etc.).

At the assemblies of the "minerval churches" members of this degree wore a green sash with a medallion, upon which was depicted an owl holding in its claws an open book bearing the initials P*(er)* M*(e)* C*(aeci)* V*(ident)*.[1]

Quarrels between Weishaupt and the more radical v. Knigge weakened the Order and on 22 July 1784 the reactionary Elector Karl Theodor, instigated by his father confessor, a Jesuit by the name of Franck, issued a decree banning all secret societies. In March of the following year another edict banned the Illuminati by name. V. Bassus's Schloss Sandersdorf was searched for documents in 1787; Weishaupt found protection under Duke Ernest of Saxe-Gotha, his influence possibly filtering through to the "catholic" education of Albert, the future Prince Consort.

In 1784 Mozart had become a mason, likewise Haydn in 1786. Mayr when in Venice in the 1790's was under the surveillance of the Council of Ten and in 1820 he was found to be a member of a Masonic lodge in Bergamo, a lodge incidentally made up of all professions, as well as the clergy! No charges were brought and the Lodge was considered to be harmless. To what extent Mayr was involved in the activities of the Illuminati is open to speculation. That he was involved, there is no doubt.

---

1 Surely, the origin of Donizetti's *Siccome gufo presi il mio volo* - (as an owl I took my flight.) See Z. 496, Zavadini: *Donizetti - vita, musiche, epistolario.*

4   Adam Weishaupt (1748 - 1830)

Since there is scant information available, a few further thoughts on Weishaupt may help to better understand Mayr's development. He was no grand magus since he was a lecturer at a small university in times of social and intellectual upheaval. He was not an atheist as some have made him out to be; his writings became increasingly involved with theological matters. He was no genius, merely a rather naive and sincere person concerned with the ignorance of his times. He was not an anarchist, nor was his order one of the causes of the French Revolution, nor was he a proto-marxist.

Blake remarked that all progress is judgement, that every movement for good carries its counterpart in the hands of ignoble souls. What would Jesus of Nazareth have said if he had to take account of all the sins committed in his name? No doubt the right and the left will fight over Weishaupt to eternity. He certainly was no messiah nor antichrist.

One discovers a mind caught between the materialism of the Enlightenment and a heroic belief in idealism and absolutes. He believed humanity could be happy through a conduct somewhat akin to the Buddhist Middle Way. Happiness is for Weishaupt a human right; it is what gives society its *raison d'être*. For Weishaupt, to understand the nature of happiness is to know the priority for which humanity should strive. But there are two vital flaws in every society which oppose society's goal: laziness and ignorance. "When we look at this goodly world, and see that every man may be happy, but that the happiness of one depends on the conduct of another; when we see the wicked so powerful and the good so weak, and that it is vain to strive singly and alone against the current of vice and oppression, the wish naturally arises . . . to form an association of the most worthy persons, who should work together removing the obstacles to human happiness . . .permanently to unite thinking men from all parts of the world, of all classes and religions, in a single society, by means of a given higher interest, without prejudice to their freedom of thought, and in spite of all their different opinions and emotions, and to make them, whether they be inferior or equals, enthusiastic and responsive to such a degree that the many act as one and desire and do of their own volition and with the truest conviction, that which no public compulsion has been able to effect since the world and mankind have existed. Such a society is the masterpiece of human reason, in its highest perfection."

He aimed at a society which would make "the most important discoveries in all the branches of Science, . . . improving the members of the Society, . . . cultivating great men and . . . assuring them, even in this world, . . . the certain prize of their perfection, . . . protecting them against persecution and suppression and . . . tying the hand of despotism in whatever shape or form . . .".

If Weishaupt is guilty, it is a charge of Pelagianism. Mayr, judging by his religious faith and the clear exposition of evil in his opera *Medea in Corinto*, was no Pelagian. Rather, he owed to Weishaupt those principles of:

- being free from prejudice.
- leading a moral life.
- a belief in the simplicity of living.
- freedom from vain honours.
- a life dedicated to study.
- acceptance of friendship and mutual forgiveness as being fundamental to the good life.
- recognizing social oppression as the result of conceit, ambition, greed, envy and thirst for power.
- contempt for false politics, false scholarship, false religion.
- that a man with all his possessions, rank, honours and titles enjoys them only through his fellow-men, and furthermore, through his fellow men he may equally lose them.
- that Nature step by step reveals her face to the seeker, that she will fill his mind with wisdom and his heart with virtue - in other words - *Natura est Deus in rebus.*
- a hierarchic and cosmological view of the created order of the universe.

Weishaupt may also have encouraged the view of history to be found in Mayr's Notebooks. Rather than a linear view of time stretching from the darkest of ages to a utopian millenium, Mayr's view is cyclic. Civilizations, societies, movements and ideas, all have their time to rise and fall on the Wheel of Fortune due to indolence and ignorance, humanity's two great enemies.

How Mayr found time to compose, write, teach, organise all that he did, is a puzzle to the modern mind caught in the stressful vortex of travel and distractions. If people are amazed at Donizetti's catalogue of works perhaps they should consider his teacher's. Mayr was anything but narrow-minded. He was a highly aware person. Every page of the Notebooks testifies to his lively mind. It was by applying Weishaupt's two enemies of humanity (indolence and ignorance) to the times he lived through, that Mayr became increasingly disturbed by the direction the arts were taking - he considered what today we might call "the excesses of romanticism" to be decadent and intellectually weakening.

Perhaps Mayr would have agreed with his teacher, that every age ultimately depends on the few souls who are not submerged under the illusions of their times, and who state in their work and life the abiding links which forge the true chain of history.

5 Tommaso Francesco Maria v. Bassus (1742 - 1815)

A short distance from Mendorf is the village of Sandersdorf with its castle. It was the property of the v. Bassus family, a family with connections in Bavaria and in the Grisons and the Valtellina. Baron Tommaso in 1767 became the Mayor of Poschiavo, a position he held until 1791. A member of his family, Giovanni Domenico, taught at Ingolstadt University, where Tommaso also studied, and where Weishaupt was lecturer in Law.

The lords of Sandersdorf were geographically the "rulers" of Mendorf. Maybe it was a v. Bassus who had wished to take the young Mayr to Vienna, an offer which his father had finally declined. At exactly what point Mayr found a patron in v. Bassus is hard to say. It is possible that the family had lent support to Mayr after the collapse of the Jesuit College in Ingolstadt. Baron Tommaso joined Weishaupt's Illuminati in 1777 and by 1779 had become the organiser of the movement in Italy. Mayr became a university student in 1781 and by 1787 he was with v. Bassus in Poschiavo (Grisons) and Tirano (Valtellina). Two years later he was in Bergamo and at 26 beginning to find his direction in life. He was 28 when he composed his first oratorio and 31 by the time of his first opera. By any account Mayr was a late starter, a fact that makes his success and opus of works even more impressive.

Baron Tommaso retained his friendship and admiration for Adam Weishaupt after the suppression of the Illuminati and public disgrace, writing in his defence and setting out the ideals of the Illuminati in 1787 when Mayr was with him in Poschiavo.

V. Bassus, or De (or Da) Bassus (or Bessus), as he is sometimes known in Italy, is an important figure in Italian history due to his publishing house at Poschiavo. The Baron continued the liberal tradition of publishing begun in Coira (Chur) by Carlantonio Pilati, who in time also joined the ranks of the Illuminati. These two men joined forces to publish books and tracts which were severely censored in Italy.

The first publication, 1780, *Le più necessarie cognizioni pei fanciulli*, was the first Italian scholastic book which dealt with the problem of educating children from various religious backgrounds. This is not surprising in the light of the role the Illuminati gave to education and the fact that Heinrich Johann Pestalozzi was a member of the Order. In the following year Goethe's *Sorrows of the Young Werther* was translated by Gaetano Grossi and published. The Illuminati attempted to persuade a more charitable view towards the problem of suicide. Perhaps Donizetti's operas, with acts of suicide such as Edgardo's in *Lucia di Lammermoor* are examples of the influence of Illuminati teaching. Pilati's two books *La riforma d'Italia* and *Riflessioni d'un Italiano* indicate the political tone of the press, likewise v. Bassus's own apologia for the Illuminati published in 1787.

The ambience of Poschiavo and Tirano must have had a fundamental influence over Mayr. It is not too far fetched to conjecture that he and v. Bassus (and separately Goethe?) left Germany to avoid embarrassment after the edicts against the Illuminati. There is nothing more potent for hardening views than persecution. Thus by 25 Mayr had been fully exposed to reforming ideas concerning education and society. He was most likely involved with editing texts during his time with v. Bassus. The influence of Goethe must have been fundamental and helps to explain Mayr's classicism as well as his leanings towards the new ideas of Romanticism. But all this has little to do with music, though it is an essential step in Mayr's life and intellectual growth. Mayr was on the side of reform, but enlightened reform, not revolution.

In 1784 v. Bassus had written to Weishaupt a depressing report on the state of new ideas in Lombardy and Milan. He saw that the attitude of the Milanese forbade any attempt to form a lodge. Maybe v. Bassus encouraged Mayr to carry illuminist ideas to Italy, arranging for him his journey from Tirano to Bergamo (a relatively short journey) and gave him letters of introduction to his next patron, Canon Count Pesenti. Bergamo could have been a distribution point for his books. If this is so, then in Italy v. Bassus looked to the arts, especially the theatre rather than politics, to communicate ideas.

Mayr arrived in Italy with the ideal of "reforming" Italian music. He had yet to learn the "business" of composition. There is a difference between publishing a few songs at Regensburg and staging an opera in Venice with that city's long musical tradition. Maybe this arrival in Italy again reflects the indirect influence of Goethe and a belief in the theatre as the true initiator which leads to enlightenment; consider for example, *Wilhelm Meister*, a work which Mayr knew and admired.

Mayr informs us that his Regensburg songs brought him success, that a certain scientist, Cavaliere Mecenate, encouraged him to dedicate his life to music, and that he travelled to Bergamo to study under Carlo Lenzi.

Mayr had turned his back on his native land.

6   Sturm und Drang

Besides the intellectual world of the French Enlightenment and the excitement of secret societies, Mayr would have found himself exposed to the passionate outpourings of the *Sturm und Drang*. Both Herder and Goethe were members of the Order of the Illuminati. Hence Mayr would have arrived in Italy as an "apostle" of German intellectual life. Perhaps with ideals comparable with Friedrich Overbeck's painting *Italy and Germany* (1811 and worked upon until 1828, Munich, *Bayerische Staatsgemäldesammlungen*).

The movement we know as the *Sturm und Drang* was a strange interplay between Rousseau's "return to nature", the sincerity of introspection and mystical pantheism associated with Pietism, the English novel, Old Norse mythology, Ossian, Spinoza's philosophy, the writings of Shaftesbury, liberal minded philanthropy, an interest in science in the widest possible context, as well as the ambience of secret and often occult societies.

Mayr was thus well integrated into the roots of the Romantic Movement; however, it should be noted that it was for his pupil Donizetti to draw out from his teacher the full implication of romanticism in works like *Anna Bolena, Lucia di Lammermoor, Maria Stuarda* and *La favorite*. Mayr remained by choice essentially a classicist.

It was the language of the passions that Mayr gleaned from writers like Herder; here was a language which amplified the theories of Rameau, D'Alembert and the French Encyclopaedists. Once words were set to music, it became easier to theorize and link the ideals of *la musique drammatique* to the classical world of the modes and the supposed quasi-magical influence of music over the emotional life. When in Venice and studying texts like Carli's *Osservazioni sulla musica* (1782) and Barca's theories on music, Mayr must have drawn together the experience of a German university training with the Italian humanist tradition dating from the Renaissance, with the writings of theorists which fascinated him, such as Gaffurio and Zarlino. Maybe it appeared to Mayr that the German tradition was revitalizing the tired world of Italian music. Here was the secret of his "reform". He would use German instrumentation to give new sonorities to the dramatic world of the Italian operatic stage. Theory had to be at the service of sensitivity; alone it was but a skeleton; with a right understanding of the passionate life it could help to move an audience. The stage he considered, was a space on which the odd amalgam of the passions could be acted out; heightened by melody, harmony and rhythm they could have an audience at their mercy. Hence Mayr's concern for taste rather than excess. The theatre rightly used could initiate an audience into the hells, purgatories and paradises dwelling within an individual's heart. "Know Thyself", the self with all its darkness (Jason and Medea) and light (Zeliska in *L'amor coniugale*).

At the core of Mayr's thought and personality is the debate bemeen the rules of the game and the role of genius. Hamann (who influenced Herder) had suggested that a poet like Homer replaced ignorance of the rules of art, rules which an Aristotle might construe at a later date. Shakespeare had broken all the classical laws. What then . . . was unrestrained genius the answer?

According to Hamann and Mayr, the direction was for the creative person to understand the genius of the archaic sources dormant within his own consciousness: "Poetry is the mother-tongue of the human race: as gardening is older than farming, painting older than writing, singing than declamation, parables than inferences, bartering than commerce. A deeper sleep was the rest of our ancestors and an ecstatic dance their movement - senses and passions speak and understand nothing but images. The whole treasure of human knowledge and happiness consists in images." (Hamann, *Aesthetica in nuce*). Hamann's sequence of thought is a fundamental concept for Mayr, for he saw the world of opera as a world of images which could be evoked and heightened through the dramatic powers of music. He would have seized upon Herder's and Winckelmann's advice: "Do not rob the Greeks of what they have invented, but rather seize upon the art of invention, composition and form!".

Haydn and Mayr consequently studied and used in their music folk tunes and popular rhythms for both composers considered that in traditional, yet spontaneous musical exclamation, lay the roots of original poetic genius. Their example was continued by

Donizetti. Since opera was the declamation of words spiced with music, then a right balance must be aimed for between the popular (in the higher sense of the word) and the science of music. Words exclaimed through the power of music could reach the "natural" in a listener, tune his awareness of emotions and their relationship to his mind and will. Words and music could confront a person with the immediate, the "pregnant" or "eternal" present through the flow of inspiration. "One can never enjoy what follows if one has not enjoyed what has gone before - one cannot fully recall what has gone before (even in amended form) without losing the present." (*Herder, Reisejournal*). Mayr was to be criticised by his public for stringing together scene after scene in a continual flow of music. A good example is in *L'amor coniugale*, 1805, from scene 14, the *Terzetto, Qual voce mi sorprende* to the opera's conclusion. The audience is "subjected" to a constant flow of musical ideas breaking with Italian operatic convention of the times. The master's influence may be felt in the pupil's *L'elisir d'amore*, 1832, Act I from Nemorino's *Caro elisir! sei mio*, until the conclusion of the act. Such qualities indicate that Donizetti was a pupil of Mayr rather than a follower of Rossini.

Thus music should confront the listener with immediacy and as such it is indestructible, for something indelible is stamped on the mind and soul. Through words and music, sense and reason intertwine, opening the dictionary of the life within. True opera (the work, the task) should provide the key to our inner being, igniting the Divine Spark, re-awakening the Prometheus within. Hence, the agony and the ecstasy evoked by the power of music. Away with "nice, dull, annoying, useless free-thinking; substitute for everything that perhaps is needed more - heart, warmth, blood, humanity, life!" (Herder, *Auch eine Philosophie der Geschichte zur Bildung der Menschheit* - 1774).

Here is the trumpet call for romanticism which Mayr, with all his classicism, took with him to Italy. Compare his sounds to those of Galuppi, Cimarosa and Paisiello; quite simply he wrought a revolution.

One final point; the *Sturm und Drang*, Herder and Goethe, revalued the Middle Ages, especially English History, which was considered "solid, cohesive, noble and splendid!". (See for example, the operas *La rosa bianca e la rosa rossa*, 1813 and *Alfredo il Grande, Re degli Anglo-Sassoni*, 1819). Once more the full impact of Mayr's background was to come to fruition in Donizetti.

Already we are stumbling across the problem of seeing Mayr as a "bridge" composer from one generation to another. Such he was, but he was a lot more too; he was a fine composer and a complete mind, authentic and personal in himself. Nothing can be farther from the truth than to smudge him somewhere between Cimarosa and Rossini.

7   Classicism

Sturm und Drang, shot through with passion, intolerance and immaturity, could only lead to loss of sanity or change of heart as the main protagonists of the movement matured. It was a young man's movement - of the kind that re-occurs in every generation, re-appearing with another mask. Once high lofty ideals and hopes met with the stark reality of experience, the understanding of the nature of "genius" had to mature.

In 1776 Goethe secured Herder's appointment in Weimar and gradually the stable world of classicism took on a different complexion. It offered all the seeds that early romanticism lacked.

These are the years of Goethe's contacts with the Illuminati, who if anything, presented the classical ideal permeating the concept of state and culture, rather than romanticism's adulation of the individual. Classicism was a notion of a land south of the Alps where spiritual rebirth through first-hand knowledge of the world of the ancients and their descendants could be experienced. Both Goethe and Mayr had to journey to Italy in order for their lives to mature.

Torquato Tasso, the tragic 16th century poet, the subject of Goethe's play and Donizetti's opera, was for the Romantics a prototype of their own kind. Tasso was the example of the poet exiled, imprisoned and destroyed due to his genius and idealized world of love.

For the new classicism, genius alone was not enough; it required tempering with well-proven science, reconciliating the individual with society. Without structure, pattern and discipline, romanticism, was like Tasso, doomed to eventual self destruction. The poet's *daimon*, the driving force of his genius, was considered also the cause of his fate which encircles him and brings him to his ultimate self destruction. He will meet either insanity, like Tasso, or nobility of personality overcoming the fear of death, like Egmont.

Schiller's *Maria Stuart* and Donizetti's *Maria Stuarda* are both works showing personal excess, being purified, and the acceptance of fate through moral reason (forgiveness), liberating the soul from the apparent finality of death. In the hands of Goethe and Schiller, Mayr and to a certain extent Donizetti, romanticism is harnessed to the theme of the classical world's sense of morality. For Mayr in particular, all had been said before in the libretti of Metastasio, the poet, who, as we shall see, became his mentor, setting *Demetrio* to music in 1824, forty-two years after the poet's death. With *Faust* "part two", Goethe remained substantially fascinated with the imagery of the occult sciences as expressions of the soul, with *Dom Sébastien, roi du Portugal* or *Maria di Rohan*, Donizetti became lost in the *maelström* of Romanticism. Mayr, at the close of his years, appears to be fulfilled, enlightened, physically blind, but awake to Eternity.

As already noted, the Notebooks show that Mayr knew *Wilhelm Meister*. Wilhelm's journey reflects his own. Lost in the agony and the ecstasy of the lives of wandering actors, caught in their vices and cabals, Wilhelm is educated through life's experience and develops the notion of a reform of the theatre. This comes about through staging

Shakespeare's *Hamlet*, the epitome of romantic genius for both Herder and the young Goethe. Enthusiasm gives way to understanding and the theatre becomes a world through which the world may be better understood; a discipline which may mature those involved. Thus romantic subjectivity is restrained by experience; in keeping with Illuminati doctrine, a right understanding of the world constitutes Wilhelm's education. The individual matures only through coming to terms with his own mistaken tendencies. The re-interpretation of the classical world for Wilhelm (i.e., Goethe and Mayr) is to "go out" and meet life and harness the *daimon* of genius. The ultimate ideal is not chaos but harmony through the recognition of real education. Wilhelm learns responsibility for those whose fate has become intertwined with his own (i.e., Mignon, the Harper and Felix) and only thus becomes prepared and fit for being received into the Society of the Tower (the Illuminati) [2]. Only through a living classicism (not an intellectual, abstract ideal) does Wilhelm become worthy of Natalie's love.

If we remove Goethe's antipathy to Christianity and submerge the *Meister* experience into traditional Catholic understanding of the soul and its pilgrimage, then we have the necessary clues to understanding Mayr's complex personality as it is revealed in his life, work and Notebooks.

II   1789 - 1802

1   The Church of *S. Maria Maggiore* and the MIA
2   Carlo Lenzi
3   Ferdinando Bertoni
4   Venice - the end of *La Serenissima*
5   Theatre and music in the late 18th century
6   The first oratorios and operas
7   Marriage and the return to Bergamo

Thus Mayr "took himself to Bergamo" - so read the *Cenni* - in order to dedicate his life to music. There, "initially, he was to place himself under the direction of Carlo Lenzi (1735 - 1805), the Kapellmeister, a well-known figure with the reputation of being a

---

2   'Illuminati'is here meant in a wider context than the first few years of Weishaupt's Order. It is meant more in line with his later thought after the Order's suppression, that is, that in every generation there is an "invisible" family of wise souls who hold the tradition together for the next generation.

composer of church music, renowned even outside of Italy". Mayr interestingly notes that he had had the advantage of meeting Lenzi during a previous journey to those parts. Mayr had therefore already been to Italy.

It is surprising that no-one has noticed this detail; that Mayr had already met Lenzi during a previous journey. The most laudable conclusion is that Mayr had been sent or taken by v. Bassus to Lombardy on "business". Perhaps Mayr had been a courier distributing his patron's publications. It is possible that if Mayr had not left v. Bassus and whatever job he was doing for his patron to follow his vocation, he would have remained an unfulfilled person, unknown to the history books, and the course of Italian music would have been very different.

Bergamo may well have been a commercial distribution point for clandestine books but it also boasted a long tradition in music, literature and the visual arts. In 1428 the Visconti of Milan had ceded the city to Venice, under whose power Bergamo remained until 1797, the year of the advent of Napoleon and the birth of Gaetano Donizetti. To this day, a visitor cannot help but feel, even know, the reality of this tradition. The amazing fact is that Mayr subsequently turned down appointments as far and wide as St. Petersburg, Lisbon, London, Vienna, Paris, Dresden, Milan and Novara. Once he had been supported by the city of his choice, his mind was made up, and the reason behind his decision to stay was the promise of founding a school to promote his teaching[3]. One might well say that his school was his true vocation (for it drew on all the resources of his training as an illuminatus), but that it was his music by which he established his reputation. As Mayr reflects, Haydn was not given a doctorate by Oxford University for writing an obscure thesis but for his abilities as a composer. No-one should become a founder or be made a principal of a music school unless he is a musician in the fullest sense, equal to Padre Martini or Stanislao Mattei of Bologna. It is quite clear from Mayr's writings that education was for him something that could only happen in relationship to a master (or masters) in the fullest sense of the word, and furthermore, on a genuine small scale.

He would have agreed with the maxim, "small is beautiful". However, it is important to note that his school became the subsequent pattern for all other Italian music schools even though they grew in size!

1   The Church of *S. Maria Maggiore* and the MIA

The focal centre of the old city (*Città Alta*) is a memorable square with a fountain. Northwards lies the splendid High Renaissance palace, now the *Biblioteca Civica A. Mai*,

---

3   Mayr's decision to stay in Bergamo and to create from scratch his own school may only be explained by recognizing the sort of education he had received from Weishaupt and v. Bassus and his ideal to reform Italian music.

where today most of Mayr's music and writings are kept. Southwards, through arches covering the old market, lies the *Cappella Colleoni* and the great church of *S. Maria Maggiore*.

Externally the church is Romanesque in the style made famous by the Comancini masons. It was built in the 12th century on the site of *S. Maria Antiqua* which dated back to 774 AD and was built close by a Roman temple dedicated to the Goddess of Mercy. We are told sacrifices used to be offered on its altars hoping to propitiate the God of Fear and the Goddess of Hope. Certainly this whole area has the feeling of being saturated in antiquity. It is as if Stonehenge had become the centre of a city and that the ancient site had been obscured by a cathedral. On the south side of the basilica, Mayr's house and school are at the distance of easy stone throws.

Internally, the church is one of the finest examples of High Renaissance decoration, anticipating the Baroque. The ceiling is a vast iconographic setting portraying in allegory and symbol the Virgin Mary as the rich flower of the Old Testament. Mayr, who was naturally attracted to the visual arts, would have made use of its images when teaching. It is easy to imagine choir boys trying to interpret the enigmatic symbols of Lorenzo Lotto's *intarsie* which surround the choir behind the high altar and the choir screen. In many ways the iconographic significance of the basilica's interior may only be unlocked through a speculative philosophical approach such as Mayr would have learnt from the Illuminati. At the furthermost western point of the building lie the tombs of Mayr and Donizetti which face eastwards towards the high altar. Inside *S. Maria Maggiore* one steps into a vast space dedicated to the feminine mysteries: mercy, compassion, charity and sacrifice. The ancient chronicler of the church wrote:

> "The greater church which is called the Church of Mercy in this city
> of ours, Bergamo, . . . it was built not only at almost incredible ex-
> pense but also with great artistic elegance, out of square cut blocks
> of stone hewn by our fellow citizens in honour of the Mercy of the
> Mother of God. It was begun by prayer in this summer season of
> 1137."

A lay order dedicated to good works was founded by Bishop Erodo; however, it was a Dominican friar, Pinamonte Brembiati, who wrote its rule in 1265, a year before his death. The fabric, liturgy and music were the responsibility of the Council (*Consorzio*) of the MIA, or *Misericordia Maggiore*, as the lay order was known. In 1449, the city fathers yielded to the MIA all its interests in the basilica, and in 1453 Pope Nicholas V liberated *S. Maria Maggiore* from all episcopal jurisdiction, a privilege continued to this day. From 1449, instruction in singing and playing was begun. Two teachers worked under a kapellmeister, a post held by musicians like Gaffurio, Pietro Vinci, Gasparo Alberti, Filippo Vitali, Legrenzi, G.B. Bassani, and Ponchielli, besides Lenzi and Mayr. Under the Venetian Republic the choir was supported by double organs, brass and viols.

Mayr was approaching an institution with a long musical tradition, a place of beauty, a sanctuary with meaning.

2   Carlo Lenzi 1735 - 1805

Mayr's remarks on Lenzi are blunt. "But realising after a few months that he [Mayr] could not get instruction in the first principles of the art of counterpoint; moreover, finding his means of sustenance diminishing he had already resolved to return to his native land, when a generous enthusiast for the art of music of that city, the late Count Canon Pesenti, had the goodness of soul to sustain him, offering him the suitable means for overcoming his fear of continuing in a musical career, and procured for him the advantage of the necessary study with the renowned Ferdinando Bertoni, then Kapellmeister of St. Mark's, Venice."

Pesenti was fundamental to Mayr's career. There is a tradition that the Count-priest not only supported Mayr because of his obvious musical talents but because Mayr had once saved him from the fury of a frightened horse. Calvi informs us that Mayr was to remain faithful to his benefactor's wish, that he would ultimately dedicate himself to the composition of sacred music, a sign of the respect he had towards Pesenti. One has the suspicion that here was a man of great sensibility who helped Mayr not only financially, but also intellectually and spiritually. Pesenti takes his place alongside Weishaupt and v. Bassus as a fundamental influence over the evolving personality and career of the composer to be.

The remark concerning Lenzi and counterpoint made by Mayr becomes clearer when it is realized that in the *Biblioteca Civica* are Lenzi's manuscripts of counterpoint studies made by the composer at Naples whilst at the school of Nicola Sala, then one of the most important schools of the period. Lenzi was in Naples between 1755 and 1760. Nicola Sala had been the pupil of Nicola Fago and Leonardo Leo, names which link Lenzi to the zenith of the Neapolitan School which excelled in the counterpoint style of religious music; for example, the Scarlattis, Francesco Durante, Nicola Porpora, Leonardo Vinci and others. Naples had been the formative influence over Lenzi's music.

When Lenzi returned to Bergamo he became deputy Kapellmeister at *S. Maria Maggiore*, due, it is recorded, to the frailty of the then Kapellmeister, Lodovico Ferronati, once the orchestra's first violinist. Ferronati died in 1767 making way for Lenzi's appointment. Lenzi was 32 and had already worked seven years for the MIA. The lay order's records show that he was commissioned to compose music regularly for services. For example: 21 March 1780 - ". . . two psalms, that is one *Domine*, one *Confitebor*; a *Magnificat*; a *Miserere* for Good Friday; *Lauds* with choir; a *Messa*, that is, a *Kyrie*, a *Gloria*; a *Salve*; an *Anthem* for *Vespers* for two choirs, organ and violone, with all the necessary parts".

From 1787 composition duties were eased on Lenzi due to his poor sight; however, he did not cease from composing until two years before his death. In 1789, it is quite possible that Mayr came across a tired, sick and virtually blind man who found it difficult to give himself to teaching. Furthermore, during Lenzi's last years music may have lost some of its lustre in *S. Maria Maggiore*. At his own request the aging Kapellmeister left his appointment on 2 June 1802 and Mayr took over his mantle on the same day. Lenzi died on 23 March 1805.

3   Ferdinando Bertoni 1725 - 1813

Mayr reached Venice at the latest by 1790. He is sometimes referred to as a pupil of Bertoni. This is an exaggeration to say the least. The *Cenni* record:

> "It was to his [Mayr's] lack of luck that also this worthy master supposed that his pupil [Mayr was 27!] possessed more knowledge of music's theoretical science than he [Mayr] had. Since he [Bertoni] was already well advanced in years, he did not wish to undertake the precise task of leading him through the troublesome course of elementary and higher rigorous instruction in harmony and counterpoint, and was content to give him only simple advice on the design and making of pieces of music. These he [Mayr] wrote according to his gifts, moreover he had to perfect his studies during those few years through reading and studying writers on musical theory, examining all types of composition, which he attempted to obtain and then copy them with indefatigable labour."

Thus it may be supposed that the greater amount of music of other composers copied out by Mayr in the *Biblioteca Civica* dates from this period, likewise the books which he copied out for study.

Mayr was a substantially self-taught composer. Bertoni would have shared with Mayr the structure of the "Italian" idiom, the "tricks of the trade" of late 18th century Venetian operatic conventions. It was the world of which Mayr wished to become master, in order to develop it and fill it with the insights of Germanic instrumentation. Burney described Bertoni's music as "graceful and interesting . . . constantly natural, correct and judicious; often pleasing and sometimes happy". Bertoni stylistically would have been midway between Galuppi (who had died in 1785) and Cimarosa (whom Mayr knew in Venice). He admired both composers and they had a formative influence over the Bavarian composer. Galuppi's music is charming, clear in intention with good use of modulation. He excelled in different genres and was a famous keyboard player. He set the pattern for *opera buffa* and was fortunate to collaborate with Goldoni as librettist. Many of Mayr's comic works echo the world of Galuppi and Goldoni; for example, *La Locandiera* (1800) and *L'avaro*

(1799). Cimarosa offered a model for tragic works, for example *Gli Orazi ed i Curiazi* (1797) and *Artemisia* (1801). Mayr gave the sound of these composers the "wound" of the *Sturm und Drang* as well as the heroic expectations brought to Italy by the cathartic and liberating presence of Napoleon. The world of Bertoni, Galuppi and Cimarosa is *aggiornamentato*, that is, brought up to date. From the first works, Mayr makes references to his own national composers, especially Gluck, Haydn and Mozart. But to return to Bertoni. Mayr would have found congenial conversations relating to Bertoni's own *Orfeo ed Euridice* (1776) for which the composer had used Calzabigi's text thus inviting open comparison with Gluck's masterpiece. Critics of the period accused Gluck of plagiarism, lifting arias from Bertoni's operas. Mayr would have been able to air his views on the relationship between classical tragedy and contemporary opera, and argue for his beloved Metastasio. His first opera *Saffo* shows the influence of Gluck in the long sections for chorus [4]. Furthermore, Bertoni's vast experience in writing sacred music would not have gone unquestioned and the early oratorios take their form from those of Bertoni and other composers of the day. But the content is new, Mayr introduced orchestral ideas from his German sources, for example, the Haydnesque, instrumental picture-painting in the arioso sections of *La Passione* (1794), as well as the mood of *The seven last words*, developed by Mayr in the crucifixion sequence. Later, Mayr performed Haydn's work in its vocal setting, to which he added a moving *Invito* or "invitation". Mayr, by the evidence of his first compositions, was calculating a form and a content which he knew would make his audience (on the verge of losing their old world for a new order wrought by revolution) sit up and take account - he was a new voice in the dramatic art of vocal music.

The *Cenni* do not provide all the facts to hand. Mayr had been to Venice before 1790. On the 7 June 1786 he was presented by Angiolo Dalmazzo to Contessa Marina Querini Benzoni and to the free life of her *salotto*. Mayr was accused of having an affair with the Contessa, as was virtually every male visitor to her *salotto*. Byron was to become her lover in 1818 when she was over sixty. Longhi painted her portrait and Antonio Lamberti composed verses to her honour:

> *La biondina in gondoletta*
> *l'altra sera go mena,*
> *dal piacer la povareta*
> *la x'è in bota indormenzà.*

Mayr set the verses to music in honour of the beauty who loved to keep hot slices of polenta safely housed in her ample cleavage, to be shared and nibbled as she journeyed along the canals! It became a song that has remained in the memories of gondoliers; to this day it is sung to tourists as they are packaged in gondolas on their expensive tours. By tradition it is the song taught to Rosina in the *Barbiere di Siviglia* during the music lesson scene. The melody was set to a sequence of variations by Ferdinando Paër and it was the most successful melody Mayr ever wrote.

---

4   Mayr copied out Gluck's *Alceste* and had all Gluck's main dramatic operas in his library.

But this detail throws into chaos Mayr's *Cenni*. 1786 is the year of the Regensburg song album, a year before Mayr said he travelled over the Alps southwards. It is fair to conclude that the elderly Mayr inadvertently got his year wrong in the *Cenni*; but why does he not add the visit to Italy alongside Poschiavo and Tirano? This would have been the year when he first met Carlo Lenzi. No doubt he was "on business" with v. Bassus; maybe the composer of popular songs was a good decoy for the distribution of books forbidden by the Inquisition. Also, from 1789, the Illuminati were known to the Venetian police. In the State Archives of Venice, envelope number 225, a dispatch to Niccolò Corner, *Capitano-vice-podestà* of Bergamo contains a reference dated 29 July 1794 (the year of Mayr's *Saffo* and *La Passione*) to Giovanni Maironi da Ponte (subsequently a friend of Mayr) with reference to a journey undertaken by v. Bassus to Bergamo and on to Venice (no doubt to see Mayr, amongst other commitments). V. Bassus is described as a "Giacobin in opinion and a member of the Sect of the Illuminati" and "that he has friends and followers in Lombardy and the Veneto . . . he has the name of "Hannibal" and is something more than just an ordinary member".

In the records of the infamous Council of Ten, Mayr is noted as a personality constantly to be seen in gallant society of the decade.

4   Venice - the end of *La Serenissima*

The secret for not being exiled or sent to rot in prison was not to rock the boat and to enjoy the merry-go-round while it lasted. Only whisper liberal views to friends in secret, wear one's wig, don the domino's mask if the *calle* (the narrow passageways) of Venice had to be negotiated anonymously, and carry on with work as normal. But never be caught with certain books or pamphlets on one's person!

It is helpful to imagine Mayr stepping into the world of Longhi's paintings, a world in which pale faces peer out at the viewer with a blank expression. Too often only the servants and peasants and rogues look real - the *cicisbei* and their ladies look as if they require a good dusting - sentiments with which Mayr would have fully approved.

The last days of the Republic thrived on careless indifference to the storm brewing in France. Molmenti writes:

> "The state which had once scaled the heights of glory, disappeared
> in a kind of voluptuous stupor, not, however, debased by aught that
> was abject. In the society of Venice during the last days there were
> more defects than faults, frivolity of sentiment rather than violence
> of passion. Corruption ever presented itself under the guise of a
> crude sensuality; it was never involved in turpitude, nor as in An-

cient Rome, did it break out into outbursts of brutality and mad lust. Venice was no worse than France, which was preparing a great Revolution, England under Anne and George . . . In Venice the poetry of the place, its singular site, the development of its art, all contributed to emphasise the corruption which was common to the rest of Europe."

When Napoleon dissolved the Venetian dream, Mayr was 34, a year short of Dante's *mezzo del cammin* of our earthly pilgrimage. His life belongs to the old order and the beginning of the new.

The years spent in Venice which saw the birth of his first oratorios, cantatas and operas were set against a political backcloth. Doge Renier died on 18 February 1789. However, so as not to disturb carnival time his death was kept secret until 2 March, in Lent! An ambitious doge, he had found few to share in his concern for the future of the Republic in the light of European events. The intelligentsia of the middle classes and nobility were being drawn together through the distribution of new ideas. With persons like Consul Smith (Canaletto's patron), Goldoni and Casanova, freemasonry was gaining ground, preparing the way for change.

In 1788 Venice's ambassador to France, Antonio Cappello, warned his fellow Venetians not to isolate themselves from other nations in order to protect their own interests. His communication was not even forwarded to the Senate, rather it was decided that booksellers should be forbidden to circulate books of a liberal substance. Comedians had to curb their humour, and even the popular coffee houses had to be careful of free and lively discussion.

On 9 March 1789, Lodovico Manin was elected doge; on 5 May the French Revolution began. Venice continued its merry-go-round of pleasure. Unarmed neutrality was believed to be the best policy by Europe's oldest republic; how could *La Serenissima* be the victim of revolution?

However, Venice was humiliated and her territories became a battlefield for the French and Austrians. Napoleon constantly sought excuses for quarrelling and his agents incited Bergamo, Brescia and Crema to revolt. The glory of Venice had ceased, but she still believed herself to be safe on her lagoons, where her fleet captured a French ship and executed the captain for his presumption in trespassing on the territorial waters of the lagoons. The general belief was that the city would be defended quite simply by its Dalmatian troops. But by 1797 Napoleon had intended to take Venice.

Any idea of resistance was laid to one side. On 30 April the Senate gathered round a weak, terrified doge. The only counsel he could offer was. "Tonight we are not sure of sleeping in our own beds!" Any would-be heroes were ignored.

Napoleon had secretly sold Venice to Austria at the Treaty of Leoben and was in no mood for coming to terms whatsoever. He declared war on 1 May. On 12 May the Great Council met for the last time. Manin burst into tears, committed Venice to the Divine Will and resigned. The first shots were heard. Venice had been humiliated. A "tree of liberty" was erected in St. Mark's Square. The populace and a few patricians danced around it. The poet Ugo Foscolo joined the new merriment, as did Contessa Marina Querini Benzoni dressed in an authentic Athenian tunic! Where was Mayr on that day?

5 Theatre and music in late 18th century Venice

The richness and complexity of 18th century Venetian art demands specialized study. Sometimes it is overlooked that artists were not a separate breed but men very much integrated into the life of their times; the borderline between decorative arts and pure painting often being consequently, misleadingly blurred. Painters could turn their talents to decorating furniture, frescoes for a villa, stage scenery, casing for a church organ, or simply a fan.

The Venetian school never had much time for academies, their own only being founded in the mid-eighteenth Century. Their tradition revolved around the family and the workshop - the Bellini, Vivarini, Bassano, Tiepolo, Guardi etc. They refused to impose theory on their art. Pietro Aretino implied one either had "it" or lacked "it"; lesser men would shrink back before genius. The one Venetian who records a little of their thought was Marco Boschini (1613 - 1678). In his poem, *La carta del navigar pittoresco* (1660), he shows how the Venetian artist considered his work akin to that of the musician. His thoughts must have formed an echo in Mayr's own.

Boschini wrote:

> "The Venetian artist is an expert musician
> who tunes and plays well his instrument.
> If occasionally he plays a few discords
> they are meant to give more spirit to the concert.
> His hand regulates, works and perfects,
> forms fugues, sonatas and bagatelles,
> toccatas, even preludes and fantasias;
> all these he modulates from key to key . . . "

The sensuousness of Venetian art is "operatic", the dexterity of paint and line, the marriage of brush and pen, colour and tone, all relates to a wide vision concerning the nature of the arts. Mayr reflects in the Notebooks, "Music is like painting with its colours and shades. Music is the art of painting with pleasing sounds the passions in such a way that the affections of the listener are moved and give rise to ecstasy." Just as one can learn to "read" the touch of the brush charged with colour, so one should learn to appreciate the tonal quality of Mayr's orchestration. Perhaps it was the sensuousness of sound to which the Venetian public related above all in Mayr's music; it had parallels in the world around them. It is unfortunate that Stendhal failed to appreciate it.

Venice was a musical world where song inspired travellers. Mayr was also noted because of the vocal quality of his songs. Many were published long before his operas and were to be found in print before 1800 and as far abroad as London - a mark of his fame. Here was a German who could beat the Italians at their own game. Goethe, writing in his *Italian Journey*, 6 October 1786, casts light on the situation, for the entry admirably catches the ambience upon which Mayr made his mark:

> "For this evening I had made arrangements to hear the famous sing-ing of the boatmen, who chant verses by Tasso[5] and Ariosto to their own melodies. This performance has to be ordered in advance, for it is now rarely done and belongs rather, to the half-forgotten legends of the past. The moon had risen when I took my seat in a gondola and the two singers, one in the prow, the other in the stern, began chanting verse after verse in turns. The melody, which we know from Rousseau, is something between chorale and recitative. It always moves at the same tempo without any definite beat. The modulation is of the same character; the singers change pitch according to the content of the verse in a kind of declamation.
>
> I shall not go into the question of how the melody evolved. It is enough to say that it is ideal for someone idly singing to himself and adapting the tune to poems he knows by heart.
>
> The singer sits on the shore of an island, on the bank of a canal or in a gondola, and sings at the top of his voice - the people here ap-preciate volume more than anything else. His aim is to make his voice carry as far as possible over the still mirror of water. Far away another singer hears it. He knows the melody and the words and answers with the next verse. The first singer answers again, and so on. Each is the echo of the other. They keep this up night after night without ever getting tired. If the listener has chosen the right spot, which is halfway between them, the further apart they are, the more enchanting the singing will sound.
>
> To demonstrate this, my boatmen tied up the gondola on the shore of the Giudecca and walked along the canal in opposite directions. I walked back and forth, leaving the one, who was just about to sing, and walking towards the other, who had just stopped. For the first time I felt the full effect of this singing. The sound of their voices far away was extraordinary, a lament without sadness, and I was moved to tears. I put this down to my mood at the moment, but my old manservant said: "*è singolare, come quel canto intenerisce, è*

---

5   Note in Mayr's opera, *Belle ciarle e triste fatti*, the gondoliers' song based on Tasso by the librettist Anelli; *Roma superba del suo vanto antico*.

molto più ben cantato". He wanted me to hear the women on the Lido, especially those from Malamocco and Pellestrina. They too, he told me, sing verses by Tasso to the same or a similar melody, and added: "It is their custom to sit on the seashore while their husbands are out sea-fishing, and sing these songs in penetrating tones until, from far out over the sea, their men reply, and in this way they converse with each other." Is this not a beautiful custom? I dare say that, to someone standing close by, the sound of such voices, competing with the thunder of the waves, might not be very agreeable. But the motive behind such singing is so human and genuine that it makes the mere notes of the melody, over which scholars have racked their brains in vain, come to life. It is the cry of some lonely human being, sent out into the wide world till it reaches the ears of another lonely human being who is moved to answer it."

The theatrical world still felt the wake left by Goldoni and his squabbles with Chiari and Gozzi. Presentations ranged from *Commedia dell'arte* performances in local squares, to tragedies and operas in theatres that have long ceased to exist.

Music, however, was the favourite amongst the arts. The State gave music its protection, ensuring that song resonated throughout the *calle*, on the gondolas, in churches and in the theatres. By the time Mayr reached Venice its greatest composers had died but their works were still proudly performed. Venice was one of the great musical centres of Europe.

Benedetto Marcello (Mayr was renowned for his accompaniment to Marcello's settings of the first fifty psalms) had died in 1739. Antonio Lotti likewise had died - so had Antonio Vivaldi. Giuseppe Tartini died in 1770 - "the Platonist" as Mayr termed him. Needless to say, Mayr studied Tartini's theoretical writings and held him in high respect. Baldassare Galuppi died in 1785.

Ferdinando Paër, the composer whom Mayr associated with his own desire for "reform", was in Venice from 1791 to 1796 before leaving for Vienna and Paris where he became Napoleon's favourite composer. Paër and Mayr both composed *Te Deums* for Napoleon's two coronations. There is a tradition that suggests Mayr helped Cimarosa, owing to sickness, with his last works. Certainly *Gli Orazi ed i Curiazi* (1796) marks the end of a generation of serious operas, whereas *Saffo* performed two years earlier, is the beginning of a new breed.

Giovanni Paisiello's *Nina pazza per l'amore* composed in 1789 still triumphed in Venice in 1796.

Mayr comments in his *Cenni*:

> "In brilliant, gay Venice, he [Mayr] had the opportunity to frequent many theatres, musical gatherings, and to hear an infinity of church compositions, then performed with extraordinary pomp, to hear oratorios composed by excellent composers and performed with much perfection in the then existing three female conservatories[6]."

He was fortunate that he caught the end of a world and its tradition before it vanished for all time.

> "Dust and ashes, dead and done with, Venice spent what Venice earned."
>
> (Browning - *A toccata of Galuppi's*)

6   The first oratorios and operas

The *Cenni* continue:

> "Moreover, after having the fortune to air one of his [Mayr's] Masses and Vespers during one of the most solemn occasions, he had the fortune to compose for the Conservatory of the *Mendicanti* an oratorio entitled: *Jacob a Labano fugiens*, which was performed in the presence of three sovereigns: Ferdinand, King of Naples; Leopold the Grandduke of Tuscany[7]; and Ferdinand, Archduke of Milan."

Thus Mayr begins his "career" (previously he had only composed songs) with his first and last love, sacred music (the mass survives and is to be found in the *Fondo Mayr, Biblioteca Civica*, Bergamo).

Jacob a Labano fugiens is in form similar to all the six oratorios. This may be termed *Venetian*, the format favoured by the four pious institutions (or conservatories, as Mayr called them) and which had been used for over a century. In a wider sense, the format may be said to be *Italian*, for similar works were given throughout the Peninsula, in keeping with the tradition inaugurated by the Oratorians. The oratorios are in two parts, the

---

6   There were in fact four such institutions rivalling each other according to the merits of the teachers, the *Incurabili*, the *Ospedaletto*, the *Pietà*, and the *Mendicanti*. The *Ospedaletto* (or *Ospedali*) was bankrupt by 1777, but it did not cut back on the production of oratorios.

7   Leopold II (1747-1792) known as "the Wise" left Florence 1790 to be crowned emperor after the death of his brother Joseph II.

first part, comprising a brief sinfonia, introductory chorus with sections for the soloists, a sequence of recitatives, arioso sections, arias and duets for the soloists, and a concluding chorus; the second part being the same except for a brief introduction. The orchestra: Violins I and II, Violas are sometimes divided for sonority, Cellos and Doublebasses, Oboes I and II, Bassoon, Horns I and II. A continuo part is understood and expected even if it is not specified in the full score. Such was the typical church orchestra of the period, a force which Mayr would extend once Kapellmeister at Bergamo. Mayr also introduces an obligato instrument if it suits his purpose. He refused permission for his sacred music to be published. The only exception is the *G Minor Requiem* which was printed without his permission.

The librettist of Mayr's first oratorio was Giuseppe Maria Foppa (1760 - 1845) who wrote a number of libretti for Mayr. He had studied at the *Mendicanti* and was a popular librettist of his period.

Goethe writes for 3 October 1786:

> "Map in hand, I tried to find my way through the labyrinth to the Church of the Mendicants. Here is the Conservatorio, which at the present time enjoys the highest reputation. The women were singing an oratorio behind the choir screen; the church was filled with listeners, the music beautiful and the voices superb. An alto sang the part of King Saul, the protagonist in the work. I have never heard such a voice. Some passages in the music were of infinite beauty and the text was perfectly singable - a kind of Italian Latin which made one smile at times but which gave the music wide scope.
>
> The performance would have been even more enjoyable if the damned conductor had not beaten time against the screen with a rolled sheet of music as insolently as if he were teaching schoolboys. The girls had so often rehearsed the piece that his vehement slapping was as unnecessary as if, in order to make us appreciate a beautiful statue, someone were to stick little patches of red cloth on the joints.
>
> This man was a musician, yet he did not, apparently, hear the discordant sound he was making which ruined the harmony of the whole. Maybe he wanted to attract our attention to himself by this extraordinary behaviour; he would have convinced us better of his merits by giving a perfect performance. I know this thumping out the beat is customary with the French; but I had not expected it from the Italians. The public, though, seemed to be used to it. It was not the only occasion on which I have seen the public under the delusion that something which spoils the enjoyment is part of it."

Mayr was among the very last composers to write for a world more easily associated with Vivaldi and Goldoni, the antics of Brighella, Harlequin and Pantaloon.

The *Cenni* adds:

> "He [Mayr] followed by writing for the same institution three other oratorios, amongst which *Sisara* had the most success; amazing approval with a continual flock of listeners, eager each time to admire the excellent and animated performance. In particular that of the famous Bianca Sacchetti[8] who was the last teacher and director of the *Mendicanti*."

Sisara was performed in 1793, *Tobiae matrimonium* in 1794, *David in spelunca Engaddi* in 1795. All three have libretti by Foppa, the last mentioned having an alternative text in Italian. All four *Mendicanti* oratorios exist in the *Fondo Mayr*; the scores are clear and invite revival. (See catalogue).

Prior to *Jacob a Labano fugiens*, he had had performed his first orchestral piece, a cantata, *Femio, ossia la musica custode della fede maritale*[9], to celebrate a marriage between two persons of famous old Venetian families, the Widemaro and Foscarini. Clearly, Mayr was moving in the right circles. This is a substantial work lasting over an hour, for three soloists, chorus and an orchestra which already shows the signs of things to come. Mayr never used instruments for the sake of noise, but quality, rather like the varying strokes of a brush when working on a canvas, or the light and shade in a Guardi or a Tiepolo painting. If he wanted a particular tonal effect he would introduce solo instruments; in *Femio* he introduced the harp, an instrument of which he was particularly fond. There are numbers for solo harp and numerous examples of its use in the operas, the best known being for its tonal qualities: Creusa's second aria in *Medea in Corinto*. Donizetti's use of flute and harp as the introduction to the fountain scene of *Lucia di Lammermoor* is an example of Mayr's influence.

But it was in 1794, at *La Fenice* where Mayr played viola in the orchestra, with the first performance of his *opera seria, Saffo ossia I riti d'Apollo Leucadio* that Mayr's fame was sealed. The opera was composed due to the following circumstances. In 1793 Mayr had been called back to Bergamo by his patron, Count Canon Pesenti, in order to spend a few days with him and consider composing exclusively *religious* music, but Pesenti suddenly died.

---

8   Bianca Sacchetti was a pupil of Bertoni and who was judged as "admirable for a very artificial sound of ligatures and subtleties which rendered pleasing a not perfect voice." Mayr wrote for her the cantata *Ero* (libretto, Foppa) 1793.

9   Libretto by Abate Boaretti.

Mayr explains that Pesenti's death came as a great shock for it left him without an income, and it was thus that he decided to compose for the stage. His decision was encouraged by Gluck's rival, Piccinni, who was in Venice for his opera *Griselda* on the 8 October at the *San Samuele*, and by Peter Winter who likewise was in Venice, for the performances of two operas at the rival *San Benedetto*[10]: *I fratelli rivali*, November 1793 and *Belisa ossia La fedeltà riconosciuta* whose first night was on 5 February 1794, twelve days before Mayr's outstanding success at *La Fenice*. Regardless of *Saffo*'s success Mayr did not compose another opera for nearly two years.

The choice of subject for his first opera is interesting (as is Donizetti's *Il Pigmaglione*), for it tells us much about Mayr. Throughout his long life he meditated upon the nature of love and knowledge; what may be termed the "Apollonian mysteries" (whereas Donizetti was torn to pieces like Dionysius in the *maelström* of passions). Solemn scenes of pagan ritual are a feature of Mayr's operas, for example *I misteri Eleusini*, 1802; *Alonso e Cora*, 1804; *Zamori*, 1804; and *I Cherusci*, 1808. It is possible to think of Mozart's *Die Zauberflöte* with its male chorus and sombre voice of Zarastro. The connection is direct; Ignaz v. Born, who commissioned Mozart's opera, was an Illuminatus and there is evidence that Mozart likewise belonged to the order. Certainly, when her husband died, Constance Mozart wrote to Mayr asking him to find a job for her son Karl Thomas, a request Mayr promptly fulfilled. Constance Mozart had met Mayr in Vienna, 1803.

Judging by the London revival of Mayr's oratorio *La Passione* (1794) in 1974 these early works are of an amazing quality. Although a late starter, it is as if Mayr was already an expert in his profession. It is nothing short of a *tour de force* of the intellect.

It is worth quoting from the *Cenni confidenziali*:

> "First of all it would be worth pondering on the fact it was already late when Mayr had the possibility of dedicating himself to the study of composition. Deprived from even a regular and basic elementary instruction in the art of counterpoint, directed only to learn as much as was necessary to maintain a job in the country of his benefactor[11], where, in a manner of saying, every composition was studied, plotted and imitated, fugues were virtually forbidden, and then suddenly thrown by fate into a theatrical career without previous study - except for that little practice acquired in writing two or three oratorios. This was at 31 years old (an age at which it can be said the fire of the imagination already begins to diminish). In contrast to younger composers like Paër and Nasolini who had repeatedly produced works in Venetian theatres, he was still at the beginning of his (personal) studies, obliged for a few years to make a living giving

---

10   Theatres in Venice, except for *La Fenice* took their names from the parish in which they were sited.

11   V. Bassus. Mayr was employed to compose what today might be called "background" music. There is confirmation of this in the *Sandersdorf papers*.

keyboard lessons, it is surprising that his productions were not filled with mistakes and absurdities. He was forced by need to live a retiring life during these study years and he was therefore not often in contact with the wide world, finding pleasure more in the conversation of good books. He considered his own affections and emotions of the heart when a poet [librettist] did not supply his libretti with sentiment, characters, dramatic situations, and failed to write with the true language of passion."[12]

Was this a criticism of Foppa? Certainly, Gaetano Rossi and Mayr's own discovery, a poet called Felice Romani, subsequently to become the most sought after poet by composers, were the librettists for whom he showed a preference.

Mayr continues with a revealing statement about himself:

> "It is true he envied Cimarosa who in his operas could find a fresh, gracious, insinuating instrumental *cantilena* for the most insignificant words."

Mayr's sudden burst into dramatic activity should not obscure the fact that he was still composing songs, e.g. the *Duettini* based on words by Metastasio, the *Canzonette Veneziane* and the *Canti Italiani e Tedeschi*. The popularity of these small gems is testified by the number of printed editions of the period.

7   Marriage and the return to Bergamo

In the autumn of 1796 Mayr married Angiola Venturali, a daughter of Venice's new, honest and upright merchant class idealized by Goldoni in his comedies. She had been one of Mayr's pupils. Abate Rubbi wrote commemorative sonnets noting that Mayr had inspired not only the science of music but also love in his young pupil. But Mayr's new found happiness "vanished like a dream". Angiola died in giving birth to a son who died thirty-six days later. (A doubly tragic event which was later to be echoed in Donizetti's marriage). Mayr submerged his emotions in ceaseless creativity, allowing the fall of the Republic to pass by as if a matter of no consequence.

---

12 This comment on librettists resembles similar quotations which may be gleaned from Donizetti's letters. Donizetti's *Poliuto*, 1839 (reworked as *Les martyrs*, 1840) owes much to Mayr. It is arguably one of the composer's best operas. Also interesting from a master-pupil view point is that *Saffo's* libretto was by Sograffi (1759 - 1818), a writer who kept alive the Goldoni style and from whom Donizetti took two plays, making them into his very own *Convenienze ed inconvenienze teatrali* (1827). Mayr composed music for Sograffi's *L'inconvenienze teatrali* (1800).

As Mayr's natural child died, so was born his spiritual son Donizetti, in Borgo Canale, Bergamo.

Mayr's operatic career now began in earnest with *La Lodoiska* (1796). The prospect of marriage no doubt had focused his mind on composing for the stage. By the time he took up his appointment at *S. Maria Maggiore* (June 1802) he had composed at least twenty-seven operas. Prior to *La Lodoiska* there were, in addition, *Saffo* and *Apelle e Campaspe*. Furthermore there might have been other works which may one day come to light. If Donizetti termed Rossini "lazy", Mayr might have added that his pupil could have worked harder!

Two important points arise when the list of operas in the catalogue section is consulted. First, Mayr gradually abandoned Foppa for Rossi, a fine librettist, who also provided Donizetti with *Maria Padilla* (1841) and *Linda di Chamounix* (1842). Secondly, and more importantly, by 1801 Mayr began composing *opere semiserie*, a genre he pioneered and at which he was most successful, leaving a lasting influence over Donizetti. Without Mayr, *L'elisir d'amore*, that masterpiece of sheer delight, could not be conceived. Yet this is the man who wanted eventually, to renounce composing for the stage and to give his life to teaching and composing religious music.

There is one more important point. Mayr's music, because of its orchestral and vocal qualities, aided the appreciation of Mozart in Italy, especially an opera such as *I misteri Eleusini*, a work which echoes *Die Zauberflöte*.

III   1802 - 1813

1   Kapellmeister
2   The Foundation of Mayr's school
3   Music for *S. Maria Maggiore*
4   The Operas and Cantatas

1   Kapellmeister

Mayr writes: "In this year (1802), he was asked by the chapter of the Basilica of *Santa Maria Maggiore* in Bergamo to accept the post of kapellmeister. On the feast of Corpus Christi were performed his first mass and vespers."

Mayr's memory may have brought two events together. It would appear that he was involved with the Easter Ceremonies of 1802 (the performance of the Mass and Vespers), because the records of the Church show that the orchestral forces were suddenly increased to 31 (this figure may also include extra singers). Of the known settings of the *Tantum ergo* (the hymn of St. Thomas Aquinas associated with the adoration of the Blessed Sacrament) listed in the catalogue, there is one in F Major (soprano, alto or tenor, 13 strings, oboes, horns, organ), dated 1803, *Corpus Domini.*[13] Mayr very rarely dates his religious compositions. The fact that a date appears on this work could just indicate that it was his first *Tantum ergo* for Bergamo.[14] Of the numerous *Domine ad adjuvandum* (for the beginning of Vespers) there is one dated, *Per il Corpus Domini del 1802*; it is in G Major and is in the same binding as a *Dixit* in D Major and versicles. There is also a *Kyrie* (separated from the *Gloria* and *Credo*), marked, *prima messa scritta da Mayr*. This must be the mass composed in 1791, rather than his first, composed for *S. Maria Maggiore*. There is also a *Confitebor tibi* in B Major belonging to the 1802 Vespers[15]; it is one of twelve settings of the psalm. His only full setting (according to the *Fondo Mayr*) of the psalm *In convertendo* is dated 25 August 1803.

Mayr had been invited to renew a flagging musical tradition. Lenzi was old and he had asked to be retired, while the Napoleonic invasion had changed the old world. The French troops had used *S. Maria Maggiore* as a dance hall, taking down from the walls the precious Flemish tapestries which still decorate the church, in order to use them as carpets. The MIA's schools had been closed - the old spirit had vanished. For example, for Easter 1798 only three extra musicians had been employed in contrast to the thirty-one of Easter 1802. Perhaps on this occasion Mayr simply took over the orchestral and vocal responsibilities and in respect kept mostly settings by Lenzi but revamped them with larger orchestral forces. He started the way he meant to go on, introducing a new orchestral and vocal sound (he was to replace the last castrati with boys from his school).

In order to understand the various settings of the liturgy by Mayr, it is necessary to realize that the size of the choir and orchestra he employed would wax and wane according to the importance of the feast day and its appropriateness in the liturgical year. This explains why certain pieces are scored for larger orchestral forces than others, and why, when consulting the orchestral parts of a piece, one can find instruments not recorded in the full score; the extra instruments being added to a subsequent performance on a day of greater liturgical importance. Thus trombones and timpani are the instruments which may suddenly appear.

---

13 The late G Major *Tantum Ergo* (?1843) is numbered by Mayr as No. 17. Here is an example of just how many of Mayr's religious compositions are mislaid or lost.

14 In general, any attempt to suggest an order may only be done by the calligraphic style, or a particular copyist, or quality of paper. Occasionally, manuscripts are marked with a number indicating the order of composition. The manuscripts bearing dates are usually very early works or those written at the end of his life on large sheets of paper with large staves, owing to Mayr's virtual blindness.

15 It is possible that all the psalms on a major feast day would generally have been sung to settings, except for the long *In exitu Israel* which, more than likely, would have been sung to Gregorian chant.

This can also happen in the secular cantatas. One may imagine a courier running down *Via Arena* from the Seminary to Mayr's house in 1816 with the news to add bassoons and trombones to the cantata *Annibale a Cartago* for the finances could be stretched to include them. The evening dedicated to the Hannibal theme was going to be more of a splash than previously thought! After all, the year was 1816. V. Bassus ("Hannibal") had died and Napoleon (often compared to Hannibal) had been defeated at Waterloo in the previous year. The three cantatas making up part of the evening's entertainment obviously had undertones for the initiated.

Basically there seem to be three sizes of orchestra, related to liturgical importance.

A   The major feasts

Voices: S A T B or S or A T B soli; 4 or 3 part choir.

Orchestra: vl I + II; vla (sometimes I + II); celli; c.bassi; flute; oboe I + II; clarinet I + II; horns I + II; bassoon; trombone (sometimes I + II); serpent; timpani; (Gran Cassa for a *Dies Irae*); organ.

Various instruments may be used as obbligato instruments - violin, cello, oboe, clarinet, cor anglais, horn etc. There is even one organ - obligato Mass.

The main "music" festivals were as follows, sung Mass being normal practice, in addition to the services listed:

The Circumcision of Our Lord	Vespers and Benediction
The Conversion of St. Paul	
The Purification	Vespers and Benediction
Palm Sunday until Easter	(except Mondays and Tuesdays)
Vigil and Feast of Pentecost	Vespers and Benediction
Corpus Christi	Vespers, Benediction, Procession
The Assumption	Vespers and Benediction
St. Bartholomew	Vespers and solemnity of relics
Nativity of Our Lady	Vespers and Benediction
Christmas	Vespers, Benediction, Office and Midnight Mass

Votive Mass of the Holy Spirit for the City at the beginning of August.
On any occasion when the Blessed Sacrament was exposed or . . . any special occasion for Our Lady.
On any occasion when music was required - e.g. St. Cecilia Festival, a celebration instituted and encouraged by Mayr and in which Donizetti became involved as a young composer.
The day for the *pubblica accademia* (that is a concert).

The following feast days were also of major importance:

Epiphany	Sundays in Feria
The Annunciation	All Saints
Second and Third feast days of Easter	All Souls
The Ascension	The nine Masses for the Dead (set
Second and Third feast days of Pentecost	throughout the year)

B   Other festivals and Sundays

Voices: S A T B; S or A T B (Mayr's terms, used by Donizetti are "*a Quat-tro*" or "*a Tre*" and/or 4 or 3 part choir).

Orchestra: vl I + II; vla (sometimes I + II); celli; c.basso; oboes I + II; clarinets I + II; bassoon; horns I + II; organ.

Obbligato use of instruments, as for "major feasts".

The following days are listed with music:

All Sundays except Lent
    and Autumn holidays
Septuagesima Sunday (morning only)
Sexagesima (morning only)

Quinquagesima (morning only)
Fourth Sunday in Lent (morning only)
Compline after mid-Lent
Trinity Sunday

plus:

January
    St. Sebastian

February
    St. Matthias

March
    St. Joseph

April
    St. Mark

May
    St. Philip and St. James
    The Holy Cross
    St. John *ante portam Latinam*
        (morning only)
    Rogationtide

June
    St. John the Baptist
    St. Peter and St. Paul

July
Visitations of Our Lady
  St. James
  St. Anne, Mother of Our Lady

August
  Our Lady of the Snows
  St. Lawrence
  St. Roch
  St. Alexander, patron saint of
    Bergamo

September
  Holidays

October
  No major feast days

November
  Presentation of Our Lady
  St. Andrew

December
  The Conception of Our Lady
  St. Thomas
  St. Stephen
  St. John the Evangelist
  St. Silvester, local saint

C Lent, Requiems, simple Vespers

3 or 4 part choir; violone and organ.

It is interesting to note that:

(a) The Passion on Holy Tuesday and Holy Wednesday were sung by 4 voices with violone.

(b) The Good Friday Passion was sung by a tenor solo (the role of Christ) with orchestra: vl I + II; vle; celli; basso; flute; oboe I + II; horn I + II; bassoon; organ; or 4 voices with violone.

(c) The Lamentations for Holy Wednesday, Maundy Thursday and Good Friday are scored for soloist, or soloist and choir, or choir, orchestra - with use of obligato instruments as appropriate. The lamentations were considered to be among Mayr's most famous compositions.

This is the amazing music tradition into which Donizetti and his fellow students took *regular* part. It helps to explain why he began his career composing religious music, why he was made Kapellmeister to the Royal Viennese Chapel, why he composed superb religious works towards the end of his career, why he contributed to Mayr's *Hymn Book*, why his letters reveal a devout person. Any attempt to imagine the impression made by the dignity of the Liturgy sung in the beauty of *S. Maria Maggiore* must stun the modern mind which, for the greater part, has lost the liturgical tradition together with its interpretation and significance.

Besides singing in *S. Maria Maggiore*, the choir was invited to sing in other churches; for example, at Novara.[16] The students were also involved in first Italian performances of Haydn's *Creation*, Mozart's *Requiem*, Beethoven's *Christ on the Mount of Olives* and Handel's *Hallelujah Chorus*, and many other works.

When approaching both Mayr's and Donizetti's religious music, the listener must accept the conventions of the period and be free from puritanical ideas that the Deity should only be worshipped with "plain" music. Alberto Moravia made an interesting comment when he singled out Verdi's *Requiem* as a *humanist* work (a work which is better explained once the Mayr tradtition is known).[17] Nothing of the sort can be levelled at Mayr's or Donizetti's religious music. One may whirl to their music like an intoxicated dervish or remain stunned by the sheer beauty of simplicity. But one will always be brought a little closer to the mystery of *knowledge* and *love* as interpreted by one of the world's main religious traditions.

2   The Foundation of Mayr's school

Mayr was a conscientious kapellmeister and still found time to compose three or four operas a year, together with building up his repertory of church music. Behind the scenes he was working hard for his projected school. Finances had to be wooed and a site found.

He writes in his *Cenni*:

> "Resulting from a project presented by [Mayr] put forward in two *Memorie*[18] to this end, there was founded by decree of the *Pio luogo della misericordia di Bergamo* (MIA) on 12th March of this year 1805, *Le lezioni caritatevoli di musica*. From then on it was maintained with continual determination by the charitable congregation with the double intention of maintaining a constant supply of national musicians for the basilica especially soprano and contralto voices, and helping the poor by providing for them with a new means of employment.

---

16 Today a city of crumbling façades. The Novara festival was held in the church of *San Gaudenzio*.

17 Verdi attended Mayr's funeral celebrations and contributed to the fund for the funerary monument to Mayr now in *S. Maria Maggiore*.

18 For example, the *Memoria*. See selected writings and bibliography.

The number of students increased to 14 [that is from 12], 8 for singing and 6 for violin studies. [All had to dedicate themselves to what today we would term "liberal studies"].[19] The school received the approval of the Ministry for Internal Affairs. The Inspectorate of public education ordered the publication of the school's rules[20] drawn up by Mayr, in which he gave the same emphasis to the task of working out a method for the choir as well as the instrumental faculty. He prepared the writing of this task in association with Sig. Francesco Salari[21], professor of the choir school, but the task remained incomplete due to the change of government. [Napoleon crowned himself in Milan Cathedral on 26 May 1805 with the 11th century Iron Crown of Lombardy, an event for which Mayr composed his famous *Te Deum*.] It is a school where charitable aid is particularly directed towards vocal training - an art form which the Province of Bergamo is noted, especially since the end of the last century and the present.[22]

In 1816 the school enjoyed the highest honour of a visit by His Highness, the most Serene Prince, the Vice-King of Italy and the Emperor. It also gained the unexpected distinction of being invited to give a concert at the royal court. This event was accomplished with a variety of pieces due to an improvement being made two years previously. Instead of 8 boy sopranos being taken by the choir school, 4 were accepted with the addition of 2 tenors and 2 basses. This new arrangement proved successful, since Trezzini, Giordani, Storti, Savj and Pagliaroli[23] etc. are already performing on the stages

---

19 Mayr taught his students literature, art history, mythology, grammar, general history, geography and arithmetic. In 1812 Abbé Baizini was appointed especially to teach liberal studies. This is a simple example of how Mayr's school became a model for future Italian music academies.

20 These were eventually published: *Regolamento delle lezioni Caritatevoli di Musica addette alla Cappella di S. Maria Maggiore sotto la Direzione della Congregazione di Carità di Bergamo.*

21 Notes on Mayr's staff follow this extract from the *Cenni*.

22 Bergamo had become famous for its tenors during the 18th century. Those most remembered today are Giacomo David (1750 - 1830); and his son, Giovanni David (1790 - 1864); Domenico Donzelli (1790 - 1873); and Giovanni Battista Rubini (1794 - 1854). It is interesting to note that Mayr composed far more cantatas for the tenor voice than for soprano or bass.

23 Carlo Trezzini was one of the boy sopranos who became a well-known tenor. Giovanni Giordani, bass-baritone, he sang in Donizetti's *L'ajo nell'imbarazzo* at *La Scala* and was recognised for his interpretation of Bellini. Giovanni Storti, a successful tenor. Savj and Pagliaroli are curiously not listed in the school registers. Could they be Salvi and Pontiroli? A certain Savi left the school due to voice problems.

of the best theatres in Italy. Furthermore, this school can congratu-
late itself for having produced Donizetti[24] whose works are constantly being received with due applause on Neapolitan and Roman
stages. The Verona Philharmonic has given its trust to Sig. Marco
Bonesi[25] for its academies and theatres. He was the great Capuzzi's
best pupil."

Mayr wrote for the school[26] a short musical primer, a method "for the most comfortable
positions of the hands on the keyboard" - a few notes on how to compose for the Corno
da Caccia - he translated from German Förster's[27] treatise on accompaniment. He
provided at his own expense all the methods (text books) of the French Conservatoire.
For the end of the academic year he wrote special compositions and in order to exercise
the pupils in the art of declamation he wrote the librettos of three small pieces adapted to
the capacities of the young pupils, *La prova dell' accademia finale*, *Il piccolo compositore*
and *I piccoli virtuosi ambulanti*.

With the foundation of his school, Mayr achieved his main ambition in life. In a letter he
expressed his gratitude to the Consortium.

"My heart does not know how to express all that it feels, however, it does comprehend
that joyous exaltation of which I do not believe myself to be worthy, is nothing more than
the effect of your supreme generosity."

Mayr had an impressive staff:

Francesco Salari (1751 - 1832) studied under Piccinni in Naples and completed his studies
in Milan. As choir master he was Donizetti's tutor. Though a Bergamasque, Mayr must
have first met him in Venice where he was a singing teacher for 28 years and composed
operas and sacred music. He was appointed in 1805 deputy Kapellmeister and must have
been "second in charge" at the school, taking on responsibilities when Mayr was absent
due to the staging of his operas.

Antonio Capuzzi (1755 - 1818) studied under Tartini and taught his method. He was
regarded as one of the best violinists of his age. He was also *violino principale* of *La Scala*

---

24 This indicates that the *Cenni* must have been written prior to Donizetti leaving Naples for Paris and
during the final years of his career. The handwriting could suggest that the *Cenni* (not the *Cenni
confidenziali*) were written as early as 1835 or even earlier.

25 Marco Bonesi (1806 - 1874), studied the violin at Mayr's school, was a friend of Donizetti (he left a few
pages of notes on the composer) and corresponded with Mayr.

26 For Mayr's teaching, see chapter V 4.

27 Emanuel Aloys Förster (1748 - 1823). Austrian composer, theorist and teacher. He knew Haydn, Mozart
and Beethoven, and composed quartets and quintets deserving revival.

orchestra. When in London in 1796 he had composed music for a ballet entitled *La villanella rapita ossia Il corsaro*. He was the composer of operas, violin concertos, quintets and quartets. A double bass concerto has been recorded by *I Musici*. Mayr and Donizetti composed music for his funeral celebrations.

Antonio Gonzales (1764 - 1830) was organist at *S. Maria Maggiore*. His restrained and serious playing was approved of by Mayr (who could be outspoken and critical of organists for their bad taste). He studied in Bergamo and Milan. He composed an opera *Il calandrino* for the *Teatro S. Moisè* Venice, where Mayr may have known him for the first time. Mayr's letters show a concern for Gonzales and his home life.

In 1812 Mayr appointed the Revd. Giovanni Battista Baizini to help him teach what today we term "Liberal studies". He was a minor poet and provided Mayr with texts for at least three cantatas: *La festa di Ercole* (1816); *Arianna e Bacco* (1817); *L'Armonia* (1825). He taught at the school until his death in 1828. Mayr outlived all the first teachers he engaged.

The various fortunes of the first 12 students registered at the school in 1806 indicate the quality of education given.

1. Antonio Ignazio Bosio left due to voice problems.

2. Marco Bonesi became, as already noted, a first-class violinist. On Capuzzi's death he substituted for his master until the appointment of Pietro Rovelli (1793 - 1838), on whose death he became violin teacher at the school. Mayr thus lived to see the appointment of one of his own students.

3. Domenico Gaetano Maria Donizetti (1797 - 1848) was born the same year as Schubert and his life span is embraced by the two major revolutionary upheavals in European history prior to the Russian Revolution. When interpreting Donizetti it is essential to realize that he did not belong to Verdi's risorgimento generation. Donizetti maintained that he was apolitical and enjoyed friendship with people like Michele Accursi, a papal spy, and the Rubini brothers, noted revolutionaries. The more his music is studied in the light of Mayr's own, the more it is clear that he remained a disciple of Mayr, though his teacher would have frowned on the excessive melodrama and the morbid streak of some of the late works.

4. Pietro Angelini was a violin student who was sent down in 1811 due to poor results.

5. Giovanni Giuseppe Manghenoni left the school in 1816 with distinction. He showed promise as a composer and was an excellent singer but died young.

6. Giuseppe Pontiroli, a noted treble who became a fine tenor. In 1832, on Salari's death, he was nominated teacher of vocal studies at the school.

7. Giuseppe Lavezzari was a disappointment; after six years of study he was expelled due to lack of co-operation.

8. Clemente Alessandro Zanetti became a fine violinist and was second violin in La Scala orchestra.

9. Giovanni Carrara left the school after a year.

10. Antonio Dolci, Donizetti's friend and a close friend of Mayr, used to read to the elderly teacher when overtaken by blindness. He was a fine pianist for whom Donizetti composed most of his piano music. On Mayr's death he took over the directorship of the school for two years, retaining his appointment as piano teacher until three years before his death in 1869.

11. Francesco Maria Davide Rotigni left the school after a year.

12. Antonio Benedetto Tavecchi was a boy soloist of distinction. He died young. Mayr composed a *Miserere* for the Requiem which was played not only at Tavecchi's funeral but also at his own.

Clearly at Mayr's school one succeeded or failed.

3   Music for *S. Maria Maggiore*

The new found security and happiness is marked by Mayr marrying, in the autumn of 1804, his late wife's younger sister, Lucrezia Venturali. They were to have no children[28], though by all accounts it was a happy marriage. Donizetti records in a letter that it was an example to the students, and clearly Lucrezia commanded the boys' respect.

There is another major problem when considering the extensive catalogue of Mayr's religious music. Not only are we confronted by the problems of chronology but by deciding which separate settings may be selected to make up a complete setting. Take for example the music for the Mass. There are 17 entries in the catalogue which are kept as integral pieces, whereas there is a profusion of pieces amongst which there must be various combinations in order to make up a series of substantial complete settings for the *Kyrie* and especially the *Gloria* during a sung Eucharist. Without Mayr at hand to indicate which piece may be played next to another, the would-be reviver is at a loss. The only solution is to assume responsibility for one's own choice.

In this section we shall concentrate on music for Sundays, that is the Mass and Benediction. (Music for Vespers, Hymns, Antiphons, Anthems, Litanies etc. will be considered in the section 1813 - 1824. Requiems and music for Holy Week, including the *Stabat Mater* will be considered in the section 1824 - 1845).

---

28 Donizetti refers to a daughter in his letters to Mayr. I have here reported the view taken by Ashbrook and others, that the marriage was childless, a point of view which I personally doubt.(See Z 231 etc.).

In Italy it was customary to sing, on a normal Sunday, the *Kyrie, Gloria* and *Credo*, though Mayr also composed separate settings of the *Sanctus, Benedictus* and *Agnus Dei*.

Problems start with settings of the *Kyrie*. Does the reviver juggle with the pieces available in order to make up additional complete settings? Could certain pieces have been sung as anthems? Were only the *Kyrie eleison* or the *Christe eleison* sung on simple Sundays? Perhaps the first *Kyrie* was repeated only on special occasions after the *Christe*? It is interesting to note that similar problems arise when Donizetti's religious music is studied.

When the folders containing the scores are opened, the orchestral and vocal parts are usually to be found - sometimes the parts have survived whilst the full-score has been lost. The parts are essential to the full score for, as already said, the parts often reveal extra instrumentation. They often clarify the full score by working out parts to greater detail. They are also important for dynamics.

Music was performed without a conductor in the modern sense. The orchestra was led by the *violino principale*, and the choir by the choir master or organist.

Thus the full score was given to the students to make parts (it is usually discovered that Mayr himself has made the lion's share), for example, a cheeky Donizetti noted on a viola part which he had just copied out: *La viola è giusta, non è sbagliata, no.* (The viola is right, it is not wrong, no.) Only occasionally did Mayr make use of professional copyists. Funds at the school were slender and part-making was then essential training for a young student. Compositions with parts in Donizetti's youthful hand help to make a corpus of works with which he was involved dating from 1806 until his departure for Bologna in 1815. On his return, in order to perfect his studies under Mayr, it is found that his manuscript has matured.

The *Gloria* was clearly the show piece for Sunday worship. The catalogue lists over a hundred pieces (See catalogue). From these a number of long substantial settings may be organised. It is possible that on less important Sundays only selected verses from the *Gloria* were sung.

There are twenty-two complete settings of the *Credo* (one being a wind reduction by Mayr of a *Credo* by Haydn) and a separate setting of the *Crucifixus* and two *Domine Jesu Christe*. The lengths vary according to Sundays in the church calendar year. Three may be singled out:

1. *The Novara Credo*, which the students (including Donizetti) sang with great success at Novara in 1815.

2. *Credo* in B flat Major, composed by invitation of Donizetti and sent to Naples, 1822.

3. *Credo* in F Major. One of the composer's last works dating from 1845. It is set for four voices. There are two versions, one for strings, the other for woodwind.

The second part of the Eucharist: *Sanctus, Benedictus, Agnus Dei.*

1. There are 10 complete settings of the *Sanctus, Benedictus* and *Agnus Dei*, clearly meant to be sung as a unit.
2. *Sanctus* . . . 7 settings (one marked "for the Ambrosian Rite").
3. *Benedictus* . . . 3 settings.
4. *Agnus Dei* . . . 2 settings (one clearly composed for a special occasion; six-part choir (SAAATB) and large orchestra).

In 1809 Mayr founded the *Pio Istituto Musicale* for old musicians, their widows or orphans - a sort of forerunner to *Casa Verdi*. The same year saw what must have been the first performance in Italy of Haydn's *The Creation*, on the occasion of which Mayr published a short life of Haydn[29] and appraisal of the oratorio which had a lasting influence over Mayr and the young Donizetti. *The Creation* seems to have been the first of a series of concerts introducing special pieces to the Italian public. Besides the works already mentioned we know Mayr had performed Haydn's *The Seasons, The Seven last words of the Saviour*, Johann Gottlieb Naumann's *Vater Unser*, and Winter's *Die Macht der Töne*. These concerts were held in the *Teatro della Società* close by *S. Maria Maggiore*, where many of Mayr's and Donizetti's operas were performed. *The Creation* was directed by Antonio Capuzzi and the soloists were Rosa Morandi, Serafino Gentili and Nicola De Gregis. The chorus was made up from Mayr's students, the Basilica choir and the "best singers in town". The performance was in aid of the *Pio Istituto*. There was a subsequent performance in Bologna. It is clear that Mayr's students were in demand, often travelling some distance to give performances.

4   The Operas and Cantatas

The years between 1802 and 1813 are marked by Mayr receiving numerous invitations to induce him to leave Bergamo, together with operatic cabals which, in the long run, had a part in his increasing lack of interest in composing for the stage. Rossini's success and popularity did overshadow Mayr's operatic works, but to explain Mayr's dwindling interest in composing operatic music in terms of the Rossini phenomenon alone is inac-

---

29 I have not yet traced this life of Haydn. The short printed "life" which is brought to one at the *Biblioteca Cicica* is certainly not the version to which Mayr refers, and which must be substantial in length - similar to his lives of Gaffurio or Handel. It would be interesting to read it in order to see if Mayr adds anything to what may be read in Carpani's life of Haydn (later plagiarized by Stendhal). Mayr had known Carpani in Venice.

curate. Consider the pressure of teaching, composing sacred music, and the fact that the years after 1813 saw Mayr developing his writing of cantatas. Some of the cantatas besides being stage pieces were composed for the school while others are *scene drammatiche* and concert pieces, i.e. *Annibale a Cartago*[30].

In 1803 he was invited to take over the direction of the *Italian Theatre*, Vienna. If Mayr had been predominantly interested in operatic success he would have jumped at the offer. The job ultimately went to Ferdinando Paër. Lisbon, St. Petersburg, Dresden and London chased him in vain for his services; Mayr remained in Bergamo. He never became a rich man. At the height of his operatic success (1813 - *Medea in Corinto*) he went through a severe financial crisis from which he never recovered. The reasons for the crisis are not known. Again this may be another reason why Mayr lost interest in composing for the stage and it may well have resulted from the "cabals" often mentioned in the *Cenni*. After all, he composed well over 70 operas.

It may well be asked how Mayr found the time and creative energy to compose as many works as he did. Even some of the cantatas amount to operas. It is interesting to note that at the end of his incomplete list of operas in the *Cenni*, he writes:

> "Mayr wrote moreover more than 50 cantatas for literary persons,
> public experiments for schools and seminaries; a quantity of arias
> for private commissions or for his own operas when performed by
> different singers or a request of singing teachers."

He then goes on to give a very incomplete list indeed of his sacred compositions. Perhaps the *Cenni* date from the early thirties? To support this view Mayr's footnotes to his own text cease after 1827. This would make sense of facts such as Mayr listing three *Stabat Maters* when there are at least five[31]. This would also imply that Mayr composed numerous sacred works right up to the age of over eighty, maintaining his skills at composition to the end.

Until Mayr's music is better known in performance I do not believe it is possible to do it justice through judgement by analysis. For those who wish to study the operas in greater detail there is Ludwig Schiedermair's basic study in which most of the operas are considered; as for the rest, much positive work is required to be done by researchers and musicians.

When writing on forgotten masters scholars can be patronizing to the extent of rudeness and lack of understanding. Surely one of the aims of scholarship is to open up the repertory rather than to limit it more and more to the security of a narrow field. Furthermore, sweeping judgements not only prejudice others but often arise from a lack of deep

---

30 Edited and revived by Ian Caddy, 1986.

31 *Stabat Mater No. 5* for four soloists (SATB) and small orchestra edited by John Allitt & Ian Caddy 1986.

knowledge and appreciation. A comment like, "Mayr's serious operas leave the impression of a cenotaph waiting for an occupant; of an eclectic artist who never overthrew and seldom disturbed a convention, but left a building swept and garnished for his successors"[32], may well have elements of truth from certain points of view, but as a helpful sequence of thought for revival, it is totally negative.

The tone of such remarks reminds one of the comments from which Donizetti's music used to suffer from during the forties and fifties. But once Donizetti's music was heard through revival after revival it not only changed opinions towards the composer, but also towards the understanding of the nature of Italian romanticism. Furthermore, I know to my own cost, that it is a folly to make pronouncements from manuscripts, even printed piano-vocal scores. Many years ago I showed Ian Caddy a piano-vocal score of Donizetti's *Requiem*. At that time Verdi ruled supreme and Donizetti was judged in the light of the later master - "Verdi would have made more of that" was a passing comment on a a few bars. Now Ian Caddy has become a most enthusiastic promoter and performer of the Donizetti *Requiem*[33]. It is fatal to judge all trees in the forest by the standards of the oak; there are many other beautiful species to admire and each has its own special qualities. Miracles can happen when the notes on a page are sensitively interpreted!

Taking the analogy of Donizetti's fortunes further, it should be remembered that it is a poor criterion to judge a composer by the odd aria, duet or sextet. Music, especially opera, needs to be heard as a whole and in preferably live performance. I remember hearing in the early fifties a radio performance of *Linda di Chamounix* - my faith in those hitherto unknown works of Donizetti was confirmed. It led in my own case to the revival of *Les martyrs*.

Today the average listener may know Mayr only as a name. A few cognoscenti may know the extracts from operas recorded by *Opera Rara*, or the not-wholly satisfactory recording of *Medea in Corinto*, and perhaps the *First Piano Concerto*. To have traced recordings of other revivals indicates a genuine interest.

A performance of a little known work is always a hazard especially in the case of an opera since so much can go wrong during a one off performance, as often is the case, when presented as a concert. Music has to be heard under various circumstances. Reviews may often indicate that a critic has not "heard" the music or has been suffering from a touch of bad digestion. Music is "the wingéd life" which cannot be encapsulated without destroying it. Music comes and goes; true music and honest music making will always leave a richness beyond the price of rubies.

---

32 Winton Dean. See Bibliography.

33 I am sure my colleague does not mind me taking a memory as an example - since both of us have often since fallen into the same old trap.

Recorded music is helpful for study and a more detailed recognition of a piece but too often it is a trap. Music must be heard in performance, live; and then it must be free to go where it wills.

Let us consider Mr Dean's comment in detail. The word "cenotaph" suggests idolatry, a concept far from Mayr's metaphysical and spiritual understanding of the nature of music. The "occupant" of his music, on one level is the spirit; on another it is the inward vision of a wise and good man. To hear that quality demands something more than the caprices of the outward ear beguiled by the tonalities of romanticism, for much of Mayr's understanding is still set within the 18th century. An "eclectic artist"? Donizetti said, no doubt following the advice of his teacher, that one should learn from the good wherever it was to be found, and Mayr learnt and borrowed ideas from Haydn, Mozart and Beethoven - the "good" he wished to introduce into Italian music. However, when the music is heard, it is the creative world of a strong personality which is encountered rather than the quirks of individualism in the modern sense. He offers "dialogue" as defined by Martin Buber. He does not beguile but he addresses. His art is essentially masculine in the true sense; he invites the listener to enter a *temenos*, an inner space, where contemplation, not agitation, reigns. In the visual arts, his "eclecticism" may be compared to the art of Giovanni Bellini who learnt from the good wherever he perceived it and who created an essentially contemplative visual world but whose pupils (Giorgione, Titian, Palma Vecchio etc.) adopted concepts as they willed and changed their master's art to suit their own development and century. Is this what is meant by "a building swept and garnished for his successors"? If so we are then speaking of a genuine creative genius in whom many found space to place their own furniture. Mayr however remains the building's architect. There is another parallel between Giovanni Bellini and Mayr. Both require insight into Catholic devotion and the inner oral tradition for their work to be appreciated in depth. Bellini produced his art when the Renaissance was about to rob Catholic art of its roots in the icon; Mayr's music comes from a pivot point in western music. It was not long after his death that late romantic trends began to disrupt the traditional science of music upon which Mayr grounded his musical expression.

It is hard to accept that Mayr "seldom disturbed a convention", for the assumption is simply not true. From *Saffo* (1794) to *Medea in Corinto* (1813) Mayr gradually changed the tonal quality of Italian music and introduced a new taste in subject matter. But he was not an iconoclast, nor was he a revolutionary simply for the sake of change. He was too sensitive towards the political, social and spiritual changes taking place in his own times and their ultimate consequences for western civilization not to consider carefully what he said in musical terms. He recognized that the Revolution and the advent of Napoleon had changed Europe. He wished for the unavoidable change to renew the western tradition, not ultimately to destroy it.

What are the general points recorded in books regarding Mayr's contribution? The one most referred to is his introduction into Italian opera of Germanic orchestration, not only in the delicacy of the woodwind but with the use of on-stage bands. He, along with others, developed what is erroneously termed the "Rossini crescendo"; the repetition of brief motives over an alternating tonic-dominant bass with a gradual thickening orchestration. He also formed the essential ingredients of the "Rossini storm" sequence. In fact the more Rossini's music is heard in the context of Mayr, the more its musical and dramatic roots are appreciated. Rossini's serious operas are very much in the Mayrian mould that dates from the first decade of the 19th century. Mayr's later development of musical ideas was to be taken up by Donizetti and brought to personal maturity from *Anna Bolena* (1830) onwards.

Particular to Mayr was his love of obligato instruments, the timbre of which were made to complement the voice or introduce a symbolic reference. The trumpet prelude introducing Ernesto's *Cercherò lontana terra* in Donizetti's *Don Pasquale* is typical of Mayr's influence over his pupil. Mayr loved the oboe, clarinet, cor anglais; he wrote extensively for the solo violin (possible with Capuzzi in mind) and used the sound of horns contrasting with cellos as to be found at the conclusion of *Lucia di Lammermoor*. He used the guitar where it was appropriate, the harp he loved, as well as experimenting with instruments such as the concertina. Though his size of orchestra increased he was not in favour of noise simply for the sake of stunning an audience. Especially characteristic is his use of solo groups within an orchestra, for example the instrumental ensemble (violin, clarinet, cor anglais, horn, cello and double bass) as Elfrido (*Alfredo il Grande, re degli Anglo Sassoni*, 1819) accompanies himself on the harp for the romanza, *Ov'è la bella vergine*? The result is sheer beauty and a delicacy which throws into context how later romanticism discarded and forgot Mayr for emphasis on the doubling of instruments for the sake of volume of sound. Such musical maturity shows up the adolescence of many who followed him and who stole the limelight from him. Mayr's operas are a constant flow of instrumental ideas busily seeking various combinations and orchestral effects. They are a delight to the ear.

He developed the chorus, drawing its role into the flow of drama enabling the change of situation and the development of arias. *Medea in Corinto* (1813) is full of examples but so is *San Luigi Gonzaga* (1822), a work which amply illustrates Mayr's development of the chorus to Donizettian proportions and use. He used the chorus, be it for priests, soldiers, women lamenting or crowd scenes, to set a dramatic mood.

He experimented in breaking up an aria into sections creating a *scena*, for example, Constantino's *Ah! se mirar potessi! (Elena)*. He was a master of brief harmonic shifts to heighten the dramatic content of the words being sung. Often the words are coloured with instrumentation that may be appreciated to be fundamental to Donizetti.

Likewise he will suggest with a few bars the change of emotion from scene to scene. He was also the master of dramatic contrast, as for example may be heard in *Medea in Corinto* where the "evil" music of Medea finds respite in arias for other characters. He will whip up the emotions of his characters into ensembles and strettas which were to become the essential language of Rossini and especially Donizetti. Though a religious piece, the *Te Deum* composed for Napoleon's coronation in Milan Cathedral (1805) offers an example of structure to be observed in the operas. A quartet of great beauty, prefiguring

Donizetti by a least a couple of decades, is preceded by dramatic modulations and leads after various sections, to a dramatic fugal conclusion. Though examples of Haydn and Beethoven may be suggested, the musical language is totally new to Italian music of the period.

As already mentioned elsewhere, Donizetti's genius for constructing a flow of musical ideas bridging various dramatic scenes is derived from the art of his teacher. Throughout Mayr's operas though the dramatic element is given full consideration, the clarity of the music and its intention are never muffled. His creative facility differs from say that of Rossini who writes for the moment and often without much substance of thought. Mayr composed music to be heard not only outwardly but inwardly, giving endless satisfaction long after its sounds have receded into silence.

His operatic subject matter offered example after example of operatic "furniture" for generations to come: military scenes, battles, storms, volcanic eruptions and hunts and so on. Lovers elope, others are buried alive, heroines throw themselves in the line of pistol fire to save their lovers, letters are read, prisoners are kept in towers, prayers are uttered, pagan rites are enacted, characters lose their senses only to regain them. He could also paint nature scenes with the suggestion of a few instruments; he fearlessly introduced popular tunes and rhythms, ländlers, waltzes, sicilianos, polkas and "alla rusticas". He attempted to introduce popular and folk music with dignity on the stage. In this he was indeed a child of the Revolution.

When Dr Cecilia Powell noticed the influence of *Medea in Corinto* on Turner's *The vision of Medea* (Tate Gallery, London), she drew attention to the way in which two men of creative genius working roughly at the same time used similar concepts in their separate arts that placed them firmly at the roots of romantic sensibility. A comparison between the two men is not amiss. Both, like Janus, looked to the past and to the future. Turner understood the classical world through his reading and the idyllic world of Claude Lorrain. He, like Mayr, had a firm grasp of the significance and use of mythology. Both men were inspired by the Celtic world of bards and druids. Both were caught up in the changes brought about in Europe by Napoleon and both created works in which his shadow may be detected. Both associated the general's rise and fall with Hannibal's ill-fated career. Turner painted *Hannibal and his army crossing the Alps* in 1812 and in 1818 he painted *The field of Waterloo*. As we have already noted, Mayr in 1816 composed three cantatas for the Seminary, Bergamo, relating to Hannibal's rise and fall - their texts may be easily interpreted as relating to Napoleon's defeat. Both men were inspired by the theme of the sublime and the beautiful, the spectacle of ravines, mountains, volcanoes, battles, storms, hunts, religious processions, folk scenes and nature in all her aspects. (Mayr's building makes space for Rossini's *Guillaume Tell*, 1829, even Verdi's *Aida*, 1871.) Mayr and Turner were founder spirits of the romantic sensibility and in their work they complemented the novel and tales of romance which were taking Europe by storm. Turner's monumental canvases may help one to visualize the world of exotic operas like *Alonso e Cora* (1803), *Zamori* (1804), *Gli Americani* (1805), *I Cherusci* (1808) etc. They also help to revalue Mayr's romantic interpretation of the classical world to be found in *I misteri*

Eleusini (1805), *Medea in Corinto* (1813), *Fedra* (1820) and *Demetrio* (1824) - together with the "English" appeal of *La rosa bianca e la rosa rossa* (1813), *Le due duchesse* (1814) and *Alfredo il Grande* (1819).

In addition to the heaviness of certain romantic themes Mayr was blest with the lightness of touch of the closing decades of the Venetian civilization, of Goldoni, Galuppi, Longhi and Guardi. It found expression in a number of operas. The title *Belle ciarle e tristi fatti* (1807) sets off in the memory the antics of Harlequin and the theatrical reforms brought about by Goldoni.

He was a pioneer of the *semiseria* genre which was to be fundamental to Donizetti's art. The combination of lyricism and *buffo* to be heard in *L'amor coniugale* (1805) lives on in his pupil's *Torquato Tasso* (1833) and *Il furioso all'isola di San Domingo* (1833) and many other works. With *Don Pasquale* (1843) Donizetti brought *opera buffa*, as favoured by Mayr, through a brilliant *tour de force* to a conclusion. In his masterpiece, it is as if Donizetti distilled everything he had learnt from Mayr to such perfection that nothing could ever be added to or subtracted from the *buffo* style. Master and pupil were both cautious reformers. They both certainly "left a building swept and garnished" (such is the gift of men of the spirit) together with a garden filled with rich soil for Verdi and others to plant their talents in. But Rossini was of a different calibre of mind and Verdi was of another generation.

Mayr and even Donizetti have a chivalrous quality of the 18th century. Their lyricism, along with Bellini's was quickly to become a value of the past. Europe after 1848 changed course and Baudelaire's aesthetic of the decadent imagination was to build up the stress to be found in imagery and content which was to lead to the eventual break up and loss of the western tradition.

IV   1813 - 1824

1   The Ateneo

A characteristic of Italian cultural life from the Renaissance onwards was the profusion of small academies which, from time to time and on various levels, have greatly influenced the course of Italian arts and politics. The Medici promoted the vogue with their platonic academy under the direction of Marsilio Ficino. Gian Giorgio Trissino's academy drew out Palladio's genius and the *Camerata Bardi* was fundamental to the birth of opera as a theatrical form. The *Ateneo* of Bergamo was a reconstituted academy in 1810 after the trauma of Napoleon's undoing of so much of Italy's traditional ways.

Mayr's Notebooks and operas testify to his interest in the intellectual world of the academies, in particular the thought of Zeno and Metastasio. In this he is an amalgam of 18th century thought and the energies that were to change Europe. Mazzini, in many ways a product of the political wing of the Illuminati and an enthusiastic supporter of Donizetti, in a sensitive essay written in 1839, singles out Byron and Goethe as "two mighty sources" of his times. Even these two poets poles apart from Zeno and Metastasio, are like Mayr; the more they are studied the more they are seen to be integrated into vital sources of traditional thought. Donizetti followed the excess of emotion found in Byron; Mayr remains far closer to the rejection of romanticism made by Goethe, becoming increasingly concerned with his century's loss of the west's once viable and vital traditional roots in the classical world.

Whilst Donizetti frequented salons and learnt to contend with unscrupulous impresarios and hysterical and egocentric sopranos, Mayr left the operatic world for the concerned, cultured world of the academies. At the age of 54 on 20 March 1817 he was elected as a member of the *Ateneo*; by 10 September 1823 he was elected its president until 2 March 1826. He turned down re-election in 1833, but remained an active member presenting a number of substantial dissertations.

The ambience of the *Ateneo* must have been congenial to Mayr. He would have had the companionship of other minds concerned with the restoration of abiding values after the collapse of the Cisalpine Republic and the rule of Beauharnais, the Prince-Viceroy. (In 1815, Lombardy and the Veneto had been united to be ruled by the Habsburgs, a rule which continued until 1859). Mayr's concerns were not only educational and for the good

70

of social welfare, he was equally concerned with the Liturgy and the devotion of the faithful, that it should be rooted in understanding as well as faith.

With the advent of Rossini he had seen opera take a course along which he did not wish to compete, a world of *gorgolismi*, patter rhythms and emotion over and against the intellect. In the company of members like Gerolamo Calvi[34] and Giovanni Finazzi[35] Mayr would have found an audience wherewith to air his own views and be rewarded with intelligent discussion.

Mayr gave new musical life to the recently reconstituted *Ateneo*. When its president, Marchese Giuseppe Terzi, once officer of Napoleon's ill-fated troops of the Russian campaign died in 1819 he ensured a memorable requiem in *S. Maria Maggiore*. The seat of the *Ateneo* at this time was the separate building beyond the basilica's east end. It is still an elegant Albertian building over a medieval site. Here the coffin had lain in state; as it was processed to the basilica a funeral march was played (a second by Donizetti was also possibly played), the Requiem Mass was by Mayr with three items by Donizetti who had recently returned from Bologna in order "to perfect himself" in Mayr's teaching. Donizetti also composed a *Marcia Lugubre* and a string quartet in memory of the Marchese (*Quartet No. 7 in F minor* dated 6 May 1819. The work is programmatic).

On 3 August 1820 Mayr read to the *Ateneo* his study on the life and work of Franchino Gaffurio. It was the first of a series of studies with which Mayr wished to form a book commemorating various figures which interested him had not blindness and death overtaken him[36]. Of particular interest, besides the study on Gaffurio are the studies on Algarotti, a formative influence over the early opera years of the composer, and Alessandro Barca, a Bergamasque writer whose studies on music theory were admired by Mayr.

On 3 April 1835 he read his biography of the humanist Michele Alberto Carrara. The long study in two parts concerning the *History of the Oratorio and the Mysteries* was read on 20 February 1839 and 24 August 1843. On this last occasion lack of sight forbade Mayr reading his text which had to be written out by the secretary, Abate Salvioni (with corrections by Mayr), and read by him to the illustrious audience. This important text deserves publication; besides being a remarkable history it is a vital key to understanding Mayr's intentions in his oratorios, sacred music and operas such as *I misteri Eleusini* and even Donizetti's *Poliuto*.

---

34 Calvi died in 1848, the same year as Donizetti. He was a patriot, writer and musical theorist.

35 Finazzi preached the commemorative sermon at Mayr's funeral

36 His wish was partically fulfilled in 1875 when Antonio Alessandri, then curator of the *Biblioteca Civica*, Bergamo, published a slender sequence of these "lives" with additional material taken from the writings of a Dominican friar, P. Barnaba Vaerini. See bibliography. In the Notebooks there are well over 1000 pages dedicated to the "lives". They are source material for many lesser known composers and musicians, and could be of benefit to future revisers of Grove's Dictionary.

The *Ateneo* encouraged Mayr to write. It is possible that the Notebooks owe much to his contact with members. Perhaps the sequence of entries not only record notes taken from reviews and reading in general but thoughts stimulated by conversation.

2   Mayr and Masonry

In 1820 the police discovered a masonic lodge in Bergamo. There were forty-eight members; amongst these were Abate Salvioni, Simon Mayr, priests, lawyers and representatives of various professions. One of the priests was Marco Alessandri who had already led a Bergamasque lodge in 1775. He seems to have been one of v. Bassus's contacts, for he was on good terms with a bookseller named Rondi who was known to distribute books frowned upon by the authorities. He worked for the Cisalpine Republic. After its collapse he gradually became disillusioned with politics and ecclesiastical bureaucracy. He spoke out against sermons "which tended to perpetuate prejudice in society" and he may have been part of the circle that encouraged Samuele Biava to render various hymns and prayers in Italian for Simon Mayr, Luigi Gambale, Donizetti and others to set to simple chants for two cantors to lead a congregation. The example of Alessandro Manzoni's *Inni Sacri* cannot be overlooked.

Marco Alessandri's catholicism (indeed that of Mayr and many other Bergamasques) was, as already suggested, eventually to find concrete expression in the reforms of Pope John XXIII, a Bergamasque, who studied the teachings of the MIA and who was a product of the Seminary in Bergamo for which Mayr composed a number of cantatas.

In the light of Mayr's life, writings and obvious spirituality, it is to be supposed that his interests in Masonry must date back to his years with Weishaupt and v. Bassus. He firmly believed that, besides the outward show of religion (in which he took an active part), there was an inner nucleus nourished by the Mysteries and the insights of sages and saints. If this kernel was ever to shrivel up, the external parade of the Church would quickly lose meaning and purpose, becoming a social convention alone. It is like the mask and the face, the letter and the spirit, or the circumference and the centre; both require the other to have life and meaning. Mayr would have been the first to throw up his hands in horror at a cheap theosophy or panacea of any kind. Without the tradition of the Church as a guiding principle, esotericism quickly becomes a deluding trap for the ego. This firm belief in the validity of the "inward" mysteries of religion helps us to understand Mayr's profound interest in musical science which is based upon proportion and number, together with their relationship to the inner life of the psyche, as well as the laws of a cosmology. It is not for nothing that his contemporaries compared him to Dante and Poussin.

Mayr believed in initiation, that each profession had its inner wisdom which gave purpose to work, transforming the routine of life into adoration and prayer. It was essential that if a person showed sensitivity towards "meaning" then he was taught according to his grade of consciousness.

There seems little doubt that Mayr was first an initiate of the Illuminati, free of anarchic political overtones and was second a Mason. His influence in these matters over his pupils must have been considerable. Donizetti was certainly initiated by Mayr and when the teaching is known then the more personal passages of his letters to his master are set into context. Even Donizetti's choice of subjects for libretti is better understood.

Mayr's initiatory knowledge also helps to explain his classicism. He considered Greece and its mystery religions as the root of the tradition. This conviction he would have harmonized with the seemingly irreconcilable insights of Judaism through the Christian tradition. For example, he would have perceived Merkabah and Kabbalah symbolism as illuminating the classical cosmology (especially the inner significance of scale and harmony). He was in the tradition of thinkers such as Marsilio Ficino and Pico della Mirandola, to whom theorists like Gaffurio, Zarlino and Galilei, Tartini, Barca etc. owe a fundamental debt. For Mayr romanticism could easily obscure such cultural roots by its failure to re-interpret the perennial wisdom in its own terms and by the adulation of emotion over contemplative insight.

The inner core of Mayr's teaching is simplicity itself - the sacredness of friendship and the necessity of forgiveness as the cornerstone of any relationship; the art of music being nothing less than intoxication and vision, Plato's "Divine Frenzy". He would have insisted that life itself was the true initiator (the Master only being a signpost or symbol) and that all the mysteries of Nature could be opened up through true science. Hence once matter ceased to be viewed as "solid" or "opaque" but as a degree of the spirit, then life became pure vision and illumination - sacramental as taught by the liturgy of the Church. Death was simply the actualization of a process already understood by the adept, the moving from one modality to another.

3   The Operas

Stendhal was no admirer of Mayr but he touched upon a reaction which must be experienced by many in relation to Mayr's operas: "I repeat: Mayr is the very genius of correctness; but Rossini is the very spirit of genius". He also added that the music of Mayr's operas has "a certain quality of its own, particularly when one has struggled and struggled and eventually become used to it".

The operas have the correctness of the classical world, the music is intellectual, everything on the score is set out rather like a Vermeer or Poussin painting and yet it moves with the drama. A profusion of ideas is always coming to the ear (and meets the eye from the score) and every incident leads on and flows to the next. It is essential, in order to enter Mayr's world, somehow to cease making comparisons with Mozart, Haydn, Cimarosa or Rossini. The 17th century Venetian painter, Sebastiano Mazzoni hit upon a major stumbling block in the appreciation of any work of art: "Show the public a work of art and they immediately start making comparisons". It is as if the untrained senses need reference points for stability when reacting to the act of creativity[37].

Stendhal records another aspect of Mayr's operas, the borrowing of ideas from other composers. Superficially it might appear to be plagiarism, but once understood the music is rather like the poetry of T. S. Eliot; the quotations and allusions are there to heighten the composer's dramatic intentions.

For example, let us consider *L'amor coniugale* and the hints of *Don Giovanni* and *Così fan tutte* in its second half. Moroski (Pizzaro in Beethoven's opera) is descending into the dungeon's abyss not as victor but like the Don, the victim of his own fate - hence the allusions to Mozart (his fellow illuminatus and Masonic brother). Did Mayr, like Beethoven and Wagner, disapprove of *Così fan tutte's* morality? Perhaps we have a hint of Mayr's rejection of the old régime, the Venice of Lorenzo da Ponte, which he had known and had seen fall to ruin under Napoleon. Zeliska (Leonora) is the reverse of the frivolous Dorabella and Fiordiligi. She turns the energies of the mock suicide scene in act one of Mozart's opera into an act of salvation and liberation. Hence Mayr's quotes from *Così fan tutte*; note the point where they come in the scene. Zeliska is proving to all to what extent she is the faithful spouse and lover. As already said, the music, especially that sung by Zeliska throughout this scene is of high inspiration[38].

In the overture and towards the end of *Medea in Corinto* there is a quotation from Haydn's *Creation*. It is the musical depiction of the flight and headlong fall of the angels of darkness and negation. Mayr's *Medea* is a profoundly moving portrayal of evil. In some ways it is consciously an unnerving and emotionally draining work. The quotation from Haydn is the only sign of hope, the hope for evil's downfall in the opera. The consciously "lighter" music of Creusa and Aegeus's aria is set into the dark woven web of Jason's and Medea's fate in order to alleviate the barrage of darkness from the stage and orchestral pit. In many ways *Medea in Corinto* is a hard work to enter into though we know it stunned audiences of the period, inspiring Turner to paint *The vision of Medea*. Within the severely classical modal world of Mayr's music dwells all the darkness of Wagner's gods and

---

37 Mayr's own version of Mazzoni's thought, to be found in the Notebooks is: "Why do people always bring up comparisons! The oak cannot be the same as the palm, or the cyprus or vice versa. A true individual cannot be compared except to himself."

38 Mayr would have interpreted Da Ponte's tale as initiatory. Mozart's opera is not so shocking when seen in its context of the Venetian stage. Disguise and reversal of roles are well-known ingredients of traditional stories.

titans. Today due to later romantic music, we have to retrain our ears to "hear" music such as Mayr's[39].

At the most dramatic Crucifixion sequence of the second part of *La Passione*, Mayr quotes, or rather hints at, the introduction to Haydn's *Seven last words of the Saviour*, with moving and telling effect.

Another example is the overture to *Elisa*. After the slow opening section, the audience is suddenly plunged into the first few bars of Haydn's *Symphony No. 82, The bear*. What is Mayr up to in this excellent sinfonia other than paying his respect to a composer he knew and loved? Is he, by using Haydn's pulsating theme, not setting the scene of *Elisa (a dramma sentimentale)* with its conscious fresh air feel of mountains, valleys, snows and avalanches? Like *L'amor coniugale*, the opera is *semi-seria*, a fore-runner of Donizetti's *Linda di Chamounix*. Haydn and Mayr paint a bucolic dance as vividly as any whirling peasants of Breugel or Rubens. Both composers, through their *Sturm und Drang* background, favoured and used popular tunes and rhythms.

This is not plagiarism but an acknowledgement of a family of souls. A few bars quoted by Mayr flood the mind with allusions and build up a mental image which will endure in the listener, feeding the imagination.

Rossini learnt from Mayr's ideas. Cinderella's song from *La Cenerentola*, is note for note, Zeliska's *romanza* sung on her descent into the prison's abyss. Ferretti's libretto for Rossini's opera indicates that the story should be taken as an initiatory tale. Does not Cinderella start out from the abyss to become a princess? Is not the tale, like the trials of Psyche, a symbolic account of the soul's descent and return? - as indeed, is *L'amor coniugale*. The more Mayr's music is known, the more Rossini's operas will be understood to be filled out with musical ideas to be found in the older composer.

From 1813 to *Demetrio* in 1824 Mayr turned more and more to his hero, Metastasio. He did not move with the times but graciously bowed out, setting before his public what he believed was true. Why did Metastasio appeal to Mayr?

> "Metastasio," wrote Mayr, "possesses a gift no-one has equalled.
> That is, the uniting of natural elocution to the heights of sentiment,
> together with the harmony of words and the flow of language with
> the magnificence of the subject. He also brings together the sheer
> richness of lyrical poetry with the sublime severity of religious
> thought."

---

39 *Mit der Leidenschaft ist nichts gethan. Sie muss da seyn und der Geist muss sie regieren. Alles genau rhythmisieren, schattieren und den Hörern verdeutlichen, darauf kommt es an.* (From the Notebooks.) "Nothing is achieved with passion alone. It (passion) has to be and the spirit must control it. It depends on rhythm, shading and on clarifying to listeners with great clarity." This is what Mayr's simple but busy and totally correct orchestral figuration is up to - it "paints" the passion being expressed in the words sung by the protagonists.

Metastasio aimed to portray the intellect in conflict with the passions and emotional life. He supports the Renaissance humanist ideal that *magnanimità* and *virtù*, exercised by the will and reason in the light of the intellect, may break the chains of fate and bring about a better world. Therefore, he chose archetypal heroes rather than individual personalities as the subjects of his libretti-types in which the audience might discover their own dilemmas.

Metastasio, explains Mayr, "knew, with those ideal heroes of his, how to paint natural virtues with admirable colours. He expressed with great perception the sentiments of faithfulness and of paternal and filial love. Who does not feel taken out of himself when Metastasio clothes, with unparalleled beauty, the most sublime arguments of religion, bringing together the most profound ideas with ornament of style, witnessing, one might say, virtually supernatural sacrifices, presented with the attraction and charm of his unforgettable language? He does all this, whilst masterfully preserving the proportion of thought to the musical expression, enabling song and harmony to present themselves spontaneously". Furthermore the static quality of Metastasio's libretti, in which singers must master gesture to heighten their art, is conducive to Mayr's music.

The last phase of Mayr's operatic creativity confirms this trend. *Medea in Corinto* was followed by Mayr's last two *opere semiserie*; it was a genre at which he excelled, making way for Rossini's *La gazza ladra* and Donizetti's *L'elisir d'amore*. There is also one *opera buffa* but eight *opere serie*.

Numerous cantatas date from the year 1816 when no operas were written due quite possibly to the consequences of Waterloo and the change of the ruling power. Mayr's cantata, *L'armonia*, was composed for the arrival of the Austrian King. It is composed for very large forces which recall Berlioz; the text is by Baizini and relates how the spirit of poetic inspiration (the voice of the Bard) may bring peace and harmony to a people and its warriors. In 1814 Mayr had set Jacopo Ferretti's words *Il voto di Jefte* as an oratorio. The *azione sacra, Ifigenia in Tauride*, set to Zeno's libretto dates from 1817. Two further *azioni sacre* were composed in 1821; *Atalia* (Romani), for the *San Carlo*, was conducted by Rossini, much to the disgust of Donizetti[40]; *Samuele* (Merelli), is a fascinating work. The libretto was written in association with Mayr; it indicates Mayr's knowledge of the Bible and his theological grasp. Both works merit revival. His last *azione sacra, San Luigi Gonzaga* (Cominazzi), enjoyed a considerable success. It dates from 1822, the year before his election as President of the *Ateneo*. In the *Cenni* Mayr's dates for membership and presidency are unaccountably wrong. His interests were by now sacred music and writing.

---

40 See Z.11. Possibly Donizetti's request to his teacher for a *Credo* was so that he could conduct (Donizetti was a sought-after conductor) Mayr and vindicate his reputation. Z. 12 reports that *Atalia* was performed in Rome. Donizetti denies rumours that he had added a new *Sinfonia*. Rather, he relates, Mayr's *Sinfonia* was not played owing to the length of the oratorio. Did Donizetti conduct the Rome performance?

4   Music for Vespers and other Devotions

Sunday in *S. Maria Maggiore* must have been memorable - music would have continued throughout the day, with the exception of the time given to lunch and digestion! As for the Office of Vespers there are settings of all shapes and sizes, from full orchestra to *a cappella*. It is assumed that according to the liturgical importance of the day more or less psalms were sung. On weekdays perhaps only certain verses were sung as anthems with the greater part of the Office being chanted. This seems to have been the case in parish churches.

The catalogue records numerous settings of the opening versicles to Vespers, permitting various combinations. Thus the Office began with a musical zeal which could last for ten minutes or more. As was the custom, the first psalm, *Dixit Dominus* was generally given pride of place. There are many settings of the verses, once more permitting different versions, lasting about 30 minutes. There are various settings of the office hymns (*Jesu Redemptor, Ave Maris stella* etc.) and numerous *Magnificats* of varying lengths. The Office might have ended with a fully orchestrated hymn or anthem. The interplay of plainchant for the antiphons and versicles must have made the service on a high day a curious combination of styles.

Vespers would have been in general followed by Benediction.

In the *Cenni*, Mayr records that up to the date of his writing he had set the psalms for Compline to music in four different versions. These unfortunately are lost. The instance serves to indicate how incomplete is the *Fondo Mayr*, regardless of its treasures. There are *Litanies of the Blessed Virgin Mary*, psalms for monastic clothing, the blessing of bells, and much more besides. Of particular interest is a musical introduction, an *invito*, to Haydn's *Seven last words*. The words set by Mayr are *Già trafitto in duro legno* (St. Alfonso Liguori).

Once more, the researcher is amazed at the quantity, variety and quality of the music. He becomes quickly lost in a labyrinth of possibilities. Unfortunately, he quickly has to accept that it is now impossible to say how all the pieces were used; whether they were solo pieces or parts of a complete setting.

V   1824 - 1845

1   The Notebooks (*Lo Zibaldone*)
2   The Hymn Book
3   Requiems and music for Holy Week
4   The Teaching
5   "His life was in no way lazy
         nor was he indolent in the art of music"

1   The Notebooks (*Lo Zibaldone*)

Machiavelli relates in a letter how, when he had retired to San Casciano, high in the Tuscan hills, he would go into his library and commune with the great of history. With an eagle's eye he analysed his times and wrote *The Prince*. As Mayr grew older, so he spent more time in his study reading musical journals, reflecting on music and life from his house, high above the city walls overlooking the Lombardy plain and the Bergamasque foothills. He too watched and observed a changing Europe. The result was the numerous Notebooks, kept from about 1830 until his loss of sight made writing too tedious.

Editing and preparing these remarkable documents is not an easy task, as the late Arrigo Gazzaniga and I have discovered. Too often the writing is difficult to read especially when Mayr writes in German with his elegant but obscure "Corinth" script. Translation is just as hard due to the need to render the impact of Mayr's thoughts without heaviness of style.

The books vary in size and it is possible to establish some sort of order through dates referred to in the text and the decline in handwriting. The following is the briefest outline of the Notebooks. Title headings are kept in the original. The order is not necessarily chronological.

Vol. 1   - *Instruzione* (sic) *elementare nella musica esecutiva*

Vol. 2   - *Elementi della musica pratica in rapporto all'esecuzione* (2 copies)

Vol. 3   - *Dottrina musicale ossia Compendio degli elementi della musica pratica in rapporto all'esecuzione (per uso della Scuola della Cappella di S. Maria Maggiore di Bergamo)*

Vol. 4   - *Applications des méthodes perfectionnées à l'enseignement de la musique.*

            Bound with:

                - teaching notes.
                - *L'esposizione de' intervalli e suoni.*

- Notes on the choir such as "Adamo Bianchi ill - replacement needed for Christmas".
- Ornamentation - *il grupetto* (sic) *e i trilli.*
- *Suoni forti e deboli.*

(*Regole per conoscere il modo ed il tuono d' un pezzo di musica.* Manuscript in the Conservatorio, Milan)

Vol. 5 - *Metodo di canto.*
- *Novo* (sic) *metodo di canto di Garandé.*
- *Dissertazione : della voce umana, delle malatti e rimedi contro di essi da Frederico Augusto.*
- *Weber von Heilbron.*
- *various notes.*

Vol. 6 - *Dissertazione sopra la coltura ed il perfezionamento dell' udito musicale.*
- *Recensione della scuola di canto di Schubert.*
- Notes on the Cembalo
- *Recensione delle lettere di Natoli sopra il canto come mezzo di provare la felicità domestica e il diletto sociale.*

Vol. 7 - *Trattato dell' accompagnamento.*

Vol. 8 - Notes on the Organ.
- *Breve istruzione pel modo di suonare il pedale cavata delle fonti più autorevoli e corredata di ogni genere di esercizi ed esercizi.*

Vol. 9 - *Il clavicembalo.*
- *Degli accidenti.*
- *Della cognizione de' tasti.*
- *Della figura e del valore delle note.*
- *De' segni della trasposizione ossia degli accidenti.*

Vol. 10 - *Sul capitolo della musica dei Greci.*
- *Musica antica.*
- *Musica bergamasca: saggio storico della musica, degli artisti, e sugli scrittori musicali a Bergamo corredato di ritratti, di brani di opere inedite di composizioni musicali.*
- *La musica in Germania.*

Vol. 11 - *Le glorie della musica sotto il fausto governo dell' imperiale reale casa d'Austria.*
- Copies of letters by Zeno from the edition of *Sig. Sansoni*, Venice 1785.
- Notes on *La letteratura musicale.*

Vol. 12 - *Letteratura musicale, scuole di musica, accademie e società filarmoniche.*

Vol. 13 - *Cenni storici intorno all' oratorio.*

Vol. 14 - *Frammenti sui violini e sui violinisti italiani.*
- *Intorno alla storia del violino.*

Vol. 15 - A history of *La stampa ed incisione dei caratteri musicali.*
- The harp.
- The clarinet.
- The serpent - corno di basso.
- The bassoon.
- The organ.
- The organ at Monte Cassino.
- The organ at Monza.
- The organ at St. Peters, Munich.
- *Dell' orgine e dell' uso della tromba presso gli antichi (del Sig. Galland).*
  (Brevi Cenni intorno alla maniera di scrivere per lo strumento musicale
  chiamato corno, o corno di caccia. Manuscript in the Conservatorio,
  Bologna.)

Vol. 16 - Notes on the violin.

Vol. 17 - *Almanaco musicale per l'anno 1826* (602 pages which attempt to give a
  picture of the state of music in Europe for that year. A fascinating document;
  i.e. Notes on the Eisteddfod held in Wrexham. Elsewhere in the Notebooks,
  La quarta grande festa Musicale di York, 1835).

Vol. 18 - *Biografie di musicisti* (This is the *Lives* already referred to - well over 1000
  pages).

Vol. 19 - Second, longer version of the history of the oratorio.
- A life of St. Cecilia and the origin of the St. Cecilia societies. (As noted in
  the next section, Mayr was involved with the institution of the St. Cecilia
  Society and was in contact with Bishop Sailer (once his lecturer) and Karl
  Proske, both founder members of the society).
- *Palestrina.*
- The Serassi Family.
- Finazzi - castrato.
- Notes on the Jesuits[41]

  (In addition, Mayr copied out a number of books. These, as already suggested,
  would appear to date from the Venetian years. See Bibliography).

Vol. 20 - Various books of notes and thoughts which contain treatises such as that on
  instruments published by Arrigo Gazzaniga.

---

41 Clearly the Jesuits fascinated Mayr because of his Illuminati background. It is suggested that he
    eventually made his peace with the followers of St. Ignatius Loyola. *San Luigi Gonazga* (1822) is a
    commemoration of an important saint of the Society of Jesus. As with the libretto to *Samuele* (1821),
    the text is carefully annotated with details and information - examples of Mayr's commitment to
    Catholic renewal.

Mayr wrote in Italian, German or French (he corresponded in French with his wife when away from home). The *Zibaldone* is filled with short quotes in English, Latin and Greek. These notes often have no order and they are simply a record of thoughts or facts to have caught Mayr's attention. Thus we may read:

> "Scherzo pour piano par *Chopin*. Breitkopf. Impassioned, as well as experimenting in the various degrees of suffering."

Again:

> "*Pasta* or *Clara Novello* - a goddess of vestal health in song."

Or:

> "He [Mayr] learnt more than he taught."
> "The richness of my goal makes me poor."
> "Life is a tunnel, a long and dark way of which we do not see the end until it is upon us."
> "Life is like a journey by train, we are soon half-way."

Or thoughts on composers:

> "Beethoven is a man whose fame for the most extraordinary and sublime art [of music] has reached not only all the civilized countries of Europe but the remotest parts of the globe. His name is remembered first of all when the subject concerns the hardest and most sublime flights of the imagination; then one mentions a vast river flowing with creativity and above all beholding music's perfection as the ruling art."

Field, Clementi, Weber, Krommer, Mendelssohn, Tomaschek and many other contemporaries meet with Mayr's seal of approval. C. P. E. Bach is singled out as a vital figure in the development of music. J. S. Bach, Handel, Tartini, Gluck, Mozart and Haydn are mentors.

The reader is surprised at first by the space given to the piano and piano music; it is necessary to remember that by the age of 10 (1773) Mayr had been known for his piano playing. Here then are the records of a pianist whose keyboard experience dated from 1773 to 1843 (assuming there are no entries after that year owing to blindness) from C. P. E. Bach and the Mannheim School to Robert and Clara Schumann! - names which conjure up the enormous change that took place in music during Mayr's lifetime.

Perhaps a page throws up a little poetic doodle:

> "Cash, cash, you don't use anything else
> if Seneca disapproves your ways
> Just listen with a smile on your face

If you've cash, you've arrived
If you've nought, you're nought
Only cash has value in both worlds
Without cash, in either, you're nought
Since arguments don't count
Not even the devil has value
What is the philosopher, the poet, the hero
What is the artist without cash?
Kepler, Mozart, Schiller, Lessing
Arrived but made no cash
Fame's tuba is brass
And brass is not gold
Ye gods, therefore give me cash
Nature give me a metallic voice
Because today we mint cash!"

Or notes on what an overture should be!:

"The overture must be a concise summary of what is to follow, a characteristic miniature of what the opera is about. In its concrete expression, complete and self-contained, the overture must enable speculative thoughts about what still remains unheard - that is, glances ahead preparing our receptivity for what is to follow - rendering our thoughts pleasant and lighter. The overture must take us to the starting line - then open the gateway."

He is critical of the tendencies in romantic opera:

"Dramatic music is quickly rushing towards degeneracy, constantly being superficial with suggested illusions and with nothing of true depth."

Then a page is turned to discover a full treatise on instruments and the art of instrumentation or on the nature of inspiration and poetic genius, or as a viola player his personal thoughts on Haydn's quartets:

"I would wish to compare Haydn's quartets to the moon, the light of which penetrates a dark room in the night. When one plays other works by more modern composers such as Onslow[42], Beethoven, Mendelssohn etc., these are enthusiasts, light fills the room, there is an explosion of ecstasy (real or put on we will not bother to enquire) and then suddenly the simpler compositions, just as fresh, original and full of humour, are forgotten and no longer spoken of. But when

---

42 George Onslow (1784 - 1853), an Anglo-French composer who only wrote chamber music.

the fanatics have left, the noise died down, then the soul desires to nourish itself quietly and to rejoice in the peace of the night's light."

The Notebooks are where we find Mayr's definitions of *Classical* and *Classicism*:

> "Classical is that which was scientifically and artistically valued as excellent and true by civilized peoples of all points of view - at least by those who stayed awake. Classicism is: perfect beauty of material and representation due to intimate perception [of thought] - a complete, perfect platting and drawing together of invention and representation."

Though Mayr believed in "rules", they were to him guidelines, the "signposts" indicating the way to create. He was no fundamentalist to whom the rules became the incarnation of the spirit. True one may find elements of a doctrine, indications of his opinions and views on life, but the overall impression is of a man totally open to all around him. However, what he encountered he filtered through the oral teaching he had received. He sought the perennial and was not distracted by the ephemeral. In other words, he was against fashion for fashion's sake; he could not abide artificiality, vain illusions or shallow concepts. As a traditional thinker he recognised the devaluing of currency (devaluing is here meant in the much wider context than that in which it is used today) as a sign of the times in which he lived, times which indulged in ever increasing adulation of industry and its products, over and against the life of the spirit. He combined a cyclic with a linear view of time. Humanity was on its own self-chosen journey to see if it could find the gates of paradise open once more, but time has its cyclic laws to which all are made to bow. Fate can both destroy and initiate. Perseverence in one's follies leads to self-destruction; thus grasping *magnanimità* and *virtù*, soaked in Christian charity was the future's only hope.

He was modern in so far as he was conscious of the implications of his age; he was a man of the 18th century in so far as he believed in order, beauty and goodness. Without respect and understanding, it is best to leave Mayr to one side. Mayr is essentially of the western civilization, a civilization which may be considered to be the result of a strange amalgam of classical and hebraic thought - a treasure trove of grace capable of the most sublime creations, but once misused or forgotten, as history has shown, capable of drawing the curtain on humanity's final act upon the stage of the Divine Comedy.

2   The Hymn Book

Schiedermair records that when Mayr was visited by the ecclesiastical musicologist, Karl Proske (1794 - 1861), on 24 August 1834, the elderly composer, like Handel, could remember little of his student days except for two lecturers who had commanded his respect: Johann Michael Sailer (1751 - 1832) and Benedikt Stattler (1728 - 1797). Sailer is a positive clue as to how Mayr's thoughts had evolved since his days in Ingolstadt and under the influence of the Illuminati.

It becomes clear that Mayr had long left far behind any negative, radical ideas he may or may not have had passed on from v. Bassus and Weishaupt. By 1834 he had become, as his writings show, something of a detached sage, involved, amongst other activities, with the compiling of a vernacular hymnbook, the *Melodie sacre*. As already stressed, he valued and believed profoundly in the role of the liturgy within a Christian society. He belonged to a generation which had lived through the Revolution and the Napoleonic reforms, he had experienced one of the greatest historical upheavals of the human spirit, and he recognized that life would never be the same again. Thus we find Mayr belonging to a group of Catholic intellectuals who realized that with the change in social structures the laity should be able to understand and to participate in the Church's prayers and praises. Again his debt to Herder is perceived; the aim was to draw together folk-wisdom, rational humanism and mystical insight.

Ultimately it was the enlightened Johann Sailer, a Jesuit who became the Bishop of Regensburg, who was to have the most influence over Mayr, not v. Bassus or Weishaupt. The Catholic neo-platonism of Mayr's old lecturer tempered his Aristotelian leanings towards a universal, encyclopaedic knowledge with a mystical insight.

Perhaps it is possible to speculate that Mayr's financial problems, which curiously came at the height of his career, were related to a conscious break with any possible radical leanings. Avenues to financial income may have abruptly come to an end owing to his choice for an enlightened orthodoxy. Maybe he broke off contacts with v. Bassus and a long-standing financial perk suddenly ceased. One thing is certain. Mayr changed direction in about 1813. He did not hesitate in the way he had chosen; he was, as the Notebooks show, a totally unprejudiced and open man who viewed the flow of history with detachment. However, he was a man to whom truth and veracity were his *raison d'être*.

Since the *Melodie sacre* (in the context of the liturgical compositions and writings) represent the culmination of Mayr's work, it will not be out of place to set out the intellectual course which he had taken.

The source which inspired the development of thought would appear to have been originally the influence of Johann Georg Hamann (1730 - 1788). Hamann reacted to Kant's philosophy and the Enlightenment's enthronement of reason over and against the other faculties of human consciousness. He balanced the contemporary vogue for French and classical quotations with Hebraic epigrams and an understanding of the Kabbalah, no doubt because of the fundamental influence of the great Lutheran mystic, Jacob Boehme (1575 - 1624). For Hamann humanity's common birthday was the poetic genius expressed throughout the ages through inspired individuals - it was not the Enlightenment's utopian day-dream of a brave new world. Like Dante, he considered the individual and his social role as a flow of three score years and ten across the stage of life, that is, from life we extract the vitality of experience, faith and a living tradition tested over generations. It was impossible for Hamann to create a dualism through the separation of form and matter, spirit and soul, mind and body.

These romantic stirrings complement rather than detract from the essential Christian teachings. Life was understood to be a way rather than an intellectual speculative game. Such a view could not exalt "education" over the innate wisdom of religion, for the poetic genius (or, in Blake's terms, the Imagination) was like a wine-press extracting nectar from what was otherwise the humdrum of so-called reality.

Hamann's thought became that of Herder (1744 - 1803) who shared his vision with Goethe (1749 - 1832).

Herder re-emphasised Boehme's perception of man and woman being macrocosmically and microcosmically part of the Creation; nature was woven into ourselves as much as into the highest heavens. He assumed that in a right minded society the rational faculties were balanced with the senses and the emotions. The aim of whatever we term "culture" should be the awakening and the care of the poetic genius (the creative imagination). Thus he considered that a healthy society respected and understood the role of myth and ritual, tale and folksong. Herder was suspicious of all those who sought to make belief reasonable thus killing the intuitive, imaginative, perceptive and visionary life of the soul. The great secret was fostering a living tradition that aided the intellect towards belief. Similarly to Blake, he considered that the Middle Ages had been a great flowering of the imagination. Both men in their separate ways sought to free, once more, that visionary genius that could build a Gothic cathedral, tabernacling all its glories from missals to vessels, from myth to liturgy.

Though a Jesuit, Johann Sailer led Catholic approval of the romantic movement in Bavaria. His clerical colleagues suspected his orthodoxy, so that his appointment as Bishop of Regensburg did not come until the last few years of his influential life.

Sailer had taught Mayr, who remained in close contact with Bavaria's royal kapellmeister, Johann Kaspar Aiblinger (1779 - 1867). Aiblinger is recorded as twice visiting Mayr. Pizzetti went as far as suggesting that Aiblinger considered himself as being a disciple of Mayr. In 1838, when Mayr returned for his only brief visit to his homeland, Aiblinger was his host; he was to become, in the forties, Donizetti's friend. The tone of the one surviving letter from Mayr to Aiblinger in which he encourages his career and a visit to Vienna for further studies, could indicate that the younger composer may well have studied under Mayr.

Mayr and Sailer openly strove to reconcile folk wisdom with a humanism grounded in the platonic view. Both were open to the positive aspects of the Enlightenment, but it was the romantic impetus of the times that encouraged and aided the reconciliation of views in order to establish a universal over-view. Both men encouraged popular participation in the liturgy, both did much to revive the dignity of early ecclesiastical music and especially favoured was Palestrina. The liturgy was considered a sacred drama through which all the complex energies of the psyche might be reconciled. Any sacred piece composed by

Mayr illustrated their outlook. First of all, the musical science permitting the composition is totally rational, but it is also a vehicle for the poetic genius, a system proven over generations, evoking correspondences between the macrocosm and the microcosm. Secondly, the appreciation and enjoyment of the music is spontaneous, free, heart-felt; the music is sound which is immediate and fresh but never vulgar or common. In other words, when a congregation sings the liturgy with the naturalness with which a peasant girl may sing the *Ave Maria* at midday in the fields, then a musical revolution has taken place.

Therefore, for Sailer the teacher, and Mayr the pupil, every faculty of human consciousness must be developed, every person must move freely and become what they truly are through the liturgical meal, marrying the temporal with the eternal, innocence with transcendence, filling time and space with love and wisdom.

Sailer also helped Mayr to appreciate art and religion as a unity:

> "If we consider the one, true, eternal religion according to its inner life in a man, we find that it is nothing more than the life of a childlike temper in the one, true God; the life of trust in God as the one immutable ground of existence. Only this religion, where it exists, is interior by nature and character, spirit and life, invisible. And yet religion, as the interior life of man, has an irresistible impulse to reveal itself, to make itself visible, audible, sensible and to form for itself a body that can be seen, heard, felt, and enjoyed. It is one and the same artistic impulse that sees in the night sky Nature's own great cathedral and conceives and produces Saint Peter's in Rome, Saint Paul's in London, the *Stephanskirche* in Vienna, and the *Frauenkirche* in Munich . . .
>
> This impulse is never content with the expression of inner life of religion in ever new forms of celestial music and sacred eloquence . . . , does not rest until the deepest feelings have been brought to their full culmination, until other instruments have been combined in marvellous harmony with the music of the spheres and become one celestial music, and the great allelujah of the heavenly choirs is echoed in the human chorus below." (from *Von dem Bunde der Religion mit der Kunst)*[43].

Even a casual browsing through the Notebooks reveals the influence of Sailer over Mayr. Their mutual aim was the restoration after social upheavals of the genuine religious spirit, which is something far more than the contemporary emphasis on sociological and politi-

---

43 Quoted from Conrad L. Donakowski, *A muse for the masses*, Chicago and London, 1972.

cal views. It is an understanding of the world, indeed the Creation, as sacrament; the mirror of art and the vehicle for beauty.

Karl Proske was Sailer's pupil. In 1834 (the year he visited Mayr) he had travelled to Rome in order to study 16th century religious music with Giuseppe Baini, the kapellmeister of St. Peter's, Rome. Sailer had died two years previously and Proske was continuing the bishop's work. At Mayr's house one of the main topics of discussion must have been the hymn book which was taking shape for publication. Mayr with his poet, Samuele Biava and his co-composer the Neapolitan, Luigi Gambale, was very much part of the Catholic re-awakening in Italy, which is more commonly associated with Alessandro Manzoni, through the novel, *I promessi sposi (The betrothed)*. The well-known story affirms the victory of a child-like faith over the intrigues of noblemen and brigands, and is in keeping with values lauded by Herder. Indeed, Goethe praised Manzoni's poems known as the *Inni sacri*, written between 1812 to 1835. Manzoni typifies the intellectual mind struggling with problems of faith, whereas Biava was someone working at the grass roots. His vernacular paraphrasing of canticles, psalms and hymns was the result of experiments in congregational worship in the vernacular over a number of years. For example, experiments were made in the valleys of the Ossola in Piedmont and by two priests, Luigi Riva and F. Carini who worked in parishes in Cassano dell'Adda, Lombardy, not far from Bergamo. The general policy was to have two cantors leading the congregation, similar to recent practice in French parochial worship. Mayr without doubt knew and was impressed by the work done at Cassano dell'Adda. In time, by about 1830, the vernacular movement resulted in a number of composers writing simple melodies to be used for congregational worship on an experimental level. For example, Donizetti's chant for the *Te Deum* and a psalm (Biava's text) still exist. Also, the so-called *Dante Ave Maria* for two sopranos results from the vernacular movement. Besides Mayr and Gambale, others listed as having contributed melodies for the experiment are: Morlacchi, Bonfichi, Pavesi, Perotti, Callegari, Donizetti, Vaccai, Rastrelli, Gabussi, Rieschi, Manna and Padre Davide, the famous Bergamasque organist and pupil of Mayr.

The preface to the first edition (1835) of the *Melodie sacre*, written by Michele Parma, explains that the melodies were not chosen for publication until the faithful themselves had chosen and accepted those which were sung not only "in sanctuaries, but in homes, factories and the fields". The result was that those of Mayr and Gambale were selected.

On 30 March 1836, the Government of Lombardy asked the dioceses to give their formal blessing to Biava's verses which were by that date being readily used. On 20 October of the same year, Pope Gregory XVI wrote a formal letter of approval. Later, in another letter dated 27 July 1837 he reaffirmed his *imprimatur* and confessed that he too used Biava's texts for his own devotions. By 1838, the *Melodie sacre* had gone through seven editions.

The preface to the 7th edition was written by Melchiale Gabba. In it he traced the historical and liturgical use of hymns in worship, commending the return to the use of the vernacular. He praised the new approach to melody:

"Such is the quality of Mayr's and Gambale's music offered in this book that it corresponds with complete precision and strength to the meters [of the verses], rhythms and the various levels of meanings of the hymns. It influences [literally "invades"] the spirit of a person through its own power, it awakens the heart and vivifies grace. It turns sorrow into joy, purifies the passions, grafting to them noble aspirations. It helps those in mourning, heals the sick, offers consolation and eases tribulation."

Gabba quoted from a review written by Francesco Vigano in the *Pirata*, 17 February 1837:

"Mayr's melodies and harmonies are not of the kind that move a person and fill him with sensuous anxieties, leaving him once the music has finished, languid and empty; rather, they touch the heart, awakening it to ideals, purifying and strengthening it. They illuminate the mind and inspire the soul to that faith which escapes definition, since it is the mysterious lifting up of the created towards the Creator. It is what a person feels and what is unfathomable in words. Mayr is the master poet, the true Dante of sacred music. His thoughts, even when they may appear as obscure, are like pictures [reflections or icons]. They are felt, they are clothed with empathy, they are clear, never abrasive. Once played they send out a harmonic sound which is most precious."

The *Melodie sacre* is divided into 5 sections:

1. Morning and evening prayers   2. Hymns
   (all set to music)
3. Canticle   4. Psalms
5. Prayers for Holy Communion. (It is curious to note that there are no contributions from Mayr for the section devoted to eucharistic worship. It seems probable that it had been agreed previously that this aspect of devotion was to be given over to Gambale.)

In all there are 29 contributions from Mayr:

1. Our Father   2. *Angelus*
3. *Ave Maria*   4. *Sanctus*
5. *Gloria*   6. Invocation to Our Lady of the
                                          People *(Sub tuum praesidium)*

7. *Ave maris stella*   8. *Stabat Mater*
9. Invocation to the Guardian Angel   10. *Requiem aeternam*
11. *Dies Ira*e   12. *Piange Lingua*

13. *O sacrum convivium*
15. *Vexilla regis prodeunt*
17. The Redemption (Canticle of the First Day)
19. *The Exodus*
21. The Mystical Joys of Our Lady
23. *Nunc dimittis*
25. The Beatitudes
27. *Miserere*
29. *Laudate Dominum, omnes gentes*

14. *Domine non sum dignis*
16. *Te Deum*
18. The Glorification of the Third Day (The Resurrection)
20. The Passion
22. *Benedictus*
24. The Song of St. John the Baptist
26. *De profundis*
28. *Cum invocarem exaudivit me Deus*

Mayr composed many chants which were not published, many may be lost. Twenty-five hymns, in the hand of a copyist, have fortunately been traced, eleven are devotions to the Passion; eight are prayers to Our Lady; there are two *Stabat Maters,* and four are on general themes. Various other hymns have fortunately survived[44].

It is sad to record that the Roman Church has for the greater part lost its musical tradition. Catholics do not have anything comparable to the *English Hymnal* or *Hymns Ancient and Modern*; if they did, then examples of Mayr (and certainly Gambale and possibly even Donizetti) as a composer of hymns would be still in use. Here is a strong case for the Catholic Church to draw together a selection of hymns from the earlist days of the Christian community (such melodies as Mayr would have considered inimitable and the purest examples) and across the centuries to the present - a new "hymns ancient and modern".

The fruition of Mayr's final aspiration as a composer is an example of his stature. He asked to be given the grace of inspiration to compose simple melodies for sacred texts, melodies which would make the sung words meaningful, melodies which would become second nature to a congregation. One is made to think of the icon painter, anonymous, with the intention of being an instrument to record a divine archetype. In a spiritual dimension, Mayr completed his pilgrimage. He had travelled through the infernal regions, he had scaled the Mount to regain the Garden of Earthly Innocence, he had been permitted to record harmonies and melodies of Paradise. He would have been the last to claim anything for himself in the eyes of the Deity. He was one of those rare, enlightened souls who taught the truth to those who came into contact with him.

Mayr still has a teaching to offer to a world increasingly caught in the vortex of its own self-judgement.

---

44 *The Library of Ugo and Olga Levi,* Venice. See catalogue for further details.

3   Requiems and music for Holy Week

The ceremonies associated with the burial of the dead must have been lavish affairs for those who could afford musicians and singers. There are seven complete settings of the Requiem Mass which so far have been traced, these are of varying lengths and musical texture, according to liturgical and personal requirements. The first vigil of the Office of the Dead is honoured with a setting of three lessons and three responsaries, these are for full orchestra, alto, tenor and bass soloists and four-part choir. There are over a hundred settings of various verses from the penitentary psalm, the *Miserere*, "Have mercy upon me, O God, after thy great goodness, according to the multitude of thy mercies do away mine offences". From the verses numerous full-settings may be organized depending on preference. There are eight *requiem aeternam, at least two contain also the Te decet* and *Kyrie*. Two are marked *con sinfonia*. There is also a *requiem aeternam* for the Ambrosian Rite used in and around Milan. There are also various settings of verses from the *Dies irae*.

Clearly, not everyone was rich enough to pay for a fully sung requiem and some people, therefore, chose the verses and settings they wished and could afford to be sung. The rest of the service would have most likely been chanted. The Notebooks record Mayr's great respect and love for Gregorian chant and he would have taken simpler services with just as much attention and devotion.

The "wind" *Requiem Mass* takes about fifty minutes to play. The *Gran Messa da Requiem in G minor* lasts for a full hundred minutes and must surely be acknowledged as a prototype for Donizetti and for Verdi, especially since it was the only religious composition by Mayr to have been published during his lifetime; it was published without his permission[45].

The Office for the Burial of the Dead exercised a profound influence over the young Donizetti. Later, when a mature composer, he wrote to Mayr in 1837:

> "I took the chance to compose a requiem mass and have it performed
> in Naples (since my soul felt ready for such a task). It was performed
> there and on this occasion I had things done according to my liking;
> that is, I had the altar moved virtually to the centre of the church;
> the apse behind the altar I had covered with a hanging black drapery,
> on which one saw simply an immense golden cross hanging from
> the arch to the ground. Thus the orchestra, etc. was behind, the public
> heard but could not see, the church being dark except for candlelight
> which made the service very sad. Thus the public's distraction was

---

45 Donizetti gave the score of his *Requiem* to Antonio Dolci in whose hands it remained until his death, after which it was performed for the first time in 1870, four years before Verdi's *Requiem*, a fact which helps to explain echoes of Donizetti in Verdi's *Dies Irae*.

curbed from seeing who was playing and who was singing, because for me in matters of death I love very much this religious sadness."

In *S. Maria Maggiore*, the musicians would have been virtually out of sight, high up in the choir galleries. It is quite possible to imagine the young Donizetti leaning forward so as to look below to observe the movement of the liturgy from the shrouded coffin and its six candles to the altar and its sacrament. In this context it is interesting to note that though Mayr's settings of the *Requiem aeternam, Te decet, Kyrie* and *Dies irae* may be long and substantial, the *Sanctus, Benedictus* and *Agnus Dei* are always short and to the point in order not to hold up the eucharistic action.

Holy Week in the Church generally, has always been known for liturgical solemnity. In Mayr's time, the orchestra and organ were, with discretion, allowed to play. The more one studies the customs of *S. Maria Maggiore*, the more one realizes that Mayr knew an age which has long disappeared from church services. One of the musical highlights of the Week was the singing of the *Lamentations*. Gerolamo Calvi notes in his list of Mayr's sacred music that: "all Mayr's *Lamentations* are to be noted, for their strength of expression, character, and freshness of colour and instrumentation, they are to be compared with the classics." These vary from two to four different settings of each lamentation, they are scored for solo voice or soloists, choir and full orchestral accompaniment. Certain verses are set with obligato instruments, giving the vocal line a timbre which in the acoustic environment of a church must have deeply moved the listener. It is to be hoped that these works are soon revived.

The Passion readings for Palm Sunday, Holy Wednesday and Maundy Thursday, are for four-part choir with violone and organ continuo. In contrast, on Good Friday, the words of Christ are set for Tenor solo and orchestra and stand in strict juxtaposition to the rest of the text set for four-part choir with the usual violone and organ continuo.

There is also a setting for three voices (ATB?) of a devotion dedicated to the *Three hours of agony on the Cross*. As might be expected, it is unaccompanied, except for the customary violone continuo. Mayr also encouraged meditative performances of Haydn's vocal setting of the *Seven last words of the Saviour*. This, as already noted, he preceeded by a full, musical invitation to devotion, using words by St. Alphonse Liguori. The scoring is in keeping with Haydn's, that is, soloists, choir and orchestra. In the *Marciana Library* in Venice, there is to be found Mayr's own setting of the *Seven last words*. The fact that it is in Venice suggests that it may be an early work.

When taken in the context of his contributions to the *Hymn Book* and his numerous simple settings of spiritual praises "for the mission field" (that is, parochial missions), Mayr's ceaseless dedication to sacred music indicates how much he yearned for a spiritual revival within the Church. For Mayr, it was a century which was awake to so many new impulses; however, in the field of theology it was "asleep". He longed for the new found popular enthusiasm regarding theatrical music to turn and to help re-kindle devotional life with evangelical richness. His last three great *azioni sacre*, (*Samuele*, 1821; *Atalia*, 1822;

S. Luigi Gonzaga, 1822, which are for all intents and purposes operas like Donizetti's *Poliuto* and *Il Diluvio Universale*) are lasting testaments to how he tried to use the popular medium of the theatre to awaken an interest in religious themes. Likewise, it is against this concern that the musical beauties of his last operas, *Fedra*, 1822, and *Demetrio*, 1824, should be appreciated. *Medea in Corinto*, 1813, the opera by which he is remembered, is only a step on the way to the final rich, theatrical flowering of genius in the early 1820s. They were his last pleadings (in the context of the theatre) with a world he considered had lost its direction due to romantic frivolities. For Mayr, all the faculties of the soul, intellect as well as emotion had to be balanced, and to this the inner life of the spirit was paramount.

Mayr had lived through the Revolution and he had stood with the Napoleonic reforms of Italy but he had observed that a deep wound had been cut into society. It was not just a shift of political power, it was the gradual trivializing of genuine traditional roots which for their vitality must draw from the life of the spirit. He aspired by his music to help lead the new society to recognize quality rather than quantity. His aspiration cannot be seen as wrong, for today, it is with music that the west has lost its connection with the genius of its much maligned and misunderstood tradition. The arts in a monetarist and materialist society become increasingly an embarrassment; they are acceptable when they can be auctioned or play the role of fashion - but when Bach's *Passions*, Handel's *Messiah* or Elgar's oratorios are played with sincerity, the spirit lives for a while and the soul is moved. When people meet to make music, be it a Haydn quartet or a Beethoven symphony, whether the performers be professional or amateur, then something of the energy Mayr knew and considered worth devoting his life to, lives on.

To know Mayr, implies to familiarize oneself with his concerns, at the heart of which is sacred music. His operatic contribution is but the shell, and it is the present writer's belief, that a genuine Mayr revival can only come about through knowing the greater religious compositions which in turn throw light on his works for the theatre. Nothing could make Mayr happier for the kernel of his creative genius would have been once again appreciated.

4   The Teaching

Mayr was among the last composers of the west to teach in the context of a meaningful oral tradition the science of music as it had evolved from ancient Greece to his own times. Though we may not eavesdrop on his teaching, the music and the manner in which it was conceived, the extensive notes and writings, together with the ethos surrounding the man, make this supposition possible.

In this section an attempt will be made to suggest the essential content of the oral teaching. However, since today schools and academies no longer know or use the oral tradition a brief digression could be useful in helping to recognize the gulf between a living tradition and modernism.

It is true that in Jungian psychology and various modern theosophies there are residues of a tradition, but an oral tradition as envisaged here may only be nourished in the context of a vital and healthy religious expression with its sources and in the case of the west, firmly at one with the roots of Judaism or Christianity. The health of an oral tradition is strictly dependent on the spirituality of the "family" and "fellowship" at a grass roots level. It is not the result of an elitist group separating itself from the main social body. During his "illuminati" years Mayr would have come into contact with esoteric tradition, but such a tradition could only have come into health and fullness once Mayr had totally identified his teaching and life with the spiritual world of Catholicism as he found it in the diocese of Bergamo.

A comment such as Apollinaire's, *On ne peut pas transporter partout avec soi le cadavre de son père* (One cannot carry around with one the body of one's father) could have arisen only in a generation totally alienated from the tradition referred to. From the modernist viewpoint it is easy to judge the teaching offered by Mayr as a *cadavre*, a dead weight. Whereas Mayr had struggled to reconcile the past with the present for the sake of the future, Apollinaire's generation extolled a confidence in a future separated from the past, an awareness which valued anarchy, revolution, materialism, and especially the new awareness brought into play through speed and the comparative ease of travel. Utopia (no-place) was again believed in and the catharsis of war and destruction was exalted. All signs of the past were to be obliterated, museums debunked and the canals of Venice drained. Such idealism found fulfilment in the bloodshed of the First World War and the Russian Revolution. The well known photograph of Apollinaire with a bandage wrapped around his head as a result of a wound sustained in the trenches is an ironic reminder of a generation's folly.

The launching of the modernist movement encouraged the emphasis of consciousness increasingly away from the contemplative hub of the past for the dynamic vortex caused by "existential" experience. Sequence, plurality, fragmentation of the whole because the order of the day demanded it to be so. Curiously, the art forms born from modernism such as the cinema and television have created a passivity within the beholder rather than a creative response. Do not these images projected in dark rooms recall with new poignancy the imagery of Plato's Cave?

The rejection of the past as irrelevant reached its zenith in the Sixties. Academic institutions declared anything that did not fit into their intellectual systems "a lie", and any residues of the past had to be intellectualized into subjects such as "comparative religions" or "psychology". Theology had fallen to such a low ebb that it no longer understood its own language of symbolism and ranted on concerning "demythologizing", a fashion still adhered to by many bishops and clergy. In despair the young turned to drugs and the east, for it seemed that the west had nothing to offer except materialism and the nightmare looming on the horizon caused by the caprices of the mind and the shallow greed engendered by materialism. The result has been illiteracy concerning the west and its tradition.

Modernism has used the term, "the language of rupture". By definition rupture implies a tearing away by excessive or misguided force. It can only be repaired by the intervention of surgery. The nostalgia for the past which today often prevails in taste cannot heal. It is concerned with fashionable externalities and the parade of residues, lacking the toughness of an inner reality. It is no more than an escape from the crudeness of the present.

Mayr was rugged and tough, no doubt blunt when called upon to be so, but he was also compassionate and loving. These qualities are attested to in Donizetti's letters to his master.

By the time Donizetti had returned from the Bologna Academy "to perfect himself in the teachings of Mayr", his master was at the height of his creative powers. Curiously, Donizetti was encouraged to compose a quantity of string quartets and music for the piano and for religious occasions[46]. Eventually in 1822, thanks to Mayr's negotiations, the young composer launched out on a career with his opera, *Zoraide di Granata*, performed in Rome. Earlier attempts at operatic composition had been local and somewhat half-hearted. In 1822 Mayr was composing music of the quality to be heard in his *azione sacra, S. Luigi Gonzaga*. Such music explains why Donizetti matured in the way he did. From 1822, until the close of the decade he struggled in the wake of Rossini. Once Rossini had settled in Paris and had opted for early retirement, Donizetti forged with his own particular spark of genius a musical expression formed out of prevalent musical fashion and the example presented to him by Mayr. His melancholy disposition made him Italy's greatest romantic composer.

But at the root of his genius there is the teaching he had received from Mayr, a teaching given expression in continual liturgical worship and the business of music making. Donizetti's early compositions must be seen not only as first attempts in the practice of his art but as the result of his musical nourishment at the hands of Mayr[47]. Besides practical advice such as Mayr himself had received from Bertoni, the usual "know-how" of melodic form and orchestration, Mayr would have passed on two essential themes of his teaching: the "rules" of music's science and how they are related to a meditative pythagorian concept of the cosmos; how these "rules" were the expression of a theological and metaphysical knowledge. Mayr would have emphasised that such insights enabled

---

46 The quartets were composed for musical evenings at the home of Alessandro Bertoli, an excellent amateur violinist. Marco Bonesi played second violin and Mayr the viola. The piano music was written mostly for Antonio Dolci and for his own pleasure. The religious music was performed in local parishes, *S. Maria Maggiore* and Mayr's *St. Cecilia Festival*.

47 Some of these compositions are of genuine interest, for example the *Tuba Mirum* (1821) and *Domine Deus* (1829) revived by Ian Caddy.

composer, performer and listener to contemplate the mysteries through music. It is interesting to note that in Italy Donizetti struggled constantly with censorship while outside Italy he was often seen as a "moral" and a "religious" composer[48]. Take three operas as examples, *Poliuto* (1839), clearly a religious work which fell foul of censorship. Mayr considered it an *azione sacra*, which indeed it is. *Linda di Chamounix* (1842), an opera which may be easily seen to be an allegory of the soul's descent and return. The librettist, Gaetano Rossi, had worked extensively with Mayr. *L'elisir d'amore* (1832) is a tale which epitomises the sort of oral teaching he would have received from Mayr[49].

There can be little doubt in the context of his writings that Mayr cast himself in the mould of a philosopher-composer. He was of the opinion that the radical change brought about in Europe by the Revolution and the advent of Napoleon laid a heavy responsibility on the shoulders of the intelligentsia for the future of Europe. As already said elsewhere, the change brought about in the social upheaval had given new weight to popular and folk music. Wrongly used, popular music could destroy the west through frivolity and the lack of understanding; rightly used it could become the roots of order. Externalities could change but substance could remain faithful to the source of the western tradition.

Maybe he considered that the stirrings of the Romantic movement could serve to purge and revitalize a stuffy classicism, to restore the essence of the western tradition to its rightful place in the order of society. Mayr would have agreed with Plato, that if philosopher-composers could responsibly communicate to their generation, they would have more influence than the law makers, for music was concerned with the heart, its passions, the knowledge of their significance, and their ordering. Similar to the ancients he would have divided his subject into *musica mundana, musica humana, musica instrumentalis*, for only thus could the right order of things be recognized. The source of music lay in the Divine Mystery itself, it flowed (emanated) to human consciousness through the heavens and spheres, planets and stars, to the earth and the natural world; it was "the health of the soul and the body" (Ficino) holding the key to the potential within a person, a society, a people; it was a science that could draw from the human voice and instruments the language of the heavens. Thus for the philosopher-composer, the art of music flows from the Divinity through the created order to the composer, musicians and audience, a gift which through their art of performing and *listening* could be returned to the Divinity. Music comes as a gift and is returned as a gift. It has little to do with the pride and arrogance of individuals who confuse with their own selves the Divinity and who fall into the same trap as poor old Lucifer, once the fairest of the angels. With Boethius, Mayr would have considered that all musicians should have the intellectual equipment and skill to carefully examine the diversity of high and low sounds by reason the senses and "possess the faculty of judging, according to the speculation or reason, appropriate and suitable to music, of modes and rhythms and of the classes of melodies and their mixtures of all those things" (Boethius).

---

48 Rudolph Angermüller, *Il periodo Viennese di Donizetti*, Bergamo, 1975.

49 John Allitt, *Donizetti, l'ultimo dei Troubadours*, Studi Donizettiani II, Bergamo 1974.

Rather than "prove" in the modernist, scientific way, Mayr would have suggested how the mathematical aspect of music may be seen to be based upon a *qualitative* significance of numbers. He would have suggested rather than have "proved" since each student was left to understand such knowledge according to his own level of consciousness. (Becoming a famous composer or not is irrelevant to the argument, for in the light of such knowledge many that would be first are last and many that are last are first. Maybe, the young Manghenoni, who died early in his career and in whom Mayr had great hopes, had more insight than the young composer from *Borgo Canale* who was to enter into the annals of musical history.)

Certainly Mayr would have drawn an analogy between music and architecture, explaining how the interplay of proportion and number enabled Leon Battista Alberti to speak of architecture as "frozen music". He would have shown how the art of composition, or reading or hearing music could enable a person to "see" architectural form due to an "inner" reading of shape and number. (Bruckner is a late example of a composer working with these insights. Here again we have a composer working closely within a devotional Catholic tradition.) It was believed that numerology and symbolic geometry was imprinted on nature and the cosmos as a Divine signature[50]. Nature was *Deus in rebus*. In the light of such teaching Mayr would have had great reverence towards the natural world; this may be observed in the Notebooks.

Thus music and architecture were seen to be reflecting the mysteries of the cosmos and of nature, of the macrocosm and the microcosm. Genuine music builds, through what Henry Corbin called the "Creative Imagination", a house, a place, a cathedral in the inner dimensions of the human soul. Music was, or should we say is, the bridge between the two worlds, that is, the hermetic understanding of what is above being echoed in what is below. Mayr's writings are full of notes on the science of sound and how he and others believed it was the great secret for the health of the soul, a society, a nation. He foresaw that the loss of such a science would lead to the "rupture" we call modernism. When Mayr noted, "Bach the metaphysician", he was thinking of that great composer's meditations on musical form as the expression of a divine numerology.

Thus music should restore to fallen humanity the recognition that it is created in the image of God. Music should awaken the contemplation of the Divine Unity reverberating in the manifold of the created order.

Music, worthy of the name, should be in sympathy with the heavenly harmony restoring health to the divided passions in conflict within the human soul. Music is, for want of an expression, the archetypal force stimulating the passionate life. Because of its nature it can restore and heal, or simply stir up the stygian depths of a person's inner life.

---

50 The growth (dance) of vegetable life, the structure of minerals and crystals, the geometry of flowers, the movements of the heavens etc. *Musica nihil aliud est quam omnium ordinem scire*. (Hermes Trismegistrus).

"What is music?" wrote Mayr at the start of his *Dottrina Musicale*, written for his young pupils and which is set out rather like a catechism: "Music is the science of sounds and their regulated combination to the end of delighting the ear and moving the heart."

Western music is built from the knowledge of melody, rhythm and harmony which tradition speaks of as the Orphic, Dionysian and Apollonian Mysteries.

The right use of melody[51] tames all creatures (the disordered passions); it can free the soul from that realm where "the good of the intellect is lost" (Dante). Melody awakens nostalgia for paradise and breaks the mind's chain of sequential logic and bestows on the soul its lost wings of freedom. Melody delights the ear and leads the soul through various states until it is liberated in ecstasy.

Rhythm[52] too induces differing states of consciousness, both negative and positive. It may be used, vainly to stimulate the passions, it may also tame the passions, purify emotion and like melody bring tears to the eyes. Mayr believed it could "dance out" poisons from the soul and heal the soul. Such knowledge is based on the relationship between time (*Chronos*, the beat and pulsation of time) and how eternal time (*Kairos*) may be known in the flow of the present.

Harmony[53] and its science for the west developed the course of Renaissance music to take on eventually the form we call "classical music"; that is, bringing together of various instruments and voices to produce the type of sound which still fills concert halls throughout the world.

Opera, the "work", was the art of drama and harmony re-binding the soul (*religere*) to the Divinity through acknowledging and understanding the passionate life. Thus it is that Mayr and others believed that mode and tonality could evoke and play with the emotional life, a highly responsible task due to the profound influence a composer may have over an audience. Mode and tonality may awaken lust, anxiety, sorrow, fear, ardour, aridity, arrogance, anger and so on. The art of harmony may also evoke chastity, yearning, purity, intense love, awe, the sense of proximity and at-oneness. Harmony may reverberate the order of the cosmos; its aim is to shatter the hardness of what Swedenborg termed the *proprium*, the ego. In the Christian mysteries music has always been associated with the angelic orders and their various ministries[54]. It was not for nothing that Mayr held the music of Palestrina in high esteem.

---

51 *"Melody is a succession of sounds that call to one another."* (St. John Damascene).

52 *"Rhythm is the order of movement."* (Plato). *"Some philosophers in the past termed rhythm as masculine and melody as feminine. It is a fact, that melody alone is nothing and without form . . . rhythm gives it form and suggests an ordered movement . . . "* (Aristides Quintilianus).

53 "Harmony is a *discordia concorde*." (Gaffurio).

54 Mayr would surely have indicated the relationship of the word "music" to the word "muse" and shown the parallels between the muses and the hierarchy of angels. He wrote a substantial study of Gaffurio who is still a major source when studying the iconography of western music.

Thus it is that the oral tradition is essentially concerned with spirituality.

Spiritual music, as envisaged by Mayr, dilutes the negativity of the passionate life[55] through its being awoken to the reality of its own negativity. The aim of spiritual music is to restore and to lead back the soul to a paradisial state.

An emblem well-known to Mayr and his contemporaries was the butterfly. Blake used it extensively in his imagery. To the butterfly is also related the imagery of the moth which inspired Blake to incise a small vignette of a moth fluttering near a candle and its flame. There are five stages in the metamorphosis of a butterfly: the egg, the caterpillar, the chrysalis, the butterfly, and dust (death). These five were traditionally understood to be related to stages of spiritual development. The egg represented the soul's spiritual poten-tial; the caterpillar represented the negative (vegetative or passionate) appetites of the soul caught in the dream-like delusions of the ego; the chrysalis represented the time for con-traction and the inward dying of the soul to the veils of the selfhood. (Here related are St. John of the Cross's masterpiece, *The Dark Night of the Soul* and poems by Michelangelo which speak of the night as the time of spiritual growth); the flight of the multicoloured butterfly represented the soul's expansion as it is flooded with Divine Love (symbolical-ly, it rises like Dante through the heavens[56]; finally the butterfly's flight in the brilliance of the sun is extinguished and its lovely form is reduced to dust. Such imagery suggested the soul being burnt up in the sheer ecstasy of its dance. Spiritually this state is the Cloud of Unknowing, the extinction of selfish rationalism, the silence of words that Dante ex-periences at the conclusion of his vision.[56] The soul has been "at-oned" and the paradox of "I am thou" or "Thou art I" (Martin Buber) swamps consciousness. Indeed, there is a limit to art poignantly experienced by masters like Michelangelo (*The Rondanini Pietà*) or Beethoven (*Opus 132*).

For Mayr's school, rhythm and harmony were fundamental to the soul's liberation, but it was melody (*bel canto*) which caused the soul to rise on Pegasus to mystic flights.

---

55 By the passionate life is meant the disordering of the psyche through the loss of "the good of the intellect". (Dante)

56 Musically, this was related to the notes rising and falling on the scale (*Scala,* ladder, Jacob's ladder, the angelic ascent and descent) and in concert producing harmony. Donizetti's Cantata dedicated to Mayr on his 78th birthday is a respectful musical joke on Mayr's teaching and is dense with meaning. It confirms what is said in this brief section. Fundamental to the choir boy's education had been the hymn to St. John which Mayr used not only to teach the musical scale (as tradition was wont) but also as holding the key to contemplative vision. Donizetti's Cantata is a joke containing the kernel of the teaching he had received. His words which he set to music are expression of his gratitude to Mayr. St. John the Evangelist with his emblem the eagle is the patron saint of contemplative vision. The relevant verses of the hymn are: UT *queant laxis;* REsonare *fibris*; MIra *gestorum*; FAmuli *tuorum*; SOLve *polluti;* LAbii *reatum; Sancte Joannes.* (In order that thy servants may sing with a full voice the marvels of your deeds, take away sin from our contaminated lips, Saint John). The text of the Cantata implies that Mayr (Johann) like St. John had opened in Donizetti and his other students the gift of ecstatic vision through music. In accordance with traditional symbolism, Donizetti relates in his verses how he too was "burnt up".

98

In the oral tradition Mayr would have drawn on Biblical imagery such as Jacob's vision and the ascent of Elijah's chariot. Indeed, he would have pointed out that the whole gamut of imagery was fulfilled in the Christian story and the tenets of the Creed. It is certain that he taught that separation from a truth known was the cause of melancholia, even madness. (Such imagery is basic to so many of Donizetti's libretti, the most famous example being *Lucia di Lammermoor* in which Donizetti put to full effect Mayr's emphasis on the symbolism of musical instruments - for example in the Mad Scene, the flute and the glass harmonica).

The union for which the pilgrim strives ends in paradox, ignorance, death, madness, extinction, which are: fulfilment, life, sanity and what St. Gregory of Nyssa termed, *epectasis*.

Mayr indicated that he knew the work of the Venerable Bede. In Bede's *Ecclesiastical history of the English people* there is recorded the incident of an ealdorman preaching to Eadwine, King of Northumberland. During his sermon a bird flew in at one window of the great hall, circled once or twice around the space in which it was trapped and then escaped through another window to its freedom. The ealdorman took this incident as a symbol of the soul descending into mortality and at death returning to the great silence that precedes and follows mortality's span of three-score years and ten. Either side of life's noise is silence.

Tradition holds that all great art is conceived from this silence and should return the beholder to it. Attributes such as awe, beauty, goodness, peace, love and union originate in this silence. Their appreciation return the beholder to their source. Spiritual music therefore originates in the contemplation of silence and returns to silence[57], for the silence is known as *pure being* and the "weeds of Athens" that we wear for our mortality can be but a reflection or shadow of "what is above". This dimension being but the "Divine Comedy" where "ignorant armies clash by night" (Matthew Arnold: *Dover Beach*).

The silence is the music of the spheres, our mortality is where fracas and deformity have their reign, except when the soul is inspired by music. Then the merry-go-round of life with its plurality of playthings is transformed by the inner song of the heart as it responds to the quest for the Beloved. There is established a strict parallel between the music of the heavens and that of the individual soul. What has been separated from the silence (*pure being*) is rebound. Religion dissolves in the act of art. The composer, the performer and the listener then become like instruments in the hands of the Deity. The song heard is his, not mine. Here there is a strict rapport with the nature of the religious icon and the icon painter.

Music is like Eve in so far as it beguiles; it is like Mary in so far as it is contemplative. Music is like Mary Magdalene in so far as it heals and restores, and leads the soul into the mystical garden to recognize the Saviour, (the Gardener and New Adam). In Mary

---

57 We think of Mayr's comments on Haydn's quartets.

Magdalene, Eve and Mary meet in the devotion of her heart (soul). Love has accomplished its quest.

That Mayr understood these matters there is no doubt. As his contemporaries responded to the sensibility of his music, the wise compared him to Dante and Poussin. It is important to note that Dante is free from romantic imprecision though he is the finest exponent of the doctrines of romantic love. He was a man who, like Mayr, was enlightened through metaphysics and theology. Poussin, like Mayr (and Dante), blended the richness of Christian and Classical sources. Anthony Blunt wrote, ". . . I believe that in creating his paintings Poussin was primarily inspired by a desire to give visible expression to certain ideas which, while not deserving the name of a philosophy[58] in a technical sense, represent a carefully thought out view of ethics, a consistent attitude to religion, and, towards the end of his life, a complex, almost mystical conception of the universe". Such could have been written of Mayr. All three men (Dante, Poussin and Mayr) knew the "rules" and knew how to reorganize them time and time again without monotony.

Dante, Poussin and Mayr were all, at some stage of their life, members of societies which offered initiation. But initiation alone can be a stumbling block giving rise to pride and elitism of the worst kind. No such charges may be laid at Mayr's door. Perhaps the hallmark of his life was that he had understood, like Blake, the Christian meaning of forgiveness. From Mayr Donizetti learnt the maxim "forgiveness is the best revenge"[59], an aspiration which places both men at the heart of the Christian Mysteries.

In Mayr and Donizetti there is that quality of understanding which comes only through life's deep wounding. This "wounding" is at the heart of the western oral tradition and is related to the much maligned and long-forgotten significance, by the greater majority of the mystical devotion to the wounds of the Saviour. The Lenten and Paschal mysteries must have been focused at the centre of their own devotional lives.

Once freed from the frivolity of fashion, their music may help to unravel the genius of the west and its tradition.

---

58 Blunt here shows his confusion between the modern understanding of the nature of philosophy with that of the ancient hermetic schools. In fact, Blunt is unable to handle Poussin's hermeticism - an interesting fact in the light of his own career.

59 See Z. 25.

5 "His life was in no way lazy nor was he indolent in the art of music"

Today we lift up for admiration the soap operas of the media. A life such as Mayr's, consciously given to values which make up a civilized society, is now rarely considered except perhaps through the fleeting imagery of a video tape. The essence of Mayr's art has very little to do with an ever changing imagery. His works have to be considered rather like symbols which remain static to the outward eye but which work inwardly. As for his music, he himself would have maintained it to be about the spirit and how it may be incarnated within a people and social life.

He was a man of extraordinary humility and objectivity:

> "Some wretched writers, spreading arrogant sarcasm and crudely invented tales, tried to undervalue his work [Mayr's], taking away the small merit which his operas had gained in times now passed, times in which they were perhaps too enthusiastically praised. Nothing is more false than what Stendhal writes in his life of Rossini: "... *il était applaudi sur les premiers théâtres: comment ne pas se croire l'égal des grands maîtres?" [... he was well received in the most important theatres, how is it not possible to believe he is equal to the great masters?"]* Such a presumption never would have found a place in his soul. Maybe it would have been to his personal gain if his character had permitted him sometimes to boast in front of others - since to certain people, in order to be esteemed by them, it is advantageous to say, "Just listen to my masterpiece of an opera! ... what a fantastic cabaletta has inspired my fresh, unsullied imagination!" He never delayed in giving full justice to those writers which were his rivals ... he has always, on every possible occasion, encouraged the gifts of young people. He foresaw, contrary to the opinion of others (as soon as he heard *L'inganno felice*), the full and worthy triumphs of Rossini. He is cheered to read that whilst once he was accused by Perotti etc. of having overloaded Italian opera with instrumentation, now he is accused of the contrary ... that whilst certain forms are now praised, they are all to be found in his own operas, even if they were once criticized ... his crescendos, mazurkas, romances, canons, unaccompanied pieces and finals ... ideas for which his successors gleaned the applause ... and the many times he was accused even of plagiarising operas written before his own. There are numerous views, regarding his style and his way of composing, to be found in Italian writers ...

> Now, far removed from the bitter and tumultuous life of the theatre, he lives in solitude, in the tranquil atmosphere of his family. He is still full of love for his art just as he was in his first youth. He oc-

cupies himself with that which his duties and work prescribe. He undertakes them for the benefit of young musicians and uses the few hours of leisure for reading a variety of books (even the most recent) together with the best literary journals concerned with the arts.

On 1 April 1844 Mayr's wife, Lucrezia, died. On 8 April Donizetti wrote from Vienna to his old friend, Antonio Dolci, a remarkable letter on the theme of death (four years to the day he himself was to die):

> "The death of Signora Lucrezia has greatly upset me, she watched over our progress in the arts, and so it seems to me yet another knot tying us from our first footsteps to the tomb has been undone . . .
>
> Every loss of friendship such as these, seems to me yet another step towards the eternal cloud of unknowing, drawing us another pace nearer to that land which we once willing left in order to be animated into this life. How I share in the Master's sorrow . . . habit has a life of its own! . . . think of him now deprived of the voice which once gave him life . . . it will be for him the greater sorrow . . . but the Divine Law is the same for all - *hodie mihi, cras tibi*, death makes all men equal. On earth remain the royal crowns and the rags of the most wretched.
>
> The dress which clothes us in order to appear before God will announce either depraved baseness or good deeds, it is the same for the king as for his subject. We shall all travel, indeed all mankind will be made to walk the same path! The loss of every treasured object only serves to give us greater encouragement to follow that path, in the hope of meeting again - this helps to infuse balsam into the rest of life . . . I know it to be so! . . . I have proved it . . . and yet few believe it to be so."

By late summer the following year Mayr had had a stroke. His finances during the last years could not have been good. Donizetti, on a visit to Bergamo, had been shocked at the poverty of his clothing and had sent him an overcoat from Vienna. Tradition would have it that his wife had been mean; more likely she had been forced to be thrifty owing to circumstances. In these last years Mayr's faithful friend was his pupil Antonio Dolci; he read letters to him in the evening and helped him in every way possible.

As Mayr's life gradually faded away, so Donizetti's own life descended into insanity and humiliation:

> "Dear Dolci,
> What? Our Mayr is not well. Is the weather a contributing factor? Even I am sick ... here in Paris the air is lighter but the rain is heavier ... my nerves become irritated every time I try to write ... patience ... The tomb! It's all over!
>
> Yours lovingly, Gaetano
> 21 August (1845)

Mayr died at the age of 82 on 2 December, 1845. Donizetti's active life, too, was over; he was taken to a sanatorium at Ivry outside Paris on 28 January 1846. The following year friends arranged for him to return to Bergamo. The faithful Dolci met the carriage at Como. Donizetti died on 8 April 1848.

Both composers' work had come to an end before the 1848 revolutions. Their art sums up a mode of thought and life which rapidly disappeared from European society. Though both were involved in the development of the Romantic movement (Donizetti is arguably Italy's greatest romantic), both had their hearts in ideals which transcend the fashions of time. These ideals imbued their art with qualities of the greatest and most enduring values.

2
Selections
from Mayr's Writings

1   Extracts from Mayr's Notebooks (*Lo Zibaldone*)

Nothing is more unjust than that which Stendhal says in his life of Rossini: *il* [Mayr] *était applaudi sur les premiers théâtres: comment ne pas se croire l'égal des grands maîtres?* Such a presumption never had a place in his heart. Perhaps it would have been to his advantage if his character had sometimes permitted him to advance himself in the presence of others. Now far removed from the bitter and tumultuous life of the theatre he lives in solitude, in the tranquil atmosphere of his family. He is still full of love for his art just as he was in his first youth. He occupies himself with that which his duties and work prescribe. He undertakes them for the benefit of young musicians and uses the few hours of leisure for reading a variety of books (even the most recent), together with the best literary journals concerned with the arts[60].

A German regards music not only as a work or object of delight, but as a revelation of the most efficacious way of development and of culture, even the beatification of humanity. Music is therefore the art of representing the soul's sensations by the means of sounds awakening analogous sentiments - and also thoughts - this requires a genial composer, a performer capable of explaining the beauties of the composition and a public capable of knowing and listening to the beauty of the composition and its execution[61].

The Ancients did not place Parnassus in a fertile plain but on the summit of a steep mountain, and to climb up there needs time and effort.

---

60 Quoted from the *cenni autobiografici* written on the occasion of his seventy-eighth birthday by request of a music society which he founded. the *Unione Filarmonica*.

61 Here Mayr is clearly referring to himself.

How beautiful is art when she comes lightly, as if on wings, bestowing rays of light on the precocious circles of daily life. Art is even more beautiful when she presents herself with a serene face and the enchanting smile which teaches humanity. She is the educator of the mind's most noble faculties - she is the canvas, the tracing-board, the picture with the temple of human consciousness. Art is beautiful to her maximum when she precedes the effort of struggle, when she appears with a transfiguring presence along the avenue of misfortune, when she is perceived as the sun rising above the plants of human destiny. Art is beautiful when her immortal breathing kisses away the sigh of the present dispelling misfortune's sad lips. And so it is that music places its most precious sacrifices on the altar of humanity and a country.

Art follows the directives of the soul according to the sentiments, the concept of life and the idea. For sentiment (in general): music, painting, sculpture . . . For the idea: paper[62]

Sentiment is hence for the soul; the more educated the sentiment, the more it is related to nature. When sentiment develops, it refines, cultivates itself, and the more it grows, the more it grows towards creative sound. By this I mean, that this last mentioned must ever newly develop itself towards spiritual sentiment - that is, if it is to correspond to its aim and mission. The human voice is the most delicate, passive and sublunar instrument in which develops all spiritual sentiment. It is therefore a duty to approach creative sound as much as possible.

Simplicity is that which has beauty in the arts, be it in theory or in practice. It is however, the hardest thing to find.

That which is simple is of necessity profound.

I am of the opinion that one must place the child destined for the art of imagination at the foothills of the mountains, so as to behold the space of that mysterious distance which will draw out at an early age unforgettable visions which will one day render him famous in his art.

The most beautiful gift is that which renders strength to one's creative genius.

The most precious things have need of time's sanction for them to mature and be appreciated.

Every artist has a limited round of ideas, in which he moves in a more or less large periphery.

Music - the art of painting with appreciable sounds the emotions in a way that the affections of whosoever is listening give birth to joy and delight.

---

62 The "sketch" or beginning of the work . . . the idea must be put on paper. It must be "incarnated". Consider, for example, Michelangelo's use of drawings in relation to his paintings, sculpture and architecture.

In the act of judgement habit makes a demand as much over the dispositions of our organs on receiving certain impressions as over the intellect. We believe that he who wishes to find the goal towards which the arts tend must labour night and day. The Beautiful is not to be found or conveniently represented at the first attempt, nor does it come haphazardly. One must take away many layers of rubbish and useless rock, similar to mining for metals in the bowels of a mountain. Genius may sometimes be likened to the dowser's twig which presumes to hold the faculty for sensing the proximity of water serpenting along underground. However, even when it has drawn one to the place where discovery is hoped for, the pick-axe and spade are still necessary to open the well and to make a profit.

More than being sensitive to the impressions of beauty, more than being capable of guessing the way that one wants to follow, inspiration is when a few rays of light are thrown and enlighten the path ahead, constantly accompanying the artist who attends with arduous and patient work in order to actualize the marvellous concept he has perceived. Initially, it is no more than a sketch caught within the first flash of intellectual inspiration. Who would dare to maintain that perseverance poisons the dignity of higher souls who harmonize a supreme virtue?

It is certain that music speaks to the Imagination as well as to the Senses. Indeed, music reaches the Heart through the Senses, imitating Nature, thus depicting, reasoning and expressing the different passions of the soul together with various sensations. This it achieves in its own particular way.

Music has in itself the Sublime. It consists in the strength of harmony and melody which may elevate, even rape the soul. Such a state comes about through the strictest union of those three elements (Greatness, Nobility, and Magnificence), with natural clarity of thought and musical sensitivity. Melody and the lively and beautiful cycle of flowing melodies must then correspond to and equal the expression of the words dressed up with the music.

Music is lost, wrote Benedetto Marcello in 1704, a man endowed with much musical genius and whose compositions contradict his opinion. He did not realize that he himself was aiding the birth of dramatic music, whilst he was preaching a sermon on the death of the arts. Music is dying sighed Rameau, without realizing what was happening in his own country, regardless of his efforts . . . music is lost, music is dying; such comments signify nothing more than the fact that music has changed form.

The study of works of the past procures various advantages. It often presents the artist with new material, for the forgotten past often becomes renewed. It helps him to acquire a clear idea of his own work. It gives a sense of purpose, understanding, diligence and continuity. It concentrates his talent and skill in a determined circle of purpose. These thoughts are of double importance in the age of the popular arts. An age which leaves the artist to run freely wherever and however he pleases. An age which permits him to use all his beautiful gifts of nature for the moment, without form, with the only aim of purchasing in the moment and only for the moment of effect.

Seb. Bach - the metaphysician.

With Mozart there flowered in our world the profound yet delicate inclination of the west besides the coloured and shining magnificence of the east - the burning, jealous passion next to the happy courageous joy of life. Child - angel.

Dies Irae - Mozart, emotional and therefore for the *anima* - Cherubini, full of calculated devices, therefore for the *animus*. However neither one or the other lacks in either composition. e.g. Cherubini - *Pie Jesu*.

During a conversation Beethoven once sat at the piano, stretched out his hands and played four notes. He smiled and said, "Well, what shall we do with that?" He was right to ask since none present were prepared for what was to emerge from those four notes which were neither a theme nor a concept. However, when the hands of the master (perhaps it was his genius) began to move over the keyboard forming immense masses of sound without ever losing the four notes, then one was lost in modulations, unimaginable and unforgettable sounds. Those around received the seriousness with a shock of admiration and with veneration for they could have wished to have kissed his hands. He opened harmony's sanctuary. It is not possible to describe the effect caused by this fantasy. It is true that he was deaf and therefore not being able to hear himself he tended to play too loud - but then, perhaps it was due to the complexity of the harmony which was always new and unexpected.

Operatic music was once divided into two distinct genres, *buffo* and serious. Paisiello appears to have been the first to have introduced a mixed style, for example his *Nina* is a most perfect model. Cimarosa treated this genre also with great success, however always blending something of the comic vein which nature gave him as the principal character of his talent. *Il matrimonio segreto* is a happy blend of the most elegant *semiseria* with the funniest of *buffo*. During the intermediary school between these two great masters and the age of Rossini, *semi-seria* gained the upper hand whilst the buffo style waned. The operas of Mayr and Paër introduced into Italian music Germanic use of harmony and orchestration, modifying the appearance and preparing a revolution. The taste of exuberance and mad joy which are characteristics of Italy, are also eminently characteristics of comic music in the past. They have brought into being some of the most attractive, gracious and refined (musical) forms.

Rossini, profiting from the development music had made with the juxtaposition of harmony, introduced the force of rhythm and the accent of modulation to a higher level than his predecessors. Even if one finds some pieces of the first order in the *opere serie* of the past, one has to admit they do not always hold your attention from beginning to end. *Otello, Tancredi* and *Semiramide* have pushed out of memory *Gli Orazzi e Curiazi*. However, true *buffo* is not Rossini's genre. His joy is more epigrammatic [i.e. one-tracked and sarcastic]. It does not intoxicate. Indeed, one finds spirit in it, a certain mockery, the personality of the author - but not absurdity, not that indefinable quality unexplainable with a word alone . . . for want of a word . . . the buffo. Perhaps there is something of this quality in *L'italiana in Algeri*. When Rossini wants to create comedy he falls back into the power of rhythm, encumbering it with a waltz. As a man of the spirit he is calculating and when one has not even the time to reflect (owing to the pace of the rhythm), one has not even a chance to be bored[63].

Donizetti[64] was born in Bergamo, where he began his studies. He went on to Bologna to continue his studies under Mattei. Afterwards he returned to his native land in order to perfect himself in the teachings of Mayr. Due to his not having much success in Milan he went to Naples where he made a happy home. There he wrote *L'esule di Roma* in which there is a fine *terzetto*. The first section is a perfect example of unity, taste and dramatic force. It radiates a perfect amalgam of melody and declamation. He then composed *Il Diluvio Universale* and *Il Paria*. On feeling himself called by his natural gifts to comedy [*buffo*] he studied carefully the *Parlanti* of Fioravanti, which are, as we have already said elsewhere invaluable models. He showed himself to be quite a good *buffo* composer with *Olivo e Pasquale, L'ajo nell'imbarazzo, La regina di Golconda* and *Le convenienze teatrali*, and we have not yet given sufficient recognition to *L'elisir d'amore*, an *opera buffa* inspired throughout with joy and happiness. He received very much praise when he presented in 1831 at the *Carcano* his tragic opera, *Anna Bolena*, a work full of beauty of the first order. He also composed *Fausta* for Naples, and for *La Scala* at carnival time, *Ugo conte di Parigi* in 1832.

Could we not liken Donizetti to Janin[65]? Compared with him even Janin would lose all his nerve and colour, regarding any subject. Moreover, Donizetti has a subtle feeling, a readiness of style which always saves him, just in time.

Donizetti's musical pen is a polypus - when he has stitched together one opera he knits together another - he is like Bosco's magic wand tapping his brain which makes operas galore jump out and *tout sans préparation*.

The organ is destined to the glorification of the divine service and the accompaniment of song. Therefore, the first thing required of an organist is that he should be convinced of the importance of his task. Furthermore, he should be diligent in the performance of his duties, keeping his attention consecrated to his task and sublime goal. For these reasons he should comport his musical talent in a manner convenient to the sublime nature of the divine office. An organist must be saturated with a religious sensibility. Thus it is neces-

---

63 A quotation which shows how Mayr understood his own place in the history of western music.

64 This and the next two quotations show how Mayr judged without preference his most famous pupil. The first is important because it bears witness to the fact that Donizetti returned after his studies in Bologna, to "perfect himself in the teachings of Mayr". The second and third quotations could be taken from the writings of contemporary journalists.

65 Janin was a well-known journalist of the period.

sary for him to be cultured in matters of the spirit . . . To distract the faithful from the contemplation of the Divine with a popular tune from a comic opera is to profane the church. Church music is something totally other than being simply "music in church". An organist does not think of himself and the displaying of his own bravura. Who would wish to present himself before the Almighty with the pride of his own spirit? Humility must penetrate the organist, he must have that understanding which is required when confronted with the sublime nature of the Holy Sacrifice.

What shall we say about Metastasio? . . . If in his own day he was judged to be the finest dramatic poet for music of all times, we can still confidently say that in this art form he was in a class of his own. Furthermore, if in our own times, when egoism scorns the cult of true sentiment, one may point out they have forgotten the dramas of this supreme and unique poet of the heart.

The oratorios are still set to music for the hundredth time by Italian and other masters. This is because Metastasio possesses a gift which no one has yet equalled. That is, the uniting of natural elocution to the heights of sentiment, together with the harmony of words and the flow of language with the magnificence of the subject. He also brings together the sheer richness of lyrical poetry with the sublime severity of religious thought.

He knew with those ideal heroes of his how to paint natural virtues with amiable colours. He expressed with great perception the sentiments of faithfulness and of paternal and filial love. Who does not feel taken out of himself when Metastasio clothes with unparallelled beauty the most sublime arguments of religion, bringing together the most profound ideas with ornament of style, witnessing one might say, virtually supernatural sacrifices presented with the attraction and charm of his unforgettable language? He does all this, whilst masterfully preserving the proportion of thought to the musical expression enabling song and harmony to present themselves spontaneously.

Melody is to music as thought is to conversation.

Music is like painting with its colours and shades.

A song must be like a proverb, written in such a way so that it passes into the mouth of all; it will be remembered when it is as true and as penetrating as a proverb.

The light of the original flame is always stronger than the light of the reflection.

The more capable you will become, the fuller will be your pleasures.

Satire is the vengeance of virtue[66].

---

66 Quotation from Parini.

Love of self hides ourselves from ourselves, and diminishes all our short-comings. We live with them, like the smells we carry about with ourselves, we do not smell them any longer and they upset only those around us.

To give is nothing, it is the way of giving which is everything (Lessing). The most beautiful gifts are those bestowed by art, the daughter of heaven. Poets and artists give everything they have to give in the moment - their spirit, all their art, all their glory; they withhold nothing of themselves.

The true rules never change even if new vogues appear to introduce a new licence. It is rather like in our own times when a new régime decides to coin new money. It rejuvenates the effigy but does little about the price.

Affectation in language and an overpowering search for means of expression confesses sterility of thought. It is a sort of false coin the property of which is but its total valuelessness.

He who wishes to write better than well writes badly.

As God loves his world so man must love the free beauty of nature.

Nature is not mastered except by following her.

Bossuet says that this century will arrive at the point when everything is held in indifference except for business and pleasure.

Why do men always wish to learn through comparisons? The oak tree is not a palm tree or a cyprus tree . . . or vice versa. A good person may not be compared except to himself. The theatre has met with the pulpit. I don't think they should argue between themselves, since in both situations we should desire that Man glorifies God and Nature (*Wilhelm Meister* - Goethe).

Whilst the austere philosopher seeks truth in a deep well, the favoured sex loves to meet it on a bed of roses.

The arts are friendly to religion, they are at one with her creating great and sublime works.

Every ten or fifteen years music will be the plaything of fashion.

The most beautiful homage is that which renders due respect to genius.

The fine arts raise man up to the dignity of morality and they beautify his life.

His spirit [Mayr's] was annoyed and disgusted by all that which presented itself to him with the graces of novelty.

Are there not two ages when truth presents itself to us as necessary? In youth to instruct us, in old age to comfort us. In the cleansing of the passions, truth is abundant.

Nature has given to womanhood three qualities: imagination, sensibility and taste - are these not the most essential for music?

Women in general are dominated by their imagination.

The education of woman has always been neglected and yet she makes for the most interesting half of life.

Simple Simon, rich in heart.

Naturalness and simplicity are today out of taste.

Whosoever is born with a talent, sees in it his most beautiful existence.

Music is the daughter of feeling and sentiment - but do all men and all nations feel in the same way?

Les grâces n'ont point d'âge.

Souvent trop d'abondance appauvrit la matière.

Si quelquefois l'art nous charme un moment, c'est quand il peut imiter la nature.

Les règles sont filles de l'art, mais l'art est fils de la nature.

Les premiers sentiments sont toujours les plus naturels.

L'ennui naquit un jour de l'uniformité.

Il est agréable d'apprendre la langue en chantant - it is not the same with morality?

Le coeur d'une mère est le chef-d'oeuvre de la Nature.

On met un peu du sien, et l'on cite beaucoup.

Le talent fut toujours l'ami de la vertu.

Cleanliness is virtue's supplement.

With a song the mother greets her new born child, with a hymn the old man descends into the dark depths of the grave.

To become passionately involved with an art is virtually to have reached half way along life's high road.

Without originality you do not found a school.

Art is eternal like the ever-conceiving matrix of the universe. Art was born from the moment of the first man's pulsebeat, summoning him to worship his Creator.

It is said the story of a people's poetry is their nation's history. One might add, it is the same matter with music and the other arts.

The age in which one begins to teach art is that of its decadence . . . Aristotle gave his precepts for the writing of tragedies when no living poet was capable of writing a tragedy.

". . que tout changement dans la musique annonce un changement dans les moeurs." Examining with a philosophical ear the character of each century's music and the changes it was subjected to, one will remark that the nation's character has changed in political and religious matters.

The general state not only in literature, but also in music, seems to have taken on some of the following characteristics:

1.   A reasoned hatred of all rules and of all ideas of control, suitability, or order in theory.

2.   A systemized imitation of the ugly and the second rate.

3.   Prevalence for the bizarre, the monstrous, the obscure, be it in ideas or in sentiment.

4.   The same with form. Form is a reflection of moral and intellectual dispositions. Does this imply a premature disorder? We witness much talk, calculated mannerisms, forced combinations, uncontrolled neologisms, all of which are signs of decadence and barbarity.

For some time now we have been invaded by "freedom of expression". Ah! This universal freedom which makes us equal with the most abject slaves in the world, each one wishing to command in his own way, who will obey?

Dramatic music is rushing towards degeneration, emptying itself in constantly more superficial appearances, devoid of value.

Acceleration of rhythm results from the spirit of the times: that is, an augmentation of means for stimulus, an envious longing to possess, an insurrection against the laws regulating form, and more directly, youth's lack of taste in matters of rhythm in music. We may observe these matters in other aspects of beauty. Today they seek art outside art. How much greater is the anxiety, far worse the pulse throb, and how much louder they stamp their feet, how much greater the enthusiasm. As for taste and that which conforms us to the laws of nature it does not affect them, it does not brighten the eyes of anyone, it does not sparkle, enflame, astonish or move to expression - it is not even observed or noticed. Every dance becomes a *tarantella*, every gallop is but the beginning of a *galopante*!

Even the art of the times is opposed to order. It confuses everything. On stage they perform as if in a concert hall or as in a church with no difference. Everywhere they wish to impress the masses, to be original, and they do so in the wrong way. To be more precise, by confusing the means of expression. We therefore impoverish ourselves and we are unable to build up ourselves and to enrich ourselves. Everywhere you hear the same (emphasis) and of consequence we shall all become the same, weak, obtuse, insensible. It is all worth nothing and must end badly.

In our times the general aspiration of men is but towards industry, the acquisition of riches and ease. Thus, it is for this reason they consume life, weary the spirit and fill the mind with preoccupations full of worry and care. And thus it is that their affections become divided. They do not ask for new thought to contemplate nor do they seek for profound sentiments which may easily lead on to more serious thought, which is of consequence heavier to bear. Patience must be with life's inevitable and already exhausted relationships. And so nothing truly adapts itself to us, one flits, jumping superficially from object to object. This makes for the passing of image upon image to one's mind - the most shallow being the easiest to understand and of consequence the quickest to be forgotten. One flies from one thing to another, novelty must follow upon novelty if we do not wish to lose fascination. Here is why the finest tragedies and best operas are no longer of interest. They ask for dances, decorations, fashion and fireworks. The same tendency is to be observed in our reading. They no longer read the master works which require both attention and reflection. Time is lacking, time is lost in every sort of bagatelle of daily bustle. Every day a new newspaper attempts to out do all others with new affectation, clever nothingness, sarcasm, dishonest judgements, arrogant and pungent manners. It offends, it falsifies, and that amuses. What amazes, in particular with new writers (even if there are some good authors who still wish to be read) is that they allow themselves to be dragged down by such vanity.

Whosoever wishes to live with the world (of fashion) must give up something to that world. This is not worth doing, even when dealing with somebody, it is better to be invisible and to pass by unnoticed. Why does the public not practise this? Why do we not permit it to our composers and poets who work openly for the tastes of the day? The variety and multiplicity of things produce always a new world, bringing us spring with its flowers and autumn with its fruits. One year is not alike another, different sorts of fruits grow better in different years. It all depends on the seasons which we are unable to regulate according to our way. Therefore, it is necessary for a man to cultivate his soul - a lot depends on external circumstances.

The new theorists wish to teach the effect. They do not realize that they are turning the whole affair about turn and making the child the father. If they do not go back to first principles how can a ray of light enlighten them?

With passion one accomplishes nothing. Yet it has to be and the spirit must direct its manifestation. An artist with much precision depends on rhythmning, shading and enlightening passion to his audience.

The horror of humanity has always been ever since the beginning of the world, but now it is no other than man himself.

Is not the misuse of the sound of the pianoforte and the organ a reason for the lack of taste in studying harmony?

A public notice has announced that: A Parisian mechanic wishes to organize an orchestra without players, that the various instruments will be played by the means of an ingenious mechanism. The leader (or conductor) will be three horses which by the means of a cylinder will put into operation many lesser cylinders. All types of music may be played on this mechanical orchestra, all with equal and admirable power, purity and precision. So as to cover the expenses of this "panorchestra" the mechanic proposes the means of a public subscription.

Everything in the world has its time; the big as well as the small take their prestige and importance simply by the dominant opinion and the circumstances of the times.

The Chinese held the opinion that the knowledge of music was intimately linked to the art of government and that those who understood the science of sounds would also be capable of governing. From this we may deduce that if any of our composers were in the position to rule, there would very soon be born a situation of total chaos.

The century is not religious and how can it be so, for religion is poetry, the sublime, the ideal?

How can a religious spirit find itself in a prosaic, positivist and materialistic century like ours?

It is a mistaken opinion to think that art is in substance something which remains totally outside of life as a thing both fantastic and exhausted, like the flight of the legendary paradise bird which it is said never touches the earth. The great artist is a child of his time. It is not until he lifts his genius in continual rapport to time that he feels linked to his nation by a thousand strands, the rise and fall of which are his most intimate joy as he obeys with gladness its laws. His happiness is in the sacredness of the pure altar of his Church and the faithful hearts of his tranquil home.

Christianity is certainly not a religion of melancholy and sadness. Rather, it is the religion of infinite serenity. It may be added that any happiness which does derive from Christianity can be no other than false intoxication, foolishness, and hidden deceit.

From a musical point of view the Greeks and the Hebrews are the supreme ancient peoples. The Romans were nothing more than imitators of their predecessors.

Music is of the Divine Essence. She fell from heaven on to the earth, she was before beings were.

Confess that wise ignorance which when it exists has true science as its fruit.

All true and abiding musical culture must derive from the music of the Church. This fact is proved by the history of music. Such a source forms the ear for melody and simple harmony, thereby it comforts the soul and receives the nourishment which no external power or energy may usurp.

Once the ancient Greeks starting from the highest principles taught that the actions of state and government depended on men, whilst the culture of the heart belonged to the feminine sex. It was thus that they gave the care of the fine arts to the Muses. Likewise also taught the Son of the Christian Church, he who made you and blessed be Thou who favours music, and who above the Muses is first in forming the heart. Yes, verily, which of the other arts besides music could so profoundly influence with such power the human heart?

Holy Mother, hear my prayer, O thou who art the most worthy protectress of the sacred art! Hear the prayer of all who approach and kneel before your altar, before which I also prostrate myself and adore.

I am certainly not with those who pretend that art must be but priestly and catholic. Today art is free, independent and vital: religious preoccupation has been broken with. However, this does not mean that we are unable to restate the origin with dignity. Modern art is incarnated in Catholicism and similar to the king she has grown up in the sanctuary amongst the fragrance of incense and sound of hymns. The adolescent when placed amidst society's bustle retains a trace which cannot be cancelled for it has been stamped on his brow by the sacred finger of priesthood. Now the young man is free but he has a tribute of homage to make to the Catholic Church, likewise his unique Mother must in turn drink to him a toast of goodwill. To follow any other cult would be a sign of ingratitude, sacrilege. In fact, it is impossible to imagine that art forgets her who has so copiously nourished him, even in the hours of privation and of misery. He cannot forget in favour of protestantism which is like a woman who in her prime of life was incapable of a drop of milk from her stony breasts[67].

Our century does not sleep, except in the field of religious thought.

When prayer has become a source of effect on the stage, being presented without object, without dignity and out of place . . . it is thus all becomes profaned.

True Catholicism, which uplifts the soul to contemplate the Sublime, was always in the past united to the arts and gave life, splendour, and consciousness.

True religion is poetry itself. It is only through religion that it is possible for there to be poetry. It is thus we are clearly shown the plight of our times, for the religious spirit is disappearing. Therefore, so will, not only poetry, but also all teaching and preparation, together with the enjoyment in the production of poetic activities.

---

67 A quotation which clearly indicates the inner struggle Mayr went through as he gradually came to question the secularizing and prevailing influences of the 19th century.

If composers (of religious music) would study Palestrina's sublime example they would regain the seriousness, strength and depth which should be theirs by nature. All the bizarre modes which are today so badly adapted to sacred texts would soon be abolished . . . They would rediscover that supremely difficult simplicity, which hand in hand with the majesty and nobility demanded by the text, communes with God and which attempts to celebrate His Glory and Incomprehensible Might, besides imploring his Mercy and Goodness.

The genuine and ancient melodies of Gregorian Chant are indeed beyond imitation. We may copy them, adapt them, heaven knows how, to other words, but to compose new ones as worthy as the ancient ones is impossible . . . without doubt the melodies of hymns are the oldest and sincerest melodies we know.

He [Mayr] explained to his students with clarity, with love and with a sense of humour how a man might understand himself to be a friend of knowledge . . .

Solitude is the diet of the soul.

It is necessary to have harmony between the Spirit and the Heart, that is to say, to have music in one's actions. Morality teaches the way in which we must put matters in agreement, so that peace and harmony of virtue is the result. Only in such a way, emanate those concepts which are worthy to echo the praises of God.

Time consumes man and man consumes time.

Our life is perhaps like a sad desert in which neither flowers nor trees grow.

It was a penetrating light which shone: it was a reflection of the nearness of immortality.

It was like a fleeting shadow thrown in a solitary place caused by the flight of a bird through the sky. The thought comes back to the mind, like recalling one's first love.

It has even been granted to me to sing the praises of the Lord - but oh! with a sound far too minute and a plectrum far too small . . . Oh! if only I had the power to express worthily here and elsewhere my gratefulness, then the profound feeling moving in my soul and the weakness impeding my lips would cease, in favour of burning and living sounds . . .

2 A Dissertation on Genius and on Composition

The origins of musical invention are analogous with what we call "poetic genius"[68] and it is a subject with little promise of a pleasing conclusion. There is however no other theme so closely linked to our understanding of the human mind. The prime aim of the present essay is that of stimulating love[69] in order to encourage an enquiring spirit into such a fascinating faculty of our nature. We shall not presume to resolve the problem adequately or to edify in any significant way our general education.

We are debtors to the existence of studies upon which this paper is dependent for any attempt at an examination of poetic genius. The poetic imagination according to Plato[70] (whose thought has influenced Aristotle, Longinius and all the philosophers who have followed in his wake) is a universal mirror in which there is an infinite reflection of objects, the origin or prototype of which wished to be traced out in the extension of the universe, thus becoming represented in a most living and faithful way. When poetry is understood in this way, as an imitative art, she no longer presents insurmountable obstacles to those who undertake to seek the origin of the mind. We may deduce from such a way of thinking that the poetic genius is derivative. The faculties of the poetic

---

68 By "poetic genius" Mayr means the inspiration which is the seed of all the arts. "The creative imagination" as defined by Henry Corbin in his book *Creative imagination in the sufism of Ibn Arabi*, London 1970, offers a most satisfactory explanation. What Mayr has to say in the following essay restates a body of teaching which the West once considered as fundamental to all the arts, the origins of which lie in what has been defined as "Tradition". One may trace it in the writings of the neo-platonic and hermetic schools; for example, Marsilio Ficino. A more immediate source for Mayr was Carli's Osservazioni sulla musica.

69 ". . . stimulating love". The purpose of art for Mayr is the manifestation of beauty so as to "rape" the soul in ecstasy, the result being an awakening of love and compassion in the beholder. "He (Mayr) explained to his students with clarity, with love and with sense of humour how a man might understand himself to be a friend of knowledge . . ." (The Notebooks).

70 Fundamental to the following paragraph is the following extract from Marsilio Ficino's *Sopra lo amore o ver convito di Platone*, Florence 1544:
"First we must realize that beauty is nothing else than a certain living and spiritual grace which through th e divine ray infuses itself first into the angles; in these are seen the figures of each sphere, which in them are called exemplars and ideas. Beauty then passes into the souls, where the figures are called reasons and thoughts, and finally into matter, where they are called images and forms. There beauty gives pleasure to all by means of reason and sight, but more or less depending on reason, which will be discussed below. This beauty shines from the one, self-same face of God into three mirrors placed in this order: the angel, the soul, and the body. In the first mirror, because of its nearness to God, it shines brightest; in the second, farther away, it is less bright; in the third, the farthest, it is very obscured. Because the angel is not impeded by a body, he reflects himself in himself and contemplates his own beauty sculptured in himself. The soul, created with the condition that it be surrounded by the earthly body, stoops to the service of the corporeal. Burdened by this condition, the soul forgets the beauty hidden in itself and, once enfolded within the earthly body, devotes itself to the use of this body; it adapts to the senses, and sometimes even reason. Consequently the soul does not behold the beauty which shines continually in it, until the body is fully grown and the reason awakened; with the aid of this the soul considers that beauty which shines from the universe into the eyes and abides in the former."

genius must be therefore directed by the accuracy and by the intensity of their own perceptions. The faculties may be thus invoked on the level of supernatural powers and ministers of incantations[71] to the purpose of teaching, upholding, awakening and beautifying. Such faculties appear to the profane and uninitiated[72] as strangely far from the sphere of possibility and the creation of a virtually divine mind. A truly poetic composition is therefore an act which excites constant wonder[73], not only through the mediating of the imitation of multiple forms and eternal energies of nature, but also through the mediation of most dissimilar things, of sentiment, of character, and of ideal essence. The combination of the eternal forms in painting[74] is infinite and the whole universe is none the less the school for painters as it is for poets, with this distinction alone, that the painter in the communicating of thought and of sentiment is bound within relationships of certain modes inherent within forms. The faculties to which we have already referred are powerful in the stimulation of awe. Every object even considered separately when represented by a painter can be familiar and recognizable to the beholder. For example, the appearance of groups or the related order of the scenes depicted may bring about an immediate new insight. However, the fundamental source of all such beauty is Nature[75] and merit depends on the faithfulness of the resemblance. Thus no matter how remarkable are the imitations, be it in painting or in poetry, the objects represented may never flatter themselves to assume other qualities outside those of the accurate first copies.

---

71 Mayr's thought is here clarified in the light of the previous quotation from Ficino. Mayr wrote "Music has in itself the Sublime. It consists in the strength of harmony and melody which may elevate, even rape the soul. Such a state comes about through the strictest union of those three elements (Greatness, Nobility and Magnificence) . . ." The "three elements" to which Mayr refers indicate that he was aware of the application of alchemic terms to the inner life of the soul. The relationship of music to the Angelic Intelligences was fundamental to Mayr's understanding.

72 Contrary to modern opinion, Mayr understood true knowledge (gnosis), the wisdom which enlightens whatever work we do, as initiatory and as accessible only to those who seek for it. "The Ancients did not place Parnassus in a fertile plain but on the summit of a steep mountain, and to climb up there needs time and effort." True initiation, though it may initially come through a teacher like Mayr, is never "valid" until it has been incarnated in the life of the person concerned, for example, Donizetti's youthful sin of pride was eradicated by his teacher through the pupil's response. (See *Donizetti and the tradition of romantic love*, London 1975, pages 43-45). One may have access to inner teachings regarding harmony and modes but one's music may still be dead. Inner knowledge in Donizetti awoke a quality of compassion that was within his soul and his finest music is a reflection of this. "Intellectual qualification must be accompanied by moral qualification. Without this it is spiritually inoperative, that is, it will not allow the man to go beyond certain limits." (F. Schuon, *Spiritual perspectives and human facts*, London 1954, page 77).

73 It is one of Mayr's themes that true beauty arouses wonder and awe in the beholder.

74 Mayr often refers in his writings to painting as analogous to music. He considered the arts to be intimately linked to one another. This is seen in the fact that much of what Mayr writes here may be found in the writings of G. P. Lornazzo and Poussin, whilst other passages in the notebooks recall the spontaneous theories of the Venetian school as exemplified in the writing of Marco Boschini.

75 Nature is here spelt with a capital letter in order to draw attention to nature as a mirror of archetypal forms.

Therefore, the source of the two arts is the vast theatre of all created forms. However, to where will we retrace the great archetypes of musical creation? From which origin or prototype will be reflected the image within the mirror of a musical inspiration? We will answer . . . as equally in nature as in the other arts. We shall now go on to see just how great is the extension.

Music is a pleasing succession or combination of sounds whose ultimate aim should be joy, as with poetry or any other of the imitative arts[76]. The capacity for this is in proportion to the faculties of the musician in uniting or in separating in a pleasing way the ordinary succession of sounds which are in nature, without breaking the laws established by her, so as to render them pleasing. Natural sounds may be considered as in part simple and in part composite; they are the products of animate or inanimate bodies.

1. Nearly all the animals are given by nature the faculty of expressing in their different ways, pleasure, pain, anger, fear. Each of these vocal expressions has a character and we give it a distinguishing name. In many cases the terms used to express the sounds are no more than a vocal description of the effects over the listener.

2. In the same way, the inanimate parts of nature also offer us ample varieties of sounds. For example, in the separate or combined operations of fire, of air, of water and of innumerable artificial bodies. To these various operations we often give epithets such as hissing, cracking, buzzing, jarring, clattering, splitting, gurgling, etc. When sounds are distinct from mere noise we associate qualities, the plaintive, the bellowing, the querulous, the howling, the lamenting, the singing, the joyous, etc. The specific character of all such sounds we find may respectively be ordered without any difficulty under general classifications which may be reduced to the following:

    a) The sublime as in the sound of mountain torrents, the blowing of gusting winds, the rumbling of thunder, the roaring of wild animals, etc.

    b) The pathetic as in the cry of new born animals, the song of the nightingale, the distant sound of bells, etc.

    c) The discordant and the bitter as in the clatter of wheels, the cry of a peacock or guinea fowl, the tuning of musical instruments, the braying of a donkey, etc.

    d) The sweet and melodious as in bird song, the soft murmuring made by the wind passing through an aperture, etc.

We should not leave the subject of natural sounds without drawing attention to the variety of truly remarkable sounds of the human voice under the diverse circumstances of anger, rebuke, kindness, ecstasy, etc. Furthermore we find in certain persons and countries (for

---

76 Imitation does not mean blind copying in a photographic or impressionistic sense. Similarly, though the sounds of nature are the source of the composer's inspiration, the composer or artist is not a recording machine. He must seek his perception of the archetype of the sound or object of which the literal, external manifestation is but a "mirror". An example of Mayr's teaching occurs in the first few bars of *L'amor coniugale* where the strings convey the activity of a girl working at a spinning wheel.

example, in Wales and Languedoc) that the ordinary course of conversation has always a certain timbre of continuous melody, more or less pleasing to the ear, according to the passion which is at the moment predominant in those who are speaking. Furthermore, it would not be amiss to observe the same characteristics in all human groups where habit of refined manners have not become an obstacle. All these matters have been fundamental to the birth of music.

All civilized peoples are especially worthy of our attention because in their manner of expression, no matter how controlled, they have a continual change of intonation, now high, now low, now accentuated, now pathetic; strong and gathering momentum in anger, whilst sometimes quite distinct owing to deliberate slowness and equality of intonation, whatever the predominant mood may be. All this goes to show that nature has associated particular combinations of sounds with certain dispositions of the mind (these may be simple or composite), thus immediately referring all reasoning creatures to the sensations from which they derive.

We have embarked upon the theme which we could entitle "primitive sound" and we are able to see how such thought might well help to contribute towards our understanding of the formation of music and its genius. When the effect of various particular sounds had been thoroughly understood and the means of reproducing artificial imitations of the sounds had been mastered, then the only difficulty met by the first composers must have been the hearing of a sufficient number of musical expressions of the same character and how to augment the required effect through a right contrast. A person's own intuitive understanding must have been enough to judge the correctness or incorrectness of the sounds used. From these one could realize which sounds were better suited to stimulate or to calm, to disturb or to comfort, to invigorate or to soothe[77]. It has been observed that the passions become aroused not so much by erudite analogies or by discordances but rather through clear and natural notes. Therefore, during music's childhood it is quite probable that the sublimity of music consisted in the use of unison since other techniques were very rare; however, the effect over the listeners must have been just as powerful. Today we are unable to gain a reliable or adequate idea of the impact of sound over those people. The souls of whom, if we may express ourselves in such a way, must have been completely at the dispositions of composers whose power must have seemed like a miraculous gift sent from heaven for ends to which they wished it to serve. Furthermore, when it was wished to explore the unharmonious and dark side of our theme, it is enough to read the amazing stories of antiquity like those of Aclepiades, Empedocles etc., together with the

---

77 Behind these thoughts lies Mayr's teaching regarding the classical understanding of the "modes". Carli's *Osservazioni sulla Musica* which he lovingly copied early in his career may be taken as a fundamental text for understanding Mayr's thought.

deeds of Linus, Orpheus, Timotheus and Antiphon[78] We should not be surprised by the verses which Pindar dedicated to his lyre: ". . . quench the powerful Lightning which gathers its flame from the immortal fire".

Musical genius, therefore, in the first theatres (*dell'arte*), consisted in the knowledge of discerning and ordering of the various sounds produced by nature with the intention of exciting in the listeners corresponding emotions through immediate impact or association. This should still be our aim in our own times, providing we do not present it with lack of taste[79]. It is all we can desire of music. In support of this assertion we shall always find men of prime value who find themselves filled with joy and happiness by simple, straightforward melodies and the old national songs of a popular origin which were inspired by taste and not by a depraved lust laden with false embellishments. Such melodies convey a genuine simplicity and the purest emotion. Their excellence is attested by the universality of their impact. For example, no man who considers himself to have any sensitivity can hope to remain indifferent to the intonation of certain old Scottish songs. Or again, take for example a tune of Gilderoy or a sad Welsh melody recalling their dead on the battlefield of Rudlan[80]. Who can listen to examples such as these without feeling the soul well up with sweet melancholy? At this point it is worthwhile noting that the effect is due to modulation in the minor. Such modulation is not the invention of art, however genuine it may be, or even the unadulterated voice of nature, it is simply the voice of agony, of desolation and of prayer. Take any person, even if he is unfamiliar with music, and ask him to listen to the *Kyrie eleison* as sung by the choir of our own

---

78 We know that Mayr insisted on mythology being taught to his students.

    a) Aclepiades of Bithynia (124 BC to 1st century BC) established the tradition of Greek medicine in Rome where his influence continued until Galen (164 AD). He believed in harmony being restored by fresh air, light, diet, hydrotherapy, massage and exercise. He was a pioneer in the treatment of mental disorders. In Mayr's long lists on the influence of sound and music over the soul there are no doubt examples taken from Aclepiades.

    b) Empedocles, born in Agrigento, Sicily 490 BC and died in the Peloponnese in about 430 BC, was a Greek philosopher and statesman. According to legend he was a self-styled god who jumped into the crater of Mt Etna in order to prove his immortality. (Mayr obviously understood the conclusion of Auber's *La Muette de Portici* in the light of this symbol, for he criticises an adverse critic of the opera by displaying his lack of knowledge in the interpretation of symbols.) Like Heracleitus, Empedocles believed in two opposing forces of love and strife, the interaction of which brings about the four elements. It is said that the mathematical teachings of Pythagoras are evident in Empedocles' analysis of bone structures.

    c) Linus was the son of Apollo who was torn into pieces by dogs at birth. Here, however, Mayr is more likely referring to the son on Ismeninus who was born at Thebes in Boetia. He taught Hercules music, who in a fit of anger struck him on the head with his lyre and killed him!

    d) Timotheus. The poet and musician of Miletus whose abilities were discovered by Euripides.

    e) Antiphon. A poet of Attica who wrote tragedies, epic poems and orations. He was put to death by Dionysius because he refused to praise his compositons.

79 This thought throws light on what Donizetti meant by "taste" (*gusto*).

80 With thoughts such as these and an opera like *La rosa bianca e la rosa rossa*, Mayr must have been a prime influence over Donizetti which helps to explain the latter's fascination with British history and romanticism.

cathedral[81]. Would he dare to deny that this was not the voice of nature? It would be as absurd to deny this as to pretend not to feel filled with strength by those choruses full of pathos by Handel such as : "We sons of Israel, let us lament" or "The total eclipse".

In order to produce such effects, it is necessary to hear the full force of each note. They are the most effective proof that: "Art is Nature to advantage dress'd". [Pope: *Essay on Criticism* (1709)]. Note however, that when an imitative art has reached a certain level of perfection, it occurs that its followers lose themselves through the over-contemplation of the finest examples and thus lose the original life of the prototype. The great, original source of nature appears prematurely poor and exhausted and its foundations ransacked. When caught amidst such apparent disadvantages, the only way to make oneself a name appears to depend upon study of the prevailing style. It is to such an attitude that we may attribute the degeneration of all the arts and the definite extinction of musical genius.

Perhaps someone might ask how the sounds of nature can become of use to the composer. We should answer such a person in the following way: such a course demands an accurate attention to one's own hearing upon which no melody or harmony may have a secure effect without first being dictated by nature. Simplicity is that which constitutes the general character of such qualities which whenever they are adopted give pleasure[82]. This the composer must intellectualize in his own particular way, without being too vague so as to stimulate awe, forcing the mysteries of his art. He must not simply pay attention to rapidity and difficulty of execution (however important these may be for contrast), for these quickly arouse the suspicion that they consist merely in artificial technique. No composer appears to have studied nature more than Haydn, a person in whom we perhaps find the highest gifts happily brought together. Here, in Italy, we hardly know his works or remain completely indifferent to them. In some of these he wished to express himself with elegance, obscurity and mischievous erudition, in place of his usual frank and spontaneous simplicity[83].

When we attentively examine the respective merits of both composers of the past and the present, "we shall take notice of them, be they popular or classical, only in proportion to their natural foundations".

After having attempted to show that our understanding of musical creativity depends on a strict attention to the effects of the prime natural sounds, we cannot help refraining from passing some comment on music today. Modern taste in the arts has, as far as we can see,

---

81 Mayr is here referring to the cathedral which is virtually "next door" to *S. Maria Maggiore*. It is typical of his self-effacement that he does not draw attention to his own choir.

82 "Simplicity is that which has beauty in the arts, be it in theory or in practice. It is however, the hardest thing to find". (Mayr)

83 Yet another example of Mayr's criticism of being "too Germanic" in composition. He would not have appreciated for example the late masses of Haydn with their "symphonic" style at the expense of religious simplicity. Donizetti in a letter to Mayr referred to composers who tended to over intellectualize as *Beethovenisti*.

impeded many quite ingenious composers by alienating them from the great lessons of nature. Sometimes, perhaps without even wishing to, they weary or distract the ear with long rapid sequences, with boring or irregular harmony, together with frequent chromatic cadenzas. Fashion encourages many embarrassments, for example, the composition of sad, pathetic arias, alas, so often introduced into concerts. They are suffocated with a flood of misplaced notes and a superfluity of ornamentation[84]. Such is to dress up an old and venerable matron with the ostentatious clothes and fancy hat of a courtesan. It is possible to observe the work of a few composers dressed up in this way. We may well ask, why the total sacrifice of taste and of judgement to the idol of fashion? Why this progress towards a more than hermetic obscurity? Surely it is now time to ban such frivolities. We should now reconsider the works of composers which up to the present won the respect of men aware of the beauties of a simple, robust style, compositions in which we may contemplate the natural dignity of various old musical forms. For example, the works of Byrd, Peter Philips or Luca Marenzio, without overlooking works by composers like Handel and Corelli.

If it happened that someone, for the sake of argument, made us study the history of music right back to its most distant origins we would affirm the point of view which maintains that the same natural principles have always existed, regardless of the changes of successive refinements in the arts. The task of the modern is not distinct or different from that of our forefathers, except in the perfecting of musical mechanisms[85]. The same laws of composition still face us and these must serve the principle of a better future. Music, which in its infancy was no other than a pleasing flow of melody, has acquired almost imperceptibly the forms and the artistic language which we now recognize as its own. Since it is difficult today for four successive notes not to become susceptible to some sort of ornamentation, which neither increases their beauty nor preserves their character of expression, we might through our study encourage the simplicity of the ancients to assume a contemporary characteristic. Such tendencies in composition futhermore, encourage expressions of a sort of secondary nature reconciling the ear to every opportune change in modulation, thus tending more than often to remove the sudden immediacy of the ancient manner of composition. Art goes onwards, receiving in its progress the additions and the contributions of innumerable composers. These additions are so much an amalgam with the essential character of early music that it would be well-nigh impossible to separate and to analyse right down to the last detail. If it was possible to know all the dates and the facts of all the composers in relative order, together with the information of who first used or helped develop the relative innovations and thus reduce the whole body of music

---

84 This explains Donizetti's many references in his correspondence to his dislike of excessive ornamentation. It is therefore wrong to tastelessly ornament both composers music. The famous flute cadenza in the mad scene of *Lucia di Lammermoor* for example, does not appear in the composer's manuscript. The embellishments were added by singers. Donizetti could do little about such tastes of the Italian operatic stage. Ornamentation should only be added for dramatic effect and with a genuine understanding of the text.

85 There was real development in the making of instruments during Mayr's lifetime, for example, the clarinet. Also compare his piano to Donizetti's own, both in the *Museo Donizettiano*, Bergamo.

to a skeleton we could then determine with better precision the progress and history of musical invention. However, such an undertaking would be more vague than useful[86]. I would on the other hand strip down not a few composers of their fame for their works would appear as a bundle of arid preconceptions or a mass of wounds thickly overlaid with bandages[87].

3   Music[88]

If beside this verdant spacious bank
you could hear Orpheus' melody divine
which frequently arrests the beat of wings
and liberates the river's rapid flow;
silent you may watch trees loose themselves
from their deeps roots, rugged mountains move,
flocks of birds take wing, the wild beasts stir,
the river pause, hearing this joyful note.

O Soul who animates these earthly shapes,
bestow their form, rejoice in harmony -
who are indeed yourself, true harmony;
behold your contours, known to you alone
radiant though as yet you dwell in sleep,
oppressed, imprisoned by the miry clay;
if with frail tongue you can utter your first origin,
speak out, that I may declare on paper
the value, order, out of music's modes.

---

86 Has our modern concern for "pigeon hole" history helped creativity in the arts? Mayr remarked elsewhere that Haydn received his doctorate for composition and not for writing a thesis!

87 Mayr at the conclusion of his essay copied out a translation by G. B. Martelli of William Collins's *The Passions - An Ode for Music*. Perhaps Mayr continued his thoughts by reading the poem and by giving an extemporary exposition emphasising how he understood the "passions" to be linked to genius and the classical understanding of the modes.

88 Mayr's note reads "from Nobile Signore Abbate Giovanni Macazi in the praiseworthy manuscript entitled *Poesie originali d'alcuni Bergamaschi* given by him to Sebastiano Muletti amongst the *Arcadiani Liudresio Ferreate*. Bergamo 1782 Vol. III."

Throughout the work proceeding from God's hand,
formed by his majesty,
nothing created equals you in beauty -
not only since you come forth from his mouth
to vivify this terrain of cold clay, as the undying spirit
to hold dominion over heaven's footstool -
but by the sign which still controls your gestures,
apart from which, you would regret your deeds,
vainly oppose his work, which you cannot disturb.
Therefore live, rejoice in your virtues
containing the harmony from which you were formed
by him who wills that you excel all living forms.

Since I compose
reveal your inspiration,
your rich inebriation.
Should my song fail
to free you from your dungeon.
yet shall you still return
to beauty,
your first habitation,
where each true melody is freely born,
compared to which
our earth is but a shadow.

If truth was uttered by Pythagoras
in the sovereign intellect, Number was the prime idea,
when he fused his First idea with ice,
thus tempering his heat,
Number was foremost in his thought.
Desirous to form man content and just,
he grounded him in Number,
from which he had created this great mass,
of stars, moon, sun -
Number was to be his first example
granting the Spirit wings to rise to the divine temple.

Since thus the soul is touched by Number's concord
as a well-tempered harp,
utters divine and ardent ecstasy.
What were the soul to hear
the various sounds concert among themselves,
as spheres, now slow, now fast, which travel the heavens?
Why does not Style, lying sick within,
beg strength from you, O Muses,

who, on the banks of Aganippe, tune
not merely golden harps -
but even the stars in their celestial cycles?

That sonorous shell, echoing the heaven's harmony -
ineffable concert -
what tongue can define?
Since world is Soul,
tunes the heavens, plays now fast now slow
- she alone is leader and inspirer:
this is the eternal arena
through which resounds
glory in lightning flash, in thunder.
No living creature could describe that sound
divine, even if he could hear it.

In part we hear it
on the golden chords of the Pelasgian or Thracian lyre;
people said it was the song of birds
when Orpheus played -
and that melting anger into pity
he restored from Dis his life's beauty.
When Amphion - sometimes called Aerius
danced to the Lydian note
moved even stones by his lyrical paces.
Thus nature played a superb symphony
rustled willows, stilled the water's ripples, yet the winds contained.

When the hearts of a primordial people
dwelling in cave and forest,
this harmonious, appealing voice
impressed a certain virtue and tradition,
attracted them away from their rough manger.
Thus it is the wise
succeed in taming the Spartans
- desiring that they should be trained by music.
The conqueror of Neptune's gates
was first taught by the Centaur
how another lovely laurel fled through song.

Surely it was this sound that moved
the heavenly messengers to Sacred verse
- which in turn the Hebrew people by the Jordan sung?
Thus, O harmony, by pouring strength and sweetness
you stimulate, attract

to where abides your origin divine.
but here my verse must cease -
too clear to me I speak too wretchedly
concerning vibrant Number's Sound -
that original sublime idea with which the Eternal Craftsman,
gave the created world both weight and measure.

Song - you are rough and indistinct -
remain amid the oaks, the beeches in the dark cold wood.
You may travel clothed, but insecure
amongst a crude people who remain in darkness,
who reject and hate, through habit,
what they do not understand.

4   Mayr's Memoria

The *Memoria* is Mayr's speech, given in March 1805 to the Council of *La Misericordia Maggiore* for the founding of a music school to be known as *Le Lezioni Caritatevoli*. The text is important for both Mayr and Donizetti studies. It should be read against the Napoleonic reforms which in northern Italy brought the old order to an end. Under the new administration Bergamo had a commune instituted and the responsibility of education was taken from the Church and societies like *La Misericordia Maggiore*. This explains Mayr's reference to the seminary (founded by the *Misericordia*) as being no longer "necessary". However the seminary exists to this day and it was where Pope John XXIII received his training for the priesthood.

Cum liquida voce, et convenientissima modulazione cantantur (res divinae) magnam huius instituti utilatem agnosco. (St. Augustine, The Confessions, Book 7, chapter 53).

It has been over a number of years now that many sensitve thinkers and excellent writers have spoken out against the obvious decadence of music in Italy. For example, Metastasio, Arteaga, Planelli, Mattei and others.

In addition to the many causes suggested, one might add the recent changes in our political life. In my opinion no one need doubt the fact that the situation has become worse rather than better. Once, in times past, the Italian nation was alone with her exclusive rule over the musical world. It was due to the excellence of her lyrical singers throughout the courts of Europe from Petersburg to Lisbon. Now she has to employ persons from Germany, Spain and ever further afield in order to supplement the lack of musicians. It is not my intention to retrace the causes which have increased the number of theatres in Italy. The fact is that in every town more theatres are being built, and even in small towns every effort is made to build theatres. Life and entertainment! *Panem et circenses!* The vogue is general. However, how are we to provide for such a hunger for musical entertainment? The immense sums spent to procure musicians of value and genuine quality result in just about enough to meet the needs of two of Italy's principal cities. All others have to be content with the mediocre even in the roles of principal singers which are taken by persons who have not even the most superficial understanding of their art. A voice with the promise of just a little disposition - that is, with the ease to execute like a parrot four runs of the scale - is enough to stimulate enthusiasm for a public hankering for satisfaction at any cost. In the meantime, hired journalists raise any beginner in his art above the stars. They destroy with their premature praise the chance of the growth of any beautiful seed within the singer.

However, if this decadence is ever-increasingly evident on the stage, it is easier to accept, since the only music composed today is for the stage. Unfortunately, it is equally to be observed in music for the Divine Liturgy. For example, and this is a hard thing to say, where in the whole of Italy is there a church which enjoys just a little reputation in the singing of its choir? No longer do we find travellers recalling an unforgettable performance of the famous *Miserere* (by Allegri) in Rome. It has simply ceased to exist. No longer are Lotti's famous *Benedictus* and *Miserere* to be heard in Venice. They have vanished. What has happened to the beautiful sounds of Ambrosian Chant once heard in Milan? What has become of the shrines at Naples and Loreto? Where are the smaller cities once so rich in famous musicians? Which of them can now boast of, at the most, two well-known singers?[89]

Furthermore, Haydn's famous oratorios, *The Creation* and *The Seasons*, Mozart's *Requiem*, all compositions admired throughout Europe as masterpieces of modern music and which have been performed with big choirs and orchestras from Vienna to the extreme east and back again to the extreme west, have not yet been heard in Italy. (*The Creation* was performed in Paris with a choir of 250. The singers were so impressed by the extraordinary beauty of the work, that out of sheer enthusiasm the musicians met together after the first part and declared that a gold medal should be struck and sent to the composer as a sincere homage from all who had taken part. Over 200 were involved in *The Seasons* produced at Vienna, 150 for the same work at Berlin. It would be impossible to record all the performances, enough to indicate that the *Requiem* [Mozart] was performed at Breslau with 130 musicians.)

At last, due to the protest of thinkers and essentially to a change in political events, it would seem that Italy wishes to clear herself from the reproach of not merely permitting,

---

89 Perhaps, in the light of this paragraph, we are fully justified in asserting that Mayr's music for *S. Maria Maggiore* was a conscious attempt at a reform in sacred music as audacious as his "reform" of operatic music. Mayr, therefore, reformed Italian operatic, orchestral and ecclesiastical music - and Italian music education! He even reformed Italian musical taste through the promotion of German music.

but of having actively encouraged the infamous custom of mutilating men, simply for the frivolous delight of hearing a voice an octave higher than others. This sudden change of opinion which bestows honour on our times, will however, leave a considerably vacant gap in our musical life.

Harmony is the most beautiful manifestation of modern music. However, due to the discovery of counterpoint, harmony was used exclusively in religious music. The appealing idea of four natural vocal lines was over the years forgotten and no one thought of returning to nature from which we had so erroneously erred. The cause was simply the whim and insatiable desire to flatter the outward ear. Soon the vacant gap will become apparent, because in a few years it will become impossible to find anyone capable of artificially imitating the natural tone of a woman's or a boy's voice. There will be no one left to sustain the vocal parts of the upper register which are so gracious, so penetrating and essential for the overall concept of vocal harmony.

Therefore let us return to prime sources and use boys between six and fourteen years of age[90]. For an emotional nation like ours it would be too dangerous to introduce women to sing at church services. They have enough power of attraction with their natural beauty, without the additional charm of their voices!

Thus, the thickening of the voice which comes about due to unavoidable laws of nature, (which may be prevented through the privation of the virile organs), makes it requisite that boys are taught at a tender age whilst they are still capable of singing such music.

Therefore, it is necessary to return once more to those means which were of so great an influence a century ago, and which brought music to the apex of perfection.

I refer to the choir and music schools. All writers, historians and thinkers agree that it would be possible to repeat once more the rapid development which music once made in Italy. We would again extend our influence through many excellent followers throughout Europe. For it is without doubt that unless there was a Peli at Modena, a Paita at Genoa, Brivio at Milan - and even more so, the great Neapolitan masters like Leo, Feo, Durante, Porpora and Scarlatti, together with their Bolognese rivals Pistocchi and Bernacchi - we would not have had a Ferri, a Farinelli, an Egiziello, a Raff, a Guadagni or a Pachiarotti.

---

90 Mayr adds an interesting footnote: "The thought of teachers of art and medicine are in agreement. Dr. Weber wrote in a report: one should begin musical training with healthy boys already from the age of five. With the not so healthy at six, and the weakest at seven and not later. The vocal chords at that age have the greatest flexibility, the ear has not yet been spoilt, the time of change of teeth is not so close and childhood illnesses have been left behind. As yet there are no signs of change in the voice and the characteristic unruly nature of boys which rebels against any attempt at education may be still easily moderated. One or two years later, this favourable period has been lost, the vocal chords lose their flexibility, education becomes a greater problem and there is little sign of progress to those who teach them and who become understandably frustrated through the loss of time."

Why are we able to hear today with so much pleasure singers like Marchesi, Crescentini, Babbini and David - although they are no longer in their prime? Do we not recognize much skill and strength in their voices? Is this not due to their devotion to training made under masters now dead but which they remember, and to the fact, that they constantly return to golden precepts taught by those worthy men?

The same may be said concerning instrumental music (which should always be an imitation of vocal music)[91]. We may recognize the same delicate and expressive quality coming from the teachings of Corelli; our fellow-bergamasque, Locatelli, Geminiani, Somis and more recently the sublime and platonic genius of Tartini from whose excellent school came Pagin, Nardini, Giardini, Borghi, Lolli, Viotti etc.

Even governments have recognized the advantage to be gained by academies of music. Hence, the emergence of famous conservatories of music at Naples and Venice. They employed only the best-known and best qualified masters and composers, thus bringing fame and reputation to such schools. Their reputation spread abroad and students of both sexes completed their course travelling to Europe's many courts to return famous and rich. Many foreigners then came to study at the academies.

What is more, many prosperous and famous travellers came to hear and to reward such outstanding examples of nature and of art.

However, when the stimulus of imitation and competition awoke in other nations, they knew (fatefully for us) how to capture the most propitious moment and take away from Italy her decisive lead in the divine art of music. Meanwhile, the ruthless teeth of time had begun to gnaw away at the foundations of our schools. Lastly, various political upheavals have caused everything to collapse. Already all private schools have ceased to exist, even the Neapolitan academies are in a great confusion. On the other hand the Tzar has founded a school for singers; colleges are multiplying in Berlin, Dresden and Leipzig, whilst other music schools have existed now for nearly half a century. The Duke of Bavaria has invited a famous Italian singer to found a music academy based on Venetian precepts and even the French have founded an academy equal to that nation's sense of prestige - but they only accomplished this on having moved to the banks of the Seine all the leading men in the operatic field, together with most of Italy's most precious monuments in this realm of study. The Library of the *Bibliotéque Nationale* of Paris is very rich in musical treasures which were collected by Kreutzer in Italy. (He is now the first violinist of His Majesty). Now even the French are making every effort to overcome all the obstacles hindering their language, appearing to wish to contradict Rousseau who

91 That is, passionate and melodic, from the heart as well as the head.

dared to negate the possibility of France ever having any good music![92]

What will Italy do? Will she quietly permit the crown to be taken away by other nations? Will she remain indifferent to the imminent decay of music? Music - the art to which she seems exclusively destined due to her climate and language, her genuine sensitivity and brilliant powers of imagination. Will she not look to repair the damage wrought by the pace of time and of fate? Will she go on begging to strangers for her musical pleasures - joys which were born from her own womb? Italy gave birth to opera and raised it to its apex. Once it was her sons of melody who filled with wonder and astonishment all Europe's nations - thus assuring homage for years to come! Ah! no! . . .

There are still in her midst men of fine intellect who have the honour and glory of their nation in their hearts. They recognize the sign of the times and understand the relationship of the fine arts to the general happiness and well-being of a people. These men are animated by the Liturgy and Offices of the Church and genuinely seek through the means of harmony and ecstasy of sound to put into practice St. Augustine's teaching: "whenever and wheresoever music is sweetly sung, the souls of the faithful are uplifted towards a greater spirituality and earnest desire for piety. They receive the power of the Spirit in proportion to their estate, for their spritual condition is stimulated by a certain occult force through voice and song".

I would embarrass my audience's modesty if I took account of all the good it has done for the people and for this holy place. You have increased in numbers and in revenue; you have encouraged the reform of both the Church and its Clergy; you have donated a considerable grant to the new grammar school; and now you are considering whether to finance the re-establishment of the art which above all others is related to holy things and which has always been known to have formed men in the finest disciplines.

Thanks to the inspired Ptolomy[93] who explained why music is related to holy things, I am able to explain and present my thoughts. I would describe myself as more fortunate if you, most worthy and esteemed citizens, would honour them with your thoughts and wise contemplation.

Let it be far from me to propose to you vast projects, for such are more or less the sons of ambition and self-interest. The difficulty of realizing such projects dooms them from the outset to the sepulchre of forgotten dreams. Should they be inconsiderately forced into

---

92 Mayr notes that Jean Jacques Rousseau wrote in his epistle on music - *Je crois avoir fait voir qu'il n'y a ni mésure ni mélodie dans la musique française, parceque la langue n'en est point susceptible; que le chant français n'est que un aboyment continuel, insupportable à toute oreille non prévenue, que l'harmonie en est brute, sans expression, et sentant uniquement son remplissage d'écolier; que les airs français ne sont pas des airs, que le récitatif français n'est point du récitatif; d'ou je conclus que les français n'ont point de musique et n'en peuvent avoir; ou que si jamais ils en ont une, ce sera tant pis pour eux.*

93 The metaphysical interpretation of the classical science of music is grounded in the Ptolemaic interpretation of the universe. The Copernican universe implies something quite different.

existence, they have but an ephemeral life for a few years. Experience has shown us by the examples left of the great masters of voice and instrument, that it is enough for one isolated man of genius to stimulate a rapid growth in his science. It is as if he electrifies those around him and that the energy communicated by his disciples stimulates thousands of others who have the talent and the will to dedicate themselves to whatever field of study is in question. (For example, Fasch, the teacher and harpsichordist of Frederick of Prussia alone taught an academy for singers which today numbers more than a hundred and fifty active members, all capable of performing the most exacting pieces of ancient or modern music. *Omnium rerum principia parva - suis progessionibus usu augentur -* Cicero).

A small music school - lessons in the practice of singing and instrumental playing - a few lessons in theory without which practice is always uncertain and over-mechanical - for twelve selected boys of the neighbourhood. This means four sopranos, four altos who will also be taught the cembalo. The remaining four would study violin. There would be need for four full-time teachers: one for singing and declamation; one for the violin: and one for general theory and who undertakes the direction of the school.

If a student was to develop a particular talent and decisive disposition for any other string or wind instrument, then a special teacher would be appointed.

To me this seems the only practical way to prevent further decadence and to reawaken the languishing science of music to a new life. We shall combine the capacity and ease of execution with direct and indirect channels of a practical nature, promoting certain rebirth. We shall aid Italy's fame, help those in need and give glory to God.

Since prejudice has never found favour in my sight, I wish you to realize that my ideas are not altogether without foundation. I will therefore indulge myself with further thoughts for discussion. Please be forbearing and give me your indulgence for a little longer.

If there has ever been a propitious time, for reasons already given, it is the present. Furthermore, it seems to me, it has become necessary to found such a school simply to keep a church alive, especially regarding its choir.

Thanks to your social work the *Misericordia* has increased in revenue.[94] Now, the ordinances and rules of the society declare in Chapter V that "those in authority in the council of the *Misericordia* regarding the administration of financial help are free and absolute".

Therefore, since you have the resources, you have ample freedom to undertake such a project without fear of prejudicing in any way whatsoever the obligations laid upon you by your office.

---

94 No doubt through gifts and perhaps what we would call today grants.

Indeed, you would be undertaking your task in the ideals of your saintly founders, by simply putting into practice the rules as laid down in Chapter VI, "the Council will have particular care in conserving, protecting and defending the reasons and well-being of the *Consortium* by using the yearly income to honour God and for the good of the poor".

Surely, there can be no one who has not realized that music has been used in holy temples throughout the ages and in all religions.

Who has not learnt about the rites and reforms of St. Ambrose or St. Gregory? His Grace Hippolitus, the Lord Bishop of Cortona wrote in one of his pastoral letters: "The Church has never esteemed a finer way to comfort its sons than with the praise of God. Therefore, we must never abandon the understanding that God's own Spirit has consecrated the art of music. (Our Redeemer praised his Eternal Father with Hymns of thanksgiving - *Hymnum pari gratias agens cantabat* - see *Matthew, 26 v. 30*).

The founders of *La Misericordia Maggiore* understood this only too well when they wrote on page 17 of the chapter we have already quoted from: "Since music encourages the souls of the faithful to devotion, because it is an outward sign of the Celestial Harmony, it gives honour to the Church and brings happiness to the laity. Therefore, it will be encouraged to keep a sufficient number of musicians (sometimes more, sometimes less), according to the needs of the times and the society's means, as it seems appropriate on occasions to the honourable Council".

Since it is your pressing duty to promote the glory of *S. Maria Maggiore* by inviting various famous foreign musicians, you will be providing for the future through the means of the music school now under consideration. You will be following the vows of your pious ancestors. You will overcome the shortage of singers and players. You will discover within your own gates a constant flow of active persons duly prepared to undertake such tasks. Furthermore, you will be enriching the church, for the pupils will be obliged to attend all the services, with good musicians. The choristers will in turn celebrate the praises of God *consonis vocibus et suavi modulatione* as required by Innocent III in his *De' Mysterio Missae,* Book I, Chapter II. May I draw your attention to the fact, that you will also be helping to eradicate the abominable custom of sacrificing the seed of generation caused by the ear's intemperance? Such in itself is a sacred deed for humanity's and God's sake. You will be following the most ancient law of Deuteronomy 23, *Non intrabit eunuchus rattritis vel amputatis testiculis e abscisso veretro Ecclesiam Domini.* We shall, through the unity of education and methods, encourage the achieving of an ideal. We shall attain the proposed goal and glorify God with praises and psalms. According to St. Basil the Great, the highest of all goods, which is Charity, recognizes itself in the chant of psalms and becomes the channel for uniting the choir in Oneness.

The School will be a most perfect work of piety and charity. The choice of the twelve boys as I have proposed will fall to only of those who have been declared after a rigorous examination to be of the very poorest in the district. Should you take boys from the various religious houses specializing in the care of the destitute in real need of charity (for example, *San Martino,* the *Pietà,* or the *Convent of the Little Sisters*) you would not lose, for you would be exempt from the cost of their keep, clothing and general welfare etc. Instead of educating them in manual work or in mechanics, which might be totally contrary to their natural genius, you would be lifting them up to a higher level. If they achieve the standard set by you, they will gain a better state for improving their future lot above the ordinary.

Such appears to me to be in accordance with the thought of the pious founders when they instituted a school for lay clerks which was not only "for the service and betterment of the Church but for the good of the poorer classes. Choice should be preferred from such citizens who are in the greatest need of help and who otherwise would have little chance of an education". But through the ravages of times the school for lay clerks has ceased to exist. We are told that the Seminary is no longer necessary. Since "the present situation and property of the place" are in your favour, is there a better idea? With what else would you substitute my proposition?

It might be said that there is no lack in our district of seats of learning, be it for the arts or for the sciences - indeed, the *Misericordia* itself contributes a considerable sum for their upkeep. For example, there are schools in the fine arts for figure and architectural drawing. They exist, it might be said, to the shame that they often substitute another art school in our city - the *Accademia Carrara.*

However, a music school does not exist in the commune or in all the Republic. Meanwhile, the general opinion and experience of other countries, whether it be true or not, is that Italy's smiling skies bestow upon its inhabitants melody and graceful song. It is furthermore said that Italy produces exclusively the finest tenor voices. In order to convince yourselves of this assertion, it is enough to remember that most of the famous tenors now gracing the capitals of Europe are Bergamasques. David along with his rival Bianchi are the cream of the best theatres in Italy. Then there is Viganoni in London, Nozzari in Paris, Perini in Spain, Bianchi in Petersburg and someone else in Naples. All receive the praise of nations. They are rich and constantly in demand. It would therefore seem that our proposed school is the best adapted to the natural genius of our inhabitants.

Nature, as it has been said by the well-known writer, Carli, imprints in a man the characteristics of a more or less marked gift in the sciences, pleasure-giving and useful arts. Happy is the man who equivocates through choice and achieves a balance of the gifts bestowed on him by Nature. He must know how to develop all his faculties, insisting on practice and dedication, thus following the path which leads to honour and perfection.

It will be an easy task for the teachers appointed by yourselves to ascertain amongst those chosen, the gifts best suited to this art. They will choose the finest and nourish them in their natural gifts.

The outcome will be certain. If by accident at the age of adolescence, with the sudden change of voice, there occurs the rare case of a sudden loss in the quality of a student's voice, he could easily apply his talents to an instrument. After all, the art of singing is the finest preparation for learning an instrument. Even if the student had no talent for playing an instrument, he would have received a basic education in grammar, arithmetic, history, geography, mythology and poetry. He would then be prepared to apply himself to the art or science of his natural vocation. The *Misericordia* would not have suffered any notable loss since the student would have served the church as a chorister for a number of years.

Development would be rapid, for besides a reasoned method based on clear and precise doctrines, a student would have occasion to perfect himself due to study, observation and performance of the finest compositions past and present, collected over time in a model library. The student would have received such encouragement for study that he could not fail but to respond. For example, the attendance at church services under the guidance of their respective teachers; concerts given each term; the encouragement and aim set by prizes awarded to those distinguishing themselves in a field of study; the eventual prospect of having a secure job in our country and fame in the most distant lands of Europe; the possibility of living in the annals of art, music and history.

So, in this way, 12 young persons taken from the lowest class possible will, after a short time, over the years, eventually procure a means of livelihood. We shall have saved from obscurity a number of varying talents which otherwise would have remained buried forever. We shall also be reviving a national industry amongst a people more destined to this art than any other. Our students will have natural gifts and will have made a decisive choice. We shall live to see the day when we shall have encouraged a realistic glory, serving the upkeep of many families and contributing in a special way towards the attraction of finance into our province. (Your own Marironi da Ponte asserts in his statistical studies that a people dependent on industry due to their land not being fertile, must endeavour to gain a living from various and many sources. No means from which a financial advantage may be gained must be overlooked. This is especially the case with that social class which finds difficulty of livelihood, for there will be less revenue and the finest minds will be lost).

I do not think that my final proposed advantage is an exaggeration. Just consider for one moment that it is owing to a lack of singers that it is always the same round of tenors who take the principal operatic roles. It is always the same singers we hear, receiving the same applause and gifts which are lavished upon them.

Let us hope we shall end the contention of the best of men, who suffer to hear Alexander, Cato or Caesar sung on our stages by deformed eunuchs with voices to make only children envious, who neglect pronunciation and expression of movement, and who are capable only of inspiring effeminacy and boredom.

We shall have no reproach of ignorance, since through attendance at the music school a pupil will receive a good education. All will receive due practice in declamation. The pupils themselves will present from time to time small musical performances adapted to their age. These will be composed in such a way that the young singers will have been pleased to have, as Metastasio said, "scratched the ear with a sonatina in the throat". We have splendid educational stimulus in acting, for the student has to find the courage to act in public. When acting out the various situations and conditions of the character they are impersonating, they will come to know the course of a distinct pronunciation enabling the word to be heard, together with the whole verse and all the changes in mood according to the various sentiments expressed. They will learn how to excite in their listeners the corresponding emotion through a dignified and effective gesture, together with the vibration and oscillation upon which sadness, happiness and ecstasy depend - just as if the human soul were being harmoniously tuned between them and their audience.

The choir will be perfected due to a right mingling of sopranos and contraltos with tenors and basses. We shall achieve the perfect melody of harmony. We shall have removed the monotony of droning voices[95].

It will be the same with the instrumental music, which is always the imitator of vocal sound. No longer will it be a disordered mass of sharp and flat sequences, of embarrassing pauses and far-fetched arabesques. We shall abandon the barbaric taste of complicated false wonders. We shall play with precision, true intonation, with sobriety concerning all embellishment. We shall seek the beautiful simplicity of Nature and beauty of sound. In this way we shall address the heart, awakening and reordering, according to music's will, all the turbulent passions.

There are many other advantages which arise from such a foundation. To those already mentioned we might add that a philosopher would stress the influence of music over education and the customs of a people. The politician would argue about its effect over society as a whole.[96] But these thoughts would lead me too far from my proposition: furthermore, nor would I presume to disturb you anymore.

It is enough that I have indulged myself as I have. Perhaps I have had the good fortune of having convinced you of:

1.   The necessity of this school -

    a.   in order to help repair the total decadence of music.

    b.   to replace with boys' voices the shortages of castrati.

---

95   Mayr adds the following footnote: "This was recognised by the Hebrews who wisely introduced harmony into the Divine Service. See *Henr. Horchio diss. de igne sacro: Patribus levitis adjungebantur filii adhuc natu minores, ad comparandam musicae varietatem et gratiam majorem . . . Neque nablio cecinerunt, aut cithara, sed ore, ut jucundam varietatem facerent, qui vox puerorum exilis eratet clara, et variegans vocem virorum.* Saintly King David was the first to found a formal song school."

96   The following footnote of Mayr's is fair comment on education today: "All that serves to make man erudite and beautify his spirit bestows health to society and nation. It is a real blessing when a government makes available to its citizens all the necessary means of growth." Maironi - *Osservazioni sul dipartimento del serio.*

c. to supply for the future the necessary voices for church music.

d. thus maintaining the beauty and dignity of the Church and its Liturgy.

2. The possibility of achievement -

a. due to the prestige bestowed by places of learning.

b. due to the increase of entries under your care.

c. due to employing the same concepts as those of the testator's original ideas, that is, simply, the welfare of the poor, the honour of God and reasonable expense.

3. The ease of achievement -

a. The choice of boys from already established religious houses for the poor, this means no cost for housing or clothing. At the most, there will be the cost of the musical instruments.

b. The choice of teachers. We have already certain teachers associated with the church. For example Maestro Gonzales for the harpsichord. There is hope that the famous Capuzzi will accept the post of the first violin together with teaching responsibilities. (It should be remembered that the Professor of Singing requires special consideration. It would be appropriate to pay him a suitable salary when you recall the number of students to which a man may exclusively dedicate himself. Signor Francesco Salari is willing to undertake this appointment. He is a Bergamasque and will be prepared to make sacrifices for his town which a foreigner would not even dream of. He is truly qualified in science and in practical ability. He made his studies at the *Naples Conservatorio* under Piccinni. Since then he has always held important teaching posts in singing in all the leading cities of Italy).

4. To have shown you the certainty of success -

a. owing to the climate which is favourable to producing good voices.

b. owing to the choice of genuine and resolved talent for training.

c. owing to the comprehensive and reasoned method for true and beautiful singing - and for instrumental playing which is equally true and expressive.

d. owing to practical exercise under the supervision of teachers in church, in school and in concert.

e. owing to the encouragement provoked by prizes and praise.

f. owing to the vigilance and guidance of the *Council of the Misericordia* which, through its presence, will know how to stimulate study and reward it with prizes and distinctions.

5.   The many various advantages to be gained -

For Art:

1.   Through the choice of special and particular talents.

2.   Through the same doctrine in method of teaching.

3.   Through the culture linking music to other necessary disciplines, especially literature and the other arts in general.

4.   Through the availability of good teachers.

5.   Through the perfecting of opera in respect to natural voices in pronunciation and declamation.

For *La Misericordia Maggiore*:

1.   Through ceasing to employ foreign teachers.

2.   Through ceasing to employ various extras for special church services.

3.   Through having the assurance of no longer lacking musicians in our own country.

For Individuals and Families:

1.   To improve the general welfare of citizens.

2.   To attract foreign currency.

3.   And perhaps as in Naples and Bologna etc. to attract foreign competition.

4.   To improve the standard of our theatre.

5.   To improve through music's influence the morals, customs and personal character.

And finally for the whole of Italy -

By giving it back its dominion in the art of music, by helping its ancient glory and superiority which other nations have at the present usurped.

And you, most honoured and illustrious citizens, you will have erected a perennial monument of gratitude and of glory.

1   A view of Mendorf.

2   Mendorf, the house where Mayr was born (right) and the Parish Church where his father was organist.

3   The organ loft, Mendorf Parish Church, where Mayr had his first organ lessons from his father.

4   *Schloss Sandersdorf*, near Mendorf, the home of the v. Bassus family.

5 View of Ingolstadt where Mayr studied.

6 Adam Weishaupt (1748-1830)
   founder of the Bavarian Illuminati.

7 Friedrich Overbeck (1789-1869), *Italy and Germany*, worked on from 1822 to 1828, oil on canvas, *Bayerische Staatsgemäldesammlungen,* Munich.

8 A view of Bergamo from S. Vigilio, drawn by A. Guesdon and lithographed by J. Jacoltet, Paris, circa 1850. In the foreground is Borgo Canale where Donizetti was born, behind which is the Seminary, the larger dome of the Cathedral and the smaller dome of *S. Maria Maggiore.* Mayr's house overlooks the city walls to the right of *S. Maria Maggiore.*

9　Mayr at the beginning of his career.

Giŏ. Simone Mayr.

10 Mayr, from a series depicting teachers at his School, dating from circa 1820.

Francesco Salari

11 Francesco Salari (1751 - 1822), choir master who was in charge of vocal studies at Mayr's School.

12 Antonio Capuzzi (1755 - 1818), pupil of Tartini, *violino principale* and a distinguished teacher at Mayr's School.

Pietro Rovelli

13 Pietro Rovelli (1793 - 1838) was appointed as violin teacher and *violino principale* after Capuzzi's death in 1818.

Antonio Gonzalez

14 Antonio Gonzales (1764 - 1838) was in charge of keyboard studies and was organist at *S. Maria Maggiore*.

15 Mayr's piano preserved at the *Museo Donizettiano*, Bergamo.

16 Mayr's School in Via Arena,
   Bergamo.

17 Mayr at the height of his operatic career. An engraving by the Scotto brothers, circa 1810.

18 Mayr, circa 1816.

19 An example of the allegorical designs in S. Maria Maggiore known to Mayr and Donizetti. These *intarsie* or in
laid wood veneers are based on drawings by Lorenzo Lotto (1480 - 1555). This particular example represents the
Pharoah as symbol of pride and vanity.

20 Mayr reading from his Notebooks, his faithful dog at his side, to a group of his students amongst which is Donizetti. *La Scala Museum*, Milan.

21 Donizetti at 18. A portrait by an anonymous artist in tempera on card. A gift to Mayr dated 5 November 1815 from Donizetti when he was a student in Bologna. *Museo Donizettiano*, Bergamo.

22 An extract from Donizetti's remarkable letter to Mayr in which he recalls his humble origins and his leaving of Bergamo in order to pursue an operatic career. *Museo Donizettiano*, Bergamo.

23 Donizetti and Mayr - pupil and master.

24 Mayr, Dolci and Donizetti consult a score: the artist Luigi Deleidi, known as Il Nebbia, records the scene; the host Michele Bettinelli looks on about to pour the wine.

25 *The sower*, a commemorative medal by the sculptor Piero Brolis struck for the rebuilding of the Seminary, Bergamo in 1967.

26 The *Ateneo* and apse of *S. Maria Maggiore*, Bergamo. Lithograph by G. Elena, circa 1870.

27, 28

Two examples of Mayr's manuscript: one
when his eyesight was good, another from
one of his last compositions written out on
large staves due to his blindness.

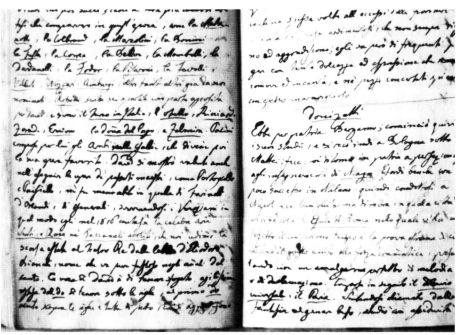

29 Mayr's notes on Donizetti in a volume from the Notebooks.

30 The title page of Mayr's copy of Algarotti's *Saggio sopra l'opera in musica*. (The Notebooks).

31 An example from Mayr's copy of Riccati's writings on musical theory. (The Notebooks).

32 A typical page of notes from the Notebooks.

33 The conclusion of the *Dissertation on Genius and on Composition*, after which Mayr has copied out in translation the *Ode to Music* by William Collins. (The Notebooks).

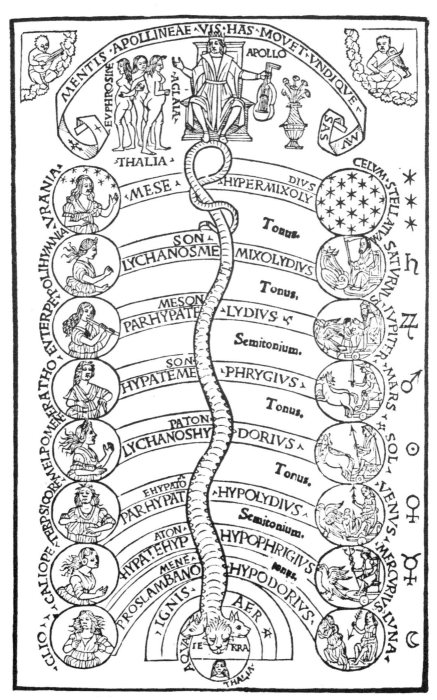

34 A diagram of the Spheres and the Muses related to the Monochord, known to Mayr due to his
studies of Gaffurio.

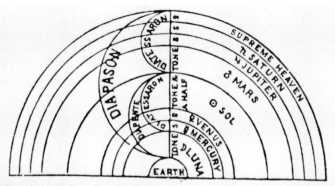

* These positions of the Pythagoreans, that the universe is framed according to musical proportion, and that all this world is enarmonic, refer to the general frame and contexture of the whole. But there are arguments in favour of music, deducible from the properties and affections of matter, discoverable in its several parts : in short, it may be said in other words, that the whole world is in tune, inasmuch as there are few bodies but are sonorous. The skin of an animal may be tuned to any given note, as is observable in the drum : a cable distended by a sufficient power is as much a musical chord as a lute string or one of wire. And Strada somewhere mentions six great guns in a fortification at Groningen, which from the sounds uttered by them in their explosion, had the names of UT, RE, MI, FA, SOL, LA. The percussion of all metals, of stones, nay of timber, or of the trunks of trees when felled, produces a musical sound : hollow vessels, as well of wood, as earth and metal, when struck do the same. Of this fact the Indian Gong, as it is called, is a surprising instance; it is an instrument of brass, or some other factitious metal, in form like a sieve, and about two feet in diameter. The late duke of Argyle had one in his observatory at Whitton, near Twickenham, in Middlesex, which being suspended edgeways by a cord, and struck with a stick muffled at the end, many times, till the quickest vibrations it could make were excited, yielded not only a clear musical sound, but the whole harmony of a diapason, namely, the unison third, fifth, and octave, so clearly and distinctly, that each was obvious to the ear. This instrument is mentioned by Capt. Dampier in one of his voyages, and is thus described by him :—

'In the sultan's mosque [at Mindanao] there is a great drum with but 'one head, called a Gong, which is instead of a clock. This gong is 'beaten at twelve o'clock, at three, six, and nine, a man being appointed 'for that service. He has a stick as big as a man's arm, with a great 'knob at the end bigger than a man's fist, made with cotton, bound fast 'with small cords; with this he strikes the gong as hard as he can about 'twenty strokes, beginning to strike leisurely the first five or six strokes, 'then he strikes faster, and at last strikes as fast as he can ; and then he 'strikes again slower and slower so many strokes : thus he rises and falls 'three times a-day, and then leaves off till three hours after.' Dampier's Voyages, vol. I. pag. 388.

Glass, and many other bodies, affected by the voice, or the vibrations of chords, return the sounds that agitate them. It is credibly reported of old Smith, the organ-maker, that he could not tune a certain pipe in St. Paul's organ till he had broken a pane of glass in the sash that incloses it.

† Stanl. Life of Pythag. pag. 393.

35 A diagram illustrating the relationship between the Monochord and the Ptolemeic system of the Universe, (*A general history of the Science and Practice of Music,* by Sir John Hawkins).

36 An academy of painting conceived in allegorical terms and engraved by Nicholas Dorigny after a drawing by Carlo Maratta. The illustration helps to set Mayr's thought in its historical and cultural context. The muses inspire the artist to perceive the archetypal world in Nature which is expressed in the divine laws of mathematics and geometry which give rise to a symbolic language.

37 *The vision of Medea* by Turner. (Tate Gallery, London).

38 Medal struck to commemorate Mayr as the founder of the *Unione Filarmonica* of Bergamo, 14
    June 1841.

39 Mayr, by Gaetano Barabini. Dated 1827. *Museo Donizettiano*, Bergamo.

40 Mayr's tomb in *S. Maria Maggiore*, Bergamo.

3
A Catalogue of Works of Johann Simon Mayr 1763 - 1845

Compiled by John Allitt for
The Mayr + Donizetti Collaboration

Introduction

Research may never attain the definitive version. In the case of Mayr's music there is still much to be traced and items to be compared. The present catalogue, therefore, is as complete as possible to date. Its aim is to convey with speed of reference the scale and scope of Mayr's work. It does not duplicate entries when more than one manuscript copy of a work exists, except in the instance of certain operas. For example there are a number of Mayr's operas in manuscript copies in American libraries which are not here listed. The search has been for autograph scores and previously unlisted works for these, it was considered, will be of immediate help in encouraging Mayr's revival.

Research has shown the unreliability of the *Fondo Mayr's* cataloguing. Certain manuscripts appear to be misplaced, others uncatalogued. Sometimes, pages missing in a *faldone* may be in another. It is now of the utmost importance that the manuscripts are properly conserved and correctly catalogued. Indeed, the greater part of this present work is dependent on information sent to the *Collaboration*. Therefore, in the near future it will have to be revised in the light of corrections and new additions.

Musicologists seriously intending to revive Mayr's music are welcome to contact *The Mayr + Donizetti Collaboration* [32 Esmond Road, London W4 1JQ] for further information.

In order that the *Collaboration's* catalogue be kept up to date, Ian Caddy and I would welcome details of new discoveries and especially of modern editions. The Collaboration's intention is the rediscovery of Mayr, a better appreciation of Donizetti, and the revaluation of early 19th century Italian music and cultural life.

Order and Abstract of the Catalogue

ORDER	CATALOGUE Nos.	No. of ENTRIES
20. Quartets with orchestra	A277	1
21. Quintets with orchestra	A278 - A279	2
22. Voice, and chorus with orchestra or pianoforte	A280 - A285	6
23. Choruses with orchestra	A286 - A297	12
24. Various pieces from unidentified operas	A298 - A338	41
25. Music for his school	A339 - A352	13
26. Collections - mostly songs	A353 - A370	18
27. Songs: voice, pianoforte guitar, etc.	A371 - A420	50
28. Sinfonie	A421 - A478	58
29. Concertos	A479 - A485	7
30. Orchestral	A486 - A492	7
31. Ballet	A493 - A494	2
32. Pianoforte with other instruments	A494 - A500	6
33. Pianoforte solo	A501 - A527	27
34. Harp	A528	1
35. Wind music	A529 - A544	16
36. Music for strings and wind instruments	A545 - A551	7
37. Guitar	A552	1
38. Organ	A553 - A560	8
39. The Mass (complete or near-complete settings)	A561 - A577	17

ORDER	CATALOGUE Nos.	No. of ENTRIES
The Proper of the Mass:		
40. Introits	A578 - A587	10
41. Graduals	A588 - A592	5
42. Offertories	A593 - A595	3
43. Sequences	A596 - A599	4
The Common of the Mass:		
44. Kyrie and Christe eleison	A600 - A648	49
45. Gloria	A649 - A804	156
46. Credo	A805 - A829	25
47. Sanctus, Benedictus, Agnus Dei	A830 - A839	10
48. Sanctus	A840 - A846	7
49. Benedictus qui venit	A847 - A849	3
50. Agnus Dei	A850 - A852	3
51. Pater noster	A853	1
Vespers:		
52. Domine ad adjuvandum	A854 - A874	21
53. Gloria Patri	A875 - A892	18
54. Sicut erat	A893 - A900	8
55. Dixit	A901 - A971	71
56. Psalms	A972 - A1035	64
57. Canticles	A1036 - A1064	28
58. Magnificat	A1065 - A1079	15
59. Hymns - full settings	A1080 - A1109	30

170

Library sigla

Note: LS refers to Ludwig Schiedermair who traced and saw scores of Mayr's music which are now lost or misplaced owing to the ravages of war or carelessness.

A: Austria
  - Wn, Vienna, Österreichische National Bibliothek Musiksammlung.
  - Wgm, Vienna, Gesellschaft der Musikfreunde.

B: Belgium
  - Bc, Brussels, Conservatoire de Musique.

CH: Switzerland
  - E, Einsiedeln, Benediktinerkloster.

D: Germany
  - Mbs, Munich, Bayerische Staatsbibliothek.
  - Bds, Berlin, Deutsche Staatsbibliothek.
  - Dlb, Dresden, Sächsische Landesbibliothek.

F: France
  - Pc, Paris, Conservatoire National de Musique.

GB: Great Britain
  - Lbl, London, British Library.
  - Lor, London, Opera Rara Collection.

H: Hungary
  - Bmm, Brno, Moravské Muzeum.

I: Italy
  - Bas, Bologna, Archivio di Stato.
  - Bc, Bologna, Civico Museo Bibliografico Musicale.
  - BGc, Bergamo, Biblioteca Civica Angelo Mai.
  - BGi, Bergamo, Civico Istituto Musicale Gaetano Donizetti.
  - BRc, Brescia, Conservatorio.
  - Bsf, Bologna, Convento di S. Francesco.
  - Ccf, Chioggia, Comunale Filippini.
  - Colombaro, Biblioteca Privata Barcella.
  - CORc, Correggio, Biblioteca Comunale.
  - CRd, Cremona, Duomo.
  - CRg, Cremona, Pio Istituto Musicale.
  - Fc, Florence, Conservatorio di Musica Luigi Cherubini.

- Fn, Florence, Biblioteca Nazionale Centrale.
- Gc, Genoa, Biblioteca Civica Berio.
- Gil, Genoa, Conservatorio di Musica Niccolò Paganini
- Ll, Livorno, Biblioteca Comunale Labronica Francesco Guerrazzi.
- Ls, Lucca, Seminario Vescovile.
- LU, Lugo, Biblioteca Comunale Fabrizio Trisi.
- MAb, Mantua, Basilica di Sant'Andrea.
- MAc, Mantua, Biblioteca Comunale.
- Mc, Milan, Conservatorio di Musica Giuseppe Verdi.
- Mr, Milan, Archivio Storico Ricordi (Publishers).
- MOe, Modena, Biblioteca Estense.
- Nc, Naples, Conservatorio di Musica S. Pietro a Majella.
- Nf, Naples, Biblioteca Oratoriana dei Filippini.
- NOVd, Novara, Archivio Musicale Classico del Duomo.
- OS, Ostiglia, Biblioteca Musicale Greggiati
- PAc, Parma, Conservatorio di Musica Arrigo Boito.
- PEsp, Perugia, San Pietro.
- PS, Pistoia, Duomo.
- Rc, Rome, Biblioteca Casanatense.
- Ria, Rome, Istituto Nazionale di Archeologia e Storia dell'Arte.
- Rsc, Rome, Conservatorio di Musica Santa Cecilia.
- Rvat, Rome, Vatican Library.
- Td, Turin, Duomo.
- Tf, Turin, Accademia Filarmonica.
- Tn, Turin, Biblioteca Nazionale Universitaria.
- Vlb, Vicenza, Biblioteca Civica Bertoliana.
- VEgs, Verona, San Giorgio in Braida.
- Vc, Venice, Biblioteca di Musica Benedetto Marcello.
- Vlevi, Venice, Fondazione Ugo Levi.
- Vnm, Venice, Biblioteca Nazionale Marciana.
- Vmc, Venice, Museo Civico Correr.
- Vqs, Venice, Accademia Querini-Stampalia.
- Vsmc, Venice, Santa Maria della Consolazione detta Della Fava.

US: United States of America
- Wc, Washington DC, Library of Congress, Music Division.
- Bm, Boston, University, Mugar Memorial Library.
- Mich, Michigan, University, Ann Arbor.

List of abbreviations

The following abbreviations apply to this section only.

A	=	alto;
B	=	bass;
cl	=	clarinets;
cr angl	=	cor-anglais;
cr	=	horns;
cr di bassetto	=	corno di bassetto;
cb	=	double bass;
fg	=	bassoon;
fl	=	flute;
ob	=	oboe;
picc	=	piccolo;
S	=	soprano;
T	=	tenor;
timp	=	timpani;
tr	=	trumpet;
trb	=	trombone;
vl	=	violin;
vl princ	=	violino principale;
vla	=	viola;
vle	=	violas.

1.   Operas

A1 SAFFO
ossia I riti d'Apollo Leucadio. Dramma per musica in 2 acts; libretto by Antonio Simone Sograffi. Venice, La Fenice, 17 Feb 1794. Autograph score: I-BGc 188.

A2 LODOISKA.
Dramma per musica in 3 acts; libretto by Francesco Gonella after Filette-Loreaux. Venice, Teatro della Fenice, 26 Jan 1796. Autograph score (incomplete): I-BGc 169; non-autograph: I-PAc, I-Gil B.5.3/5.D.7.10/12, I-Fc (2 copies), I-Mc, I-Bc, I-PAc, I-Nc. Revised as an opera buffa for Parma in 1799 but not performed. Again revised, as a dramma per musica, in 2 acts for La Scala, Milan, 26 Dec 1799. [see A17]. The ballet performed with the original *Lodoiska* had the title *Cook, ossia gl' inglesi in Othaiti.*

A3 UN PAZZO NE FA CENTO
(I rivali delusi), (La contessa immaginaria). Dramma giocoso in 2 acts; libretto by Giuseppe Maria Foppa. Venice, San Samuele, 8 Oct 1796. Partly autograph score: I-BGc 180; non-autograph: D-Dla, I-OS B.50.1-2, I-Fc A.11.147-152.

A4 TELEMACO
nell'isola di Calipso. Dramma per musica in 3 acts; libretto by Antonio Simone Sograffi. Venice, La Fenice, 16 Jan 1797. Partly autograph score: I-BGc 167.

A5 L'INTRIGO DELLA LETTERA
(Il pittore), (Il pittore astratto), (L'imbroglio della lettera). Farsa in 1 act; librettoby Giuseppe Maria Foppa, Venice, San Moisé, 24 Sept 1797. Partly autograph score and non-autograph score: I-BGc 172.

First item of a double-bill [see A6] I-NC 28.2.10. [See also A31 and A70].

A6 IL SECRETO
(Il segreto), (Il matrimonio per concorso). Farsa in 1 act; libretto by Giuseppe Maria Foppa. Venice, San Moisé, 24 Sept 1797. Autograph score with additions and cancellations: I-BGc 172, I-PAc. Second item of a double-bill [see A5]. When given under the title: *Il matrimonio per concorso,* Bologna, 1809, reworked as a dramma giocoso in 2 acts.

A7 (UN) L'AVVISO AI MARITATI.
Opera buffa or Dramma giocoso in 2 acts; libretto by Francesco Gonella. Venice, San Samuele, 15 Jan 1798. Partly autograph score: I-BGc 180.

A8 LAUSO E LIDIA.
Dramma per musica in 2 acts; libretto by Giuseppe Maria Foppa after Marmontel. Venice, La Fenice, 14 Feb 1798. Non-autograph score: I-BGc 191.

A9 ADRIANO IN SIRIA.
Dramma per musica in 3 acts; libretto adapted from Metastasio. Venice, San Benedetto, 13 Apr 1798: B-Bc (LS); 9 ms pieces in Italy.

A10 CHE ORIGINALI
(Gli originali), (Il trionfo della musica), (Il fanatico della musica), (La musicomania), (Il pazzo per la musica), (Le melomane). Farsa or opera buffa in 1 act; libretto by Gaetano Rossi. Venice, San Benedetto, 18 Oct 1798. Non-autograph score: I-Mc Noseda G3, D-Mbs, I-GL B.5.6-7, H.1.9, I-Fc, I-Mc etc.

A11 AMOR INGEGNOSO.
Farsa in 1 act; libretto by Caterino
Mazzolà. Venice, San Benedetto, 27 Dec
1798. Autograph score: I-BGc 174. With
L'ubbidienza per astuzia as double-bill
[see A12].

A12 L'UBBIDIENZA PER ASTUZIA.
Farsa in 1 act; libretto by Caterino
Mazzolà. Venice, San Benedetto, 27 Dec
1798. Autograph score: I-BGx 174. With
Amor ingegnoso as double-bill [see A11].

A13 ADELAIDE DI GUESCLINO.
Dramma per musica in 2 acts; libretto by
Gaetano Rossi after Voltaire, Venice, La
Fenice, 1 May 1799. Nearly complete
autograph score: I-BGc 195; non-
autograph score: I-PAc.

A14 L'ACCADEMIA DI MUSICA.
Farsa giocosa in 1 act; libretto by
Gaetano Rossi. Venice, San Samuele,
Aug 1799. Autograph score with many
cancellations: I-BGc 2, non-autograph:
I-Fc A.111.104-106.

A15 LABINO E CARLOTTA
(Werter e Carlotta), (Sabino e Carlotta),
Farsa in 1 act; libretto by Giuseppe Maria
Foppa, Venice, San Benedetto, 9 Oct
1799. Non-autograph score with
autograph additions and corrections for
Genoa, 1801; I-BGc 174; non-autograph
score: I-Mc Tr.MS.205.

A16 L'AVARO.
Farsa in 1 act; libretto by Giuseppe Maria
Foppa after Goldoni after Molière.
Venice, San Benedetto, Nov 1799. Partly
autograph score with corrections: I-BGc
178; non-autograph score: I-Fc A.IV.70.

A17 LODOISKA.
Opera semi-seria in 2 acts. For Parma,
1799 but not performed. Ms score with

autograph corrections but incomplete:
I-BGc 292; non-autograph: I-Fc, I-Nc,
other scores in numerous libraries and
many extracts available [see A2].

A18 LA LOCANDIERA
(La bella locandiera). Farsa in 2 acts;
libretto by Gaetano Rossi after Goldoni.
Vicenza, for the inauguration of the
Teatro Berico, Spring 1800. Ms mostly
autograph but incomplete and 17 vocal
scored pieces: I-BGc 298 (and many extracts); non-autograph score: I-Nc 1,2,8/9.

A19 IL CARETO DEL VENDITORE
D'ACETO
(L'oro fa tutto), (L'acetaio), (Il barile por-
tentoso). Farsa giocosa in 1 and 2 acts;
libretto by Giuseppe Maria Foppa after L.
S. Mercier. Venice, Sant'Angelo, 28 June
1800. Non-autograph score with
autograph notes and additions: I-BGc
175, I-Bc; I-Fc D.111.424, I-Fc
A.111.119-121, I-PAc, I-Tn etc.

A20 L'IMBROGLIONE E IL
CASTIGA-MATTI.
Farsa in 1 act; libretto by Giuseppe Maria
Foppa. Venice, San Moisé, Autumn
1800. Score lost?

A21 L'INCONVENIENZE TEATRALI.
Farsa in 1 (?) act; libretto after Sograffi.
Venice, San Luca, Autumn 1800. Score
lost; Non autograph sinfonia: I-OS
B.1405. Quintet: Sì, sì, si allegri I-BGc
319, 1800 is the year of Sograffi's play.
It is possible that the play was performed
with music by Mayr.

A22 L'EQUIVOCO
ossia Le bizzarie dell'amore (I due viag-
giatori). Dramma giocoso in 2 acts; libretto by Giuseppe Maria Foppa. Milan, La
Scala, 5 Nov 1800. Non-autograph

scores: I-BGc 181, 182, I-Fc A.11.153-158, I-Mc 213.

A23 GLI SCITI.
Dramma per musica in 2 acts; libretto by Gaetano Rossi after Voltaire. Venice, La Fenice, 26 Dec 1800. Mostly complete autograph score: I-BGc 291; non-autograph scores: I-Fc A.VI. 137-142; D.1.356-357; I-Mc (Noseda); I-Nc 28.2.23.

A24 I VIRTUOSI
(I virtuosi a teatro). Farsa in 1 act; libretto by Gaetano Rossi. Venice, San Luca, 26 Dec 1801. Incomplete partly autograph score: I-BGc 175. LS saw a full-score which presumably was destroyed in second world war: I-Mr.

A25 GINEVRA DI SCOZIA
(Ariodante), (Ginevra ed Ariodante). Dramma serio eroico per musica in 2 acts; libretto by Gaetano Rossi from Ariosto's *Orlando Furioso*. Trieste, for the inauguration of the Teatro Nuovo, 21 Apr 1801. Autograph score: I-Mr; partly autograph, incomplete: I-BGc 241, and in many other libraries.

A26 LE DUE GIORNATE
(Il portatore d'acqua), (Le due giornate di Parigi). Dramma eroicomico per musica in 2 and 3 acts; libretto by Giuseppe Maria Foppa, after J. N. Bouilly. Milan, La Scala, 18 Aug 1801. Autograph score: I-Mr; non-autograph score with 2 sinfonias and additions: I-BGc 138, I-Fc B.1.83-84, I-Nc 28.2.1-2.

A27 ARGENE.
Dramma eroico per musica in 2 acts; libretto by Gaetano Rossi based on V. Monti's tragedy *Aristodemo*. Venice, La Fenice, 28 Dec 1801. Partly autograph incomplete score: I-BGc 192.

A28 I MISTERI ELEUSINI
(Polibete), (Antinoo in Eleusi). Dramma per musica in 2 acts; libretto by Giuseppe Bernadoni. Milan, La Scala, 16 Jan 1802. Autograph score: I-Mr; Ms score with autograph corrections: I-BGc 192. Extra non-autograph scene for La Scala, 1807: I-BGc 192, Ms scores in other libraries.

A29 I CASTELLI IN ARIA
ossia Gli amanti per accidente. Farsa in 1 act; libretto by Giuseppe Maria Foppa. Venice, San Benedetto, May 1802. Score lost?

A30 ERCOLE IN LIDIA.
Dramma per musica in 2 acts; libretto by Giovanni de Gamerra. Vienna, Burgtheater, 29 Jan 1803. Non-autograph score: A-Wgm, I-Fc A.VII. 81-92.

A31 GL'INTRIGHI AMOROSI.
Dramma giocoso in 2 acts; libretto by Giuseppe Bertati. Parma, Teatro Ducale, Carnival 1803. Score lost? This may be a reworking in 2 acts of *L'intrigo della lettera* - [see A5 and A70].

A32 LE FINTE RIVALI.
Melodramma giocoso in 2 acts; libretto by Luigi Romanelli. Milan, La Scala, 20 Aug 1803. Non-autograph scores: I-BGc 184, I-Nc 28.2.7, I-Bc, I-Fc A.11.159-164.

A33 ALONSO E CORA
(La vergine del sole). Dramma per musica in 2 acts; libretto by Giuseppe Bernadoni after Marmontel's *Les Incas*. Milan, La Scala, 26 Dec 1803. Autograph score: I-Mr; incomplete non-autograph score (different sinfonia): I-BGc 195, I-Fc A.VII. 93-94; A.I. 112-117; D.I. 347-348 [see A61].

A34 AMOR NON HA RITEGNO
(La fedeltà delle vedove). Melodramma

eroicomico in 2 acts; libretto by Francesco Marconi from Carlo Gozzi's play *La
donna contraria al consiglio*. Milan, La
Scala, 18 May 1804. Non-autograph
score: I-Mc Noseda F.71/1.11, I-Bc. Ls
saw autograph score in I-Mr.

A35 ELISA
(Il Monte San Bernardo), (Il passagio di
Monte San Bernardo). Dramma sentimen-
tale in 1 act (2 parts); libretto by Gaetano
Rossi, after Saint-Cyr. Venice, San
Benedetto, 5 Aug 1804. Non-autograph
scores: I-Fc B.82 A.111.107-109 and
other copies, I-Os B.51, I-PL, I-Ro MS
2534-35, I-Nc 28.2.5, I-Mc, I-Bsf, I-Gil,
I-LI, I-PAc, I-Rsc, I-Vnm, etc.

A36 ZAMORI
ossia L'eroe dell'Indie. Dramma musicale in 2 acts; libretto by Luigi Prividali
and N.N. Piacenza, 10 Aug 1804. Non-
autograph scores: I-BGc 194, I-Rc Ms
2528.8.C.112-147, I-GL Sc 93. This
opera was reworked as *Palmira* in
Florence, 1806, [see A43].

A37 ERALDO ED EMMA.
Dramma eroico per musica in 2 acts;
libretto by Gaetano Rossi. Milan, La
Scala, 8 Jan 1805. Non-autograph scores:
I-Fc A11.132-133; D.1.333-334, I-PAc
[see A65].

A38 DI LOCANDA IN LOCANDA E
SEMPRE IN SALA.
Farsa in 3 acts (parti); libretto by L.
Giuseppe Buonavoglia based on
*D'auberge en auberge ou Les
préventions* by E. Mercier-Dupaty.
Venice, San Moisé, 5 June 1805.
Autograph score: I-BGc 21.

A39 L'AMOR CONIUGALE
(Il custode di buon cuore). Farsa sentimentale in 1 act (2 parts); libretto by

Gaetano Rossi after J.N. Bouilly based on
Léonore set by Pierre Gaveaux. Padova,
Teatro Nuovo, 26 July 1805. Autograph
scores: I-Mr, I-BGc 280; Non-autograph
scores: I-Bsf, I-Fc A.111.110-112;
D.1.335; D.1.336; D.11.372; B.1.128,
I-GiL, I-Mc, I-Nc 6.4.41; R.8.6-7, I-Rsc,
I-Vnm etc.

A40 LA ROCCIA DI FRAUENSTEIN
(Gli emigrati di Franconia). Melodramma
eroicomico in 2 acts; libretto by Gaetano
Rossi, after Angelo Anelli's *I fuorusciti
di Firenze*. Venice, Teatro della Fenice,
26 Oct 1805. Non-autograph scores: I-
Mc, I-Nc 28.2.21-22.

A41 GLI AMERICANI
(Idalide). Melodramma eroico in 2 acts;
libretto by Gaetano Rossi. Venice, La
Fenice, 26 Dec 1805. Autograph score:
I-BGc 198, US-Wc.

A42 IFIGENIA IN AULIDE.
Azione seria drammatica; libretto by
Apostolo Zeno. Parma, 1806. Score lost?
Carnival 1811, an opera intitled *Il
Sacrifizio d'Ifigenia*, an azione seria
drammatica in 2 acts with libretto by
Cesare Arici after Du Roullet and music
by Mayr, was produced at the T. Nuovo,
Bescia, for the opening of the theatre. It
is probable that this was a revision of
Ifigenia in Aulide. [See A54 and A120]

A43 PALMIRA
(Il trionfo della virtù e dell'amore). Dram-
ma per musica in 1 act (2 acts into 1 act).
Florence, Teatro La Pergola, Autumn
1806. Non-autograph scores: I-Fc
A.111.113-115, I-PAc. Reworking of
Zamori. [See A36]

A44 IL PICCOLO COMPOSITORE DI
MUSICA.
Farsa. Venice, San Moisé, 1806. Score

lost? Mayr later wrote libretto and music of an opera with a similar title for his school, Donizetti in the title role. [See A109]

A45 ADELASIA ED ALERAMO.
Melodramma serio in 2 acts; libretto by Luigi Romanelli. Milan, La Scala, 28 Dec 1806. Non-autograph scores: I-Mc 243.187, I-Fc A.1.124-131; D.1.339-34; P.1.104-5, I-Nc 28.3.32-33, I-OS B.1704.

A46 NÉ L'UN, NÉ L'ALTRO.
Dramma giocoso in 2 acts; libretto by Angelo Anelli. Milan, La Scala, 17 Aug 1807. Autograph score: I-BGc 203 (possible completed by item in I-Mc).

A47 BELLE CIARLE E TRISTI FATTI
(L'imbroglio contra l'imbroglio). Dramma giocoso in 2 acts; libretto by Angelo Anelli. Venice, La Fenice, Nov 1807. Autograph score: I-Mr.

A48 I CHERUSCI.
Dramma per musica in 2 acts; libretto by Gaetano Rossi. Rome, Teatro Argentina, Carnival 1808. Autograph score Act II Sc8: D-Mbs, LS records a full score in B-Bc, otherwise lost?

A49 UN VERO ORIGINALE
(La finta sposa), (Il barone burlato). Burletta per musica in 2 acts. Rome, Teatro Valle, 1808. Non-autograph scores: I-BGc 185, I-Rsc G. Mss 643-644.

A50 IL RITORNO DI ULISSE.
Azione eroica per musica in 2 acts; libretto by Luigi Prividali. Venice, La Fenice, Carnival 1809. Autograph score: I-BGc 199.

A51 RAOUL DI CREQUI.
Dramma per musica in 2 acts; libretto by Luigi Romanelli after Monvel *Raoul, Sire de Crequi*. Milan, La Scala, 26 Dec 1810. Autograph score: I-Mr; MS (incomplete): I-BGc 200.

A52 AMORE NON SOFFRE OPPOSIZIONI
(Amore irresistibile). Opera giocosa, opera buffa in 2 acts; libretto by Giuseppe Maria Foppa. Venice, San Moisé, Carnival 1810. Autograph score: I-BGc 185.

A53 L'AMOR FILIALE
(Il disertore). Farsa sentimentale in 1 act; libretto by Gaetano Rossi. Venice, San Moisé, Carnival 1811. Non-autograph score: I-BGc 178.

A54 IL SACRIFIZIO D'IFIGENIA.
Azione seria drammatica per musica in 2 acts; libretto by G. Arici, after Du Roullet. Brescia, Teatro Grande, Carn. 1811. Non-autograph score with title, *Ifigenia in Aulide*, Palermo, Teatro Carolina, 1820: US-Bm. Sinfonia and seven scenes exist in Italian libraries. [See A42 and A210]

A55 TAMERLANO.
Melodramma serio in 2 acts; libretto by Luigi Romanelli based on *Tamerlan* by Morel. Milan, La Scala, 26 Dec 1812. Autograph score: I-Mr; Non-autograph: I-BGc 202.

A56 LA ROSA BIANCA E LA ROSA ROSSA
(Il trionfo dell'amicizia), (Le due rose). Melodramma eroico in 2 acts; libretto by Felice Romani based on a libretto by G. de Pixerecourt (set by Gaveaux). Genoa, S. Agostino, 21 Feb 1813. Non-autograph scores: I-BGc 289, I-Fc A.IV. 66-67, I-Nc H.2.17-18, I-Rsc G. Mss 161-162.

A57 MEDEA IN CORINTO.
Melodramma tragico in 2 acts; libretto by
Felice Romani. Naples, San Carlo, 28
Nov 1813. Autograph score: I-Mr; Part
autograph: I-BGc 320. Ms scores in many
other libraries.

A58 ELENA
(Elena e Costantino). Dramma
eroicomico per musica in 2 acts; libretto
by Andrea Leone Tottola. Naples, Teatro
dei Fiorentini, 28 Jan 1814. Autograph
score: I-BGc 189, I-Bc, I-Fc A.IV. 64-65,
I-Nc 28.2.3-4, I-Mc, I-OS.

A59 ATAR
(Il serraglio d'Ormus). Melodramma
serio in 2 acts; libretto by Felice Romani
based on Beaumarchais's *Tarare*. Genoa,
S. Agostino, June 1814. Autograph score:
I-Mr.

A60 LE DUE DUCHESSE
(La caccia dei lupi), (Le due amiche).
Dramma semiserio in 2 acts; libretto by
Felice Romani. Milan, La Scala, 7 Nov
1814. Autograph score: I-Mr; Non-
autograph score: I-BGc 186-187; (Sinfonia in I-BGi XXXI.F.328.4486).

A61 CORA
(Complete reworking of *Alonso e Cora*).
Dramma per musica in 3 acts; libretto by
Marchese Francesco Berio di Salsa, ac-
cording to Naples simply Francesco
Berio. Naples, San Carlo, 27 March
1815. Non-autograph scores: I-Nc
28.3.36-37; 28.3.38-39. [See A33]

A62 MENNONE E ZEMIRA
(La figlia dell'aria ossia La vendetta di
Giunone). Dramma per musica in 3 acts;
libretto by Gaetano Rossi. Naples, San
Carlo, 22 March 1817. Autograph score:
I-Nc 14.2.12-14.

A63 AMOR AVVOCATO.
Commedia per musica in 1 act. Naples,
Teatro dei Fiorentini, Spring 1817. Non-
autograph scores: I-Nc X.6.713 (2 copies).

A64 LANASSA.
Melodramma eroico in 2 acts; libretto by
Gaetano Rossi and Bartolomeo Merelli
after Lemierre's *La veuve du Malabar*.
Venice, La Fenice, Dec 1817. Score lost?
Duet and Sinfonia in I-BGc. Mayr
records that this opera was subject to
numerous "cabals" of such bad taste that
he composed his last operatic works with
"malincuore". This could explain why the
full-score has disappeared.

A65 ALFREDO IL GRANDE, RE
DEGLI ANGLO SASSONI.
Melodramma per musica in 2 acts; libretto by Bartolomeo Merelli, after Rossi.
Bergamo, Teatro della Società, 26 Dec
1819. Autograph score: I-BGc 201, Non-
autograph score: I-Mc. Same subject, but
new work, as *Eraldo et Emma*. [See A37]

A66 LE DANAIDE (Danao).
Melodramma serio in 2 acts; libretto by
Felice Romani. Rome, Teatro Argentina,
Carnival 1819. Autograph score: I-Mr;
Non-autograph score: I-Fc A.IV. 71-72.

A67 FEDRA.
Melodramma serio in 2 acts; libretto by
Luigi Romanelli. Milan, La Scala, 26
Dec 1820. Autograph score: I-Mr; Non-
autograph score: I-Mc.

A68 DEMETRIO.
Dramma per musica in 2 acts; libretto
after Metastasio. Turin, Teatro Regio,
Carnival 1824. Score lost? Twelve
scenes, sinfonia and intermezzo: I-BGc,
I-Tf.

2.   Other Operas traced

A69 GLI AMANTI COMICI.
Sinfonia (reduction for pianoforte): I-Os
B3755.

A70 GL'INTRIGHI AMOROSI.
Dramma giocoso in 2 acts; libretto by
Giovanni Bertati. Parma, Teatro Ducale,
Carnival 1803. Most likely a revision or
alternative title. Ferrari in *Spettacoli in
Parma* (1844) does not suggest that it was
a new work (Don White). [See A5 and
A31]

A71 IL FINTO COMMANDANTE.
Opera buffa in 2 acts. Non-autograph
score: I-BGc 247. Traces of Donizetti's
hand - the score has no title, but libretto
would suggest that it belongs to the opera
of this title listed in *Dictionary of Opera
and Operetta*.

A72 IL MATRIMONIO SCOPERTO.
Farsa in 2 acts. 1 act and 2 act version:
I-Fc A-IV. 73; A.IV. 74-75.

A73 LA FIGLIA D'ARCIERE.
Title listed in *Dictionary of Opera and
Operetta*. Title confused with *La figlia
dell'aria*?

A74 PAMELA NUBILE.
Libretto probably based on Goldoni's
play after Richardson. Title listed in *Dictionary of Opera and Operetta*.

A75 RINALDO D'ASTE.
Opera semiseria in 2 acts. Naples, 1825.
A score of this title is in I-Nc said to have
been composed in 1825 but manuscript is
closer to 1800; the opera according to
Don White is not by Mayr: I-Nc 28.20.

3.   Operas for which Mayr composed Arias and Duets, etc.

A76 L'ADELINA.
Aria - Te di quest'anima: I-Mc.

A77 ADEMIRA.
Milan, Carnival 1797. Duet for SS -
Giuro ch'altro mai: I-Mc Tri Ms 665.

A78 ARMIDA.
(opera by Mysliweczek?) Aria for B -
Sorte ci arride: I-BGc 318.

A79 DI STUPOR, DI MERAVIGLIA.
Florence, Teatro di S. Maria, Summer
1804. Aria: I-Nc.

A80 ELFRIDA.
(Another title for *Eraldo ed Emma*?)
Naples. Aria for T (sung by Davide in
Naples) - Nel mirar sì vaghi oggetti:
I-BCc 311, I-BRc soncini 113, I-PS
B139/13.

A81 ELFRIDA RENDI AMORE.
(Il caro bene). Aria for S (or B).
Autograph score & non-autograph score:
I-BGc 318.

A82 EZIO.
(opera by Bertoni or Lampugnani?) Aria
for S - Quanto mai felici siete. I-BGc 310.

A83 GINEVRA DEGI ALMIERI.
(Opera by Farinelli?) Aria for S: I-Fc.

A84 GIULIETTA E ROMEO.
(Opera by Zingarelli?) Dramma per
musica. Verona (?). Aria written for Cres-
centi: Tutti al tuo cenno, O padre: I-Os
B.1402.

A85 GLI ZINGARI IN FIERA.
Farsa(?) in 1 act (?). Milan, 1805. Scena
Aria S (Principessa) - Come frà tante
pene: I-Gc Sc 147.

A86 IL BARONE DELUSO
(Cimarosa). Two duets
a) Chi ode frutti miei
b) D'amore mi moro mia sposa vibramo.
Published score GB-Lor.

A87 IL FINTO SORDO.
An aria for Farinelli's farsa: GB-Lor.

A88 IL RITORNO DI SERSE.
(Portugallo) Aria sung by Madame
Catalani - Oh! come scorrono tardi i
momenti. Printed in London 1810: GB-
Lor.

A89 LA SERVA INAMORATA.
Aria - Sulla tua cara mano: F-Pc.

A90 LA FORTUNA SOVRANA.
Cavatina for B (Nadir): I-BGc 318.

A91 LA MOLINARA.
1799. Cavatina for S - Oh! come è dolce
goder la libertà: I-Gc P.3.7.91.Sc3nn.

A92 LA PRINCIPESSA FILOSOFA.
Aria: Già un dolce raggio. Published Birchall: GB-Lor.

A93 LA SPOSA BISBETICA.
Sinfonia arranged for piano. Published
Imbault, Paris c1810: GB-Lbl.

A94 LE ASTUZIE FEMMINILI.
(Cimarosa). [See A370b]

A95 LE CANTATRICI VILLANE.
(Fioravanti) Duet - Son cavaliere amante.
Published Carli: GB-Lor.

A96 LE VIRTUOSE IN PUNTIGLIO.
Aria for S - Contento il cor nel seno
(Polacca). Composed for Luigi Marchesi,
also sung by Madame Salvini. Published
1791: GB-Lbl G.199(14); H.2831.a.(18).

A97 ORFEO ED EURIDICE.
(Bertoni) Chorus (TTB) - Ah! se intorno
a quest'urna funesta: I-BGc 314.

A98 PIRAMO E TISBE.
(Andreozzi?). Duet for S (Tisbe) and T
(Piramo) - L'estrema tua sorte: I-Tf
10.11.4.24.

A99 SIGISMONDO.
Aria for S and chorus: Da me che vuolsi,
o barbari: I-BGi XXVIII G 323.4467.

A100 TORQUATO TASSO.
(Opera or Cantata for school?) Terzetto
for SSS (Egina, Filinto, Tasso) -
O misero infelice: I-BGc 311.

A101 ZAIRA
(Winter). [See A370q]

A102 ZULEMA IN FIRENZE.
Recit. & Duet for S (Zulema) & T
(Gonslavo) - Ecco in sen verso la morte:
I-Mc (Noseda); I-Nc.

4. Pastiches

A103 ANNA VON EBERTSTEIN.
Vienna, 1867.

A104 BROKEN PROMISES.
Londonm Theatre Royal, 1805. Sinfonia
arranged for piano with flute obbl. by
Tho. Valentine. Welsh & Hawes 1825:
GB-Lbl.

A105 I COMMEDIANTI.
Opera buffa. Edited by Heinrich Bauer.

A106 IL CINNA.
"Opera con musica di diversi autori."
Opera made up of music of various com-
posers: I-Fc D.39.

A107 LA FINTA GALATEA.
By Marcello Bernardini, with music by
Mayr, Cimarosa and Nasolini: I-Mc
(Noseda).

A108 GINEVRA DI MONREALE.
Drama in 4 parts by Pietro Combi. Milan
1840. This is not an opera by Mayr as
often recorded but a play dedicated to
him. [Donizetti dedicated to Mayr: *San-
cia di Castiglia* (1832)].

5. Oratorios

A109 JACOB A LABANO FUGIENS.
Oratorio in 2 parts; text in Latin by
Foppa. Venice, Mendicanti, 1791?
Autograph score: I-BGc 161.

A110 SISARA.
Oratorio; text in Latin by Foppa. Venice,
Mendicanti, 1793. Non-autograph scores:
I-BGc 161, I-Mc 188.

**A111 TOBIA or TOBIAE
MATRIMONIUM.**
Oratorio in 2 parts; text in Latin and
Italian. Non-autograph scores: I-BGc
162, I-Mc 187bis.

A112 LA PASSIONE.
Oratorio; text N. N. & Metastasio. Forlì,

1794. Autograph score: I-Mc 189, Non-
autograph with autograph corrections:
I-BGc 162.

**A113 DAVID IN SPELUNCA
ENGADDI.**
Oratorio in 2 parts; text in Latin and
Italian. Venice, Mendicanti, 1795.
Autograph scores: I-BGc 160, I-Mc 185-
1. Last oratorio to be performed in the
Mendicanti before collapse of Venice
under Napoleon.

A114 IL SACRIFIZIO DI JEFTE.
Oratorio in 2 parts. Forlì. Non-autograph
scores: I-BGc 160, I-Mc 186.1.

6.   Azioni Sacre

A115 IL RITORNO DI JEFTE or IL VOTO INCAUTO.
Libretto by Jacopo Ferretti. Rome, Teatro Valle, Lent 1814. Ashbrook gives 1816. Score lost?

A116 GIOAS SALVATO.
Teatro Carolino, Palermo, 1816-17. This work was composed before *Atalia* (same subject).

A117 SAMUELE.
Text by B. Merelli (with Mayr?), Bergamo 1821. Autograph score: Ch-E, I-BGc 171 (parts only), I-Fc 2492; Non-autograph: I-PAc.

A118 SAN LUIGI GONZAGA.
Text by Pietro Cominazzi (with Mayr?), Bergamo, 1822. Autograph score: I-BGc 163-165.

A119 ATALIA.
Oratorio/Azione sacra in 2 acts; text by Felice Romani. Naples San Carlo, Lent 1822. Autograph score: I-Nc 15.3.12-13. Many Ms extracts I-BGc.

120 IFIGENIA IN TAURIDE.
Azione sacra; text by Apostolo Zeno. Florence, La Pergola, Spring 1817. Score lost? [See A42 and A54]

7.   Oratorio/Azioni Sacre - Miscellaneous

A121 SAULLE.
Lost oratorio? Recit and prayer - Ma qual sarà di quelli oscurissimi sensi. Sommo clemente Dio. T and orchestra. Non-autograph score: I-Mc, Tr Ms.656.

A122 "Frà le rosate nubi".
Autograph Ms. D-Bds. Aria from an oratorio.

8.   Cantatas - Staged

A123 FEMIO ossia LA MUSICA CUSTODE DELLA FEDE MARITALE.
Cantata, STT soli, SATB coro & orchestra in 2 acts/parts; text by Abate Boaretti. Venice, 1791. Autograph score: I-BGc 147. Mayr's first composition with orchestra.

A124 ARISTO E TEMIRA (TEMIRA E ARISTO).
Cantata drammatica scritta per Giuseppina Grassini (contralto) e coro; libretto NN. Venice, Teatro della Fenice, Spring 1795. Autograph score (not complete):

I-BGc 146. Recit and cavatina - vo cercando sventura: I-OS, I-Vc, I-Vnm.

A125 APELLE E CAMPASE.
Cantata. Venice, Teatro della Fenice, 1795. Score lost?

A126 TRAIANO ALL'EUFRATE
Cantata for S (Belloc), S (Testori), T (Alipraudi) and chorus; libretto by Angelo Anelli. Milan, La Scala, 1807. Autograph score: I-BGc 147. For Napoleon's birthday and for the Peace of Tilsit. Also, Ms: I-Mc W45-46 with title *St. Napoleone*.

A127 EGERIA.
Cantata (also listed as an azione drammatica) for TTS soli, TTB coro & orchestra in 2 acts; libretto by Cesare Arici. Brescia, 1816. Autograph score: I-BGc 78. For the arrival of the Emperor Francis at Brescia.

A128 IL SOGNO DI PARTENOPE.
Cantata, Azione Teatrale in 3 acts/parts; libretto by Carlo Schmidt. Naples, San Carlo, 13 Jan 1817 (per l'apertura del riedificato Teatro di San Carlo). Non-autograph score:, Act II only: I-Nc 64.N.230.

A129 ARIANNA E BACCO.
Cantata for soloists, chorus & orchestra in 3 parts; libretto by Bartolomeo Merelli. Bergamo, Music School, 2 May 1817. Autograph score: I-BGc 151. Composed for the Pio Istituto Musicale (home for musicians) on occasion of the plague (morbo petecchiale).

A130 ARIANNA A NASSO.
Soloists, ?chorus, orchestra. Naples? Autograph score: I-Nc 17.2.18. (dated 17:2:1818 - same title as a cantata by Haydn composed for single voice.)

9. Cantatas for more than one voice

A131 LA SVENTURA DI LEANDRO.
Cantata per voce sola, coro e orchestra; libretto by Contessa Velo. Vicenza, 1797. Autograph score: I-BGc; Autograph score (reduction for school): I-BGc 146; sinfonia: I-Mc. Written for Count Carcano.

A132 CANTATA IN MEMORY OF HAYDN'S DEATH.
Tenor, chorus & orchestra. Autograph score: I-BGi XXVIII G 335 4509. Text by Mayr. Haydn died 31 May 1809.

A133 ALCIDE AL BIVIO.
Cantata a più voci. (Sung in the school version by Donizetti, Dolci, Manghenoni, Tavecchi etc), coro e orchestra; libretto by Metastasio. Bergamo, Summer 1809. Autograph score: I-BGc 148. Autograph score (reduction for School): I-BGc 149.

A134 FERRAMONDO (or FAR(A) MONDO).
Cantata for S solo, chorus and orchestra; libretto by Count Carrara-Spinelli. Milan?, 1810. Autograph score: I-BGc 150. For Napoleon's marriage (27 March

1810) to Maria Luisa, daughter of Francis I of Austria. [See A135]

A135 CANTATA (WAR AND PEACE).
STB soli, SATB coro & orchestra; libretto by Count Carrara-Spinelli. Milan?, 1810. Autograph score: I-BGc 150. For the marriage of Napoleon with Maria Luisa of Austria. [See A134]

A136 NUMA POMPILIO.
Cantata for SST soli, STTB coro and orchestra; libretto by Count Carrara-Spinelli. 1811. Autograph score: I-BGc 78. On the occasion of the birth of the King of Rome (Napoleon's son). [See A137, A153]

A137 CANTATA.
For STTB soli, TTB coro & orchestra; libretto by Muletti. Bergamo, School, 1811. Autograph score: I-BGc 150. For the birth of the King of Rome.
[See A136, A153]

A138 LE FESTE D'ERCOLE.
Cantata for STT soli, TTB coro & orchestra; libretto by Abate Baizini. Bergamo, 1816. Autograph score: I-BGc 78. For the visit of the Emperor Francis I to Bergamo.

A139 L'ARMONIA.
Cantata in two parts for STB soli, SSAATTBB coro & large orchestra; libretto by Abate Baizini. Bergamo, 1816 (Mayr says 1825). Autograph score: I-BGc 158. Date 1825 according to Mayr who also says it was for the departure and not the arrival of Francis I. Gazzaniga gives 1816.

A140 INNO A PALLADE.
Cantata; libretto by Vincenzo Monti. Milan, 1820, not performed. Score lost?

A141 CANTATA FOR THE DEATH OF ANTONIO CAPUZZI.
For 2 voices, chorus & orchestra; libretto by Muletti. Bergamo, (Capuzzi: 1/8/1755 - 28/3/1818). Autograph score: I-BGc 151; for missing items see I-BGc 151, 184, 321.

A142 PICCOLA CANTATA.
Cantata for SATB ensemble with soli & orchestra; libretto by Mayr (?). Bergamo, 1822. Autograph score: I-BGc 158. For Mayr's election as president of the Ateneo, Bergamo.

A143 L'INNALZAMENTO AL TRONO DEL GIOVANE RE GIOAS.
Cantata for STB, chorus, large orchestra and stage band. 1822. Autograph scores: I-Bc 00.302, I-BGc 71.

A144 L'AUTUNNO.
Cantata in C Major. 1824. I-BGc 309. Only bass part and a terzetto for soloists and chorus traced.

A145 CANTATA FOR THE DEATH OF BEETHOVEN.
SATB Solists, chorus & orchestra. Bergamo, 1827. Non-autograph score: I-BGi XXVII F 3304496. Text by Mayr.

A146 SCHIERA DI FAUSTI EVENTI.
Cantata for SSTB soli, STTB coro, orchestra & pianoforte. Autograph score: I-BGc 77. For the arrival of the Emperor Ferdinand (of Austria) at Bergamo 1838.

A147 ALZANO ESULTANTE.
Cantata for Bass, chorus & orchestra. Autograph score: I-BGc 156. "Per il ricevimento del Vescovo Gritti-Morlacchi in Alzano."

A148 CANTATA (PORTRAIT CANTATA).
For STB soli, TTB coro & orchestra; libretto by Luigi Cominazzi. Bergamo. Autograph score: I-BGc 158. On the occasion of the unveiling of the portrait (paid for by Mayr) of Mons. Mai painted by Moriggia and placed in the Ateneo.

A149 COME IL SOLE
(Marriage cantata). For TTB & orchestra; libretto by Muletti. Autograph score: I-BGc 150.

A150 IL PADRE AI SUOI DILETTI FIGLI.
Cantata for SST & orchestra. Autograph score: I-BGc 310.

A151 IL PO, IL TEBRO, LA SENNA.
Cantata for STB & orchestra. Autograph score: I-BGc 155.

10. Cantatas for Soprano

A152 ERO.
Cantata per voce sola e orchestra; libretto by Giuseppe Foppa. Venice, 1793. Autograph score: I-BGc 146. Composed for Bianca Sacchetti, director of the Mendicanti.

A153 CANTATA FOR THE BIRTH OF THE KING OF ROME.
Soprano & harp obbligato and orchestra. 1811. Autograph score: I-BGc 79. [See A136, A137]

A154 LA MOGLIE DI ASDRUBALE.
Cantata for Soprano & orchestra; libretto in the style of Metastasio. For the Seminary-No. 3, 1816. Autograph score: I-BGc 152. [See A161, A176]

A155 ETTORE.
Cantata in F Major for soprano & orchestra. Autograph score: I-BGc 310.

A156 LA SENNA.
Cantata for soprano & orchestra. Autograph score: I-BGc 155.

11. Cantatas for Tenor

A157 L'AMICO TRADITO.
Cantata No. I for tenor & orchestra. Autograph score: I-BGc 153.

A158 AGAMENNONE.
Cantata for tenor & orchestra. 1813. Autograph score: I-BGc 153.

A159 LO SPAVENTO.
Cantata for tenor & orchestra. 1816. Autograph score: I-BGc 152.

A160 LA TEMPESTA.
Cantata for tenor & orchestra. For the school, 1816. Autograph score: I-BGc 152.

A161 ANNIBALE.
Cantata for tenor & orchestra. For the
Seminary-No. 1, 1816. Autograph score:
I-BGc 79. [See A154, A176]

A162 LA VITA CAMPESTRE.
Cantata for tenor and orchestra. Per-
formed 24 April 1823. Autograph score:
I-BGc 159.

A163 ACHILLE IN SCIRO.
(adapted also as Sansone.) Cantata for
tenor & orchestra. After 1831. Autograph
score: I BGc 79.

A164 ALLA TOMBA DELL'AMICO.
Cantata for tenor & orchestra. Autograph
score: I-BGc 155. Bound with two arias,
the first with clarinet obbligato.

A165 CONTRO L'INVENTORE
DELL'ORO.
Cantata for tenor & orchestra. Autograph
score: I-BGc 153.

A166 IL CORAGGIO RIANIMATO.
Cantata for tenor & orchestra. In C
Minor. Autograph score: I-BGc 156.

A167 IL POETA SCORAGGIATO.
Cantata for tenor & orchestra. Autograph
score: I-BGc 155.

A168 LA FANTASIA.
Cantata for tenor & orchestra. Autograph
score: I-BGc 159.

A169 LA POESIA AVVILITA.
Cantata for tenor, orchestra and harp obbligato. Autograph score: I-BGc 159.

A170 LA SOLITUUDINE.
Cantata for tenor, orchestra and violin obbligato. E Major. Autograph score: I-BGc
157.

A171 LEONIDA.
Cantata for tenor & orchestra. In B flat.
Autograph score: I-BGc 157.

A172 NABUCCO.
Cantata for tenor & orchestra. Autograph
score: I-BGc 310. Sung by Giacomo
David.

A173 NUMA POMPILIO.
Cantata for tenor, clarinet obbligato & orchestra. Autograph score: I-BGc 157.

A174 L'ORO NELLO SCRIGNO
DELL'AVARO.
Cantata for tenor and orchestra.
Autograph score: I-BGc 79.

A175 THREE CANTATAS: AGILULFO.
Lo splendore di tua virtude, LIUTPRAN-
DO L'istante è . . . ,AGILULFO La
regina s'appressa . . . All three for tenor
& orchestra. In E flat, D Major and F
major respectively. Autograph score:
I-BGc 156. For the Academy of Monza.

12.   Cantatas for Bass

A176 ANNIBALE A CARTAGO.
Cantata for bass & orchestra. For the
Seminary-No. 2, 1816. Autograph score:
I-BGc 159. [See A154, A161]

A177 LA FANTASIA RISCALDATA.
Cantata buffa for bass. For the School,
1816. Autograph score: I-BGc 152.

A178 L'EFFETTO DELLE RICCHEZZE.
Cantata for bass & orchestra. Autograph
score: I-BGc 157.

A179 IL BAGNO DI VINO.
Cantata buffa for bass & orchestra.
Autograph score: I-BGc 154. Composed
for the "Unione Filarmonica".

A180 IL POETA IMMAGINARIO.
Cantata buffa for bass & orchestra.
Autograph score: I-BGc 154.

A181 IL POLTRONE.
Cantata buffa for bass & orchestra.
Autograph score: I-BGc 154.

A182 IL SECOL D'OR.
Cantata buffa for bass & orchestra.
Autograph score: I-BGc 154.

A183 RODOMONTE.
Cantata for baritone & orchestra.
Autograph score: I-BGc 157.

A184 QUAL TERRIBILE VENDETTA.
Cantata sacra con sinfonia; libretto by
Metastasio. 1794. Non-autograph score:
I-Mc 193.10. [From La Passione, see
A112]

A185 LA MORTE DI ADONE.
Scena for voice (?) and pianoforte.
Autograph score (not complete): I-BGi
XXV.E.251.3766.

A186 CANTATAS.
uncatalogued I-Fn NA 711 MS.

13.   Concert Arias, etc.

A187 AMOR PERCHÉ M'ACCENDI.
Cavatina. C Major. S and orchestra. Non-
autograph-scores: I-Bas Malvezzi-Cam-
peggi IV.87/747b; with guitar accomp:
I-Rc 2853.7.c149-153, I-Tn.

A188 A UN COR GENTILE.
Scena. S, guitar, vl obbli. and orchestra.
Aria - A un cor gentile, Recit - Ne ancor
si vede il duca. Cavatina - Mio bello, mio
caro. Deh! vieni al tuo bene. Non-
autograph scores: I-Mc 661, I-Rsc.

A189 DOV' IL MIO BENE.
T, cl obbl and orchestra. Performed Trent
(Trento), Spring 1800. Non-autograph
score: I-GiL V.I.26.D.3.44, I-OS B.171.6.

**A190 DOVE SON IO, OVE
M'INOLTRO?**
Scena ed aria. T, corni obbli. and or-
chestra. Non-autograph score: I-BGi
XXVIII E.247.3618.

A191 GODI, AH! GODI, OROBIA.
Aria. A Minor. B and orchestra.
Autograph score: I-BGc 301.

A192 MIO BELLO, MIO CARO.
Cavatina. A Major. S, guitar and violin
obbli. and orchestra. Non-autograph
score: I-Rsc G.Mss.18.7.

A193 OR SEI TROPPO TENERELLA.
Aria. B, oboe and strings. "Aria 1834".
Non-autograph score (incomplete): I-BGc
323.

A194 SE IL PIO DOLCE
SENTIMENTO.
Aria. S(?), orchestra with violin obbl.
Non-autograph score: I-BGi
XXVIII.C.101.948.

A195 SUI COLLI OROBICI.
Serenata for T and chorus. Dedicated to
Rubini. Non-autograph score: I-BGi
XXVIII F324.4474.

A196 TORNA IN SEN LA DOLCE
CALMA.
Aria. S and orchestra. "Aria cantata della
Dalman". Non-autograph score: I-PAc.

A197 VIENI COLÀ T'ASPETTO
(Per il divertimento della Signora Paola
Corsi). Quartet. D Major. S (Argeo), S
(Sarpedonte), T (Ricciardo), B (Aclaste)
and orchestra. Non-autograph score:
I-Rsc G.Mss.214.

14. Soprano Arias with Orchestra

Note: Many of these soprano arias and
cavatinas may well have been composed
for use within Mayr's School, especially
those which are still to be found in Bergamo.

A198 AH! DOVE SEI, SPOSINO.
Aria. B flat. Autograph score: I-BGc 318.

A199 AH! NON MORIR.
F Major. Autograph score: I-BGc 318.

A200 AH! TROPPO DISSI (Recit).
SEMPRE QUEL CARO OGGETTO
(Aria).
E flat. Non-autograph score: I-BGc 330.

A201 ALLE DELIZIE IN SENO.
Aria. A Major. Autograph score: I-Mc
26/6a.

A202 AMOR È UN RAGAZZO.
Aria. Autograph score (incomplete):
I-BGc 323.

A203 AMOR POVERINO È CIECO.
Aria. G Major. Autograph score (incomplete): I-BGc 323.

A204 CALMA IL DUOLO, O MIA
SPERANZA.
Recit and Cavatina. F Major. Non-
autograph score: I-Mc Noseda.

A205 CALMA I TORMENTI MIEI.
Cavatina. A Major. Non-autograph score:
I-Mc Noseda.

A206 CHE PIÙ BRAMI AMOR
TIRANNO.
Scena ed aria. B flat. Non-autograph
score: I-Mc Q.10.5.

A207 CREDEI CHE AVESSE A UDIR.
Aria. G Major. Non-autograph score:
I-Mc Noseda.

A208 DEH! SE PIETOSA SEI.
Aria. Autograph score: I-BGc 311.

A209 DI QUEI LUMI A QUEL
SEMBIANTE.
Aria. B flat. Non-autograph score: I-Mc
Noseda.

A210 LA SPERANZA IN COR MI
DICE.
Aria. F Major. Autograph score: I-BGc
302.

A211 NATO SON GIÀ.
Scena and Cavatina. Venice. Non-
autograph score: I-Vnm. Performed by
Sig Crescentini (Castrato) at the Fenice.

A212 NEL COR PIÙ NON MI SENTO.
Aria. G Major. Autograph score: I-BGc
318.

A213 NELLA SORTE MIA FUNESTA.
Cavatina.
1. S and orchestra. E flat. Autograph
score: I-BGc.
2. S and piano. Autograph scores: I-BGc
303, 311.

A214 NEL SENO MI DESTI.
Cavatina. S and basso - continuo. Non-
autograph score: I-Lu (Malerbi C.199).

A215 OH! COME INTORNO TUTTO
S'INGOMBRA (Recit). ACCESO È
QUESTO CORE D'AMORE (Cavatina).
Scena. D Major. Non-autograph score:
I-Mc 658.

A216 PRESTO, MA IL PIÙ VACILLA.
Cavatina. B flat. S and strings. Autograph
score: I-BGc 311.

A217 PUPULLE CARE VI VOGLIO
AMARE.
Aria. D Major. Non-autograph score: I-
Mc Tr.mus.647.

A218 QUAL BUON RAMO.
Aria. C Major. Autograph score: I-BGc
323.

A219 QUEL CHE MOVE IL CIEL.
Aria. B flat. Autograph score: I-BGc 330.

A220 SARÀ SOL MIA GUIDA AMORE.
Cavatina. Non-autograph score: I-Bc.

A221 SON DONNA DELICATA.
Aria. Autograph score: I-BGc 247.

A222 SUONATORE SVENTURATO.
Aria. A Minor. Autograph score: I-BGc
318.

A223 VO CERCANDO L'ORE IN-
VANO.
Cavatina. D Major. Non-autograph score:
I-BGi 17850.

15.   Tenor Arias with Orchestra

A224 AH! CHI MI PARLA.
Scena ed aria. C Major. Autograph score:
D-Bds 5.

A225 A PENSIER DI TANTE PENE.
Cavatina. C Major. Cl, 2 ob, 2cr, string.
Non-autograph score: I-Ccf.

A226 È IN UN BARBARO COR.
Recit and aria. Autograph score: D-Bds 4.

A227 FRÀ CIMENTI DI SANGUE.
Aria. C Major. Autograph score (incomplete): I-BGc 323.

A228 FREMO GEMENDO IN POENA.
Aria. C Minor. Autograph score (incomplete): I-BGc 310.

A229 FRENA IL NEMICO E PALPITA.
Cavatina. E flat. Non-autograph score:
I-Mc Tr MS.660.

A230 GUARDA L'AFFANNO MIO.
Aria. B flat. Autograph score: I-BGc 318.

A231 NO! NO, D'ABBANDONARLA
SENZA UN ADDIO (Recit). ARIA DI
MIA PATRIA.
(Aria). G Major. T and strings.
Autograph score (incomplete): I-BGc 311.

A232 NON TEMER DI TRISTI AFFAN-
NI.
Aria. A Major. Autograph score: I-BGc
330.

A233 OR CON VOI M'È GRATO
ANCORA.
Aria. G Minor. Autograph score (incom-
plete): I-BGc 310.

A234 QUAL FIERO PALPITO.
Aria. C Major. Autograph score (incomplete): I-BGc 302.

A235 SE PIETOSO ALFIN.
Aria. C Major. Autograph score: I-BGc
321.

16. Bass Arias with Orchestra

A236 AMA L'INVIDIA INVANO.
Aria. C Major. Autograph score (incomplete): I-BGc 323.

A237 FA D'UOPO CHE S'ACCENDA.
Aria. F Major. Autograph score: I-BGc
Mayr M.1.318.15.

A238 FREMO GEMENDO.
Aria. D Minor. Autograph score (incomplete): I-BGc 319.

A239 FUGGITA È LA NOTTE.
Aria. E flat. Autograph score: I-BGc 318.

A240 IO NON SO PERCHÈ DA TANTI.
Cavatina Buffa. F Major. Non-autograph
score: I-Bc.

A241 NON È PIÙ IL TEMPO.
Cavatina. Non-autograph score (incomplete): I-PAc.

A242 SEMPRE UN ORRENDO
SPIRITO.
Aria. B Minor. Autograph score (incom-
plete): I-BGc 299.

17. Arias for unspecified voice and orchestra

A243 AH! COME SCORRONO.
Cavatina. Non-autograph score: I-Nc
4.N.27.

A244 CHI VIDI, CHE ASCOLTAI.
Aria. Non-autograph score: I-Nc 34.3.12.

A245 COME VIVERE POTREI.
Rondo. Ms parts only: I-Mc.

A246 ESSER MESTE NON DOVETE.
Aria. Autograph score: I-BGi
XXVIII.E.257.3816.

A247 LASCIAI DEL CAMPO.
Cavatina. Non-autograph score: I-Fc
B.747-749-751-752.

A248 OH! QUANTO È MAI DIFFICILE.
Recit and Cavatina. Non-autograph score:
I-Nc 22.2.4

A249 OMBRA DOLENTE E PALLIDA.
Scena ed rondo. ?S and orchestra. Non-
autograph score: I-MAc Mss 44/31.

A250 OVE SON IO?
Scena ed cavatina. Non-autograph score:
I-Nc 6.3.34.

A251 PAVENTI UN CORE.
Scena et aria. Non-autograph score: I-Fc
B.747-749-751-752.

A252 SE PIETÀ DELLE MIE PENE.
Cavatina. Non-autograph score: I-Nc
64.N.27.

18. Duets with orchestra

A257 GIÀ PARTO, SON PAGO.
ST and strings. Autograph score (incomplete): I-BGc 323.

A258 IO PENELOPE NOVELLA.
Buffo duet. D Major. SB. Non-autograph
score: I-Bc.

A259 MIO BEN, A TE ACCANTO.
B flat. St. Non-autograph score: I-Mc
Noseda.

A260 PERCHÈ SE VUOI.
Scena e duet. Non-autograph score: I-Fc
B.747-749-751-752.

A253 AH! CHE A SI GRAN CONTEN-
TO.
SS. Autograph score (incomplete): I-BGc
311.

A254 AMANTE MI SARAI.
ST. I-Vnm IV 1616 also I-PAc, I-Fc,
I-Mc, I-Nc.

A255 COME SCORDAR POTREI.
Scena ed aria. TT. Non-autograph score:
I-MOe.

A256 EH, DIMMI DA CHI SEI.
BB. Non-autograph score: I-PAc.

A261 PRESTO, PRESTO, ALL'ARMI.
B flat. BB. Non-autograph score: I-Bc.

A262 QUAL TENERO MOMENTO.
Recit and duet. Non-autograph score:
I-Nc 64.N.27.

A263 SE A QUEL DIO CHE AGLI
ASTRI IMPERA.
Scena and duet. SS. Non-autograph
score: I-PAc.

A264 SPEME DILETTA.
G Major. SS. Autograph score: I-BGc
330.

A265 TI LASCIO, MIA VITA.
Non-autograph score: I-Nc 64.N.26.

A266 VADA FRÀ L'ARMI.
Duetti. Non-autograph score: I-Fc 747-
752.

19. Terzettos with orchestra

A267 CEDI SUPERBO E MORI.
F Major. SST. Non-autograph score: I-Rc
2290,5.

A268 CHE BEL PIACERE AL CORE.
G Major. SSS. Autograph score: I-BGc
327. For school?

A269 COLL'INEFFABILE POTER.
(Seguito del terzetto). F Major. SST.
Autograph score (incomplete): I-BGc 302.

A270 FRÀ L'OMBRE PLACIDE.
F Minor. TBB, 2cr, fg, string. Non-
autograph score: I-BGc 316.

A271 LEI SI CINGA D'UNA SPADA.
S T B.Non-autograph score: I-Tf
211.33.c.77-96.

A272 MIA DESTRA ADORATA.
Non-autograph score: I-PAc.

A273 ODI FRAGOR.
Non-autograph score: I-Fc B105.

A274 OH! COME PALPITA IL COR
NEL SENO.
SSS, orch, fl, ob, cl, 2cr, strings.
Autograph score: I-BGc 61.

A275 O SPOSA AMABILE.
A Minor. SSB and orchestra. Autograph
score: I-BGc 327.

A276 QUAL ANGELLIN.
D Major. SSA. Autograph score: I-BGc
306. For school?

20. Quartets with orchestra

A277 PRESENTARSI A LEI
CONVIENE.
STBB. Non-autograph score: I-Tf
2.11.33.c45-76.

21. Quintets with orchestra

A278 AH! ME MESCHINA.
Quintet followed by scena and CEDO
CRUDEL (Aria for T). Non-autograph
score: I-BGc 330.

A279 SI, PARLEREMO MA POI.
SSTBB. Non-autograph score: I-Tf
1.IV.4.c.176-200.

22. Voice and chorus with orchestra or pianoforte

A280 SE SAPESSE IL MIO
TORMENTO.
Scena ed aria e coro. S with orchestra,
pianoforte and violin. Non-autograph
score: I-Bc.

A281 QUEST' ANIMA CONSOLA.
Cavatina. Voice, chorus and orchestra.
Non-autograph score: I-MAc Mss Mus
44/27.

A282 O CONTENTO.
Aria con coro. C Major. A, TB (coro) and
orchestra. Autograph score: I-BGc 305.

A283 AMELIA SVENTURATA & GIÀ
SPUNTÒ L' AMICA.
Cavatina: SSB Coro. Cavatina in A
Minor. Orchestra. Non-autograph score:
I-BGc 329. See also: Già spuntò l'amica,
coro & cavatina in A Minor. S, SSS
(coro). Autograph score: I-BGc 330.

A284 DI MIA MORTE S'HAI DESIO.
Scena, aria, finale. Voice, chorus. Non-
autograph score: I-Rc.

A285 AMELIA SVENTURATA.
Cavatina: and chorus. S, orchestra. Non-
autograph score: I-BGc 329.

23. Choruses with orchestra

A286 CAVALIER SE MORTE
ASPETTI.
A Minor. TTB. Autograph score: I-BGc
323.

A287 ECCHEGGI IN SÌ BEL GIORNO.
D Major. TTB. Autograph score: I-BGc
311.

A288 E GIÀ SORTO IL BRUNO VELO.
F Major. STTTBB. Autograph score (incomplete): I-BGc 314.

A289 GRATI ALLA DIVA I VOSTRI
INCENSI.
Non-autograph score: I-BGc 251.

A290 O GIOVE SOMIGLIA.
A Major. SSTB. Autograph score (incomplete): I-BGc 301.

A291 PIANGE L'ARMONIA.
E flat. SATB. Autograph score (incomplete): I-BGc 298.

292 SOTTO IL BEL VEZZO A MENO.
G Major. "a quattro voci." Autograph
score: I-BGc 323.

293 STELLA PIÙ FULGIDA.
Nocturne. F Major. SSB. Autograph
score: I-BGc 327.

A294 TACCIA IL FUROR DELL'ARMI.
Autograph score: I-BGc 184.

A295 TU CHE DEL FULMINE.
B flat. Autograph score (incomplete):
I-BGc 303.

A296 VIENI CHE L'ANIME QUI
TUTTE.
E flat. STB. Autograph score (incomplete): I-BGc 323.

A297 VITTORIA, VITTORIA.
D Major. TB. Autograph score: I-BGc
302.

24.   Various pieces from unidentified operas

Note: Various pieces which have been
traced to operas do not appear in this section or in this catalogue. Clues are given
in this list by the names of characters.

A298 AH! CHE FATE? (Recit),
CHETI, CHETI, COLLE BUONE (Aria)
(Marianna).
S and orchestra. Autograph score (incomplete): I-BGc 301.

A299 AH! DI FREZENE FATAL
DESTINO (Teramene).
G Major. B, chorus and orchestra.
Autograph score (incomplete): I-BGc 303.

A300 AH! INVANO CONTRO
AMORE, LA TUA SFORZA, AMORE.
Aria. B flat. T and orchestra. Autograph
score (incomplete): I-BGc 323 Sung by
"Cavaliere".

A301 AL TUO DESTIN TI LASCIO.
Duetto. SS (Mandane and Arbice) and orchestra. Non-autograph score: I-OS 1717.

A302 ATTENDI IL SOMMO INTERPRETE. (Act 1 No 1).
Duet and chorus. B flat Major. BB (Euristeo and Gran Sacerdore), TTB, chorus
and orchestra. Autograph score: I-BGc
298.

A303 ATTENTI LA MANO.
Quartet. C Major. S (Paolina), T
(Basilio), BB (Coscinnato and Tommaso)
and orchestra. Autograph score (incomplete): I-BGc 323.

A304 CAPRICCIOSO È IL DIO
D'AMORE (Lucilia).
Aria. D Minor. S and orchestra.
Autograph score: I-BGc 301.

A305 CHI DEL CIELO LA VOCE
COMPRENDE.
Trio. Capo de'Bardi, Capo de'Guerrieri,
Capo del popolo. G Major. STB (Trio),
SSTTB (Chorus) and orchestra.
Autograph score: I-BGc 301. [From cantata L'Armonia, see A139?]

A306 COME, CHE SENTO! (Act II).
Duet. F Major. S (Lauriana), B (Don
Crepazio) and orchestra. Autograph score
(incomplete): I-BGc 303.

A307 COME SOAVE IN PETTO.
Aria. A Major. S (Pippo), chorus (TB)
and orchestra. Autograph score: I-BGc
319.

A308 CON PAZIENZA
SOPPORTIAMO.
Recit and duet. B flat Major. S (Tintilla),
B (Marchese Ventinove) and orchestra.
Non-autograph score: I-Tf.

A309 DEH! TOGLIMI, AMORE. SI
FARÀ SENTIRE.
Quartet. G Major. SS (Marianna &
Dorina), T (Medoro), B (Conte) and or-
chestra. Autograph score (incomplete):
I-BGc 299.

A310 DIFFONDI IN NOI LA TUA
DIMORA (Act II No 5).
Coro. C Major. TTB and orchestra.
Autograph score (incomplete): I-BGc 302.

A311 DOVE RESPIRA L'AMATO
BENE.
Duet. Bellvue, (sic) 27 June 1813. S?
(Eugenia), T? (Eugenio) and strings. Non-
autograph score: I-GL H.1.8.

A312 DUE SOLDATI BRUTTI,
BRUTTI.
Quartet. B flat. S (Olivella), TT (Brunetto
and Nardo), B (Ministro) and orchestra).
Autograph score (incomplete): I-BGc 323.

A313 E FIA VER, AMATO BENE.
Quartet. C Major. S (Stefanino), AAT
and orchestra. Autograph score: I-BGc
318.

A314 ECCOLÀ, È DESSA (Recit),
VIENI, O FIGLIA DI REGI (Chorus)
(Act 1 No 2).
G Major. TTB and orchestra. Autograph
score: I-BGc 303.

A315 FIGLIO MIO - SEGUI - NON
POSSO.
Duet. F Major. TT (Adrasto and Autino)
and orchestra. Non-autograph scores:
I-Mc Noseda, I-Fc B.9. and 64.N.26.

A316 FRÀ IL TIMORE E LA
SORPRESA
(Per uso di Capranica). Terzetto. E flat
Major. BBB (Carlo, Martino, Pomponio)
and orchestra. Non-autograph score:
I-Bsf.

A317 GODI, ESULTA
(Marked Cavatina No 2). Trio. F Major.
TTB and strings. Autograph score: I-BGc
305.

A318 HO VISTO DA 'STE BANDE. LA
FORTEZZA È RESA (Act I No 6).
Aria. C Major. S (Marianna) and or-
chestra. Autograph score (incomplete):
I-BGc 303.

A319 IL COR IN PETTO (Recit),
ECCOMI A VOI (Aria).
G Major. S (Tusnelda) and orchestra.
Autograph score (incomplete): I-BGc 303.

A320 INCENSI E VITTIME.
Priests' chorus. F Major. TTB and
strings. Autograph score: I-BGc 319.

A321 INFELICE CHIARA CHE MAI
SARÀ DI TE (Recit), AMOR PIETOSO
AMORE (Aria).
S (Chiara) and orchestra. Non-autograph
score: I-Tf 2.VII.4.C.43-57.

A322 IO SARÒ SESTO (Finale Act I).
G Major. S (Costanza), T (Armando), B
(Michele) and orchestra. Autograph score
(incomplete): I-BGc 298.

A323 IO SON D'ALLEGRO UMORE.
Aria and chorus. E flat. S (Contessa),
chorus TB and orchestra. Non-autograph
score: I-BGc 314.

A324 LA FORTUNA SOVRANA.
Aria - Cavatina. E flat. B (Nadir). Non-
autograph score: I-BGc 318.

A325 LO CONOSCO, LO
COMPRENDO.
Cavatina. E flat. B (Biaggio) and or-
chestra. Autograph score (incomplete):
I-BGc 323.

A326 LUCINDA AMABILE.
Aria. A Minor. T (Dorante). With or-
chestra: autograph score (incomplete):
I-BGc 311. With piano: autograph score:
I-BGc 298.

A327 MIA CARA ZUCCHERINA.
Duet. F Major. A (Fiorina) and B
(Gaudenzio) and orchestra. Autograph
score (incomplete): I-BGc 311.

A328 O CIDIPPE SPIETATA.
Scena. G Major. S (Acronzio) and or-
chestra. Autograph score (incomplete):
I-BGc 311.

A329 O QUAL CONTENTO.
Aria. G Major. S (Tanso) and orchestra.
Autograph score (incomplete): I-BGc 318.

A330 SE ACCENDI L'ANIMA.
Aria. A Major. T (Valerio) and orchestra.
Autograph score: I-BGc 318.

A331 SE FRÀ L'ARMI.
Aria. ? (Montabano) and orchestra.
Autograph score: I-BGc 184.

A332 SENZA DI TE MIO SPOSO
COME VIVER POTRÒ (Recit), SENZA
IL CARO AMATO BENE (Duet).
B flat. S (Nina), B (Nane) and orchestra.
Non-autograph score: I-Mc Tr.Ms.652.

A333 SE PER VOI LE ARMATE
SPONDE.
Aria. D Major. S (Montalba), chorus, cr,
strings. Autograph score: I-BGc 317.

A334 SE QUELLA MAN MI CEDI
(Act 1 No 4). Aria. G Major. T (Tenente)
and orchestra. Autograph score: I-BGc
314.

A335 SON TUTTA GIUBILO.
Aria. S (Contessa), vl obbl and orchestra.
Non-autograph score: I-Lugo Malerbi
C.197.

A336 T'ASPETTA, T'ASPETTA.
Duet. Cavatina. A Major. S (Sabina), T
(Adriano) and orchestra. Autograph
score: I-BGc 302.

A337 VENTI QUATTR'ORE AL
PIÙ/BASTA QUEL RISO.
Cavatina. D Major. B (Tarabara) and
strings. Autograph score: I-BGc 298.

A338 VOI VEDRETE CHE A
PAOLINA.
Duet. G Major. B (Cincinnato) and B
(Tommaso) and orchestra. Autograph
score: I-BGc 301.

25.   Music for his school

Note: The following list is incomplete for it is presumed that a number of compositions and songs written for soprano voice and voices were for his students. Elsewhere in the catalogue, wherever a composition suggests it was used for students, an appropriate note is made. In the case of the religious music, "written for his school" means that a piece was composed especially with his choristers in view and not as a "school piece" in the limited sense.

A339 ACCADEMIA DEL 1810.
Scherzo musicale; libretto by Mayr, Bergamo, 1810. Autograph score (incomplete): I-BGc 126.

A340 IL PICCOLO COMPOSITORE DI MUSICA
(La prova dell'accademia finale). Scherzo musicale in 2 acts; libretto by Mayr. 1811. Autograph score: I-BGc 61. [See A44]

A341 I PICCOLI VIRTUOSI AMBULANTI.
1 act; libretto by Bartolomeo Merelli. Summer 1819. Autograph score: I-BGi, I.1a.A.b. See Jeremy Commons, Donizetti Society Journal No 2, 1975.

A342 UN BUON CUORE FA PERDONARE DELLE INCONSIDERATEZZE.
Scherzo musicale in 2 acts; libretto by Mayr. 1820. Autograph score: I-BGc 126.

A343 GIUSEPPE.
Azione drammatica in 3 acts; libretto by Mayr and students. 1830. Autograph score: I-BGc 128.

A344 IL GIOVEDÌ GRASSO.
Scherzo musicale in 1 act. Non-autograph score: I-BGc 173.

A345 FANCIULLI ANCORA E ALUNNI DI CARITÀ.
Chorus for 3 soprano parts and orchestra. Autograph score: I-BGc 318.

A346 Various unlisted compositions for the School. Autograph scores: I-BGc 173.

A347 Solfeggi for S.
Autograph score: I-BGi XI.E.247.3621.

A348 Solfeggi for S.
Autograph score: I-BGi XI.G.373.4762.

A349 Duet.
SS/pianoforte. Te sola adorai. Autograph score: I-BGc 303.

A350 Quartet for SSSS.
Pria che di nuovo. F Major. Autograph score: I-BGc 319.

A351 Sextet for SSSSSS, orchestra.
Quali accenti. A Major. Autograph score: I-BGc 319.

A352 Song: Qual infuocata quaglia (from Petrarch).
Composed for Donizetti when a student. S, piano and instruments. F Major. Autograph score (incomplete): I-BGc 314.

26. Collections - mostly songs

Note: Song titles may appear in more than one collection.

A353 LIEDER BEIM KLAVIER ZU SINGEN,
von J. Simon Mayr, Regensburg (Joh. Leopold Montags Erben) 1786. Non-autograph score: GB-Lbl, GB-Lor etc.

a) Lied: Ich gieng unter Erlen am kühligen Bach.

b) Gute Nacht an mein Mädchen: Vom blauen Himmel hell und fein.

c) Der Talisman: Lebt' ich in goldnen Feenzeiten.

d) Lied: Ich ging im Mondenschimmer.

e) Lied eines Mädchens: Noch bin ich jung von Jahren.

f) Ständchen: Wenn die Nacht in süßer Ruh.

g) Zufriedenheit: Ich bin vergnügt.

h) Lied eines nordischen Wilden: Mein Weib, mein süßes Weib ist hin!

i) Mädchensitte: Ein hübsches sanftes Knäbchen saß.

j) Die Nachtigall: Ich sah ein Mädchen.

k) Der Händedruck: Der Geliebten Hand berühren.

l) An Laura. Das Schweigen der Liebe: Treu geliebt und still geschwiegen.

A354 8 ITALIAN AND GERMAN SONGS.
Contralto and pianoforte. Autograph score: I-BGc 47.

a) Da chi naqui il nutrimento.

b) Gute nacht

c) La pace de' santi.

d) Sie Schwalben ziehn.

e) Perchè si mesto, oh Zeffiro.

f) Die Wasser ziehn.

g) Luci mie belle.

h) Still ist die heilge Nacht.

A355 12 CANZONETTE.
Non-autograph score: GB-Lor.

a) Quando pensate o quell'istante.

b) Per carità Bettina.

c) Dime aveta abonoriva.

d) Per ti Nina (La domanda).

e) La farfaletta.

f) Donne l'amore è un scaltro.

g) Cattina bellina graziosa (La stracavata).

h) Sempre più t'amo (Ad Amalia).

i) Compagni amor lasciate.

j) La mia Ninetta.

k) Se amor mai da vu se vede (El conseggio).

l) Non xè l'età freschissima.

A356 3 ITALIAN CANZONETTES.
T. Monzani. 1800. Harp or piano or flute with tambourine. Non-autograph score: GB-Lbl G.424(b).

a) La farfaletta.

b) L'amore.

c) La primavera.

A357 8 ARIAS.
Voice and pianoforte. Autograph score: I-BGc 317.

a) Come è dolce cosa goder.

b) Tu di quest'anima delizia e amore.

c) Ah! quando stringesti.

d) Dolce sono invan.

e) Amante mi sarete.

f) Ma che miro?

g) Chi vive senza amore.

h) Resta o caro amor.

A358 FIVE ARIAS FOR ONE AND TWO VOICES.
SS and pianofore. Non-autograph score: I-Vmc.

a) Calma, tormenti miei - S.

b) Caro oggetto che io sospiro - S.

c) Chi dice mal d'amore - S.

d) Qual tremendo sentier - SS.

e) Ah! non so dirti addio - SS.

A359 11 SONGS IN VENETIAN DIALECT.
Voice and pianoforte. Non-autograph score: I-Vmc Correr 161-196, 192.

a) Per carità Bettina.

b) Dime aveta abonoriva.

c) Per ti Nina pien d'affetto.

d) La mia Ninetta se fatta.

e) Cattina bellina (La stracavata).

f) Se amor mai da vu se vede (El conseggio).

g) Non xè l'età freschissima.

h) Si xè verissimo.

i) La mia Bettina.

j) Mico ti vedo.

k) Sentì mio core.

A360 5 ARIAS, TRIOS, DUETS.
STTB, pianoforte. Drinking songs. Autograph score: I-BGc 318.

a) Voi che cerchio amici fate - STT. [See A420]

b) Viva Bacco e chi n'appresta - STT.

c) Bacco di Bacco - T.

d) Viva Bacco - ST.

e) ? - ?

A361 THREE ARIAS.
S and pianoforte. Autograph score: I-BGc 318.

a) Qui sospirò, là rise.

b) O cara memoria di tenero affetto.

c) Se posso spirare.

A362 TWO SONGS.
S and pianoforte. Non-autograph score: I-BGc 231.

a) Per valli, per boschi.

b) No, mia bella il sol.
(Accompaniment not completely realized.)

A363 Voice, vl, cello and pianoforte.
Non-autograph score: I-BGc 47.

a) Swedish song.

b) Bavarian song.

A364 SIX SONGS.
S and pianoforte. Non-autograph score: I-OS B.3766.

a) Quando penso a quell'istante.

b) Per ti Nina pien d'affetto.

c) Donne, l'amore è un scaltro.

d) Sempre più t'amo.

e) Se amor mai da vu se vede (El conseggio).

f) Per carità Bettina.

A365 13 SONGS.
S and pianoforte. Autograph score:
I-BGc 47.
a) Vicino a Nina.

b) Per carità Bettina.

c) Donne l'amore è un scaltro.

d) Non xè l'età freschissima.

e) La mia Ninetta.

f) Ho già penato.

g) Compagni, amor lasciate.

h) Cattina bellina.

i) Si xè verrissimo.

j) Se amor mai da vu se vede.

k) Per ti Nina pien d'affetto.

l) Dime aveta abonoriva.

m) Mico ti vedo.

A366 Arias and duet for SS and
pianoforte.
Non-autograph score: I-PAc.
a) Povero cor, tu senti - S.

b) Spirar se m'è dato - S.

c) Idol mio, sempre così - SS.

A367 CANZONETTE E DUETTINI.
2 Voices and pianoforte. Non-autograph
score: I-BGc 231.
a) Bella Dea - song.

b) Dolce sogno - song.

c) Amante mi sarete - duet.

d) Nato son già alle lagrime - song.

e) Chi vive senza amore - song.

f) Quel tremendo sentier - duet.

A368 COLLECTIONS - 14 "PICCOLI
PEZZI PER PIANOFORTE, CANTO E
PIANOFORTE".
Autograph score: I-BGc 310.
a) La primavera - S and piano.

b) Allegretto - piano.

c) Allegro - piano.

d) La pace - SS (Duet).

e) Clori e Fileno - S and piano.

f) Walzer - piano.

g) Andantino - piano.

h) La bellezza - S and piano.

i) Allegro molto - piano.

j) Allegro - piano.

k) Già la notte s'avvicina - S and piano.

l) Allegro - piano.

m) Minuet - piano.

n) Chi non intende che cossa è amore - S
    and piano.

A369 CAVATINE ED ARIE.
Voice and pianoforte. Non-autograph
score: I-Ls C40.

A370 VARIOUS PRINTED SONGS.
Autograph score: GB-Lor.
a) Ad Amalia - London, Canzonetta
    VIII. "Sempre più t'amo".

b) Amante me sarete - Birchall. Sung in
    Cimarosa's opera *Le astuzie femminili*.

c) Amato fileno - Birchall. A favourite
    duet. 1800.

d) Chi non intende - Birchall. A
    favourite air.

e) Campagni amor lasciate - London,
    Canzonetta IX.

f) El consegio - Monzani & Cimador,
    Canzonetta Veneziana.

g) La domanda - London, Canzonetta IV, Per ti Nina pien d'affetto.

h) Dove sono? Oh ciel che sento? - Cianchettini & Sperati, Ariette Italiane.

i) La farfaletta - Monzani. Canzonetta No 12.

j) Idolo mio sempre così - The author, Duettino.

k) Ariette e Duettini - Cappi, Vienna.

l) A Bettina - Monzani & Cimador, Canzonetta Veneziana.

m) 2 Canzonette ed 1 Duettino - Artaria.

n) Donne l'amore - Lavenu, Venetian canzonet.

o) Grazie agli inganni tuoi - Walker, Canzonetta.

p) Luci mie belle - Artaria, Romanza.

q) Nel mirar quel vago oggetto - Holst, Aria sung in Winter's *Zaira*.

r) Per quell'amabile dolce sembiante - Romagnesi, Paris, Song.

s) Povero core intendo i tuoi sospiri - Ariettes Italiènnes, Paris, Cavatina.

t) La mia Ninetta è fatta a calazetta - London, Canzonetta X.

u) Mio bello, mio caro - Monzani & Hill, Cavatina, 1820.

v) Nice dorme - Meissonier, Cavatina. 1820 (acc. lyre or guitar).

w) Non mi sprezzar Fileno - Author, No 4.

x) Quando penso a quell'istante - Monzani & Cimador.

y) Se amor mai da vu - London, Canzonetta XI.

z) Sicuro asilo e placido - Author, No 6.

aa) Non x'è età freschissima - London, Canzonetta XII.

bb) La stracavata - London, Canzonet VII, "Cattina bellina graziosa vu se ".

cc) Tornasti o primavera - Birchall, A favourite canzonet.

dd) Vecchiarello vecchiarello - Birchall, A favourite duet.

27. Songs: voice, pianoforte, guitar, etc.

A371 ALFIN RITORNA, O CARO (Recit), ECCO A TE ME GUIDA AMORE (Aria).
Arranged by Dr. J. Clarke. Pianoforte. London, 1815? Non-autograph score: GB-Lbl H.2815.c.(28).

A372 ALTA È LA NOTTE.
Aria. E flat. S and pianoforte. Autograph score: I-BGc 323.

A373 AMANTE MI SARAI.
Duet. ST with pianoforte. London, 1804. Non-autograph score: I-BGi (785). "For the use of Mrs. Cattina Grazioni". Printed score: GB-Lbl H.2815.c.(29).

A374 ARDE L'ARA SULL'ALE DE'VENTI.
Chorus. D Major. TTB. Autograph score (incomplete): I-BGc 314.

A375 AU MARDI QUI VIENT.
Chorus. D Major. SSTTB and pianoforte.
Autograph score (incomplete): I-BGc 302

A376 BARBARO, IO NON
COMPRENDO.
Quartet. C Major. SSTT and basso-continuo. Autograph score: I-BGc 311.

A377 BELLE, CHE AMOR.
A Major. T, 2 vl and fl. Autograph score
(incomplete): I-BGc 317.

A378 CARO MIO BEN.
Cavatina. D Major. S and pianoforte.
Non-autograph score: I-Mc Noseda.

A379 CEDERÀ LA MIA COSTANZA.
Aria. T and pianoforte. Autograph score:
I-BGc 318.

A380 CHI DICE MAL D'AMORE.
Cavatina. Voice and guitar. Beilage zur
Allgemeinen Musikalischen Zeitung.
Printed score: I-BGc 310. [See A358c]

A381 CHI VIVE SENZA AMORE.
S and pianoforte. Non-autograph score:
I-Mc Noseda. [See A357g]

A382 DEH! M'ASCOLTA.
Octet for voices. Non-autograph score:
I-Tn Giordano 284.

A383 DOLCE FIAMMA DEL MIO
CORE.
Aria. Voice and pianoforte. Cianchettini
& Sperati, London 1808. Printed score:
GB-Lbl F1888a(1). With flute obbli. by
C. M. Sola, 1830. G.811.n.(21).

A384 DOVE SONO?
Aria. Arranged for pianoforte by G. Spontini. Chez Mlles Erard, Paris 1805?
Printed score: GB-Lbl G.811.a.(25).

A385 GLI INFELICI E CARI OGGETTI.
Scena & aria. C Major. Tenor and
pianoforte. Non-autograph score: I-BGc
Mayr B.11.2.

A386 GRAZIE AGLI INGANNI TUOI.
Canzonetta. Voice and harp or
pianoforte. Monzani, 1800. Printed score:
GB-Lbl G.424(10). [See A387]

A387 GRAZIE AGLI INGANNI TUOI.
Song. Metastasio. S and pianoforte.
Autograph score: I-BGc 316. [See 386]

A388 IDOLO MIO.
Duet. G Major. ST and pianoforte. Non-
autograph score: I-BGc 327.

A389 INCERTO S'AGGIRA.
Cavatina. S and orchestra. Orchestrated
by Benedetto Donelli. Non-autograph
score: I-Bc. Originally a song.

A390 IO CHE INTESI.
Duet with pianoforte. Non-autograph
score: I-MAC 44/28.

A391 LA BIONDINA IN
GONDOLETTA.
Song. Voice and guitar. Printed score:
I-Mc. [See, Un secolo di canzoni p. 268]

A392 LA GONDOLETTA.
Song. Voice and pianoforte. From Raccotta di canzonette popolare, Veneziane.
Ricordi 1839. I-Mc. [See N.16]

A393 LIEVI AURETTE.
Aria. F Major. T, 2 fl, harp and corno di
bassetto. Autograph score (incomplete):
I-BGc 323.

A394 LOIN DE NOUS.
Song. G Minor. Voice, ob and pianoforte.
Autograph score: I-BGc 314.

A395 MES SOUVENIRS.
Song. Paroles de M. Waninka. Musique
et accomp. de guitare par Mayer. Chez
Frère fils: Paris 1815? Non-autograph
score: GB-Lbl E.1717.p.(51).

A396 NON MI SPREZZAR, FILENO.
Song. S and guitar. Zamboni & Maina,
Venice, 1808. Printed score: I-BGc 231.

A397 OH! COME SCORRONO TARDI
I MOMENTI.
Song. S and guitar. Autograph score (in-
complete): I-BGc 318.

A398 OH! QUANTO T'AMO.
Aria. E flat. S and pianoforte. Autograph
score: I-BGc 318.

A399 OHIMÈ QUAL INCERTO
ORACOLO.
Motet. E flat. STB and pianoforte.
Autograph score: I-BGc 61.

A400 OMBRE DE' RE D'EROI.
Aria. B flat. T, strings and basso-continuo. Autograph score: I-BGc 302.

A401 OVE SON?
Motet. C Minor. B, 2 ob, 2 cr and strings.
Autograph score: I-BGc 62.

A402 PARTO SE VUOI MIA VITA.
Duet. Pianoforte. Monzani & Cimador,
London, 1804. Non-autograph score: GB-
Lbl, H.1980(3).[See A403]

A403 PARTO SE VUOI MIA VITA.
Duet. Pianoforte. Monzani & Cimador,
London, 1804. Printed score: GB-Lbl,
H.1980.j.(3).[See A402]

A404 PER QUELL'AMIABILE DOLCE
SEMBIANTE.
Cavatina. Pianoforte. Birchall, London,

1820? Printed score: GB-Lbl,
G.806.c.(39).

A405 PERCHÈ SÌ MESTO, O ZEFFIRO.
Song. G Minor. Voice and pianoforte.
Autograph score (incomplete): I-BGc
298. [See A354e]

A406 POVERO COR.
Arietta. E Major. S and pianoforte.
Autograph score: I-BGc 318; Non-
autograph score: I-Nc 6.2.36.

A407 QUALE AMABILE CONCENTO.
Terzetto with pianoforte. Non-autograph
score: I-Nc Arie 186.

A408 QUANDO DA TE LONTANO.
Romanza. E flat. Voice and pianoforte.
Non-autograph score (incomplete): I-BGc
302.

A409 QUANDO PENSO A
QUELL'ISTANTE.
Canzonet. Monzani & Cimador, 1800?
Printed score: GB-Lbl H.2831.a.(20).
[See A410]

A410 QUANDO PENSO A
QUELL'ISTANTE.
(Different version?) Canzonet. G Major.
Voice and piano. Printed score: D-Mbs.
[See A409]

A411 QUESTO SERTO.
Arietta. Voice and pianoforte. Artaria,
Milan. In Trovatore italiano. I-Mc. [N.43]

A412 QUESTA VITA CHI MI DIEDE.
Aria. G Major. S and pianoforte.
Autograph score: I-BGc 327.

A413 SE MI METTO.
Cavatina. B flat. S, fl and strings.
Autograph score: I-BGc 323.

A414 SE POSSO MIRARE IN
BRACCIO AL MIO BENE.
Cavatina. S and pianoforte. "Per uso delle
Signore Gerardi". Non-autograph score:
I-Nc Arie 186.

A415 SE TI RIVEDRÒ.
Song. S and strings. Autograph score (incomplete): I-BGc 323.

A416 SENTO NEL CORE UN PALPITO.
Ariettina. B flat. S and pianoforte. Non-
autograph score: I-Mc Noseda.

A417 SPIRAR SE M'È DATO IN
BRACCIO AL BIO BEN.
Arietta. F Major. Voice and pianoforte.
Non-autograph score: I-Nc. Capece
minutolo 6.2.36, Ms No 241-244.

A418 SPIRAR SE POTESSI.
Aria. S and pianoforte. Autograph score:
I-BGc 327.

A419 VENETIAN SONG FOR 3
VOICES.
Autograph score: I-BGi
XXV.D.198.2575.

A420 VOI CHE CERCHIO AMICI
FATE.
Bacchic Chorus for male voices. TTTBB.
Autograph score: I-BGc 318. [See A360a]

28.   Sinfonie

The following are catalogued as sinfonie
(rather than overtures) since the pieces do
not have titles and were most likely items
composed for orchestral concerts or special occasions or as new overtures for successful operas. They are:
1. Sinfonie with a full-score.

2. Sinfonie with a violino principale (of
    these the orchestral parts only have
    survived).

3. Sinfonie with parts only, the full score
    being lost.

4. Unfinished Sinfonie scores.

The overtures bound with manuscripts of
operas are not listed here. Mayr's overtures present an enormous problem. It is
hard often to state which overture was
specifically composed for which opera,
since Mayr often wrote new overtures for
revivals. The following is a tentative listing.

I   Full Scores

A421 SINFONIA IN C MAJOR.
Autograph score: I-BGc 329.

A422 SINFONIA IN C MAJOR.
Andantino 6/8-Allegro 4/4. Gift by Mayr
to the Accademia (Milan). 28 parts.
Autograph score: I-Mc. A.61.185.3.

A423 SINFONIA A GRANDE
ORCHESTRA N.9. C MAJOR.
Non-autograph score: I-Nf.

A424 SINFONIA IN C MAJOR.
Maestoso-Allegro. Non-autograph score:
I-OS B.3752.

A425 SINFONIA IN C MAJOR.
Largo-Allegro. Non-autograph score:
I-OS B.3752.

A426 SINFONIA IN C MAJOR.
Non-autograph score: I-PAc.

A427 SINFONIA IN C MINOR
"ATTO V".
Allegro moderato. Autograph score:
I-BGc 311.

A428 SINFONIA IN D MAJOR.
Autograph score: I-BGc Calvi 2.33.

A429 SINFONIA IN D MAJOR.
Autograph score: I-BGc 311.

A430 SINFONIA IN D MAJOR.
Autograph score: I-BGc 318.

A431 SINFONIA IN D MAJOR.
Autograph and non-autograph scores:
I-BGc 329.

A432 SINFONIA IN D MAJOR.
Non-autograph score: I-Tf.

A433 SINFONIA PER L'APERTURA
DI PIACENZA L'ESTATE 1804.
D Major largo. Maestoso-Allegro. Non-
autograph score: I-OS B.3759. [See A36?]

A434 SINFONIA MAYER.
D Major. Maestoso-Allegro vivace. Non-
autograph score: I-OS B.3760.

A435 SINFONIA IN D MAJOR.
Largo-Allegro. Non-autograph score:
I-PAc.

A436 SINFONIA BREVE IN E FLAT.
Autograph score: I-BGc 251.

A437 SINFONIA IN E FLAT.
Autograph score: I-BGc 301.

A438 SONFONIA IN E FLAT.
Maestoso-Allegretto vivace - Allegro-
vivace. Also reduction for piano/G. Pres-
tinanari 1801. Non-autograph score: I-OS
B.3761.

A439 SINFONIA.
Non-autograph score: I-CORc.

SINFONIA IN D MAJOR.
[See A1502, section 74]

II Sinfonie with Violin principale

Parts only survive - 19 in each case; fl,
2ob, 2cl, fg, 2cr, tr, trb, timps, Vl I princ,
Vl I, Vl II princ, Vl II, 2Vle, cello, ob
listed in order: No
6,1,2,3,4,7,8,9,10,11,12, (No 5 misplaced)

SINFONIA No 1 I MISTERI
ELEUSINI, see A28.

A440 SINFONIA No 6 IN C MAJOR.
Larghetto-Allegro.

A441 SINFONIA No 2 IN D MAJOR.
Larghetto non tanto-allegro vivace.

SINFONIA No 3 ELISA, see A35.

A442 SINFONIA No 4 IN D MINOR.
Andante sostenuto-allegro vivace.

A443 SINFONIA No 7 IN C MAJOR.
Allegro maestoso-Allegro vivace.

A444 SINFONIA No 8 IN D MINOR.
Largo-Allegro.

A445 SINFONIA No 9 IN B FLAT
MAJOR.
Andantino-allegro.

A446 SINFONIA No 10 IN C MAJOR.
Largo-Allegretto.

A447 SINFONIA No 11 IN C MAJOR.
Allegro maestoso-Allegro vivace.

A448 SINFONIA No 12 IN C MAJOR.
Maestoso-Allegro

III Sinfonie with Parts only

A449 SINFONIA IN C MAJOR.
Largo C; Allegretto 6/8; Allegretto 2/4. I-
Mc A.61.185.5.

A450 SINFONIA IN D MAJOR
(PRIMA COPIA).
Maestoso 4/4; Grazioso 6/8; Allegro
vivace 2/4. I-Mc A.61.185.6.

A451 SINFONIA IN D MAJOR.
I-Tf 51x286.

A452 SINFONIA IN D MINOR.
Andantino - Allegro. I-Mc A.61.186.1.
Mayr copied parts for the Academy in
Milan 1826.

A453 SINFONIA IN TEMPO DI
POLLONESE IN D MAJOR.
I-Tf H.1.26.

A454 SINFONIA IN D MINOR.
Allegro con Brio 4/4. I-Mc A.61.186.2.

A455 SINFONIA IN D MAJOR.
I-BGi XXX.I.F329.4491.

A456 SINFONIA IN D MAJOR.
I-BGi XXXI.G.331.4501.

A457 SINFONIA IN E FLAT.
Maestro cantabile - Allegro vivace.
I-CRg.

A458 SINFONIA CONCERTATA A
GRANDE ORCHESTRA: E FLAT.
Largo-Allegro vivace. I-CRg.

A459 SINFONIA IN F MAJOR.
2ob, 2cr, strings. I-BGc 306.

A460 SINFONIA IN G MAJOR.
I-OS B.47.

A461 SINFONIA CON MOLTI
STROMENTI OBBLIGATI.
Apertura Piacenza, 1805. I-Gil Sc41.

A462 SINFONIA.
I-BGi XXXI.G.331.4502.

IV Sinfonias with incomplete autograph orchestral scores

There is no certain explanation why there
are so many incomplete autograph orchestral scores. It is possible that Mayr
composed directly into parts in order to
save himself work. Generally, they would
have not been performed with a conductor in the modern sense but directed by
the Violino Principale.

A463 SINFONIA IN C MAJOR.
Autograph score: I-BGc 301.

A464 SINFONIA IN C MAJOR.
Autograph score: I-BGc 301.

A465 SINFONIA IN C MAJOR.
Autograph score: I-BGc 311.

A466 SINFONIA IN C MAJOR.
Autograph score: I-BGc 329.

A467 SINFONIA IN C MINOR.
Autograph score: I-BGc 302.

A468 SINFONIA IN C MINOR.
Autograph score: I-BGc 311.

A469 SINFONIA IN C MINOR.
Autograph score: I-BGc 323.

A470 SINFONIA IN C MINOR.
Autograph score: I-BGc 323.

A471 SINFONIA IN D MAJOR.
Autograph score: I-BGc 301.

A472 SINFONIA IN D MINOR.
Autograph score: I-BGc 314.

A473 SINFONIA IN E MINOR.
Autograph score: I-BGc 302.

A474 SINFONIA IN E MINOR.
Autograph score: I-BGc 323.

A475 SINFONIA IN E MINOR.
Autograph score: I-BGc 302.

A476 SINFONIA IN F MAJOR.
Autograph score: I-BGc 302.

A477 SINFONIA IN F MINOR.
Autograph score: I-BGc 323.

A478 SINFONIA/OUVERTURE.
B flat. Larghetto maestoso/Allegro. Non-autograph score: I-Ria Ms219.

29. Concertos

A479 PIANO CONCERTO NO.1 IN C.
Autograph and Non-autograph scores:
I-BGi XXIX.E.213.3022; I-Colombaro,
Biblioteca privata Barcella.

A480 PIANO CONCERTO NO.2 IN C.
I-BGi XIV.E.213.3023.

A481 SINFONIA CONCERTATA FOR
THREE VIOLINS.
Autograph score: I-BGi
XXIX.F.283.4208.

A482 SINFONIA CONCERTATA FOR
PICCOLO/FLUTE/CLARINET/BASSET
HORN.
Autograph score: I-BGc C.4.36. "for the
use of Sig Giovanni Sangiovani.

A483 CONCERTINO FOR BASSOON
AND ORCHESTRA.
Autograph score (incomplete): I-BGc 252.

A484 GOD SAVE THE KING
(incomplete). For 4 hands, Pianoforte and
orchestra. Modern edition completed by
Ian Schofield. Autograph score: I-BGi
Piatti Lochis 9689.

A485 VARIAZIONI FOR THE YOUNG
PIATTI, IN G MAJOR.
Circa 1830. Cello and orchestra.
Autograph score: I-BGc 49. Incomplete
score.

30. Orchestral

A486 INTERMEZZO IN D.
Autograph score: I-BGc 301.

A487 INTERMEZZO IN E MINOR.
Autograph score: I-BGc 311.

A488 INTERMEZZO IN F.
Autograph score: I-BGc 323.

A489 MARCIA IN E.
Autograph score: I-BGc 252.

A490 MARCIA IN D.
Autograph score: I-BGc 252.

A491 MARCH - GRAND MARCH OF
GEN. DE LA ROMANA.
The Rising of the Sun. 1810. Autograph
score: GB-Lbl H.1480.X.(21).

A492 INTRODUZIONE.
Atto I. In F Major. Autograph score:
I-BGc 314. L'intrigo della lettera.

PAS DE DEUX.
(See A494 under section: BALLET).

31. Ballet

A493 LA NOCE DI BENEVENTO.
(1812).
a) Contradanza in D (for guitar). I-
    Colombaro Biblioteca Privata Barcel-
    la 39h.p.15.
b) Introduction for witches and devils
    (for piano). I-OS B.3743.

c) Terzetto danced by Salvatore Viganò
    (for band). I-OS B.3742.

A494 PAS DE DEUX.
(From La noce di Benevento?). In D
Major. Full score. Autograph score:
I-BGc 311.

32. Pianoforte with other Instruments

A495 SIX FIORETTI.
For piano and bassett horn. Non-
autograph score: I-BGc II.1 II 38.

A496 TWO PIECES FOR HORN AND
PIANOFORTE.
F Minor and F Major. Autograph score:
I-BGc 314.

A497 SONATE PER FLAUTO E
PIANOFORTE.
Autograph score: I-BGi XXI.D.198.2573.

A498 SONATA "A 3" IN F MAJOR.
For clarinet, violone and pianoforte.
Autograph score: I-BGc 248. Erroneously

catalogued "by Mayr": by Guiseppe Manghenoni.

A499 SONATA "A 3" IN B FLAT.
For cl, violone and pianoforte. Autograph score: I-BGc 248. Erroneously catalogued "by Mayr": by Giuseppe Manghenoni.

A500 SONATA FOR VIOLIN AND PIANOFORTE.
Autograph score: GB-Lor.

33.   Pianoforte solo

A501 ALLEGRO DI SIMON MAYR PER PIANOFORTE.
Transcription? Non-autograph score: I-OS B.4448.

A502 ADAGIO NO 15 (E FLAT) FOR PIANOFORTE.
Autograph score: I-BGi XXIV.G.376.4782.

A503 NEAPEL UND DIE NAPOLETANER FOR PIANOFORTE.
Aldenburg, 1840. Non-autograph score: I-Mc Noseda C.1.

A504 LA DAMA SOLDATO: SONATINA FOR PIANOFORTE.
Non-autograph score: I-MOe F708. This is an example of Mayr taking a theme from Orlandi's opera, *Per voi frà mezzo all'anni.*

A505 LITTLE PRELUDES & EXERCISES FOR PIANOFORTE.
Composed for the inauguration of the piano school 1805. Various pieces. Autograph score: I-BGi XIV.E.214.3025; VIV.E.214.3033; II.E.214.3032.

A506 PICCOLI PEZZI.
For pianoforte. (Volume bound with soprano songs). Allegreto; Allegro;

Allegro, minuet, walzer, andantino, Allegro motto, allegro. Autograph score: I-BGc 310.

A507 SIX SHORT PRELUDES.
For pianoforte in D Minor. Autograph score: I-BGi XIV.E.214.3030.

A508 EIGHT DIVERTIMENTI.
For piano;
a) Allegro, b) marcia, c) polacca, d) tempo di minuetto, e) Allegretto, f) allemande, g) allegro, h) 5 variations on "Nanetta sventurata", and: Divertimenti per l'anno 1820. Non-autograph score: I-OS B.3764/a/b. Belonged to Marianna Anelli - daughter of librettist?

A509 TWO DIVERTIMENTI.
Per cembalo. Non-autograph score: I-Vnm Cod It IV 1486, Cod It IV 486.

A510 VARIATIONS.
For pianoforte on a theme in "Cora". Non-autograph score: I-Mc Noseda.

A511 VARIAZIONI E SUONATE IN D MAJOR.
Ad uso d'orchestra per il clavicembalo. Maestoso - cantabile - Allegretto - Allegro. Non-autograph score: I-OS B.3765.

A512 VARIAZIONI PER CEMBALO.
In B Major. Non-autograph score:
I-Colombaro, Biblioteca Privata Barcella.

A513 FIFTEEN STUDIES FOR
CEMBALO.
Non-autograph score: I-BGc NC.1.16.

A514 FORTY THREE STUDIES FOR
CEMBALO.
Autograph score: I-BGc Cass.I.i.II39-42.

A515 SONATINA, MINUETTI E
VALZER.
For clavicembalo. Non-autograph score:
I-Vnm Ms.c.9.

A516 DUE SONATINE PER
CEMBALO.
A 4 Mani. Autograph score: I-BGi
XV.D.168.1753.

A517 SONATINE PER CEMBALO.
Autograph score: I-BGi XIV.E.214.3031.

A518 SONATA IN D MAJOR FOR
CEMBALO.
1816. Non-autograph score: I-PEsp
M.CXXXII/42.c7-9.

A519 THREE SONATAS FOR
CEMBALO.
Non-autograph score: I-Vnm Cod It IV
1486.

A520 SPAGNUOLA, COSSACCA
and another piece for cembalo.
Autograph score: I-BGc 47.110.

A521 SUONATE, RONDÒ ED
ANDANTE PER CEMBALO.
Non-autograph score: I-OS B.3763/1-4.

A522 TRE SINFONIE PER
FORTEPIANO.
Non-autograph score: I-MOe F.705.707.

A523 THREE SINFONIE FOR
CEMBALO
Non-autograph score: I-TN (Foà Gior-
dano) 361.

A524 SINFONIA IN E FLAT MAJOR.
"For the use of Mauro Bini". No 60. Non-
autograph score: I-PEsp M.CXXXI/31.

A525 SINFONIA IN D MAJOR.
Non-autograph score: I-Colombaro,
Biblioteca Privata Barcella.

A526 SINFONIA IN D MAJOR.
Andante maestoso 4/4, Allegro 2/4. Non-
autograph score: I-Vqs C1.VIII 29-1129.

A527 SINFONIA IN C MAJOR FOR
PIANOFORTE.
Maestoso-allegretto-allegretto vivace.
Non-autograph score: I-OS B.2035. Pos-
sibly transcription not by Mayr.

34. Harp

A528 SUITE OF EIGHT PIECES FOR
HARP.
Autograph score: I-BGc 248.

35. Wind music

A529 TWENTY-NINE PIECES FOR TWO HORNS.
Non-autograph score: I-BGc B.8.7.

A530 BAGATELLA.
"a quattro", fl, cl, cr, fg. Autograph score: I-Mc Noseda. Authenticated by Andrea Gottogna.

A531 MARCIA IN E FLAT.
2 ob, cl, cr, 2 fg. Non-autograph score: I-BGc 252.

A532 MARCIA LUGUBRE.
In C Minor. For fl, ob, cl, cr di bassetto, 2 cr, 3 tr tomp, timp, fg, gr cassa, cb. Autograph score: I-BGc 47.

A533 EIGHT SONATAS "A SEI".
For 2 cl, cr di bassetto, 2 cr, fg. Autograph score: I-BGc 306.

A534 SEVEN SEPTETS FOR WIND INSTRUMENTS.
For ob, 2 cl, 2 cr, 2 fg, basso. Autograph score: I-BGc 252.

A535 SEXTET.
For 2 cl, 2 cr, 2 fg. In E flat. Autograph score (incomplete): I-BGc 319.

A536 SEXTET.
For 2 cl, 2 cr, 2 fg. Andante in B flat Major. Autograph score: I-Mc 26/6.

A537 TWO SONATAS "A SETTE".
For 2 cl, cr di bassetto, viola, 2 cr, fg. Autograph score incomplete, 15 pages only: I-BGc 306.

A538 TWO SEPTETS.
For 2 cl, 3 cr, 2 fg. 1) In E flat, 2) In B flat. Autograph score: I-BGc 302.

A539 SEPTET.
For 2 fl, 2 cl, 2 cr, cr di bassetto. In F Major. Autograph score: I-BGc 319.

A540 SEPTET NO 7 "ALLA FRANCESE".
In G Minor. For 2 cl, 2 ob, 2 cr in C, 1 cr in G. Autograph score (incomplete): I-BGc 299.

A541 OCTET.
For fl, 2 cl, 2 cr, fg, 2 bassi/celli. In D Minor. Autograph score: I-BGc 314 (in volume of misc. music).

A542 OCTET.
For 2 cl, 2 ob, 2 cr, fg, tr. In C Minor. Autograph score (incomplete): I-BGc 317.

A543 OCTET.
For 2 ob, 2 cl, 2 b, 2 tr. Autograph score: H-Bmm.

A544 FOUR NOCTURNES - NONETS.
For fl, 2 (?) cl, 2 cr, 2 fg, tr, trb. Parts only. Autograph score: I-BGi XXIV.1.576.9751.

36. Music for Strings and Wind instruments

A545 TRIO.
In E flat. For clarinetto, violino e basso.
Autograph score: I-BGc 299.

A546 QUINTET FOR STRINGS IN E
FLAT.
For vl 1 & 2, vla 1 & 2, cello. Autograph
score: I-BGc 299.

A547 SEXTET.
No 1. For cl, 2 vli, 2 cr, basso/cello. In
C Major. Autograph score: I-BGc 251.

A548 SEXTET.
No 2. For cl, 2 vli, 2 cr, cello/double
bass. C Major. Autograph score: I-BGc
251.

A549 40 CONTRAPPUNTI.
For 2 double basses. Autograph score:
I-BGc 318.

A550 SINFONIA (FOR CEMBALO).
In C Major. Transc. (possibly not by
Mayr) for 2 vl, vla, cello. Largo-allegro.
Non-autograph score: I-OS B.3753.

A551 LARGO IN 2 MOVEMENTS
WITH EXTENDED BASSOON SOLO.
For ob, 2 cr in E flat, 2 cl in B flat, tr in
E flat, 2 fg, 2 vl, 2 vla. Autograph score:
GB-Lor.

SOLO PER VIOLINO.
[See A1503, section 74]

37. Guitar

A552 LA NOCE DI BENEVENTO.
Contradanza in D.
[See A493 under section: BALLET]

38. Organ music

A553 BREVE ISTRUZIONE PEL
MODO DI SUONARE IL PEDALE.
Cavata dalle fonti più autorevoli e cor-
redata di ogni genere di esercizj e
esempj. Non-autograph score: I-BGc
Salone N95/5; Autograph score: I-BGi
III.E.275.4155.

A554 GLORIA.
Non-autograph score: I-VIb Busta 14.

A555 TWELVE PRELUDES.
Autograph score: I-BGi XVII.E.275.4156.

A556 PRELUDIO & FUGUE IN A
MAJOR FOR ORGAN.
Autograph score: I-BGc 315.

A557 SINFONIA.
In C Major. Maestoso-allegretto, allegro
vivace. Non-autograph score: I-OS
B.2035.

A558 ORGAN: SINFONIA D MAJOR.
Andante/Largo. Non-autograph score:
I-BRc Paisini 18.

A559 SINFONIA "I MISTERI
ELEUSINI".
1. Organ. 2. Sextet: 2 vl, 2 vla, cello,
basso. (transcription most likely not by

Mayr). 3. Piano. Non-autograph score:
I-Mc Noseda.

A560 SONATA FOR ORGAN.
A Major. Adagio-Allegro moderato-
Fugue. Autograph score: I-BGc 315.

39. The Mass (complete or near complete settings)

A561 MESSA DI GLORIA.
Autograph score: Private Collection
(offered for sale at Sotheby's 1986).

A562 MASS.
Soloists, choir and orchestra. "Pater Gall
Morel". 28/5/1826. Autograph score:
CH-E.

A563 MASS IN C.
SATB, orchestra: fl, ob, cr, strings.
Autograph score: I-BGc 95.

A564 TWO MASSES FOR HOLY
WEEK.
1. In F Major, 2. C Major. S (or A) TB,
violone. Autograph score: I-BGc 95.

A565 MASS WITH WIND
INSTRUMENTS.
E flat Major. SATB, fl, ob, cl, fg, cr, tr,
timps, trb, violone, organ. Autograph
score: I-BGc 96.

A566 MASS IN F MINOR (WITHOUT
CREED).
SATB, fl, ob, cl, cr, strings. Autograph
score: I-BGc 114.

A567 MASS.
C Major. STB, ob, cr, strings, organ obbl.

1826. Autograph score: I-BGc 114, ?I-Fc
E255.

A568 MASS (Missa Breve).
F Major. SSTB Kyrie, ob, cl, cr, strings,
SATB for rest of setting. Autograph
score: I-BGc 179.

A569 MASS FOR PALM SUNDAY.
SATB, organ solo. Autograph score: I-
BGc 179.

A570 MASS.
B flat Major. STB, violone. Autograph
score: I-BGc 95.

A571 MASS (KYRIE & GLORIA).
F Major. Orchestra. Autograph score:
I-BGc 121.

A572 MASS.
STB, organ. Non-autograph score: I-Vnm
Cod. It. IV 1196.

A573 MASS.
C Minor. SATB, orchestra. Non-
autograph score: I-Mc Noseda, I-Nc Mus.
rel. app. lett. M.

A574 MASS.
E flat. (No Kyrie) Autograph score:
I-BGc 264.

A575 MASS.
E flat Major. SATB, "con grande
orchestra". Autograph score: Authenticated by Donizetti, I-Bsf 125.

A576 MESSA DI GLORIA E CREDO.
C Major. Choir and orchestra. Parts only.
Autograph score: CH-E.

A577 MESSA DI GLORIA E CREDO.
E flat. SATB, orchestra. Autograph
score: I-BGc 96.

The Proper of the Mass:

40.   Introits

A578 HAEC DIES.
F Major. Easter Day. T solo and STB
chorus, orchestra. Autograph score:
I-BGc 13.

A579 INTROIT FOR CORPUS
CHRISTI.
D Major. SATB, orchestra: fl, ob, cl, cr,
strings. Autograph score: I-BGc 123.

A580 QUASI ARCUS.
Antiphon, Introit, Gradual, Offertory. 15
May 1831. Autograph score: I-BGc 67.
For visit (to *S. Maria Maggiore*) of
Bishop Gritti-Morlacchi.

A581 INTROIT FOR THE FEAST OF
THE SORROW OF THE VIRGIN.
G Major. SATB, orchestra. Autograph
score: I-BGc 123.

A582 INTROIT FOR THE MOST
SACRED RELICS
(Multae tribulationes). D Minor. SATB,
orchestra. Autograph score: I-BGc 123.

A583 LOQUEBAR - INTROIT FOR
THE FEAST OF ST. CECILIA.

B flat Major. SATB, orchestra.
Autograph score: I-BGc 123.

A584 REDEMISTI NOS.
C Major. SATB, sinfonia "for the use of
F. Mosconi". Autograph score: I-BGc 64.

A585 SALUS AUTEM.
C Major. SATB, orchestra. Autograph
score: I-BGc 123.

A586 INGRESSA
(Entrance/Introit). "Dixit Dominus" (sic)
("Dominus dixit", for Christmas Day -
first service). B flat Major. Mass etc.
SATB, fl, ob, cl, trb, tr, timps, strings.
Autograph score: I-BGc 58.

A587 ADJUTOR NOSTER.
C Major. "a quattro". Non-autograph
score: I-BGi 1015.D.114. Marked as "In-
troiti generali" i.e. more than one or for
use with various texts.

JUBILATE -
Introit for third Sunday after Easter.
[See A973]

41.   Graduals

A588 FOR SAN LUIGI GONZAGA.
"Domine spe mea". F Major. SSS &
wind: fl, cl, fg, cr, tr, trb, timp, Cb, organ.
Autograph score: I-BGc 72.

A589 FOR THE HOLY CROSS.
B flat Major. SSTB chorus, picc, fl, ob,
cl, fg, cr, tr, timp, organ obbligato,
strings. Autograph score: I-BGc 74.

A590 FOR A CONFESSOR: JUSTUS
UT PALMA FLOREBIT.

B flat Major. SATB coro e soli, piccolo,
fl, ob, cl, fg, cr, strings. Autograph score:
I-BGc 74 and sala D.8.23.

A591 ALLELUIA.
F Major. Gradual. STB unaccompanied.
7 vocal parts: I-BGi 1018.D.114.

A592 BENEDICTUS DOMINUS.
F Major. SATB and orch. "con canto
fermo ideale". Autograph score: I-BGc
33. Noted as gradual and not as a canticle.

42.   Offertories

A593 BENEDICAM DOMINUM.
F Major. Offertory, Mass. SATB, orch,
fl, cl, fg, cr, tr, trb, strings. Autograph
score: I-BGc 67.

A594 MISIT ME DOMINUS.
F Major. SSTB, fl, ob, cl, fg, cr, tr, trb,

timp, strings. Autograph score: I-BGc
Sala 32.D8.22.

A595 QUIA FECIT MAGNA.
B flat Major. SATB, orchestra: fl, cl,
obbl, tr, trb, cr, fg, strings. Parts only.
Non-autograph score: I-BGc 67.

43.   Sequences

A596 VICTIMAE PASCHALI LAUDES.
Easter sequence and 2nd Mass of Easter
Day Mass.
1. Easter Sequence 1st Mass of Easter
Day. B flat Major. SATB, orchestra: fl,
ob, cl, cr, strings. Autograph score:
I-BGc 72.
2. Easter Sequence 2nd Mass of Easter
Day. G Major. SATB, orchestra: fl, ob,
cl, cr, strings. Autograph score: I-BGc 72.

A597 SEQUENCE FOR PENTECOST
(Veni sancte Spiritus). B flat Major.

SATB, orchestra: fl, ob, cl, cr, strings.
Autograph score: I-BGc 72.

A598 LAUDA SION.
(Sequence for Corpus Christi) E flat
Major. SATB, orchestra. Autograph
score: I-BGc 72.

A599 JERUSALEM SURGE -
RESPONSORIUM.
Responsary. Autograph score: I-BGc 299.

See also - DIES IRAE (section 67).

The Common of the Mass:

44. Kyrie and Christe Eleison

A600 KYRIE.
TTB, organ/violone. Non-autograph
score: I-BGi 1014.E.114.

A601 KYRIE.
STB, organ/violone. Non-autograph
score: I-BGi 1047.B.49.

A602 KYRIE.
Voices, orchestra and organ. Non-
autograph score: I-Fc E.1.284.

A603 KYRIE I & II.
C Minor - I, C Major - II. SATB, fl, ob,
cl, fg, cr, tr, timps, strings, serpent & con-
tra-bassoon. Autograph score: I-BGc 112.

A604 KYRIE.
C Minor. SATB "con sinfonia". 1830.
2 ob, 2 cr. Three non-autograph scores:
I-BGi 1013.D.114, 474.D.115; I-Mc 193.2

A605 KYRIE.
D Major. SATB, fl, ob, cl, fg, cr, tr, trb,
timps, strings. Autograph score: I-BGc
109.

A606 KYRIE.
D Major. SATB, ob, 2 cr, strings. Non-
autograph score: I-BGi 1012.D.114.
Copied by Francesco Maria Zanchi.

A607 KYRIE II.
D Major. SATB soloists & chorus,
orchestra. Non-autograph score: I-BGi
479c.D.116.

A608 KYRIE.
D Minor. SATB soloists & chorus,
orchestra. Non-autograph score: I-BGi
479a.D.116.

A609 KYRIE I KYRIE II.
G Minor/G Major. SSTB, fl, ob, cl, fg, cr,
trb, timps, strings. Autograph score:
I-BGc 101.

A610 KYRIE I KYRIE II.
SATB, fl, ob, strings. Autograph score:
I-BGc 113.

A611 KYRIE I KYRIE II.
G Major/G Minor. SATB, fl, ob, cl, cr, tr,
trb, timps, 2 vla, strings. Autograph
score: I-BGc 117.

A612 KYRIE.
C Minor. SATB, ob, fg, tr, trb, strings.
First Mass written by Mayr: 1791.
Autograph score: I-BGc 179. See also
Gloria and Cum Sancto. [See A667]

A613 KYRIE & CHRISTE.
SATB, ob, cr, strings. Autograph score:
I-BGc 119.

A614 KYRIE.
C Minor. SATB, orchestra. Autograph
score: I-BGc 299.

A615 KYRIE.
D Major. SATB, 2 ob, 2 cr, strings. Non-
autograph score: I-BGi 1012.D.114.
Copied by F. M. Zanchi.

A616 KYRIE/CHRISTE/KYRIE.
D Major. SATB, fl, ob, cl, fg, cr, tr, trb,
timp, strings. Autograph score: I-BGc
116.

A617 KYRIE AND CHRISTE.
D Major. SATB, ob, cl, cr, tr, strings.
Autograph score: I-BGc 119.

A618 KYRIE A 4 VOCI DEL CELEBRE
M° SIMONE MAYR.
D Major. Orchestra. 2 May 1858. Non-
autograph score: I-OS B.317. Copied by
Luigi Provaglio.

A619 KYRIE.
D Major. SATB and orchestra.
Autograph score: I-BGc 109.

A620 KYRIE.
D Minor. SATB, orchestra. Autograph
score: I-BGc 302.

A621 KYRIE/CHRISTE/KYRIE.
E Minor. SATB, fl, ob, cl, fg, cr, trb,
strings. Autograph score: I-BGc 108.

A622 KYRIE A 4 VOCI.
E Minor. 25 April 1838. Non-autograph
score: I-OS B.318. Copied from "another
manuscript of Luigi Provaglio, Mantova
2 May 1858".

A623 KYRIE/CHRISTE/KYRIE.
E flat Major. SATB, fl, ob, cl, cr,
strings.Autograph score: I-BGc 88.

A624 KYRIE/CHRISTE/KYRIE.
E flat Major. SATB, orchestra. Parts
only: I-BGc 179.

A625 KYRIE/CHRISTE/KYRIE.
E flat Major. SATB, orchestra. Late
work. Autograph score: I-BGc 110.

A626 KYRIE/CHRISTE/KYRIE.
F Major. SATB, fl, ob, cl, fg, cr, tr, trb,
timp, strings. Autograph score: I-BGc 93.

A627 KYRIE I KYRIE II.
F Major. SATB, fl, ob, cl, fg, cr, tr, trb,
timps, strings. Autograph score: I-BGc
107.

A628 KYRIE IN F.
SATB and strings. Autograph score:
I-BGc 297.

A629 KYRIE (no Christe) & GLORIA
(In excelsis and cum Sancto Spirito).
F Major. STB, ob, cr, strings. Autograph
score: I-BGc 121.

A630 KYRIE I/KYRIE II.
G Major. SATB, orchestra. Autograph
score: I-BGc 117.

A631 KYRIE.
G Minor. SATB, orchestra. Autograph
score: I-BGc 120.

A632 KYRIE.
B flat Major. SSTB, orchestra. Autograph
score: I-BGc 63.

A633 KYRIE/CHRISTE/KYRIE.
B flat Major. Orchestra. Autograph score:
I-BGc 118.

A634 KYRIE PASTORALE.
C Major (6/8). SATB, fl, ob, cl, cr,
strings. Autograph score: I-BGc 122.

A635 KYRIE "di Novara".
SATB, orchestra. 1815? (No Christe).
Autograph score: I-BGc 111.

A636 KYRIE/CHRISTE/KYRIE.
E flat Major. SATB, orchestra.
Autograph score: I-BGc 96.

A637 KYRIE.
SATB, orchestra. Autograph score:
D-Bds N.2.

A638 CHRISTE ELEISON.
F Major. T solo, fg, cl obbl, orchestra.
Autograph score: I-BGc 97.

A639 CHRISTE ELEISON.
B flat. T solo, ob obbl, orchestra.
Autograph score: I-BGc 97.

A640 CHRISTE ELEISON.
E flat. BT soli, viola obbl, and orchestra.
Autograph score: I-BGc 97.

A641 CHRISTE ELEISON.
G Major. B solo, fl obbl, orchestra.
Autograph score: I-BGc 97.

A642 CHRISTE ELEISON.
F Major. SS soli, orchestra. Autograph
score: I-BGc 100.

A643 CHRISTE ELEISON.
B flat. SS soli, orchestra. Autograph
score: I-BGc 97.

A644 CHRISTE ELEISON.
B flat. TT soli, 2 cl obbl, and orchestra.
Autograph score: I-BGc 98.

A645 CHRISTE ELEISON.
B flat. TT soli, ob, cl, fg obbl, orchestra.
Autograph score: I-BGc 100.

A646 CHRISTE ELEISON.
G Major. SSS soli, orchestra. Autograph
score: I-BGc 100. (For School?)

A647 CHRISTE ELEISON.
G Major. SSS soli, orchestra. Autograph
score: I-BGc 100. (For School?)

A648 CHRISTE ELEISON.
B flat. SAT soli, STB coro. Autograph
score: I-BGc 98.

45. Gloria

GLORIA IN EXCELSIS (Gloria)

A649 GLORIA IN EXCELSIS.
E flat Major. SATB: fl, ob, cl, fg, cr, tr,
trb, timp, strings. Autograph score: I-BGc
96.

A650 GLORIA IN EXCELSIS and CUM
SANCTO.
B flat Major. SSTB, fl, ob, cr, strings.
Autograph score: I-BGc 93. On a vocal
part of the Cum Sancto written "Per
Donizetti".

A651 GLORIA IN EXCELSIS and CUM
SANCTO.
C Major. SATB, fl, ob, cl, cr, strings.
Autograph score: I-BGc 88.

A652 GLORIA IN EXCELSIS.
B flat Major. SST, fl, ob, cl, fg, cr, tr, trb,
timp, strings. Autograph score: I-BGc 93.

A653 GLORIA IN EXCELSIS.
C Major. SATB, orchestra. Autograph
score: I-BGc 99 and 101. In two versions,
the second slightly larger orchestral forces.

A654 GLORIA IN EXCELSIS and CUM
SANCTO.
A Major. SATB, fl, ob, cl, fg, cr, tr, trb,
timp, strings. Autograph score: I-BGc
107.

A655 GLORIA IN EXCELSIS.
C Major. SATB, fl, ob, cl, fg, cr, tr, timp,
strings. Autograph score: I-BGc 108.

A656 GLORIA IN EXCELSIS.
D Major. SATB, fl, ob, cl, fg, cr, tr, trb, timp, strings. Autograph score: I-BGc 109.

A657 GLORIA IN EXCELSIS and CUM SANCTO.
E flat Major. SATB, fl, cl, ob, 2 cr, fg, tr, trb, timp, strings, (parts only). Autograph score: I-BGc 110.

A658 GLORIA IN EXCELSIS and CUM SANCTO.
D Major. SATB, fl, ob, cl, fg, cr, 3 tr, trb, timp, strings (two scores). Autograph score: I-BGc 112.

A659 GLORIA IN EXCELSIS and CUM SANCTO.
A Major. SATB, parts only. Autograph score: I-BGc 113.

A660 GLORIA IN EXCELSIS and CUM SANCTO.
D Major. SATB, fl, ob, cl, fg, 2 tr, timp, strings. Autograph score: I-BGc 115. Exists also for wind instruments, 2 scores.

A661 GLORIA IN EXCELSIS and CUM SANCTO.
D Major. SATB, fl, ob, cl, fg, 2 cr, 2 tr "a chiavi" obbli, trb, timp, strings. Autograph score: I-BGc 116.

A662 GLORIA IN EXCELSIS and CUM SANCTO.
G Major. SATB, fl, ob, cr, tr, trb, timp, strings. Autograph score: I-BGc 117.

A663 GLORIA IN EXCELSIS and CUM SANCTO.
C Major. SATB, fl, ob, cl, cr, tr, trb, timp, strings. Autograph score: I-BGc 118.

A664 GLORIA IN EXCELSIS and CUM SANCTO.
C Major. SATB ob, cr, strings. Autograph score: I-BGc 119.

A665 GLORIA IN EXCELSIS and CUM SANCTO.
D Major. SATB, ob, cl, cr, tr, strings. Autograph score: I-BGc 120.

A666 GLORIA IN EXCELSIS and CUM SANCTO.
B flat Major. SATB, fl, ob, cr, strings. Autograph score: I-BGc 120.

A667 GLORIA IN EXCELSIS and CUM SANCTO.
SATB, ob, fg, tr, trb, strings. Autograph score: I-BGc 179. (From Mayr's first Mass - 1791? SEE A612)

A668 GLORIA IN EXCELSIS.
F Major. Autograph score: I-BGc 121.

A669 GLORIA IN EXCELSIS and CUM SANCTO (Pastorale).
SATB, fl, ob, cl, cr, strings. Autograph score: I-BGc 122. For Christmas.

A670 GLORIA IN EXCELSIS.
F Major. SATB, cl, ob, cr, tr obbl, fl, ob, cl, tr, trb, timp, strings. Autograph score: I-BGc sala 32.D.8.12.

A671 GLORIA IN EXCELSIS and CUM SANCTO.
E flat Major. SATB, fl, ob, cl, tr, trb, cr, strings. 27 August 1843. Autograph score: I-BGc sala D.8.2/5; sala D.8.2/4. Mayr's last composition. 80 years and two months. Also for wind instruments only.

A672 GLORIA IN EXCELSIS.
B flat Major. TTB, organ. Autograph score: I-BGi 1004.D.114.

A673 GLORIA IN EXCELSIS.
C Major. SATB, orchestra. 1833.
Autograph score: I-BGi 1005.D.114.

A674 GLORIA IN EXCELSIS.
C Major. SATB, orchestra. 1830.
Autograph score: I-BGi 1003.D.114.

A675 GLORIA IN EXCELSIS.
C Major. SATB, 2 ob, 2 cr, strings.
Autograph score: I-BGi 473.D.115.

A676 GLORIA IN EXCELSIS.
D Major. SATB, orchestra. Autograph
score: I-BGi 1002.D.114.

A677 GLORIA IN EXCELSIS.
D Major. SATB, orchestra. Autograph
score: I-BGc 264.

A678 GLORIA IN EXCELSIS.
E flat Major. SATB, instruments.
Autograph score: I-BGc 96.

A679 GLORIA IN EXCELSIS.
E flat Major. SATB, chorus, orchestra.
Autograph score: I-BGi 479.D.116.

A680 GLORIA IN EXCELSIS.
B Minor. 2 part choir/organ. Non-
autograph score: I-Mc PV.BU.3-3.

ET IN TERRA PAX (Gloria)

A681 ET IN TERRA PAX and
LAUDAMUS.
F Major. B solo, SATB, chorus, fl, ob, cl,
fg, 2 cr, tr, timp, strings. Autograph
score: I-BGc 103.

A682 ET IN TERRA PAX and
LAUDAMUS.
A flat Major. T solo, cl obbl, fl, cr,
strings. Parts only: I-BGc 103.

A683 ET IN TERRA PAX.
B flat Major. ST (soli), fl, ob, cl, cr, fg,
strings. Parts only: I-BGc 103.

A684 ET IN TERRA PAX and
LAUDAMUS.
C Major. T solo, cl, or, ob obbl, ob, cr,
strings. Autograph score: I-BGc 104.

A685 ET IN TERRA PAX and
LAUDAMUS.
A flat Major. T solo, cl obbl, fl, ob,
strings. 1843. Autograph score: I-BGc
sala 32.D.8.9.

LAUDAMUS TE (Gloria)

A686 LAUDAMUS TE.
G Major. T or S solo with flute obbl,
orchestra. Autograph score: I-BGc 100.

A687 LAUDAMUS TE.
D Major. A and flute obbl, orchestra.
Autograph score: I-BGi 479e.D.116.

A688 LAUDAMUS TE.
C Major. T solo, ob obbl, orchestra.
Autograph score: I-BGc sala 32.D.8.19.

A689 LAUDAMUS TE.
C Major. T solo, ob obbl, orchestra.
Autograph score: I-BGc 103.

A690 LAUDAMUS TE.
E flat Major. T solo, cl obbl, orchestra.
Autograph score: I-BGc 104.

A691 LAUDAMUS TE.
G Major. T solo, orchestra. Autograph
score: I-BGc 104.

A692 LAUDAMUS TE.
T solo, fl obbl, orchestra. Autograph
score: I-BGc XXXV522.10085.

A693 LAUDAMUS TE.
D Major. B solo, fl & cl obbli, orchestra.
Autograph score: I-BGc 100.

A694 LAUDAMUS TE.
G Major. B solo, fl obbl, orchestra.
Autograph score: I-BGc 100.

A695 LAUDAMUS TE.
G Major. B solo, orchestra. Autograph
score: I-BGc 103, I-Mc 193.4, I-Vc XI39.

A696 LAUDAMUS TE.
G Major. B solo, 2 fl, 2 cr, strings. 1830.
Non-autograph score: I-BGi 1018A.

A697 LAUDAMUS TE.
G Major. T B soli, 2 fl, orchestra.
Autograph score: I-BGc 103.

A698 LAUDAMUS TE.
B solo, orchestra. Non-autograph score:
I-Vc X.139.

A699 LAUDAMUS TE.
D Major. B solo, orchestra. Autograph
score: I-BGc 104.

A700 LAUDAMUS TE.
G Major. T solo, orchestra. Autograph
score: I-BGc 104.

A701 LAUDAMUS TE.
C Major. T solo, orchestra. Autograph
score: I-BGc 104.

A702 LAUDAMUS TE
(with Et in terra pax).
A flat Major. T solo, cl obbl, orchestra.
Autograph score: I-BGc 104.

A703 LAUDAMUS TE
(with Et in terra pax).
F Major. B solo, SATB coro, orchestra.
Autograph score: I-BGc 103.

GRATIAS AGIMUS (Gloria)

A704 GRATIAS AGIMUS.
E flat. B solo, cl and corno da caccia
obbli, orchestra. Non-autograph score:
I-BGi 1009.D.114.

A705 GRATIAS AGIMUS.
B flat Major. S solo, cello, ob, cl, fg obbl,
fl, cr, trb, strings. Autograph score:
I-BGc 86.

A706 GRATIAS AGIMUS.
B flat Major. T solo, cl obbli, fl, ob, cl,
fg, cr, tr, trb, strings. Autograph score:
I-BGc 86.

A707 GRATIAS AGIMUS.
E flat Major. B solo, cl & cr obbli, ob, cr,
strings. Autograph score: I-BGc 86.

A708 GRATIAS AGIMUS.
B flat Major. T solo, ob, cr, strings. 1830.
Autograph score: I-BGc 86. (Copies in
I-BGi and I-Mc.)

A709 GRATIAS AGIMUS.
F Major. B solo, cr obbl, fl, ob, cl, cr,
strings. Autograph score: I-BGc 89.

A710 GRATIAS AGIMUS.
F Major. B solo, strings. Autograph
score: I-BGc 89.

A711 GRATIAS AGIMUS.
B flat Major. S solo, cl obbl, fl, ob, cr,
strings. Autograph score: I-BGc 89.

A712 GRATIAS AGIMUS and
DOMINE DEUS.
E flat Major. B solo, cr obbl, fl, cr,
strings. Autograph score: I-BGc 89.

A713 GRATIAS AGIMUS.
D Major. S solo, fl, ob, cl, fg, cr, trb,
strings. Autograph score: I-BGc 102.

A714 GRATIAS AGIMUS.
F Major. T solo, fl, ob, cl, fg, cr, trb, strings. Autograph score: I-BGc 102.

A715 GRATIAS AGIMUS.
B flat Major. S solo, cello obbl, fl, 2 ob, cl, fg, cr, trb, strings. Autograph score: I-BGc 102.

A716 GRATIAS AGIMUS.
F Major. A solo, string quartet, organ. Autograph score: I-BGc 102.

A717 GRATIAS AGIMUS and DOMINE DEUS.
C Major. S solo, ATB coro, vla obbl, fl, ob, cl, cr, strings. Autograph score: I-BGc 102.

A718 GRATIAS AGIMUS.
F Major. B solo, cello obbl, strings. Autograph score: I-BGc 102.

A719 GRATIAS AGIMUS and DOMINE DEUS.
E flat Major. B solo, vla or cl or cr obbl, cl, cr, strings. Autograph score: I-BGc 105.

A720 GRATIAS AGIMUS.
E flat Major. B solo, cr obbl, fl, ob, cl, fg, 2 cr, trb, strings. Autograph score: I-BGc 105.

A721 GRATIAS AGIMUS.
B flat Major. T solo, cl obbl, cl, cr, strings, organ. Autograph score: I-BGc 105.

A722 GRATIAS AGIMUS.
A Major. T solo, cl obbl, fl, ob, cr, strings. Autograph score: I-BGc 105.

A723 GRATIAS AGIMUS and DOMINE DEUS.

A solo, fl obbl, fl, ob, 2 cr, fg, strings. Autograph score: I-BGc 91.

A724 GRATIAS AGIMUS.
B flat Major. T solo, cl obbl, fl, ob, cl, cr, fg, tr, trb, strings. Autograph score: I-BGc 125.

A725 GRATIAS AGIMUS.
F Major. T solo, cello & ob & cl & cr obbli, fl, ob, cr, strings. Non-autograph score: I-BGc 125.

A726 GRATIAS AGIMUS.
F Major. SATB soli, SATB coro, fl, ob, cl, cr, strings. Autograph score: I-BGc 125.

A727 GRATIAS AGIMUS.
B flat Major. T solo and orchestra. Autograph score: I-BGc 323.

DOMINE DEUS (Gloria)

A728 DOMINE DEUS.
D Major. B solo, fl obbl, orchestra. Autograph score: I-BGc 82.

A729 DOMINE DEUS.
B flat Major. SS soli, orchestra. Autograph score: I-BGc 82.

A730 DOMINE DEUS.
G Major. SS soli, orchestra. Autograph score: I-BGc 82.

A731 DOMINE DEUS.
B flat Major. TS soli, cello & ob obbli, orchestra. Autograph score: I-BGc 82.

A732 DOMINE DEUS.
D Major. S solo, vl obbl, orchestra. Autograph score: I-BGc 90.

A733 DOMINE DEUS.
D Major. B (solo), ob & cr obbli, orchestra. Autograph score: I-BGc 90.

A734 DOMINE DEUS.
D Major. S solo fl & ob & cb obbli, orchestra. Autograph score: I-BGc 90.

A735 DOMINE DEUS.
E flat Major. B solo, orchestra. Autograph score: I-BGc 90.

A736 DOMINE DEUS.
A Major. B solo, orchestra. Autograph score: I-BGc 91.

A737 DOMINE DEUS.
F Major and E flat. B solo, cr di bassetto obbl, orchestra. Autograph score: I-BGc 91.

A738 DOMINE DEUS.
G Major. S solo, fl obbl, orchestra. Autograph score: I-BGc 91.

A739 DOMINE DEUS.
G Major. TTB, orchestra. Autograph score: I-BGc 94.

A740 DOMINE DEUS.
D Major. STB soli orchestra. Autograph score: I-BGc 94. Non-autograph scores: I-BGi 994.D.107 (con sinfonia), I-Mc Ms.193.6.

A741 DOMINE DEUS.
B flat Major. T solo, vl, cl, cr & cello obbli, orchestra. Non-autograph score: I-BGc 94.

A742 DOMINE DEUS.
F Major. B (solo), cr obbl, orchestra. Non-autograph score: I-BGc 94.

A743 DOMINE DEUS.
B flat Major. SSB soli, orchestra. Autograph score: I-BGc 94.

A744 DOMINE DEUS.
B flat Major. TT (soli), harp or organ obbl/orchestra. Autograph score: I-BGc 94.

A745 DOMINE DEUS.
G Major. STB soli, fl & fg obbli, orchestra. Autograph score: I-BGc 125.

A746 DOMINE DEUS.
D Major. B solo, cr obbl, orchestra. Autograph score: I-BGc 125.

A747 DOMINE DEUS.
F Major. B solo, fg obbl, orchestra. Autograph score: I-BGc 125.

A748 DOMINE DEUS.
B flat Major. T solo, vl & cl & cr & cello obbli, orchestra. Autograph score: I-BGc 82.

A749 DOMINE DEUS.
B flat Major. T solo, vl & cl & cr & cello obbli, orchestra. Late work. Autograph score: I-BGc sala 32.D.8.21.

A750 DOMINE DEUS.
F Major. B solo, orchestra. 1843. Autograph score: I-BGc sala 32.D.8.6.

A751 DOMINE DEUS.
C Major. SS soli, TTB/TTB double choir, orchestra. Non-autograph score: I-BGi 479f.D.117.

A752 DOMINE DEUS.
B flat. T (solo), vl, cello, cl, cr obbl, orchestra. Autograph score: I-BGc 82.

QUI TOLLIS (Gloria)

A753 QUI TOLLIS.
A Minor. T solo, 2 vl obbli, fl, ob, cl, cr, strings. Autograph score: I-BGc 75.

A754 QUI TOLLIS.
C Major. T solo, vl solo, fl, ob, cl, cr, tr, strings. Autograph score: I-BGc 75.

A755 QUI TOLLIS.
E Major. T solo, STB coro, 2 vl obbli, fl, ob, cl, cr, tr, trb, fg, timp, strings. Autograph score: I-BGc 83.

A756 QUI TOLLIS.
A Major. T solo, vl obbl, fl, ob, cl, fg, cr, trb, trb, timp, strings. Autograph score: I-BGc 83.

A757 QUI TOLLIS.
D Minor. B solo, fg obbl, fl, ob, cl, cr, trb, strings. Late work. Autograph score: I-BGc sala 32.D.8.10.

A758 QUI TOLLIS.
D Minor. STB soli, organ obbl, orch, ob, cr, strings. Non-autograph score: I-BGc 83.

A759 QUI TOLLIS.
F Major. S solo, cello obbl, and STB coro. Non-autograph score: I-BGi 1028A, I-Mc 193.7.

A760 QUI TOLLIS.
E flat Major. SATB "concertanti", fl, ob, cl, cr, strings. Autograph score: I-BGc 83. "Qui tollis e Suscipe a fuga piena".

A761 QUI TOLLIS.
A Minor. T solo, 2 vl obbli, fl, ob, cl, cr, fg, strings. Autograph score: I-BGc 83.

A762 QUI TOLLIS.
F Major. S solo, ATB coro, cello obbl, fl, ob, 2 cl, fg, cr, strings. Autograph score: I-BGc 99.

A763 QUI TOLLIS.
F Major. T solo, harp obbl, cello pizzicato, fl, cl, cr, strings. Autograph score: I-BGc 99.

A764 QUI TOLLIS.
D Minor. B solo, cr obbl, fl, ob, cl, fg, 2 cr, strings. Autograph score: I-BGc 99.

A765 QUI TOLLIS.
C Minor. T solo, fl, ob, cl, cr, strings. Autograph score: I-BGc 100.

A766 QUI TOLLIS.
C Major. T solo, SATB coro, fl, ob, cl, cr, strings. Autograph score: I-BGc 99.

SUSCIPE DEPRECATIONEM (Gloria)

A767 SUSCIPE DEPRECATIONEM.
A Minor. SATB, orchestra. Autograph score: I-BGc 299. [See also A760]

QUI SEDES (Gloria)

A768 QUI SEDES.
E flat. S solo, fl, ob, cl, fg, cr, trb, strings. Autograph score: I-BGc 106.

A769 QUI SEDES.
F Major. T solo, vl obbl, ob, cr, strings. Autograph score: I-BGc 106.

A770 QUI SEDES and QUONIAM.
E flat Major. T solo, vl & ob & cl & cr angl (or fl) obbli, orchestra, cr, strings. Autograph score: I-BGc 106.

A771 QUI SEDES.
G Major. S solo & fl obbl, cl, ob, cr, fg, tr, strings. Autograph score: I-BGc sala 32.D.8.17.

A772 QUI SEDES.
D Minor. T solo, fl obbl, fl, 2 ob, cr, strings. Autograph score: I-BGc sala 32.D.8.18. Late work.

A773 QUI SEDES.
F Major. S solo, cr obbl, fl, cr, strings. Autograph score: I-BGc 106.

A774 QUI SEDES.
B flat Major. T solo, cl, vla, cello obbl, 2 ob, cr, strings. Autograph score: I-BGc 106.

A775 QUI SEDES.
B flat Major. S solo, 2 ob obbli, fl, cr, fg, strings. Autograph score: I-BGc 81.

A776 QUI SEDES.
G Major. T solo, bassett horn obbl, fl, ob, cr, strings. Autograph score: I-BGc 81.

A777 QUI SEDES.
F Major. T solo, cl obbl, fl, ob, fg, cr, trb, strings. Autograph score: I-BGc 81.

A778 QUI SEDES.
E Major. S solo, 2 cr obbli, fl, ob, cl, fg, strings. Autograph score: I-BGc 84.

A779 QUI SEDES (Per il centenario del santuario di Caravaggio).
T solo, cr obbl, fl, ob, cr, fg, tr, strings. Autograph score: I-BGc 84. Sung by Rubini.

A780 QUI SEDES.
B flat Major. T solo, cl obbl, fl, ob, cr, fg, tr, strings. Autograph score: I-BGc 84.

A781 QUI SEDES.
G Minor. T solo, cl obbl, fl, ob, cl, cr, strings. Autograph score: I-BGc 84.

A782 QUI SEDES.
E flat. T solo, vl obbl, fl, ob, cl, fg, cr, tr, strings. Autograph score: I-BGc 85.

A783 QUI SEDES.
D Major. S solo, vl obbl, fl, cl, cr, tr, strings. Autograph score: I-BGc 85.

A784 QUI SEDES.
E flat Major. B solo, vl obbl, fl, cl, cr, tr, strings. Autograph score: I-BGc 85.

A785 QUI SEDES.
G Major. T or S solo, cr di bassetto obbl, orchestra. Autograph score: I-BGc 81.

A786 QUI SEDES.
G Major. S solo, strings. Autograph score: I-BGc 314.

A787 QUI SEDES.
B flat. S solo, cr obbl, orchestra. Autograph score: I-BGc 84.

A788 QUI SEDES.
C Major. T solo, orchestra. Non-autograph score: I-BGi 479h.D.117.

A789 QUI SEDES.
E flat. T solo, orchestra. Non-autograph score: II-Mc 193.8.

A790 QUI SEDES.
D flat. B solo, orchestra. Autograph score: I-BGc 57.

A791 QUI SEDES.
E flat. B solo, tr obbl, orchestra. Autograph score: I-BGc 85.

CUM SANCTO SPIRITU (Gloria)

A792 CUM SANCTO SPIRITU (A due voci con strumenti).
C Major. ST soli, orchestra, 2 cl, 2 cr, tr, trb, timp, organ. Non-autograph score: I-BGi 992.D.107.

A793 CUM SANCTO SPIRITU.
C Major. TTB. Autograph score (incomplete): I-BGc 297.

A794 CUM SANCTO SPIRITU.
C Major. SATB, con sinfonia. Non-autograph score: I-BGi 990.D.106.

A795 CUM SANCTO SPIRITU.
D Major. SATB, orchestra. Autograph score: I-BGc 109.

A796 CUM SANCTO SPIRITU.
D Major. SATB, orchestra. Autograph score: I-BGc 112.

A797 CUM SANCTO SPIRITU.
D Major. SATB, orchestra. Autograph score: I-BGc 116.

A798 CUM SANCTO SPIRITU.
E flat. SATB, orchestra. Non-autograph score: I-BGi 479i.D.117.

A799 CUM SANCTO SPIRITU.
F Major. SATB. Autograph score: I-BGc 121.

A800 CUM SANCTO SPIRITU.
F Major. SATB, orchestra, fl, ob, cl, fg, cr, tr, trb, timp, strings, organ. Late work. Autograph score: I-BGc sala 32.D.8.20.

A801 CUM SANCTO SPIRITU.
G Major. SATB, orchestra. Autograph score: I-BGc 117.

A802 CUM SANCTO SPIRITU.
G Major. SATB, orchestra, con sinfonia. Non-autograph score: I-BGi 991.D.106.

A803 CUM SANCTO SPIRITU.
A Minor. SATB, orchestra. Autograph score: I-BGc 108.

A804 CUM SANCTO SPIRITU.
B flat. SSTB, orchestra. Autograph score: I-BGc 93.

46.   Credo

A805 CREDO.
C Major. TTB soli, orchestra. Non-autograph score: I-Cf Prov. G. M. Griguolo.

A806 CREDO.
3 voices (?STB), orchestra, organ. Non-autograph score: I-Vsmc.

A807 CREDO.
C Major. 3 voices (?STB), coro ad libitum, orchestra. Non-autograph score: I-Gil sc.21.n.n.

A808 CREDO.
C Major. SATB, orchestra. Autograph score: I-BGc. Non-autograph score: I-Mc 193.9.

A809 CREDO (Credo di Novara).
C Major. SATB, orchestra. Autograph score: I-BGc 87.

A810 CREDO.
C Major. SATB, orchestra. Autograph
score: I-BGc 92.

A811 CREDO.
D Major. SATB, orchestra. Autograph
score: I-BGc 92.

A812 CREDO.
D Major. SATB, orchestra. Autograph
score (unfinished): I-BGc 323.

A813 CREDO.
F Major. SATB, fl, cl, ob, tr, trb, timp,
fg, strings, organ. Non-autograph score:
I-BGc 80.

A814 CREDO.
F Major. SATB, orchestra. Autograph
score: I-BGc 92.

A815 CREDO.
F Major. a) SATB, strings. b) SATB,
wind. 1843. Autograph score: I-BGc sala
D.8.2.6 and sala D.8.2.7.

A816 CREDO.
F Major. SATB, orchestra. Non-
autograph score: I-MAb (2Ms).

A817 CREDO.
F Major. Parts (9 vocal) (29 instrumental). Conservatorio Donizetti. (prov. *S.
Maria M.*) which could be complements
to one of the credos in F Major.

A818 CREDO.
A Minor. SSTB, orchestra. Autograph
score: I-BGc 68.

A819 CREDO.
B flat. SATB, orchestra. Autograph
score: I-BGc 92. Credo composed for
Donizetti and sent to Naples 1822.

A820 CREDO
(Credo a più voci con sinfonia).
B flat. Non-autograph score: I-BGi
988.D.106.

A821 CREDO.
B flat Major. SATB, orchestra.
Autograph score: I-BGc 331.

A822 CREDO
(a quattro voci concertate).
Non-autograph score: I-Vlb Busta 14 Ms.

A823 CREDO.
C Major. SATTBB, orchestra. Non-
autograph score: I-BGi 4706.E.131.

A824 CREDO (Credo a sei voci con
accompagnamento instrumentale).
Non-autograph score: I-Rvat Mus 138 Ms.

A825 CREDO.
A Major. 2 part choir/organ. Non-
autograph score: I-Mc PVBU 3-3.

A826 CREDO.
B flat. By Haydn. Wind reduction by
Mayr. Autograph score: I-BGc 315.

MISCELLANEOUS

A827 CRUCIFIXUS.
E flat. STB, orchestra. Non-autograph
score: I-BGc 80.

A828 DOMINE JESU CHRISTE
(A quattro).

E flat. SATB, orchestra. Autograph
score: I-BGc 44.

A829 DOMINE JESU CHRISTE.
B flat. STB, strings (parts only). Non-
autograph score: I-BGi 478.D.115.

47.   Sanctus, Benedictus, Agnus Dei

SANCTUS BENEDICTUS AGNUS DEI

A830 SANCTUS, BENEDICTUS, AGNUS DEI.
C Major. SATB, fl, ob, cl, fg, cr, strings. Autograph score: I-BGc 73.

A831 SANCTUS (Pastorale), BENEDICTUS, AGNUS DEI.
C Major. SATB, fl, ob, cl, fg, cr, tr, trb, timp, strings. Autograph score: I-BGc 73. For Christmas.

A832 SANCTUS, BENEDICTUS, AGNUS DEI.
D Major. SATB, orch, fl, ob, cl, fg, cr, tr, trb, timp, strings. Autograph score: I-BGc 73.

A833.SANCTUS, BENEDICTUS, AGNUS DEI.
E flat Major. SATB, fl, ob, cl, fg, cr, tr, trb, serpent, timp, strings. Autograph score: I-BGc 73.

A834 SANCTUS, BENEDICTUS, AGNUS DEI.
B flat Major. STB, orch, ob, cl, cr, tr, trb, timp, strings. Autograph score: I-BGc 77.

A835 SANCTUS, BENEDICTUS, AGNUS DEI.
D Major. T solo, B solo, TTB coro, orchestra. Autograph score: I-BGc 77.

A836 SANCTUS, BENEDICTUS, AGNUS DEI.
D Major. SATB, orch, fl, ob, cl, fg, tr, trb, timp, strings. Autograph score: I-BGc 77.

A837 SANCTUS, BENEDICTUS, AGNUS DEI.
SATB, orchestra. Non-autograph score: I-BGi 1048.B.49.

A838 SANCTUS, BENEDICTUS, AGNUS DEI.
SATB, orchestra. Autograph score: I-BGc 77.

A839 SANCTUS, BENEDICTUS, AGNUS DEI.
TTTB, orchestra. Autograph score: I-BGc 77.

48.   Sanctus

A840 SANCTUS.
Double choir, violone, organ. Autograph score: D-Mbs. "Va attaccato dopo il gloria in G."

A841 SANCTUS.
2 cantors (TT), organ. Non-autorgraph score: I-Mc PVBU33. "Concenti a più voci" p. 8.

A842 SANCTUS
(For the Ambrosian Rite).
D Major. SATB, orchestra, fl, ob, cl, fg, cr, tr, trb, timp, strings. Autograph score: I-BGc 40.

A843 SANCTUS.
B flat Major. SATB, fl, ob, cl, fg, cr, tr,
trb, timp, strings. Autograph score: I-BGc
44, I-BGi 479m.D.118.

A844 SANTUS.
G Minor. SATB, fl, cl, cr, strings.
Autograph score: I-BGc 47.

A845 SANCTUS.
D Major. SATB, orchestra. Non-
autograph score: I-OS B.2302.

A846 SANCTUS.
B flat. STB, strings. Non-autograph
score. I-BGi 478.D.115.

49.   Benedictus Qui Venit

A847 BENEDICTUS QUI VENIT.
B flat. TTB, orchestra. Autograph score:
I-BGc 16.

A848 BENEDICTUS QUI VENIT.
G Minor. SSSS, orchestra. Non-
autograph score: I-BGc 316. Presumably
composed for school.

A849 BENEDICTUS QUI VENIT.
A Major. Solo, fl, cr di bassetto, fg, cr,
strings. Late work. Autograph score:
I-BGc sala 32.D.8.8.

50.   Agnus Dei

A850 AGNUS DEI, also SANCTUS,
HOSANNA.
SATTTB, orchestra. Non-autograph
score: I-BGc sala 32.D.8.8.

A851 AGNUS DEI.
F Major. SATB and orchestra. Autograph
score: I-BGc 44.

A852 L'AGNELLO DI DIO (Agnus Dei).
C Major. 2 cantors (TT), choir, organ.
Non-autograph score: I-Mc PVBU3-3.
Printed in "Concenti a più voci" p. 18.

51.   Pater Noster

A853 PATER NOSTER.
B flat. 2 part chorus, organ. Non-
autograph score: I-Mc PVBU3-3.
In "concenti a più voci."

52.   Vespers

DOMINE AD ADJUVANDUM

Vespers, Opening Versicles.

A854 DOMINE AD ADJUVANDUM.
C Major. SATB, orchestra. Complete
Vespers. 1791. Autograph score: I-BGc
139.

A855 DOMINE AD ADJUVANDUM.
SATB, violone, organ. Nearly complete
setting of Vespers. Autograph score: I-
BGc 139.

A856 DOMINE AD ADJUVANDUM.
G Major. SATB, orchestra (& Dixit).
Autograph score: I-BGc 136.

A857 DOMINE AD ADJUVANDUM.
G Major. SATB, orchestra (& Dixit).
Autograph score: I-BGc 137. "Per il Corpus Domine del 1802". Part of Mayr's
first Vespers for *S. Maria Maggiore*.

A858 DOMINE AD ADJUVANDUM.
B flat Major. SATB and orchestra (with
Dixit and Magnificat). Parts only: I-BGc
139.

A859 DOMINE AD ADJUVANDUM.
G Major. SATB, orchestra (with Dixit).
Autograph score: I-BGc 139.

A860 DOMINE AD ADJUVANDUM.
C Major (with Magnificat). TTB, wind,
organ violone. Autograph score: I-BGc
139.

A861 DOMINE AD ADJUVANDUM.
C Major. SATB, orchestra. Autograph
score: I-BGc 60.

A862 DOMINE AD ADJUVANDUM.
G Major. SATB, orchestra. Autograph
score: I-BGc 60.

A863 DOMINE AD ADJUVANDUM.
F Major. SSTB and orchestra. Autograph
score: I-BGc 60.

A864 DOMINE AD ADJUVANDUM.
B flat Major. SATB, orchestra.
Autograph score: I-BGc 60.

A865 DOMINE AD ADJUVANDUM.
C Major. SATB, orchestra. Autograph
score: I-BGc 62.

A866 DOMINE AD ADJUVANDUM.
F Major. SATB, orchestra. Autograph
score: I-BGc 62.

A867 DOMINE AD ADJUVANDUM.
E flat Major. SATB, orchestra.
Autograph score: I-BGc 62.

A868 DOMINE AD ADJUVANDUM.
C Major. SATB, orchestra. Autograph
score: I-BGc 62.

A869 DOMINE AD ADJUVANDUM.
D Major. SATB, orchestra. Autograph
score: I-BGc 124.

A870 DOMINE AD ADJUVANDUM.
F Major. SATB, orchestra. Autograph
score: I-BGc 124.

A871 DOMINE AD ADJUVANDUM.
G Major. SATB, 2 cr & trb obbli,
orchestra. Autograph score: I-BGc 124.

A872 DOMINE AD ADJUVANDUM.
B flat Major. T (solo) chorus SATB,
cl obbl, orchestra. Autograph score:
I-BGc 124.

A873 DOMINE AD ADJUVANDUM.
E flat. Chorus SATB, orchestra. Parts
only: I-BGi 492a.D.119.

A874 DOMINE AD ADJUVANDUM.
C Major. SATB, orchestra. Non-

autograph score: I-Nc musica rel. 1200.
No doubt taken by or sent to Donizetti
when he was living and working in
Naples.

53. Gloria Patri (Vespers)

A875 GLORIA PATRI N1.
C Major. T solo, fl, ob, tr, cr, strings.
Autograph score: I-BGc 2.

A876 GLORIA PATRI N2.
F Major. S (or A or B) solo, 2 ob, 2 cr,
fg, strings. Non-autograph score: I-BGc 2.

A877 GLORIA PATRI N3.
A Minor. S solo, vl obbl, fl, ob, cl, cr, fg,
timp, strings. Autograph score: I-BGc 2.

A878 GLORIA PATRI N4.
A flat Major. S (or A), vl & cello (or fg)
obbli, fl, cl, ob, cr, trb, strings. Non-
autograph score: I-BGc 2.

A879 GLORIA PATRI N5.
F Major. S (or A) solo, ATB coro, vl
solo, fl, cl, cr, strings. Autograph score:
I-BGc 2.

A880 GLORIA PATRI N6.
F Major. S solo & coro (SATB?), fl, ob,
cl, fg, cr, trb, strings. Autograph score:
I-BGc 2.

A881 GLORIA PATRI N7.
G Major. S solo, fl obbl, ob, cl, fg, cr, trb,
strings. Autograph score: I-BGc 2.

A882 GLORIA PATRI N8.
G Major. S solo, fl & cello obbli, fl, ob,
fg, cr, tr, strings. Autograph score:
I-BGc 4.

A883 GLORIA PATRI N9.
A flat Major. S solo, cl obbl, fl, ob, cr,
strings. Autograph score: I-BGc 4.

A884 GLORIA PATRI N10.
E flat Major. A (or S) solo, cr inglese
obbl, fl, ob, ce, strings. Autograph score:
I-BGc 4.

A885 GLORIA PATRI N11.
A flat Major. S solo, vl solo, fl, cr, cello
solo, vle, basso. Autograph score:
I-BGc 11.

A886 GLORIA PATRI N12.
F Minor. S solo, ob or cr obbl, ob, cr,
strings. Autograph score: I-BGc 4.

A887 GLORIA PATRI N13.
B flat Major. S or B solo, ob, fg, cr,
strings. Non-autograph score: I-BGc 4.

A888 GLORIA PATRI.
F Major. S solo, Sicut erat (F Minor),
SATB coro, orchestra, fl, ob, cl, fg, cr, tr,
trb, strings. Autograph score: I-BGc 66,
I-BGi 1007.D.114.

A889 GLORIA PATRI.
F Major. 2S, TB (coro), fl, ob, cl, cr, fg,
tr, trb, timp, strings. Autograph score:
I-BGc 69.

A890 GLORIA PATRI.
E Minor. T solo, cr obbl, orchestra. Non-autograph score: I-BGi 492f.D.120.

A891 GLORIA PATRI.
Italian trans: Samuele Biava for Hymn Book? S, organ. Autograph score: I-BGc 283.

A892 GLORIA PATRI.
E Minor. 2 cantors (TT), choir. Non-autograph score: I-Mc PVBU3-3. In concenti a più voci p. 3. (Same as A891?)

54.   Sicut Erat (Vespers)

A893 SICUT ERAT.
C Major. SATB, orchestra, fl, ob, cl, fg, cr, tr, trb, timp, strings. Autograph score: I-BGc 70.

A894 SICUT ERAT.
C Major. SATB and orchestra (as above). Autograph score: I-BGc 129.

A895 SICUT ERAT.
E flat Major. SATB, orchestra. Autograph score: I-BGc 129. See also I-BGc 134. (Belongs to Dixit in E flat in same Faldone)

A896 SICUT ERAT.
D Major. SATB, orchestra. Autograph score: I-BGc 130.

A897 SICUT ERAT.
E Major. SATB, orchestra. Autograph score: I-BGc 134. Belongs to Dixit "dei sorbetti" in same Faldone.

A898 SICUT ERAT.
C Major. STB, coro, orchestra. Non-autograph score: I-BGi 492g.D.120.

A899 SICUT ERAT.
C Major. SATB, orchestra. Autograph score: I-BGc 129.

A900 SICUT ERAT.
D Major. SATB, orchestra. Non-autograph score: I-Nc 1209.

55.   Dixit (Psalm 109)

DIXIT DOMINUS (Dixit)

A901 DIXIT.
B flat. STB, 2 ob, 2 cr. Non-autograph score: I-BGi 997.D.112.

A902 DIXIT.
C Major. SATB, orchestra. Autograph score: I-BGc 70.

A903 DIXIT.
C Major. SATB, violone, organ. Autograph score: I-BGc 139.

A904 DIXIT.
C Major. SATB "con piccola orchestra". Autograph score: I-BGc 139.

A905 DIXIT.
C Major. Tenore solo con repieni,
"A Quattro", SATB and orchestra.
Autograph score: I-BGc 133.

A906 DIXIT.
C Major. "Con versetti e sicut erat".
SATB, orchestra. Autograph score:
I-BGc 133.

A907 DIXIT.
C Major. SATB, orchestra. Non-
autograph score: I-BGi 2926.D.119.

A908 DIXIT.
D Major. SATB and orchestra.
Autograph score: I-BGc 130.

A909 DIXIT.
E Minor. SATB and orchestra, 4 tr obbli.
Autograph score: I-BGc 130.

A910 DIXIT.
D Major. SATB, orchestra. Parts only:
I-Mc MS.184-2.

A911 DIXIT.
D Major. SATB, orchestra. Autograph
score: I-BGc 76.

A912 DIXIT.
D Major. SATB, orchestra. Autograph
score: I-BGc 76. Also Juravit,
De torrente, Gloria, Sicut.

A913 DIXIT.
E flat Major. SATB, orchestra.
Autograph score: I-BGc 129. Also
Sicut erat.

A914 DIXIT.
E flat. SATB, orchestra. Autograph
score: I-BGc 69. Also Sicut erat.

A915 DIXIT.
F Major. SATB, orchestra. Autograph
score: I-BGc 132. Also Sicut erat.

A916 DIXIT.
F Major. SATB, orchestra. Autograph
score: I-BGc 66.

A917 DIXIT.
F Major. SATB, orchestra. 1802. Non-
autograph score: I-BGi 996.D.112. Part
of Mayr's first Vespers for S. Maria Maggiore.

A918 DIXIT (Dei sorbetti).
G Major. SATB, orchestra. Autograph
score: I-BGc 134. See also I-BGc 129.
Also Sicut erat.

A919 DIXIT.
B flat Major. SATB, orchestra.
Autograph score: I-BGc 69.

A920 DIXIT.
C Major. SATB, orchestra, with Sicut
erat. Autograph score: I-BGc 129.

A921 DIXIT.
B flat Major. SATB, orchestra. 1842.
Autograph score: I-BGc sala 32.D.815.

A922 DIXIT.
C Major. SATB, orchestra. Autograph
score: I-BGc 139. Part of complete
setting of Vespers.

A923 DIXIT.
Autograph score: I-BGc 139. Part of near
complete setting of Vespers.

A924 DIXIT & VERSETTI.
G Major. SATB, orchestra. Autograph
score: I-BGc 136.

A925 DIXIT & VERSETTI.
G Major. SATB, orchestra. Autograph score: I-BGc 137. "Per il Corpus Domini del 1802". Part of Mayr's first Vespers for *S. Maria Maggiore*.

A926 DIXIT.
B flat Major. SATB, orchestra. Parts only: I-BGc 139.

A927 DIXIT.
G Major. SATB, orchestra. Autograph score: I-BGc 139.

DIXIT - See A1035.

VIRGAM VIRTUTIS (Dixit)

A928 VIRGAM VIRTUTIS & TECUM PRINCIPIUM.
B flat Major. T solo, cello obbl, orchestra. Autograph score: I-BGc 138.

A929 VIRGAM VIRTUTIS.
C Major. T solo, ob, cl, fg obbl, orchestra. Autograph score: I-BGc 138.

TECUM PRINCIPIUM (Dixit)

A930 TECUM PRINCIPIUM.
G Major. S solo, fl obbl, orchestra. Autograph score: I-BGc 138.

A931 TECUM PRINCIPIUM.
E flat Major. T solo, cl & cr obbli, ob, cl, fg, cr, trb, strings. Autograph score: I-BGc 141.

A932 TECUM PRINCIPIUM.
G Major. S (or T) solo, orchestra. Autograph score: I-BGc 141.

A933 TECUM PRINCIPIUM.
G Major. SS soli, orchestra. Autograph score: I-BGc 141.

A934 TECUM PRINCIPIUM.
F Major. T solo, ob obbl, fl, cl, fg, cr, tr, strings. Autograph score: I-BGc 142.

A935 TECUM PRINCIPIUM.
C Major. T solo, ob obbl, orchestra. Autograph score: I-BGc 142.

A936 TECUM PRINCIPIUM.
B flat Major. T solo, fl or cl obbl, orch. Autograph score: I-BGc 142.

A937 TECUM PRINCIPIUM.
G Major. B solo, fl obbl, orch. Autograph score: I-BGc 142.

A938 TECUM PRINCIPIUM.
B flat. S solo, cello obbl, orchestra. Non-autograph score: I-BGi 1031.A.7.

DOMINUS A DEXTRIS (Dixit)

A939 DOMINUS A DEXTRIS.
D Major. T solo, chorus (?SATB), 4 tr obbl, orchestra. Autograph score: I-BGc 141. Also Juravit Dominus.

A940 DOMINUS A DEXTRIS.
C Major. TT soli, SSB coro, orchestra. Autograph score: I-BGc 143. Also Judicabit and De torrente.

A941 DOMINUS A DEXTRIS.
B flat Major. T solo, cl obbl, orchestra. Autograph score: I-BGc 143.

A942 DOMINUS A DEXTRIS.
D Major. T solo, vl obbl, orchestra. Autograph score: I-BGc 143.

A943 DOMINUS A DEXTRIS.
D Minor. T solo, vl obbl, orchestra. Autograph score: I-BGc 143.

A944 DOMINUS A DEXTRIS.
F Major. S solo, orchestra. Autograph score: I-BGc 143.

A945 DOMINUS A DEXTRIS.
C Major. T solo, chorus (?SATB), orchestra. Autograph score: I-BGc 143. Also De torrente.

A946 DOMINUS A DEXTRIS.
D Major. SATB, orchestra. Autograph score: I-BGc 144. Also De torrente - Basso solo.

A947 DOMINUS A DEXTRIS.
B flat Major. T solo, cl obbl, orchestra. Autograph score: I-BGc 144.

A948 DOMINUS A DEXTRIS.
C Major. B solo, orchestra. Autograph score: I-BGc 144.

A949 DOMINUS A DEXTRIS.
D Major. B solo, orchestra. Autograph score: I-BGc 144.

A950 DOMINUS A DEXTRIS.
D Minor. SATB, orchestra. Autograph score: I-BGc 144.

JUDICABIT (Dixit)

A951 JUDICABIT.
D Major. T solo, orchestra. Parts only: I-BGi 492d.120.

A952 JUDICABIT.
D Major. B solo "con corni", orchestra. Autograph score: I-BGc 145.

A953 JUDICABIT.
E flat Major. B solo, tr, cr & trb obbl, orchestra. Autograph score: I-BGc 145.

A954 JUDICABIT.
E flat Major. Duet TB, cl & fg obbli, orchestra. Autograph score: I-BGc 145.

A955 JUDICABIT.
A Minor. T solo, orchestra. Autograph score: I-BGc 145.

JURAVIT DOMINUS (Dixit)

A956 JURAVIT.
D Major. A solo, vla obbl, orchestra. Autograph score: I-BGc 140.

A957 JURAVIT.
C Minor. B solo, cl & cr obbli, orchestra. Autograph score: I-BGc 140.

A958 JURAVIT.
E flat Major. B solo, cl obbl, orchestra. Non-autograph score: I-BGi 1016.D.114.

A959 JURAVIT.
C Minor. B solo "con ripieni", orchestra. Non-autograph score: I-BGi 492d.B.120.

A960 JURAVIT (and DOMINUS A DEXTRIS).
D Major. T solo "con ripieno e 4 trombe", orchestra. Autograph score: I-BGc 141.

A961 JURAVIT.
E flat Major. B or A solo, cl (ob or fg) obbl, orchestra. Autograph score: I-BGc 141.

A962 JURAVIT.
E flat Major. B solo, orchestra. Autograph score: I-BGc 140.

963 JURAVIT.
E flat Major. B solo, cl obbl, orchestra. Non-autograph score: I-BGc 140.

A964 JURAVIT.
B solo "con clarinetti", orchestra. Non-autograph score: I-Nc Musica religiosa 1201.

A965 JURAVIT.
F Major. B solo, cr angl, fg obbl, orchestra. Autograph score: I-BGc 140.

A966 JURAVIT.
F Major. TTB, cl & cr obbli, orchestra. Autograph score: I-BGc 140.

DE TORRENTE (Dixit)

A967 DE TORRENTE.
E flat Major. T solo, orchestra. Autograph score: I-BGc 1.

A968 DE TORRENTE.
B flat. T solo and orchestra. Autograph score: I-BGc 1.

A969 DE TORRENTE.
A Major. B solo, vl obbl, orchestra. Autograph score: I-BGc 1.

A970 DE TORRENTE.
C Major. TT or SS, orch, 2 ob, 2 cr, strings. Autograph score: I-BGc 1.

A971 DE TORRENTE.
B flat. SS or TT, TB, orchestra. Autograph score: I-BGc 1.

56. Psalms

AFFERTE DOMINO (Psalm 29, in Book of Common Prayer)

A972 AFFERTE DOMINO
(Unaccompanied). Non-autograph score: I-BGc 11.

JUBILATE (Psalm 100)

A973 JUBILATE.
D Minor. SATB, orchestra, ob, cl, cr, fg, tr, timp, strings. Non-autograph score: I-BGc 67. (Used as Introit for Third Sunday after Easter).

DIXIT DOMINUS (Psalm 109)
See: Section 55.

CONFITEBOR TIBI (Psalm 110)

A974 CONFITEBOR TIBI.
C Major. STB soli. 1794 N.1. Non-autograph score: I-Vsmc.

A975 CONFITEBOR TIBI.
C Major. SATB soli, SATB coro. 1795. N.2. Non-autograph score: I-Mc MS 191.3.

A976 CONFITEBOR TIBI.
B flat. "A quattro concertati" (SATB), orchestra. 1802, Corpus Domine N.3. Autograph score: I-BGc 3. Part of Mayr's first Vespers for *S. Maria Maggiore*.

A977 CONFITEBOR TIBI.
B flat. T solo, vl & cello obbli, orchestra. N.5. Autograph score: I-BGc 3.

A978 CONFITEBOR TIBI.
B flat. T solo, orchestra. Autograph
score: I-BGc 3.

A979 CONFITEBOR TIBI.
F Major. B solo, coro, fl & cr obbli,
orchestra. Autograph score: I-BGc 5.

A980 CONFITEBOR TIBI.
B flat. SAB (soli) "con piccola
orchestra". Autograph score: I-BGc 5.

A981 CONFITEBOR TIBI.
C Major. SATB soli, orchestra.
Autograph score: I-BGc 3.

A982 CONFITEBOR TIBI.
F Major. SATB soli, orchestra.
Autograph score: I-BGc 139.

A983 CONFITEBOR TIBI.
F Major. SATB Chorus, orchestra. Non-
autograph score: I-BGi 492h.E.121.

A984 CONFITEBOR TIBI.
G Major. Double chorus SATB, 2 vl, 2
violoni, organ. Autograph score: I-BGc 5.

CONFITEBOR TIBI - See A1035.

BEATUS VIR (Psalm 111)

A985 BEATUS VIR.
G Major. S solo, fl obbl, orchestra.
Autograph score: I-BGc 6.

A986 BEATUS VIR.
F Major. S solo, ATB chorus, orchestra.
Autograph score: I-BGc 6.

A987 BEATUS VIR.
E flat. SATB chorus, orchestra.
Autograph score: I-BGc 327.

A988 BEATUS VIR.
A Minor. SATB soli, "a piccola orchestra". Autograph score: I-BGc 139.

A989 BEATUS VIR.
F Major. SATB, orchestra. Autograph
score: I-BGc 6. "I salmi intermedj ed
Inni pel Casnigo."

BEATUS VIR - See A1035.

LAUDATE PUERI (Psalm 112)

A990 LAUDATE PUERI.
B flat Major. SATB, orchestra.
Autograph score: I-BGc 9.

A991 LAUDATE PUERI.
C Major. SATB, orchestra. Autograph
score: I-BGc 9.

A992 LAUDATE PUERI.
B flat Major. SSST, harp obbl, orchestra.
Autograph score: I-BGc 9.

A993 LAUDATE PUERI.
C Major. SATB soli, SATB coro,
orchestra. Autograph score: I-BGc 10.

A994 LAUDATE PUERI.
E flat Major. No 6. B solo, cl & cr obbli,
orchestra. Autograph score: I-BGc 5.

A995 LAUDATE PUERI.
C Major. SAB, orchestra. Autograph
score: I-BGc 309.

A996 LAUDATE PUERI
(Psalmo piccolo).
SATB, orchestra. Autograph score:
I-BGc 139.

A997 LAUDATE PUERI.
SATB soli, SATB coro, orchestra.
Autograph score: I-MC MS 191.2.

A998 LAUDATE PUERI.
B flat Major. SATB soli, ripieni
(ie. coro), orchestra. Autograph score:
I-BGi 492i.E.121.

LAUDATE PUERI (Psalm 113) - See
A1035.

IN EXITU ISRAEL (Psalm 113)

These following scores make up two settings of the psalm:
a) an early version
b) a late version: substantially a rewrit-
ing of the earlier version. Parts; complete full scores.

A999 IN EXITU ISRAEL.
C Major. SATB soli, chorus, orchestra.

A1000 SIMULACRA GENTIUM.
A Major. B, orchestra.

A1001 DOMUS ISRAEL.
F Major. Duet; AB, orchestra.

A1002 QUI TIMENT DOMINO.
B flat Major. T, orchestra.

A1003 DOMINUS MEMOR FUIT.
G Major. SATB soli, coro, orchestra.

A1004 BENEDICITI.
C Major. T solo, SSB coro, orchestra.

A1005 NON MORTUI.
E flat Major. SATB soli, coro, orchestra.

A1006 NON MORTUI.
SATB soli, coro, orchestra.

A1007 GLORIA PATRI.
SATB soli, coro, orchestra.

A1008 SICUT.
SATB soli, coro, orchestra.

(All of the above): Autograph scores:
I-BGc 11 and Sala 32.D.8.27. (Both of
these settings are major compositions.)

IN EXITU ISRAEL - See A1035.

CREDIDI (Psalm 115)

A1009 CREDIDI.
E flat. T solo, orchestra. Autograph
score: I-BGc 12.

A1010 CREDIDI.
SATB (chorus, indicated by number of
parts), strings. Autograph score: I-BGc
12.

CREDIDI - See A1035.

LAUDATE DOMINUM
(Psalm 116)

A1011 LAUDATE DOMINUM.
E flat Major. SATB, orchestra, or wind
only. Autograph score: I-BGc 8.

A1012 LAUDATE DOMINUM.
B flat Major. SATB, cello obbl, orchestra. Autograph score: I-BGc 8.

A1013 LAUDATE DOMINUM.
B flat Major. T solo, SATB coro, organ.
Only a few MS parts survive: I-BGc 8.

A1014 LAUDATE DOMINUM.
G Major. SATB, orchestra. Autograph
score: I-BGc 8.

A1015 LAUDATE DOMINUM.
C Major. SATB, orchestra. Autograph
score: I-BGc 8.

A1016 LAUDATE DOMINUM.
G Major. SATB, "piccola orchestra".
Autograph score: I-BGc 139.

LAUDATE DOMINUM - See A1035.

LEVAVI OCULOS (Psalm 120)

A1017 LEVAVI OCULOS.
A Major. SATB, orchestra. Autograph score: I-BGc 11.

LAETATUS SUM (Psalm 121)

A1018 LAETATUS SUM.
G Major. B solo, fl obbl, fl, ob, cl, cr, strings. Autograph score: I-BGc 7.

A1019 LAETATUS SUM.
E flat Major. SATB, fl, ob, cr, strings. Autograph score: I-BGc 7.

A1020 LAETATUS SUM.
F Major. T solo, cl obbl, coro (T), ob, cl, cr, strings. Autograph score: I-BGc 7.

A1021 LAETATUS SUM.
E flat Major. SSB, organ. Also Nisi Dominus, Magnificat in G Major, SSB soli, S coro, organ. Autograph score: I-BGc 11.

LAETATUS SUM - See A1035.

IN CONVERTENDO (Psalm 125)

A1022 IN CONVERTENDO.
C Major. SATB, ob, cr, strings. 25 August 1803. Autograph score: I-BGc 12.

IN CONVERTENDO - See A1035.

NISI DOMINUS (Psalm 126)

A1023 NISI DOMINUS.
D Major. B solo, cr obbl, SATB coro, fl, ob, 2 cr (1 obbl), strings, organ. Autograph score: D-Dlb Mus 4104.E.1.1.

A1024 NISI DOMINUS.
D Major. B (or A) solo, cr obbl, coro, orchestra. Autograph score: I-BGc 7.

A1025 NISI DOMINUS.
G Major. S (or A) & ripieni di TBB, orchestra. Autograph score: I-BGc 7.

A1026 NISI DOMINUS.
F Major. SATB, orchestra. Autograph score: I-BGc 7.

A1027 NISI DOMINUS.
G Major. SSSB, organ. Autograph score: I-BGc 11.

A1028 NISI DOMINUS.
SATB, violone, organ. Autograph score: I-BGc 139.

NISI DOMINUS - See A1035.

BEATI OMNES (Psalm 127)

BEATI OMNES - See A1035.

DE PROFUNDIS (Psalm 129)

A1029 DE PROFUNDIS.
D Minor. SATB, orchestra. Autograph score: I-BGc 11.

DE PROFUNDIS - See A1035.

MEMENTO DOMINE DAVID (Psalm 131)

MEMENTO DOMINE - See A1035.

ECCE QUAM BONUM (Psalm 132)

A1030 ECCE QUAM BONUM.
C Major. SATB, orchestra. Autograph score: I-BGc 11. (See, For the clothing to the religious life.)

DOMINE PROBASTI ME
(Psalm 138)

DOMINE PROBASTI - See A1035.

LAUDA JERUSALEM (Psalm 147)

A1031 LAUDA JERUSALEM.
F Major. SATB soli & coro, 2 ob, 2 cl,
fg, 2 cr, strings, organ. Autograph score:
D-Dlb Mus 4104.E.1.2.

LAUDA JERUSALEM (Psalm 147
verses 12 - 20)

A1032 LAUDA JERUSALEM.
A flat Major. SS, fl, ob, cl, cr, strings.
Autograph score: I-BGc 12.

A1033 LAUDA JERUSALEM.
F Major. SATB, orchestra. Autograph
score: I-BGc 12. May also be sung as
Beatus vir.

A1034 LAUDA JERUSALEM.
SATB, orchestra. March 1821.
Autograph score: I-BGc 00.304.
Presented by Mayr to Bologna Academy.

LAUDA JERUSALEM - See A1035.

A CAPPELLA PSALMS and CANTICLES

A1035 DOMINE AD ADJUVANDUM
(Versicle response); DIXIT DOMINUS
(Ps 109); CONFITEBOR TIBI (Ps 110)
(4 settings); BEATUS VIR (Ps 111);
LAUDATE PUERI (Ps 112); LAUDATE
DOMINUM (Ps 116); LAETATUS SUM
(Ps 121); NISI DOMINUS (Ps 126)
(2 settings); LAUDA JERUSALEM
(Ps 147) (2 settings); CREDIDI (Ps 115);
IN CONVERTENDO (Ps 125);
DOMINE PROBASTI ME (Ps 138);
IN EXITU ISRAEL (Ps 113);
MEMENTO DOMINE DAVID (Ps 131);
BEATI OMNES (Ps 127) (2 settings);
DE PROFUNDIS (Ps 129);
MAGNIFICAT (Canticle),
SATB, violone, organ. Autograph score:
I-BGc 66.

57.   Canticles

TE DEUM

A1036 TE DEUM.
D Major. SAATB soli, SSAATTBB coro,
orchestra. Milan Cathedral 26 May 1805.
Autograph score: I-BGc 306.
For Napoleon's Coronation. The set of
parts in I-BGc represent a simpler
orchestration, possibly for *S. Maria
Maggiore*.

BENEDICTUS

BENEDICTUS DOMINUS (Benedictus)

A1037 BENEDICTUS DOMINUS.
F Major. A solo, fl, cr bassetto, fg, cr,
strings. Late work. Autograph score: I-
BGc sala 32.D.88.

A1038 BENEDICTUS DOMINUS.
F Major. B solo, orchestra. Autograph
score: I-BGc 315. Also: Sicut locutus,
B flat Major, T solo, cl obbl, orchestra;
Et tu puer, A flat Major, T solo,
orchestra; Ut sine timore, E flat Major,
SATB and orchestra; Per viscera,
F Minor, SATB, orchestra.

A1039 BENEDICTUS DOMINUS.
TB soli, SATB coro. Late work. 1841.
Autograph score: I-BGc sala 32.D.8.2.8.

A1040 BENEDICTUS DOMINUS.
C Major. SATB, orchestra. Non-
autograph score: I-BGc 315.

A1041 BENEDICTUS DOMINUS.
C Major. SATB, orchestra. Autograph
score: I-BGc 315.

A1042 BENEDICTUS DOMINUS.
D Major. SATB, orchestra. (Full setting
with solists). Non-autograph score:
I-BGc 34.

A1043 BENEDICTUS DOMINUS.
D Major. SATB, orch. Parts only:
I-BGc 293.

A1044 BENEDICTUS DOMINUS.
E flat, SATB, orch. Autograph score:
I-BGc 312.

A1045 BENEDICTUS DOMINUS
with Et tu puer and Per viscera. SATB,
orchestra. Autograph score: I-BGc 331.

A1046 BENEDICTUS DOMINUS
F Major. SATB, orchestra. "sul canto
fermo dell'iste confessor." Autograph
score: I-BGc 35.

A1047 BENEDICTUS DOMINUS
B flat. SATB, wind, organ. Autograph
score: I-BGc 312.

A1048 BENEDICTUS DOMINUS
B flat. SATB, orchestra. Autograph
score: I-BGc 35.

A1049 BENEDICTUS DOMINUS
B flat. SATB, orchestra. "sul canto
fermo." 1831. Autograph score: I-BGc 33.

A1050 BENEDICTUS DOMINUS
Double choir SATB/SATB, orchestra.
Autograph score: I-BGc 331.

SICUT LOCUTUS EST
(Benedictus)

A1051 SICUT LOCUTUS EST.
G Major. A solo, 2 fl, ob, cr, strings.
Autograph score: I-BGc 312.

A1052 SICUT LOCUTUS EST.
B flat Major. T solo, fl, ob, cl, cr, strings.
Autograph score: I-BGc 34.

AD FACIENDAM
MISERICORDIAM (Benedictus)

A1053 AD FACIENDAM
MISERICORDIAM
C Major. T solo, fl obbl, orchestra.
Autograph score: I-BGc 312.

A1054 AD FACIENDAM
MISERICORDIAM
E flat Major. AA soli, orchestra.
Autograph score: I-BGc 312.

A1055 AD FACIENDAM
MISERICORDIAM
A Major. S solo, orchestra. Autograph
score: I-BGc 312.

JUSJURANDUM (Benedictus verse)

A1056 JUSJURANDUM.
F Major. B solo, fl, ob, cl, cr, strings.
Autograph score: I-BGc 34.

ET TU PUER (Benedictus)

A1057 ET TU PUER.
A Major. SAT chorus, fl, ob, cl, cr,
strings. Autograph score: I-BGc 34.

A1058 ET TU PUER.
E flat Major. SSAAB soli, 2 cr, vle, cello,
violone. Autograph score: I-BGc 312.

A1059 ET TU PUER.
B flat Major. S solo, harp obbl, fl, ob, cr,
strings. Autograph score: I-BGc 312.

A1060 ET TU PUER.
C Major. T solo, cl, ob, cr, strings.
Autograph score: I-BGc 312.

A1061 ET TU PUER.
A flat. T solo, orchestra. Autograph
score: I-BGc 315. 20th century Ms in
BGi 999.D.112.

PER VISCERA (Benedictus)

A1062 PER VISCERA.
D Major. SATB, fl, ob, cl, cr, strings.
Autograph score: I-BGc 34.

A1063 PER VISCERA.
F Minor. SATB, orchestra. Autograph
score: I-BGc 315.

A1064 PER VISCERA.
B Minor. SATB, orchestra. Autograph
score: I-BGc 34.

58.   Magnificat

A1065 MAGNIFICAT with Gloria Patri.
C Major. SATB, orchestra. Autograph
score: I-BGc 19.

A1066 MAGNIFICAT with Gloria Patri.
F Major. SATB, orchestra. Autograph
score: I-BGc 19.

A1067 MAGNIFICAT.
D Major. SATB, orchestra. Autograph
score: I-BGc 19.

A1068 MAGNIFICAT.
C Major. SATB, orchestra. Autograph
score: I-BGc 19.

A1069 MAGNIFICAT.
C Major, SATB, orchestra. Autograph
score: I-BGc 20. In 2nd movement SA
soli, vl & cl soli.

A1070 MAGNIFICAT.
D Major. SATB, orchestra. Autograph
score: I-BGc 20.

A1071 MAGNIFICAT.
B flat Major. SSTB, strings. 1842.
Autograph score: I-BGc sala 32.D.8.3.

A1072 MAGNIFICAT
with Domine ad adjuvandum, Dixit, Nisi
Dominus, Ave maris stella. C Major.

SATB, violone. Autograph score: I-BGc
139.

A1073 MAGNIFICAT
with Domine ad adjuvandum and Dixit.
B flat Major. SATB, orchestra.
Autograph score: I-BGc 139.

A1074 MAGNIFICAT
with Domine ad adjuvandum. C Major.
TTB. Autograph score: I-BGc 139.

A1075 MAGNIFICAT
with Laetatus sum, Nisi Dominus. E flat
Major. SS soli, S coro, B, organ.
Autograph score: I-BGc 11. (For school).

A1076 MAGNIFICAT
"a canto solo con ripieni". B flat Major.
Non-autograph score: I-BGi 492m.E.121.

A1077 MAGNIFICAT.
SATB, orchestra. "sul tuono del canto
monasticale". Non-autograph score: I-Ls
C15.

A1078 MAGNIFICAT.
F Major. SATB, orchestra. Non-
autograph score: I-Nc musica religiosa
1202.

A1079 MAGNIFICAT.
B flat Major. "a Cinque", orchestra,
organ. Non-autograph score: I-Novd.

MAGNIFICAT - See A1035.

59.   Hymns - full settings with orchestra

A1080 A SOLIS ORTUS CARDINE.
(Christmastide hymn). "A Quattro".
Autograph score: I-BGc 16.

A1081 AH! CESSATE LACRYMANTIS
SATIS POENA.
T. Autograph score (incomplete): I-BGc
323.

A1082 AMOR JESU DOLCISSIME.
Hymn. E flat. SSA. Autograph score:
I-BGc 327.

A1083 CRUDELIS HERODES.
Hymn, Epiphany. G Major. SATB, fl, ob,
cl, cr, strings. Autograph score: I-BGc 13.

A1084 INVICTE CHRISTI SIGNIFER.
(For the feast of St. Alexander). Hymn.

E flat Major. T solo, orch, ob, cl, cr,
strings. 1805. Autograph score: I-BGc 15.

A1085 ISTE CONFESSOR.
Vespers, Hymn. C Major. "A Quattro"
SATB. Non-autograph score: I-BGi
4921.E.121.

A1086 JESU DULCIS MEMORIA.
Hymn, Motet. E flat Major. "A Quattro
concertati", SSTB, vl principale, ob, cl,
cr, fg, trb, strings. Autograph score:
I-BGc 73.

A1087 JESU REDEMPTOR.
G Major. "A Quattro", fl, ob, cl, cr, tr,
timp, strings. Autograph score: I-BGc 13.

A1088 JESU REDEMPTOR
(For New Year's Day). C Major. TTB, fl,
ob, cl, cr, strings. Autograph score:
I-BGc 13.

A1089 JESU REDEMPTOR
(For Christmas). G Major. SATB, fl, ob,
cl, cr, tr, timp, strings. Autograph score:
I-BGc 13.

A1090 JESU QUEM VELATUM.
G Major. SAT, 5 vocal parts; or SSAAT
(ie boys & tenor, for school). Non-
autograph score: I-BGi 477.D.115.

A1091 JESU QUEM VELATUM.
G Major. 2 Cantors (TT), organ. "Per la
Cappella Colleoni." I-BGc 30.

A1092 O MAGNE PRESUL
(may also be used as Exultet orbis).
C Major. SATB. Autograph score: I-BGc
14; Non-autograph score: I-BGi 1026.A.

A1093 O QUET UNDIS
(For Our Lady of Sorrows). Hymn. B
flat. SATB, "a fiato". Autograph score:
I-BGc 15.

A1094 O VITTIMA DI PACE.
Hymn. B flat. SSB, 2 vl, basso-continuo.
Autograph score: I-BGc 299.

A1095 O VITTIMA DI PACE.
F Major. SSB, strings. Autograph score
(incomplete): I-BGc 302, I-BGc 61
(Ms: SSB with pianoforte).

A1096 PLACARRE CHRISTE.
Hymn for All Saints. C Major. TTB.
Autograph score: I-BGc 16.

A1097 SALUTIS HUMANAE
(Ascension Day). SSTB. Autograph
score: I-BGc 13.

A1098 SANCTA MATER ISTUD AGAS.
F Major. T solo, vl princ. Autograph
score: I-BGc 25.

A1099 SANCTORUM MERITIS.
Hymn. F Major. SATB, fl, ob, cl, cr,
strings. Autograph score: I-BGc 15.

A1100 SERBA, O DIO, L'AMATO
AUGUSTO
(National Hymn). F Major. SATB.
Autograph score: I-BGc 308.

A1101 SI QUAERIS MIRACULA
(For the feast of St. Anthony). E flat
Major. SATB, cl, cr, strings. Autograph
score: I-BGc 15.

A1102 TE JOSEPH CELEBRENT
(Hymn for St. Joseph's Day). C Major.
STB, cr, ob, organ. Autograph score:
I-BGc 16.

A1103 TRISTES ERANT APOSTOLI.
Hymn. G Major. SATB, organ. 1803.
Autograph score: I-BGc 16.

A1104 VEXILLA REGIS.
Hymn Passiontide. C Major. T solo, vl,
ob, cl, cr, strings. Autograph score:
I-BGc 15.

A1105 VEXILLA REGIS
(For Procession). Hymn Passiontide.
G Major. Non-autograph score: I-BGi
433.E.122.

A1106 VENI CREATOR SPIRITUS.
Hymn Pentecost. B flat Major. STB coro.
"Pentecost 180..." Autograph score: I-
BGc 13. This piece could have been com-
posed for Mayr's first Pentecost at
S. Maria Maggiore.

A1107 VENI CREATOR SPIRITUS.
Hymn Pentecost. C Major. SATB.
Autograph score: I-BGc 13.

A1108 VIENI CREATOR SPIRITO.
G Major. 2 cantors, coro, organ. In "Concenti a più voci". Non-autograph score:
I-Mc PVBU3-3.

A1109 INNO PER S CECILIA.
C Major. SATB coro, fl, ob, cl, fg, cr, tr,
trb, timp, strings. Autograph score:
I-BGc 16.

See A 1501, VENI SANCTE SPIRITUS.

60.   Hymns and Spiritual Praises

A1110 HYMN BOOK
(Inni, Motetti, Antifone, Salmi). Words
by Samuele Biava. SS (boys/cantors) and
organ.
I-BGc 283. GB-Lbl, etc.

23 HYMNS AND 2 STABAT MATER
For use in the Mission field.
I-Vlevi CF.B.38.
Numbers A1111 - A1134, in the following order, are in one collection.

A1111 CROCIFISSO MIO SIGNOR.
G Major. TT. Non-autograph score.

A1112 PACE MIO DIO CHE GIÀ MI
PENTO.
G Major. TT. Non-autograph score.

A1113 PECCATI MAI PIÙ.
E Minor. TT. Non-autograph score.

A1114 PERDONO MIO DIO.
G Major. TT. Non-autograph score.

A1115 FERMATE O BARBARI NON
PIÙ.
G Major. TT. Non-autograph score.

A1116 GESÙ MIO CON DURE FUNI.
G Major. TT. Non-autograph score.

A1117 SU PENSIERI AL CIEL
VOLATE.
G Major. TT. Non-autograph score.

A1118 ALMA CONTRITA RALLEGRA
IL CORE.
G Major. TT. Non-autograph score.

A1119 RALLEGRISI OGNI ALMA.
G Major. TT. Non-autograph score.

A1120 CORRETE O MORTALI.
G Major. TT. Non-autograph score.

A1121 SU FIGLI CANTATE.
G Major. TT. Non-autograph score.

A1122 LODATE MARIA O LINGUE
FEDELI.
G Major. TT. Non-autograph score.

A1123 VERGINE AMABILE ARDO
PER TE.
G Major. TT. Non-autograph score.

A1124 O BELLA MIA SPERANZA.
G Major. TT. Non-autograph score.

A1125 VERGINE BELLA DEL CIEL
REGINA.
G Major. TT. Non-autograph score.

A1126 O DEL CIEL GRAN REGINA.
G Major. TT. Non-autograph score.

A1127 DEL TUO CELESTE TRONO.
G Major. TT. Non-autograph score.

A1128 SOCCORRI MARIA BENIGNA
SOCCORRI.
G Major. TT. Non-autograph score.

A1129 2 STABAT MATER.
G Major. TT. Non-autograph score.

A1130 NON ANCH'ERA IL MONDO.
G Major. TT. Non-autograph score.

A1131 SEI PURA SEI PIÙ BELLA
MARIA.
G Major. TT. Non-autograph score.

A1132 TU SCENDI DALLE STELLE.
G Major. TT. Non-autograph score.

A1133 FIGLI OGGI COMPIESI
L'ANNO FESTOSO.
G Major. TT. Non-autograph score.

A1134 VANITÀ DI VANITÀ OGNI
COSA È VANITÀ.
G Major. TT. Non-autograph score.

A1135 CANZONCINE SACRE
POPOLARI.
Non-autograph score: I-Vnm Cod.It.
IV.1219.

A1136 CANZONETTE SACRE.
"A 2 e più voci senza accomp." Non-
autograph score: I-Vnm Cod.It. IV.486.

A1137 PECCATORI, SE TRÀ MORTE.
F Major. TT. Non-autograph score:
I-BGc Mayr Nc 1.11.20.p.15.

A1138 SIAM REI DI MILLE ERRORI.
B flat. TT. Non-autograph score: I-BGc
Mayr Nc 1.11.17.p.13.

A1139 SEI PURA, SEI PIA.
G Major. TT. Non-autograph score:
I-Mayr Nc 1.11.18.p.13-14.

LAUDI SPIRITUALI
(Presumably for Hymn Book)

A1140 LAUDI SPIRITUALI FOR 2 & 3
VOICES.
Non-autograph score: I-BGc 283. With
works by Salari and others. Also Novena
& Birth of Our Lord Jesus Christ, words
by St. Alphonse de'Liguori.

A1141 NOSTRO AVVOCATO
(for the feast of S. Luigi Gonzaga).
G Major. SSB. Non-autograph score:
I-BGc 283.

A1142 TERZETTO: O VITTIMA DI
PACE.
TTB, piano. Autograph score: I-BGc 61.

61. Eucharistic Hymns

A1143 HYMN FOR THE PROCESSION
OF THE MOST BLESSED SACRA-
MENT.
Benediction, Corpus Christi or Holy
Thursday. G Major. 2 cantors, organ.
Autograph score: I-BGc 30.

PANGE LINGUA (Holy Thursday)

A1144 PANGE LINGUA.
A Major. SATB, fl, ob, cl, cr, strings.
Autograph score: I-BGc 13.

A1145 PANGE LINGUA.
C Major. SATB, fl, ob, cl, cr, tr, trb, strings. Autograph score: I-BGc 17.

A1146 PANGE LINGUA.
G Major. STB, organ. Autograph score: I-BGc 30.

A1147 PANGE LINGUA.
C Major. SATB, wind. Autograph score: I-BGc 16.

O SALUTARIS HOSTIA
(Benediction)

A1148 O SALUTARIS HOSTIA.
C Major. STTB, violone, organ. Non-autograph score: I-BGc 15.

A1149 O SALUTARIS HOSTIA.
D Major. ATTB, violone. Non-autograph score: I-BGc 15.

A1150 O SALUTARIS HOSTIA.
G Major. TTB, ob, cl, cr, fg, trb, strings. Autograph score: I-BGc 15.

A1151 O SALUTARIS HOSTIA.
B flat Major. TTB, fl, ob, cl, fg, cr, tr, trb, organ. Autograph score: I-BGc 15.

A1152 O SALUTARIS HOSTIA.
F Major. TTB, fl, ob, cl, cr, fg, tr, strings. Autograph score: I-BGc 15.

A1153 O SALUTARIS HOSTIA.
B flat Major. SATB, cl, ob, cr, fg, trb, organ. Autograph score: I-BGc 15.

A1154 O SALUTARIS HOSTIA.
E flat Major. SATB, fl, ob, cl, cr, trb, strings. Autograph score: I-BGc 15.

A1155 O SALUTARIS HOSTIA.
C Major. TTTB, organ. Autograph score: I-BGc 15.

A1156 O SALUTARIS HOSTIA.
B flat. SSSS, wind, 2 cr, tr, 4 trb, organ. Autograph score: I-BGc 15. (For school).

TANTUM ERGO (Benediction, Holy week)

A1157 TANTUM ERGO.
D Major. S solo, organ. Autograph score: I-BGc 15. Meant to be sung by boys in unison. 11 parts.

A1158 TANTUM ERGO.
B flat Major. T solo, SATB coro, fl, ob, cl, fg, cr, tr, trb, timp, strings. Autograph score: I-BGc 17.

A1159 TANTUM ERGO NO 17.
G Major. B solo, TTB, coro, fl obbl. 1843. Autograph score: I-BGc 17.

A1160 TANTUM ERGO.
E flat Major. S solo, ATB coro, fl, cl, cr, strings. Autograph score: I-BGc 17.

A1161 TANTUM ERGO
(or Pange Lingua). C Major. SATB, organ, orchestra. Non-autograph score: I-BGc 18.

A1162 TANTUM ERGO.
B flat Major. SATB, fl, ob, cl, cr, strings. Autograph score: I-BGc 18.

A1163 TANTUM ERGO.
F Major. S (or A or T) B, orchestra. Autograph score: I-BGc 18.

A1164 TANTUM ERGO.
E flat Major. B solo, TTB coro, orchestra with cl obbl. Autograph score: I-BGc 18.

A1165 TANTUM ERGO.
B flat Major. T solo, cl obbl, coro. Non-autograph score: I-BGc 18.

A1166 TANTUM ERGO
(Gloria patri, sicut erat). D Major. SATB,
orchestra. Autograph score: I-BGc 49.

A1167 TANTUM ERGO.
E flat Major. S solo, coro, orchestra.
Autograph score: I-BGc 17.

A1168 TANTUM ERGO.
E flat Major. T solo, orchestra. 1820.
Non-autograph score: I-Cf.

A1169 TANTUM ERGO.
B flat Major. SAT, strings. Non-
autograph score: I-BGc 297.

ECCE PANIS (Mass, Motet)

A1170 ECCE PANIS.
T solo, coro SATB, vl obbl, orchestra.
Non-autograph score: US-Mich M.2020
M47.E3.17-b.

O SACRUM CONVIVIUM
(Mass, Motet)

A1171 O SACRUM CONVIVIUM
(Per Novara). G Major. ATTB, orchestra,
organ. Autograph score: I-BGc 15. Non-
autograph score: I-NOVd.

A1172 O SACRUM CONVIVIUM.
F Major. S, pianoforte/organ. Autograph
score: I-BGc 310. (For school).

62. Hymns to Our Lady

A1173 SALVE REGINA.
B solo, SAB coro, fl, ob, cl, fg, 2 cr, trb,
strings. Autograph score: D-Mbm
Coll.Mus.Max.238.

A1174 SANCTA MARIA SUCURRE.
Motet. C Major. ATTB, fl, ob, cl, cr,
strings. Autograph score: D-Mbm
Coll.Mus.Max.237.

A1175 SANCTA MARIA
(Per Novara). C Major. ATTB, organ.
I-BGc 59; I-NOVd.

A1176 INVOCATION TO OUR LADY.
Hymn. STB, coro. Non-autograph scores:
I-OS B.2295, I-Vnm Cod.It. IV.486.

A1177 AVE MARIA.
E Major. Non-autograph score: I-BGc 13.
Only the soprano line exists.

ALMA REDEMPTORIS
(Hymn to Our Lady, Vespers etc.)

A1178 ALMA REDEMPTORIS.
B flat Major. T, wind. Autograph score:
I-BGc 15.

A1179 ALMA REDEMPTORIS.
A Major. STB, orchestra. Autograph
score: I-BGc 15.

A1180 ALMA REDEMPTORIS.
B flat. T, orchestra. Autograph score:
I-BGc 15.

AVE MARIS STELLA
(Hymn to Our Lady, Vespers etc.)

A1181 AVE MARIS STELLA.
F Major. SATB, orchestra. Autograph
score: I-BGc 13.

A1182 AVE MARIS STELLA.
F Major. SATB, violone, organ.
Autograph score: I-BGc 139.

A1183 AVE MARIS STELLA.
G Major. SATB, "con sinfonia", 2 ob,
2 cr, strings. 1803. Autograph score:
I-BGc 13; Non-autograph score: I-BGi
985.D.105.

A1184 AVE MARIS STELLA.
G Major. SATB, orchestra. Autograph
score: I-BGc 13.

AVE REGINA
(Hymn to Our Lady, Vespers etc.)

A1185 AVE REGINA.
B flat Major. SAB soli, orchestra.
Autograph score: I-BGc 307.

A1186 AVE REGINA.
E flat. SSTB, orchestra. Autograph score:
I-BGc 307.

A1187 AVE REGINA.
F Major. SATB, violone, organ.
Autograph score: I-BGc 47.

A1188 AVE REGINA.
G Major. SATB, orchestra. Non-
autograph score: I-Mc 190.1.

REGINA COELI
(Hymn to Our Lady, Vespers etc.)

A1189 REGINA COELI.
G Major. S solo, ob, cr, fg, strings. Non-
autograph score: I-BGc 307.

A1190 REGINA COELI.
B flat Major. T solo, 2 ob, fg, cr, strings.
Autograph score: I-BGc 307.

SALVE REGINA
(Hymn to Our Lady, Vespers etc.)

A1191 SALVE REGINA.
S solo, 2 ob, 2 cr, fg, violone, organ.
1798. Non-autograph score: I-Vc Correr
52-60.

A1192 SALVE REGINA.
"a Cinque". Autograph score: I-Fc E.427.

A1193 SALVE REGINA.
F Major. SB soli, orchestra. Autograph
score: I-BGc 307.

A1194 SALVE REGINA.
F Major. S solo, orchestra. Autograph
score: I-BGc 307.

A1195 SALVE REGINA.
B flat Major. T solo, fl, ob, cl, cr, strings.
Autograph score: I-BGc 307.

A1196 SALVE REGINA.
F Major. B solo, SAB, coro, orchestra.
Autograph score: I-BGc 307.

A1197 SALVE REGINA.
F Major. S solo, 2 ob, cr, strings.
Autograph score: I-BGc 307.

A1198 SALVE REGINA.
B flat Major. T solo, ob, fg, cr, strings.
Autograph score: I-BGc 307.

A1199 SALVE REGINA No 5
(May also be sung as Iste Confessor).
F Major. B solo, 2 ob, 2 cr, fg, strings.
Autograph score: I-BGc 307.

A1200 SALVE REGINA.
C Major. S solo, 2 ob, 2 cr, violone,
organ. Autograph score: I-BGc 307.

A1201 SALVE REGINA.
F Major. 2 cantors, choir, org. In "Con-

centi a più voci". p 17. Non-autograph score: I-Mc PVBU 2-3.

AVE MARIA (The Angelic Salutation ⤸ Hymn to Our Lady)

A1202 L'AVE MARIA.
F Major. 2 part coro, organ. In "Concenti a più voci" p 6. Non-autograph score: I-Mc PVBU 3-3.

THE ANGELUS

A1203 L'ANGELUS DOMINI.
F Major. 2 cantors, coro, organ. In "Concenti a più voci" p 5. Non-autograph score: I-Mc PVBU 3-3.

DEVOTIONAL HYMNS TO OUR LADY

A1204 DAL TUO CELESTE TRONO.
Canzonetta. G Major. TT. Non-autograph score: I-BGc NC.1.11.2.

A1205 LODATE MARIA.
G Major. TT. Non-autograph score: I-BGc NC.1.11.13.

A1206 O BELLA MIA SPERANZA.
G Major. TT. Non-autograph score: I-BGc NC.1.11.1.p.1.

A1207 O DEL CIEL GRANDE REGINA.
G Major. TT. Non-autograph score: I-BGc NC.1.11.3.3.

A1208 O VIRGO IMMACULATA
(Ah miseri). C Minor. T solo, orch. Non-autograph score: I-Mc 191.1.

A1209 SANCTA MARIA.
C Major. "a Cinque" organ. Non-autograph score: I-NOVd.

A1210 SANCTA MARIA.
C Major. SATB, orchestra. Non-autograph score: I-BGi 1023A.

A1211 SANCTA MARIA
(Per Novara). C Major. ATTB, organ. Autograph score: I-BGc 59.

A1212 SANCTA MARIA SUCCURRE MISERIS (Per Novara).
C Major. SATB, organ, orchestra. Autograph score: I-BGc 59.

A1213 SOCCORI MARIA.
Canzonetta religiosa. G Major. TT. Non-autograph score: I-BGc NC.1.11.5.

A1214 VERGINE AMABILE
(Offerta del proprio cuore a Maria).
G Major. TT. Non-autograph score: I-BGc NC.1.11.6.

A1215 VERGINE BELLA
(Offerta del proprio cuore a Maria).
G Major. TT. Non-autograph score: I-BGc NC.1.11.9.

A1216 VERSES TO OUR LADY FOR THE MONTH OF MAY.
Non-autograph score: I-CEsm.

A1217 VIRGO IMMACULATA.
D Minor. T solo, orchestra. Autograph score: I-BGc 59.

STABAT MATER (Passiontide Hymn by Jacopone da Todi).
Verses:
Quando corpus; Eja mater; Q quam tristis; Pro peccatis; Virgo Virginum; Inflammatus et accensus; Flammis ne urar succensus; Christe cum sit; Fac ut animae donetur.

A1218 STABAT MATER
& Quando corpus. F Minor. SATB, ob,
cl, cr, strings. Autograph score: I-BGc 24.

A1219 STABAT MATER
& Quando corpus. C Minor. SATB, cl,
ob, cl, cr, strings. Autograph score:
I-BGc 24.

A1220 STABAT MATER
& Quando Corpus. G Minor. SATB, ob,
cl, cr, strings. Autograph score: I-BGc 24.

A1221 STABAT MATER,
Eja Mater, Quando Corpus. F Minor.
SATB, ob, cl, cr, vl solo, strings.
Autograph score: I-BGc 23.

A1222 STABAT MATER
"a Quattro con picciola orchestra. N.5."
C Minor. SATB, ob, cr, strings.
Autograph score: I-BGc 23.

A1223 STABAT MATER.
G Major. SATB, wind. Autograph score:
I-BGc 16.

A1224 STABAT MATER.
F Major. SATB, wind. Autograph score:
I-BGc 16.

A1225 O QUAM TRISTIS.
B flat Major. SATB, fl, ob, cl, cr, strings.
Autograph score: I-BGc 23.

A1226 O QUAM TRISTIS.
A flat Major. T solo, cl or fg obbl, cl,
strings. Autograph score: I-BGc 23.

A1227 O QUAM TRISTIS.
F Major. S solo, cello or fg or cr obbl, cl
obbl, cr, strings. Autograph score:
I-BGc 23.

A1228 O QUAM TRISTIS.
B flat Major. TT soli, cl (or ob) obbl, cr,
strings. Autograph score: I-BGc 23.

A1229 QUIS EST HOMO.
C Minor. S solo, cello or ob or fg obbl, fl,
ob, cl, strings. Autograph score: I-BGc 25.

A1230 QUIS EST HOMO.
D Minor. T solo, ob or fl obbl, ob, cl, cr,
strings. Autograph score: I-BGc 25.

A1231 PRO PECCATIS.
F Minor. B solo, ob, cl, cr, strings.
Autograph score: I-BGc 25.

A1232 EJA MATER.
F Minor. SATB, orch. Autograph score:
I-BGc 23.

A1233 EJA MATER.
E flat Major. SATB, orchestra.
Autograph score: I-BGc 25.

A1234 EJA MATER.
E flat Major. B solo, cr obbl, orchestra.
Non-autograph score: I-BGc 25.

A1235 EJA MATER.
G Major. SATB, orchestra. Autograph
score: I-BGc 25.

A1236 EJA MATER.
F Major. SATB, orchestra. Autograph
score: I-BGc 25.

A1237 EJA MATER.
F Major. SATB, 2 ob, cl, 2 cr, violone,
?organ. Autograph score: I-BGc 25.

A1238 SANCTA MATER.
F Major. T solo, vl obbl, ob, cl, cr,
strings. Autograph score: I-BGc 25.

A1239 VIRGO VIRGINUM.
F Major. S solo, fl, ob, cl, cr, trb, strings.
Autograph score: I-BGc 25.

A1240 VIRGO VIRGINUM.
A Major. T solo, vl or cl obbl, fl, cr, fg, trb, strings. Autograph score: I-BGc 25.

A1241 INFLAMMATUS ET ACCENSUS.
F Major. B solo, ob, cr, strings. Autograph score: I-BGc 27.

A1242 FLAMMIS NE URAR SUCCENSUS.
E flat Major. B solo, fl, ob, cl, 2 cr, strings. Autograph score: I-BGc 316.

A1243 CHRISTE CUM SIT.
C Major. T solo, fl, ob, cl, cr, strings. Autograph score: I-BGc 27.

A1244 FAC UT ANIMAE DONETUR.
C Major. STB, cl, cr, tr, trb, strings. Autograph score: I-BGc 316.

A1245 STABAT MATER.
C Minor. TTB, organ. Non-autograph score: I-Mc 193.

A1246 STABAT MATER.
G Minor. SATB, orchestra. Non-autograph score: I-OS B.256/1.
O Quam tristis, Andante, 3/4, B flat; Eja mater, adagio, 4/4, G Major; Inflammatus, All. mod, 4/4, C Major; Flammis ne urar, Andantino, 3/4, C Major; Quando corpus, adagio, 4/4, G Major.

A1247 STABAT MATER.
SATB. Non-autograph score: I-CEsm.

See also HYMNS AND SPIRITUAL PRAISES

63.   Music for Holy Week

LAMENTATIONS (LESSONS) FOR HOLY WEDNESDAY

A1248 No I, in C Minor.
T solo, fl, cl, cr, strings. "Quo modo sedet". Autograph score: I-BGc 27.

A1249 No I, in A Major.
SSTB, fl, cl, cr. "Incipit lamentatio". Autograph score: I-BGc 27.

A1250 No I, in D Minor.
B solo, coro, fl, cl, cr & violino princ. Autograph score: I-BGc 27.

A1251 No II, in D Minor.
B solo, ob, cr, strings. No 4, 1804, "Vau

et egressus est". Autograph score: I-BGc 27.

A1252 No II, in F Major.
S solo, fl, ob, cl, cr, strings. "Egressus est". Autograph score: I-BGc 27.

A1253 No III, in E flat Major.
T solo, cl & cr obbli, orchestra. "Jod manum suam". Autograph score: I-BGc 26.

A1254 No III, in F Major.
A solo, cr obbl, ob, cr, strings. "Manum suam". Autograph score: I-BGc 26.

LAMENTATIONS (LESSONS) FOR HOLY THURSDAY

(Maundy Thursday)

A1255 No I, in F Major.
B solo, fl, ob, cl, cr, strings. N.2, "Incipit lamentatione". Autograph score: I-BGc 29.

A1256 No I, in F Major.
B solo, vla obbl, fl, ob, cl, cr, strings. N.3, "De lamentatione". Autograph score: I-BGc 29.

A1257 No I, in A Major.
S solo, vl princ, ob, cl, cr, strings. Autograph score: I-BGc 29.

A1258 No II, in G Minor.
T solo, coro, orchestra. Autograph score: I-BGc 28.

A1259 No II, in A Minor.
T solo, SSTB coro, orchestra. Autograph score: I-BGc 28.

A1260 No III, in E flat Major.
A solo, orchestra. 2nd half "Jerusalem", ATB. Autograph score: I-BGc 28.

A1261 No III, in G Major.
S solo, SSTB coro, orchestra. Autograph score: I-BGc 28.

LAMENTATIONS (LESSONS) FOR GOOD FRIDAY

A1262 No I, in D Minor.
SSTB, organ. Autograph score: I-BGc 30.

A1263 No I, in C Major.
S solo, orchestra. Autograph score: I-BGc 32.

A1264 No I, in E flat Major.
S solo, orchestra. Autograph score: I-BGc 32.

A1265 No I, in E flat Major.
T solo, cl & cr obbli, orchestra. Autograph score: I-BGc 32.

A1266 No I, in D Major.
AT soli, orchestra. N.7. Autograph score: I-BGc 32.

A1267 No II, in B flat Major.
TB soli, orchestra. Autograph score: I-BGc 31.

A1268 No II, in E flat Major.
B solo, vla & cr obbli, orchestra. Autograph score: I-BGc 31.

A1269 No II, in C Minor.
B solo, cr obbl, orchestra. N.5. Autograph score: I-BGc 31.

A1270 No III, in F Major.
SA soli, TTBB coro, orchestra. Autograph score: I-BGc 31.

A1271 No III, in E Minor.
S solo, vl obbli, SSTB coro, orchestra. Autograph score: I-BGc 31.

A1272 No III, in G Minor.
TT soli, 2 celli obbli (or cl dolci), orchestra. Autograph score: I-BGc 30.

A1273 No III, in F Minor.
SSTB, orchestra. Autograph score: I-BGc 30.

THE PASSION

A1274 THE PASSION.
For Palm Sunday. SATB, violone, organ. 41 verses. Non-autograph score: I-BGi 483.D.118.

A1275 THE PASSION.
For Holy Tuesday. G Major. SATB, violone, organ. "Non in die ista". Autograph score: I-BGc; Non-autograph score: I-BGi 484.D.118.

A1276 THE PASSION.
For Holy Wednesday. C Major. SATB, violone, organ. Autograph score: I-BGc 30.

A1277 THE PASSION.
For Good Friday. SATB, violone, organ. 34 verses. Non-autograph score: I-BGi 486.D.119.

A1278 THE PASSION.
For Good Friday. B flat. Fl, ob, 2 cr, 2 fg, strings, organ. The role of Christ - "Scitis quia post tridum".

THE THREE HOURS ON THE CROSS

A1279 THE THREE HOURS ON THE CROSS (Tre ore dell'agonia).
3 voices, violone. Non-autograph score: I-VEsg.

THE WAY OF THE CROSS

A1280 THE WAY OF THE CROSS.
Two devotional settings: Sancti Crucis. Non-autograph scores: A-Wgm.

THE DEVOTION OF THE SEVEN LAST WORDS OF THE SAVIOUR

A1281 GIÀ TRAFITTO IN DURO LEGNO
(An Invitation for Haydn's *Seven last words of the Saviour*). Words by St. Alphonse de'Liguori. G Minor. SATB coro, orchestra. Autograph score: I-BGc 225. [In Mayr's Library there are the vocal and the quartet versions of Haydn's masterpiece.]

64.   The Office of the Dead

FIRST VIGIL OF THE OFFICE FOR THE DEAD

A1283 1st LESSON.
G Minor. B solo, fl, ob, cl, fg, tr, trb, strings. Autograph score: I-BGc 37.

A1284 1st RESPONSORY.
G Major. SATB, fl, ob, cl, fg, tr, trb, strings. Autograph score: I-BGc 37.

A1285 2nd LESSON.
B flat Major. T solo, fl, ob, cl, fg, tr, trb, strings. Autograph score: I-BGc 37.

A1286 2nd RESPONSORY.
B flat Major. SATB, fl, ob, cl, fg, tr, trb, strings. Autograph score: I-BGc 37.

A1287 3rd LESSON.
E flat Major. A solo, fl, ob, cl, fg, tr, trb, strings. Autograph score: I-BGc 37.

A1288 3rd RESPONSORY.
G Minor. SATB, fl, ob, cl, fg, tr, trb, strings. Autograph score: I-BGc 37.

65. Requiem Mass (Complete Settings)

A1289 MESSA DA REQUIEM.
E flat Major. SATB, fl, cl, fg, cr.
Autograph score: I-BGc 36.

A1290 MESSA DA REQUIEM.
F Major. STB, orchestra. Autograph
score: I-BGc 47. Short requiem 12
"carte".

A1291 MESSA DA REQUIEM.
D Minor. SATB, orchestra. Autograph
score: I-BGc 47.

A1292 MESSA DA REQUIEM.
G Minor. TTB, tr, trb. Late work.
Autograph score: I-BGc sala 32.E.8.25.

A1293 MESSA DA REQUIEM.
C Minor. SATB soli, SATB coro,
orchestra. Non-autograph score:
I-Mc 192.2.

A1294 MESSA DA REQUIEM.
G Minor. SATB soli, SATB coro, 2 fl,
2 ob, 2 cl, 2 cr di bassetto, 2 fg, 4 cr, 3 tr,
trb, timp, strings, organ. 1819 (printed
score). In most libraries, GB-Lbl, I-BGc,
etc.

A1295 MESSA DA REQUIEM.
SATB, orchestra. Non-autograph score:
I-Fc E.800.

66. Requiem Aeternam (Requiem: Introit)

A1296 REQUIEM AETERNAM.
C Minor. SATB, fl, cl, ob, strings, organ
obbl. Autograph score: I-BGc 37. A part
signed "Donizetti".

A1297 REQUIEM AETERNAM, TE
DECET, KYRIE.
SATB, fl, ob, cl, cr, tr, trb, timp, strings.
Autograph score: I-BGc 37.

A1298 REQUIEM AETERNAM, TE
DECET, KYRIE.
G Minor. SSAT, "Tenore di ripieno,
Bassi", orchestra, 2 fl, ob, cl, cr di basset-
to, fg, 2 cr, 3 tr, trb, timp, strings, organ.
Late work. Autograph score: I-BGc sala
32.D.8.16.

A1299 REQUIEM AETERNAM.
D Minor. STB, violone. Non-autograph
score:I-BGi 489.D.119.

A1300 REQUIEM AETERNAM.
F Major. STB, violone. Non-autograph
score:I-BGi 490.D.119.

A1301 REQUIEM AETERNAM CON
SINFONIA.
SATB, orchestra. Non-autograph score:
I-BGi 1029.A.7.

A1302 REQUIEM AETERNAM CON
SINFONIA.
D Minor. SATB, orchestra. "Per uso di
F. Mosconi". Autograph score: I-BGc 64.

A1303 REQUIEM AETERNAM.
A flat. 2 part choir, organ. In "Concenti a
più voci" p 19. Non-autograph score:
I-Mc PVBU 3-3.

A1304 REQUIEM AETERNAM.
"Per il Rito Ambrosiano". C Minor.
SATB coro, fl, ob, cl, fg, cr, tr, trb, timp,
strings. Autograph score: I-BGc 40.

67.   Dies Irae (Requiem: Sequences, Hymn)
(Words by Thomas of Celano)

A1305 DIES IRAE.
C Minor. "A più voci" STB, strings. Non-autograph score: I-BGi 478a.D.115.

A1306 DIES IRAE.
C Minor. "a Quattro corni ed anche a 2 come co' soliti strumenti di fiato". (also Huic Ergo: see A1309). SATB, fl, ob, cl, cr, tr, trb, timp, strings, organ. Autograph score: I-BGc 39.

A1307 DIES IRAE.
D Minor. "a quattro con grande orchestra" (also Tuba Mirum). SSTB, 4 cr, and "grande orchestra con solisti di fiato". Autograph score: I-BGc 40.

A1308 DIES IRAE.
D Minor. SATB, large orchestra, cr di bassetto obbl. Late work. Autograph score: I-BGc sala 32.D.8.15.

HUIC ERGO (Requiem, Dies irae)

A1309 HUIC ERGO.
D Minor. 4 soli (or coro?), fl, ob, cl, cr, strings; second band: 2 cr, tr, trb, timp, gran cassa, cb, organ. Autograph score: I-BGc 39.

TUBA MIRUM (Requiem, Dies irae)

A1310 TUBA MIRUM.
E flat Major. B solo, trb obbl, orchestra. Autograph score: I-BGc 41.

A1311 TUBA MIRUM.
F Major. B solo, orchestra. Non-autograph score: I-Mc 192.3.

A1312 TUBA MIRUM.
C Minor. "a basso solo con grande orchestra". Autograph score: I-BGc 40.

LIBER SCRIPTUS
(Requiem, Dies irae)

A1313 LIBER SCRIPTUS.
B flat Major. T solo, cl obbl, orchestra. Autograph score: I-BGc 41.

A1314 LIBER SCRIPTUS.
F Major. T solo, fg obbl, orchestra. Autograph score: I-BGc 41.

A1315 LIBER SCRIPTUS & ECCE ENIM.
B flat Major. Vla obbl. Autograph score: I-BGc 41.

INTER OVES (Requiem, Dies irae)

A1316 INTER OVES.
C Major. "a Cinque con coro", SSATB, fl, ob, cl, fg, cr, tr, trb, timp, strings. Autograph score: I-BGc 41.

RECORDARE (Requiem, Dies irae)

A1317 RECORDARE.
F Major. SSS, concertina or arcordian obbl, strings. Autograph score: I-BGc 41.

A1318 RECORDARE.
C Major. T solo (or S or A), ob, fg. Autograph score: I-BGc 41.

INGEMISCO (Requiem, Dies irae)

A1319 INGEMISCO.
A Minor. T solo, vl obbl, fl, ob, cl, fg, cr, strings. Autograph score: I-BGc 41.

A1320 INGEMISCO.
F Minor. S solo, fl & cello obbli, fl, cl, cr, trb, strings. Autograph score: I-BGc 41.

ORO SUPPLEX (Requiem, Dies irae)

A1321 ORO SUPPLEX.
E Major. S, instruments. Autograph score: I-BGc 302.

A1322 ORO SUPPLEX.
E flat. TB, cl & cr obbli, 2 ob, fg. Non-autograph score: I-BGi 1027A.

A1323 ORO SUPPLEX.
E flat. B, cr obbli, orchestra. Autograph score: I-BGc 44.

A1324 ORO SUPPLEX.
E flat Major. A, orchestra. Autograph score: I-BGc 44.

A1325 ORO SUPPLES.
E flat Major. STB, cl & cr obbli, orchestra. Non-autograph score: I-BGc 44.

LACRYMOSA (Requiem, Dies irae)

A1326 LACRYMOSA.
Finale. C Minor. "più voci ed archi". Non-autograph score: I-BGi 478.D.115.

A1327 LACRYMOSA.
E flat Major. SATB, picc, fl, ob, cl, fg, cr, tr, trb, strings. Autograph score: I-BGc 40.

68.   Libera Me and Subvenite Sancti
(Requiem)

A1328 LIBERA ME.
G Minor. SATB, violone, organ. Autograph score: I-BGc 47.

A1329 LIBERA ME.
C Minor. SATB soli, SATB coro, orchestra. Non-autograph score: I-BGi 478e.D.115.

A1330 LIBERA ME.
D Minor. "a Quattro"; "a grande orchestra". Autograph score: I-BGc 47.

A1331 LIBERA ME
from Requiem Mass, by Iganz Xavier von Seyfried. Reduction for wind by Mayr. Autograph score: I-BGc 47.

A1332 SUBVENITE SANCTI.
G Minor. SATB, orchestra. Autograph score: I-BGc 47.

69. Miserere (Psalm 50)

Sung at Requiems and during Lent and Holy Week

A1333 MISERERE.
F Minor. SATB, fl, ob, cl, cr, fg, tr, trb,
timp, strings. Autograph score: I-BGc 38.

A1334 MISERERE.
D flat Major. SATB, fl, ob, cl, cr, strings.
Autograph score: I-BGc 38.

A1335 MISERERE.
G Minor. SATB, fl, ob, cl, cr, serp, trb,
strings. Autograph score: I-BGc 42.

A1336 MISERERE.
F Minor. SATB, ob, cl, cr, fg, strings.
Autograph score: I-BGc 42. One part
marked "Donizetti".

A1337 MISERERE and TUNC
ACCEPTABIS.
C Major. SATB, fl, ob, cl, cr, organ obbl,
strings. Autograph score: I-BGc 43.

A1338 MISERERE and TUNC
ACCEPTABIS.
D Minor. SATB, ob, cl, cr, strings.
Autograph score: I-BGc 43.

A1339 MISERERE.
C Minor. SATB, fl, ob, cl, cr, tr, trb,
timp, strings. Autograph score: I-BGc 45.

A1340 MISERERE and TUNC
ACCEPTABIS.
G Minor. SATB, fl, ob, cl, cr, trb, strings.
Autograph score: I-BGc 45.

A1341 MISERERE.
C Minor. SATB, fl, ob, cl, cr, strings.
Autograph score: I-BGc 45.

A1342 MISERERE.
D Minor. SATB, fl, ob, cl, fg, cr, tr, trb,
timp, strings. Autograph score: I-BGc 46.

A1343 MISERERE and TUNC
ACCEPTABIS.
G Minor. STB, fl, ob, cl, cr, tr, trb, timp,
strings. Autograph score: I-BGc 46.

A1344 MISERERE and TUNC
ACCEPTABIS.
D Major. SSTB, fl, ob, cl, cr, strings.
Autograph score: I-BGc 48.

A1345 MISERERE and TUNC
ACCEPTABIS.
F Minor. SATB, fl, ob, cl, cr, strings.
Autograph score: I-BGc 48.

A1346 MISERERE.
E flat Major. Alternating double coro, fl,
ob, cl, cr, strings. Autograph score: I-
BGc 49.

A1347 MISERERE.
G Minor. SATB, fl, ob, cl, cr, strings,
violone, organ. Autograph score: I-BGc
49.

1348 MISERERE
and Amplius, Tibi soli, Cor mundum,
Redde mibi, Libera me, Quoniam si
voluisses. Benigne fac. D Minor, TTB,
ob, cl, cr, fg, strings. Non-autograph
score: I-BGc 50.

A1349 MISERERE and TUNC
ACCEPTABIS.
F Major. SATB, fl, ob, cl, cr, strings.
Autograph score: I-BGc 52.

A1350 MISERERE.
A flat Major. SATB, fl, ob, cl, cr, trb, strings. Autograph score: I-BGc 52.

A1351 MISERERE.
D Minor. SATB, ob, cr, strings. 1803. Autograph score: I-BGc 204.

A1352 MISERERE.
G Minor. SATB, ob, cr, strings. 1803. Autograph score: I-BGc 204.

A1353 MISERERE.
SATB, cl, cr, tr, trb, timp. Autograph score: I-BGc 214. Written for the funeral of Tavecchi 1st Sop of *S. Maria Maggiore* and used at Mayr's own requiem - published by Ricordi.

A1354 MISERERE.
D Minor. 1843. Autograph score: I-BGc sala D.8.24/1. Incomplete.

A1355 MISERERE.
STB "viole e strumenti a fiato". Non-autograph score: I-Fc B.2351.

A1356 MISERERE.
D Minor. ATTB, Autograph score: I-BGc 295. Incomplete.

A1357 MISERERE.
SATB and orchestra. Autograph score: D-Bds "Mayr 3".

AMPLIUS AND TIBI SOLI
(Miserere)

A1358 AMPLIUS.
E flat. T solo, orchestra. Autograph score: I-BGc 214.

A1359 AMPLIUS & TIBI SOLI.
C Major. T, orchestra. Autograph score: I-BGc 214.

A1360 AMPLIUS & TIBI SOLI.
B solo, fl obbl, orchestra. Autograph score: I-BGc 214.

TIBI SOLI (Miserere)

A1361 TIBI SOLI.
C Major. T solo, cello obbl, orchestra. Autograph score: I-BGc 208.

A1362 TIBI SOLI.
C Major. B solo, ob obbl, orchestra. Autograph score: I-BGc 208.

A1363 TIBI SOLI.
C Major. T solo, fl & ob & cl obbli, orchestra. Autograph score: I-BGc 208.

A1364 TIBI SOLI.
E flat Major. S solo, ob obbl, orchestra. Autograph score: I-BGc 208.

A1365 TIBI SOLI.
B flat Major. S (or A) solo, cl, ob, cello obbl, coro ATB and orchestra. Autograph score: I-BGc 208.

A1366 TIBI SOLI.
C Major. T solo, ob obbl, orchestra. Autograph score: I-BGc 212.

A1367 TIBI SOLI.
C Major. T solo and orchestra. Autograph score: I-BGc 212.

A1368 TIBI SOLI.
C Major. T solo, ob obbl, orchestra. Autograph score: I-BGc 212.

A1369 TIBI SOLI.
B flat Major. T solo, cello solo, orchestra. Autograph score: I-BGc 213.

A1370 TIBI SOLI.
B Minor. T solo, fl, ob obbl, orchestra. Autograph score: I-BGc 213.

A1371 TIBI SOLI.
G Major. SSSSA, orchestra. Autograph score: I-BGc 213.(For School).

A1372 TIBI SOLI.
B flat Major. T solo, cl obbl, orchestra. Autograph score: I-BGc 213.

ECCE ENIM (Miserere)

A1373 ECCE ENIM.
E flat. S solo, cl or ob or cello obbl and orchestra. Autograph score: I-BGc 207.

A1374 ECCE ENIM.
E flat. T solo, orchestra. Autograph score: I-BGc 207.

A1375 ECCE ENIM.
B flat. T solo, 2 cl obbli, orchestra. Autograph score: I-BGc 207.

ASPERGES ME (Miserere)

A1376 ASPERGES ME.
D Major. S solo, vl obbl, orchestra. Autograph score: I-BGc 211.

A1377 ASPERGES ME.
G Major. S solo "con ripieno", ATB coro, orchestra. Autograph score: I-BGc 209.

A1378 ASPERGES ME.
G Major. S solo, 2 fl obbli, orchestra. Autograph score: I-BGc 210.

A1379 ASPERGES ME.
G Major. S solo, fl obbl, orchestra. Autograph score: I-BGc 211- Same as I-BGc sala 32.D.8.7.

A1380 ASPERGES ME.
G Major. S solo, vl obbl, orchestra. 1834. Autograph score: I-BGc 209. I-BGi 984.D.105.

A1381 ASPERGES ME.
G Major. T solo, fl obbl, orchestra. Autograph score: I-BGc 210.

A1382 ASPERGES ME.
D Major. B solo, fl obbl, orchestra. Autograph score: I-BGc 210.

A1383 ASPERGES ME.
E flat. B solo, cr obbl, orchestra. Autograph score: I-BGc 215. Followed by Redde mihi.

A1384 ASPERGES ME.
C Major. B solo, ob obbl, orchestra. Autograph score: I-BGc 215.

A1385 ASPERGES ME.
F Major. B solo, vla obbl, orchestra. Autograph score: I-BGc 210.

A1386 ASPERGES ME.
C Major. SATB "con fuga". Autograph score: I-BGc 215.

A1387 ASPERGES ME.
G Minor. SATB, orchestra. Autograph score: I-BGc 215. 40 parts on which are found the names of the following students: Tavecchi, Manghenoni, Pontiroli.

A1388 ASPERGES ME.
F Major. SSBB soli, choir SATB?, orchestra. Autograph score: I-BGc 209.

AVERTE FACIEM TUAM
(Miserere)

A1389 AVERTE FACIEM TUAM.
D flat. S solo, cl obbl, orchestra. Autograph score: I-BGc 217.

A1390 AVERTE FACIEM TUAM.
E flat. T solo, cello & cr obbli, orchestra. Autograph score: I-BGc 216.

A1391 AVERTE FACIEM TUAM.
D Major. S or B solo, orchestra.
Autograph score: I-BGc 218.

A1392 AVERTE FACIEM TUAM.
E flat. B solo, SATB coro, fl, ob, cl, 2 cr,
strings. Autograph score: I-BGc 218,
I-BGi (MS)986.D.105.

A1393 AVERTE FACIEM TUAM.
E flat. B solo, cr obbl, orchestra.
Autograph score: I-BGc 216.

A1394 AVERTE FACIEM TUAM.
F Major. B solo, orchestra. Autograph
score: I-BGc 218.

A1395 AVERTE FACIEM TUAM.
F Major. B solo, "con ripieni", SATB
chorus, vla & cello obbli, orchestra.
Autograph score: I-BGc 217.

A1396 AVERTE FACIEM TUAM.
F Major. B solo, cello obbl, orchestra.
Autograph score: I-BGc 217.

A1397 AVERTE FACIEM TUAM.
B flat Major. B solo, cr obbl, orchestra.
Autograph score: I-BGc 218.

A1398 AVERTE FACIEM TUAM.
F Major. AT soli, orchestra. Autograph
score: I-BGc 216.

A1399 AVERTE FACIEM TUAM.
F Major. SSS, wind instruments.
Autograph score: I-BGc 216.

A1400 AVERTE FACIEM TUAM.
E flat. SATB, ob & 2 cr obbli, orchestra.
Autograph score: I-BGc 216.

COR MUNDUM (Miserere)

A1401 COR MUNDUM.
A flat. S solo, cl obbl, orchestra.
Autograph score: I-BGc 221.

NE PROYCIAS ME (Miserere)

A1402 NE PROYCIAS ME.
D Major. A solo, 2 vl obbli, ob, 3 cr,
strings. Non-autograph score: I-BGi
1024A.

DOCEBO (Miserere)

A1403 DOCEBO.
D Major. S solo, SATB coro, fl obbl,
orchestra. Autograph score: I-BGc 220.

A1404 DOCEBO.
B flat Major. STB soli, TTB coro, orchestra. Autograph score: I-BGc 220.

A1405 DOCEBO.
B flat Major. STB soli, orchestra.
Autograph score: I-BGc 220.

A1406 DOCEBO.
A Minor. TT soli, vl obbl, orchestra.
Autograph score: I-BGc 220. Also fol-
low: Libera, Sacrificium, Benigne fac
Domine.

A1407 DOCEBO.
E flat. B solo, orchestra. Autograph
score: I-BGc 221.

A1408 DOCEBO.
C Major. B solo, orchestra. Autograph
score: I-BGc 221.

A1409 DOCEBO.
C Major. B solo, orchestra. Autograph
score: I-BGc 221.

A1410 DOCEBO.
D Major. A solo, 2 vl obbli, orchestra.
Autograph score: I-BGc 221.

DOMINE LABIA MEA (Miserere)

A1411 DOMINE LABIA MEA.
A flat Major. T solo, cl obbl, orchestra.
Autograph score: I-BGc 219.

A1412 DOMINE LABIA MEA.
B flat Major. T solo, cello obbl,
orchestra. Autograph score: I-BGc 219.

A1413 DOMINE LABIA MEA.
A Major. T solo, vl obbl, orchestra.
Autograph score: I-BGc 219.

A1414 DOMINE LABIA MEA.
G Major. SA soli, orchestra. Autograph
score: I-BGc 219.

A1415 DOMINE LABIA MEA.
A flat. T solo, cl or cr obbl, orchestra.
1834. Non-autograph score: I-BGi
995.D.107.

QUONIAM SI VOLUISSES
(Miserere)

A1416 QUONIAM SI VOLUISSES.
F Major. S solo, ob, cr, strings.
Autograph score: I-BGc 223.

A1417 QUONIAM SI VOLUISSES.
F Major. T solo, vl obbl, fl, ob, cl, cr,
strings. Autograph score: I-BGc 223.

A1418 QUONIAM SI VOLUISSES.
C Minor. T solo, ob obbl, cl, cr, cello.
Autograph score: I-BGc 223.

A1419 QUONIAM SI VOLUISSES.
F Major. S solo, 2 ob, cr, strings.
Autograph score: I-BGc 223.

A1420 QUONIAM SI VOLUISSES.
E flat Major. T solo, cr & cl obbli,
orchestra. Autograph score: I-BGc 223.

A1421 QUONIAM SI VOLUISSES.
D Major. B solo, 2 ob, 2 cr, strings.
Autograph score: I-BGc 104.

SACRIFICIUM (Miserere)

A1422 SACRIFICIUM.
F Major. S solo, cr di bassetto obbl, fg,
cr, strings. Autograph score: I-BGc 222.

A1423 SACRIFICIUM.
G Major. Same as above except with cl
(b flat) obbl. Autograph score: I-BGc 222.

A1424 SACRIFICIUM.
A flat Major. B solo, cl, cr obbl, fl, ob,
cr, fg, trb, strings. Autograph score:
I-BGc 222.

A1425 SACRIFICIUM.
F Minor. B solo, cr inglese & cr obbli, fl,
strings. Autograph score: I-BGc 222.

A1426 SACRIFICIUM.
G Minor. T solo, fl & cello obbli, fl, ob,
cl, cr, strings. Autograph score: I-BGc
222. Donizetti wrote on viola part, which
he had copied, "La viola è giusta, non è
sbagliata, no".

A1427 QUONIAM & SACRIFICIUM.
E flat Major. T solo, cl & cr obbli, fl, ob,
cr, strings. Autograph score: I-BGc 223.

A1428 SACRIFICIUM.
D Minor. T solo, vl obbl, fl, ob, cl, cr,
strings. Autograph score: I-BGc 224.

A1429 SACRIFICIUM.
C Minor. T solo, vl solo, fl, ob, cl, cr,
strings. Autograph score: I-BGc 224.
Proceeded by Domine Labia mea.

A1430 SACRIFICIUM.
A Major. T solo, vl obbl, fl, ob, cl, cr,
strings. Autograph score: I-BGc 224.

A1431 SACRIFICIUM.
A Minor. T solo, vl obbl, ob, cr, strings.
Autograph score: I-BGc 224.

TUNC ACCEPTABIS (Miserere)

A1432 TUNC ACCEPTABIS
F Major. SATB, orchestra. Autograph
score: I-BGc 38.

A1433 TUNC ACCEPTABIS
C Minor/E Minor. SATB, orchestra.
Autograph score: I-BGc 38.

A1434 TUNC ACCEPTABIS
G Minor. SATB, orchestra. Autograph
score: I-BGc 42.

A1435 TUNC ACCEPTABIS
F Minor. SATB, orchestra. Autograph
score: I-BGc 42.

A1436 TUNC ACCEPTABIS
C Minor. SATB, orchestra. Autograph
score: I-BGc 45.

A1437 TUNC ACCEPTABIS
C Minor. SATB, orchestra. Autograph
score: I-BGc 45.

A1438 TUNC ACCEPTABIS
D flat Major. SSTB (coro). Autograph
score: I-BGc 46.

A1439 TUNC ACCEPTABIS
C Minor. SATB, orchestra. Autograph
score: I-BGc 46.

A1440 TUNC ACCEPTABIS
E flat Major. SATB alternating double
choir. Autograph score: I-BGc 49.

A1441 TUNC ACCEPTABIS
G Major. SATB, orchestra. Autograph
score: I-BGc 49.

A1442 TUNC ACCEPTABIS
A Minor. SATB, orchestra. Autograph
score: I-BGc 50.

A1443 TUNC ACCEPTABIS
E flat Major. SATB soli, SSSS coro,
orchestra. Autograph score: I-BGc 50.
(For School).

A1444 TUNC ACCEPTABIS
B flat Major. SATB, orchestra.
Autograph score: I-BGc 52.

A1445 TUNC ACCEPTABIS
F Major. SATB, orchestra. Autograph
score: I-BGc 52. "Dieu a inspiré Mayr".

A1446 TUNC ACCEPTABIS
E flat Major. SATB, strings. 1843.
Autograph score: I-BGc sala D.8.24/2.

A1447 TUNC ACCEPTABIS
G Minor. SATB, orchestra. Autograph
score: I-BGi 1032.A.7.

A1448 TUNC ACCEPTABIS
B Minor. SATB, orchestra. Autograph
score: I-BGc 42.

A1449 TUNC ACCEPTABIS
B Minor. STTB alternating double choir,
orchestra. Autograph score: I-BGc 49.

70.   Motets

A1450 A FACIENDAM
MISERICORDIAM.
A Major. T, orchestra. Autograph score:
I-BGc 312.

A1451 A FACIENDAM
MISERICORDIAM.
S, orchestra. Autograph score: I-BGc 312.

A1452 A FACIENDAM
MISERICORDIAM.
E flat. AA soli, orchestra. Autograph
score: I-BGc 312.

A1453 AL SOMMO ETERNO
CREATOR.
E flat, T, orchestra. "copiato in Ostiglia il
l dicembre 1814". Non-autograph score:
I-OS B.1719.

A1454 BENEDICAMUS DOMINO.
D Minor. SATB, orchestra. Autograph
score: I-BGc 67.

A1455 BENEDICAMUS DOMINO.
F Major. SATB, ob, cl, fg, cr, strings.
Autograph score: I-BGc 67.

A1456 BENEDICTI VOS A DOMINO.
a) C Major. T solo, orchestra. Autograph
score: I-BGc 11; b) C Major. STB,
orchestra. Autograph score: I-BGc 11.
Both pieces have the same melodic line.

A1457 BENIGNE FAC, DOMINE.
E flat. T solo, orchestra. Autograph
score: I-BGc 224.

A1458 CHRISTE CUM SIT.
C Major. T solo, fl, ob, cl, cr, strings.
Autograph score: I-BGc 27.

A1459 CHRISTUS NATUS EST.
Motet for Christmas. A Major. SATB,
orchestra. "per la festa di S. Natale".
Autograph score: I-BGc 58.

A1460 DELLA TUA GLORIA,
DE' TUOI PORTENTI.
B flat, STB, orchestra. Autograph score:
I-BGc 61.

A1461 DELLA DUA GLORIA,
DE' TUOI PORTENTI.
B flat, TTB, orchestra. Non-autograph
score: I-BGc 77.

A1462 DELLA DUA GLORIA,
DE' TUOI PORTENTI.
B flat, STB, orchestra. Autograph score
incomplete: I-BGc 232.

A1463 DOMINUS MEMOR FUIT.
G Major. SATB, orchestra. Autograph
score: I-BGc 11.

A1464 EXAUDI NOS.
B flat, 5 voices, organ. Non-autograph
score: I-Nd.

A1465 EXULTATE PASTORES.
G Major. TTB, chorus, vli, vle, fl, ob, cl,
cr, trb, (basso, ie organ/violone). Non-
autograph score: I-BGc 58.

A1466 EXURGE ANIMA & REDIRE.
Exurge anima in D Major. Redire in
G Major. S solo, ob, cr, strings.
Autograph score: I-BGc 62.

A1467 GAUDENT IN COELIS.
D Major. "a Quattro", orchestra. Non-
autograph score: I-BGi 1001.D.114.

A1468 FLOS CARMELI.
Motet for the Feast of S. Luigi Gonzaga.
SSTB soli, TTB coro, fl, ob, cl, fg, cr,
organ, strings. Autograph score: I-BGc
59.

A1469 IN BEATO AGABITO.
F Major. 5 voices, organ. Non-autograph
score: I-Nd.

A1470 LAUDEM VOLO CANTICARE.
B flat Major. B solo, orchestra.
Autograph score: I-BGc 59.

A1471 LAUDEM VOLO CANTICARE.
Slightly different version of above. Non-
autograph score: I-BGc 77.

A1472 LODE A DIO.
Motet based on Psalm 117. "Confitemini
Domino quoniam bonus". E flat Major.
SSSTTB, orch. Autograph score: I-BGc
308.

A1473 ME MISERUM QUID HOC.
C Minor. S solo, ob, cr, fg, strings.
Autograph score: I-BGc 62. Non-
autograph score: I-Mc MS.190.2.
Followed by aria, Aure placide spirate.

A1474 O LUX BEATISSIMA.
Double four part choir. Autograph score:
A-Wn 33.759.

A1475 OH DEUS QUOD ME.
Allegro animato. E flat. S, orchestra. Non-
autograph score: I-BGi 1011.D.114.

A1476 OMNES DE SABA.
Motet for Epiphany. SATB, orchestra.
Autograph score: I-BGc 58.

A1477 PRO PECCATIS SUAE GENTIS.
F Minor. B solo, 2 ob, cl, 2 cr, strings.
Autograph score: I-BGc 25.

A1478 PROPITIUS ESTO.
A Minor. "a Cinque", organ. Autograph
score: I-NOVd.

A1479 PUERI EBREORUM IN
DOMENICA PALMARUM.
Palm Sunday. G Major. SATB, organ or
violone. Non-autograph score: I-BGi
487.D.119.

A1480 QUIS ANGOR QUIS
TUMULTUS.
C Minor. T solo, 2 cl, 2 cr, strings. 1820.
Non-autograph score: I-Cf.

A1481 QUAL COLPA, ETERNO DIO.
C Minor. T solo, orchestra. Segue aria -
Ombre meste. Non-autograph score: I-Mc
MS.190.

A1482 QUI LOCUTUS EST.
G Major. A solo, orchestra. Autograph
score: I-BGc 312.

A1483 UBI SUM.
S solo, instruments. Non-autograph
score: I-Td.

A1484 UT SINE TIMORE.
E flat. SATB, orchestra. Autograph
score: I-BGc 315.

A1485 VIR DEI.
G Major. "a Cinque", violone, organ.
Autograph score: I-Nd.

A1486 THREE RELIGIOUS MOTETS.
B solo, fl, 2 cl, cr, fg. Non-autograph
score: I-BGc 77.

A1487 OVE SON, QUAL MI SCOSSE.
C Minor. B solo, ob, cr, strings.
Autograph score: I-BGc 62.

A1488 THREE MOTETS: MATER
CHRISTI; SOMMO BEN, MIO SIG-
NOR; LODATO SEMPRE SIA.
Based on litanies. SATB. Non-autograph
score: I-BGc 305.

A1489 MOTET FOR SOLO VOICE.
S, orchestra. Non-autograph score: I-Vmc
52-60.

71.   Litanies

LITANIES (Benediction, Devotional)

A1490 LITANY OF OUR LADY.
F Major. SATB, orchestra. Autograph
score: I-BGc 316.

A1491 LITANY OF OUR LADY.
C Major. SATB, orchestra. Autograph
score: I-BGc 316.

A1492 LITANY OF OUR LADY.
A Major. S solo, SATB coro, orchestra.
Autograph score: I-BGc 22.

A1493 LITANY OF OUR LADY.
G Minor. SATB, orchestra. Autograph
score: I-BGc 22.

A1494 LITANY OF OUR LADY.
SATB, orchestra. Non-autograph-score:
I-Vnm.

A1495 LITANY.
SATB, orchestra. Non-autograph-score:
I-Vnm.

A1496 LITANY.
G Minor. SATB, orchestra. Autograph
score: I-Mc 192-1.

72.   For the blessing of bells

A1497 VIDERUNT TE.
D Major. "a Tre" STB, wind, organ obbl.
Autograph score: I-BGc 11.

73.   For the clothing of the religious life

See A1030 ECCE QUAM BONUM
(Ps. 132). C Major. SATB, orchestra.
Autograph score: I-BGc 11.

A1498 LAETATUS SUM
(Ps. 121). B flat Major. T solo, cl obbl,
orchestra. Autograph score: I-BGc 11.

A1499 LEVAVI OCULOS MEOS.
F Major. SATB, vl obbl, ob, cl, cr,
strings, organ. Autograph score: I-BGc
11.

A1500 HAEC ACCIPIET
(For the clothing of Nuns). F Major.
4 soli, cl or ob, cr, strings. Autograph
score: I-BGc 67.

A1501 VENI SANCTE SPIRITUS
(Hymn). B flat Major. 4 soli, orchestra.
Autograph score: I-BGc 67.

74.   New Entries

A1502 SINFONIA IN D.
Fl, 2 ob, fg, 2 cr, strings. USA - Edwin
A. Fleisher Collection, Free Library of
Philadelphia.

A1503 SONATA PICCOLA
for violin solo. Edited Heinrich Bauer.

A1504 SOLO FOR VIOLIN.
Edited Spada; ms refer Spada.

A1505 MESSA DI REQUIEM
(No 6). E flat Major. Soli & coro SSTB,
fl, 2 cl, cr di bassetto, 2 fg, 2 cr, tr, trb,
timp, strings (no violins), organ.
Autograph score: I-BGc 306.

A1506 SINFONIA A DUE VIOLINI
OBBLIGATI.
B flat. 2 ob, fg, 2 cr, 2 vl obbli, 2 vl, 2
vle, violone. Autograph score: I-BGc 329.

A1507 SINFONIA IN D MAJOR.
Larghetto-allegro, ob, cl, fg, 2 cr, strings.
Autograph score: I-BGc 329.

A1508 SINFONIA IN D MAJOR.
Maestro-allegro vivace, fl, 2 ob, 2 cl, fg,
2 cr, 2 tr, timp, strings. Autograph score:
I-BGc 329.

A1509 SINFONIA IN B FLAT.
Andantino-allegro, parts only. Autograph
score: I-BGc 329.

A1510 CONCERTONE No2,
the following parts only, fl, 2 vla, cello
obbl, 1 violone 1+2. Autograph score:
I-BGc 254.

Appendix I

Mayr's Librettists

ANGELO ANNELLI (Anelli)
1761 - 1820.
1. Né l'un, né l'altro, 1807.
2. Belle ciarle e tristi fatti, 1807.

CESARE ARICI.
1. Il sagrifizio d'Ifigenia, 1811.
2. Eregia (cantata), 1816.

ABATE G. B. (Giovanni Battista)
BAIZINI.
1. La festa di Ercole (cantata), 1816.
2. Arianna e Bacco (cantata), 1817.
3. L'Armonia (cantata), 1825.

MARCHESE FRANCESCO BERIO DI
SALSA.
Cora. Librettist of Rossini's Otello.

GIUSEPPE BERNADONI.
1. Alonso e Cora, 1804.
2. I misteri Eleusini, 1802, 1807.

L. G. BUONAVOGLIA
Da locanda in locanda e sempre in sala,
1805.

PIETRO COMINAZZI.
S. Luigi Gonzaga, 1822.

JACOPO FERRETTI.
1784 - 1852.
Il ritorno di Jefte ossia Il voto incauto,
1816.

GIUSEPPE MARIA FOPPA.
1760 - 1845.
1. Jacob a Labano fugiens, 1791.
2. Sisara, 1793.
3. Tobiae Matrimonium, 1794.

4. ?La Passione, Metastasio and another
hand, 1794.
5. David in spelunca Engaddi, 1795.
6. Il sagrifizio di Jefte, 1795.
7. Un pazzo ne fa cento, 1796.
8. Il secreto, 1797.
9. L'intrigo della lettera, 1797.
10. Lauso e Lidia, 1798.
11. L'avaro, 1799.
12. Il caretto del venditor d'aceto, 1800.
13. L'equivoco, 1800.
14. L'imbroglione ed i castigamatti,
1800.
15. Le due giornate, 1801.
16. I castelli in aria, 1802.
17. Amore non soffre opposizione, 1810.

GIOVANNI (de) GAMERRA.
1743 - 1803.
Ercole in Lidia, 1803.

URBANO LAMPREDI.
Il sogno di Partenope, (cantata), 1817.
Also described as a *melodramma
allegorico*.

CATERINO (CATTARINO) MAZZOLÀ.
Latter half of 1700 - 1806.
1. Amor ingenoso, 1799.
2. L'ubbidienza per astuzia, 1799.

FRANCESCO MARCONI.
Amor non ha ritegno.

METASTASIO (PIETRO TRAPASSI).
1698 - 1782.
1. Numerous songs and duets, 1791.
2. La Passione, 1794 (and other hand,
G. M. Foppa?)
3. Adriano in Siria, 1799 & NN.

4. Alcide al bivio, 1809.

5. Demetrio, 1824.

BARTOLOMEO MERELLI.
1794 - 1879.

1. Arianna e Bacco, 1817, (cantata in 2 acts).

2. Lanassa, 1818, with G. Rossi?

3. Alfredo il grande, re degli Anglo Sassoni 1821.

4. Samuele, 1821.

LUIGI PRIVIDALI (PREVIDALI).
Second half of 1700 - circa 1850.

1. Zamori/Palmira, 1804, with Mayr.

2. Il ritorno di Ulisse, 1809.

MICHELANGELO PRUNETTI.
Un vero originale.

FELICE ROMANI.
1788 - 1865.

1. La rosa bianca e la rosa rossa, 1813.

2. Medea in Corinto, 1813.

3. Atar, 1814.

4. Le due duchesse ossia La caccia de'lupi, 1814.

5. Le Danaidi, 1819.

6. Atalia.

LUIGI ROMANELLI.
1751 - 1839.

1. Le finte rivali, 1803.

2. Adelasia ed Aleramo, 1807.

3. Raoul di Crequi, 1810.

4. Tamerlano, 1813.

5. Fedra, 1820.

GAETANO ROSSI.
1774 - 1855.

1. Che originali, 1799.

2. Adelaide de Guesclino, 1799.

3. Labino e Carlotta, 1799.

4. L'accademia di musica, 1799.

5. Gli Sciti, 1800.

6. La locandiera, 1800.

7. Ginevra di Scozia, 1801.

8. I virtuosi, 1801.

9. Argene, 1802.

10. Elisa, 1804.

11. Eraldo ed Emma, 1805.

12. L'amor coniugale, 1805.

13. La roccia di Frauenstein, 1805.

14. Gli Americani, 1807.

15. ? I Cherusci, 1808.

16. L'amor figliale, 1811.

17. ? Mennone e Zemira ossia La figlia dell'aria.

18. Lanassa, 1818, (with B. Merelli).

ANTONIO SIMONE (SIMEONE) SOGRAFFI.
1759 - 1818.

1. Saffo ossia I riti d'Apollo Leucadio, 1794.

2. Telemaco nell'isola di Calipso, 1797.

3. Le inconvenienze teatrali.

ANDREA LEONE TOTTOLA.
Latter part of 18th century - 1831.
Elena, 1814.

APOSTOLO ZENO.
1668 - 1750. Ifigenia in Aulide, 1806.

Appendix II

An Outline of the religious music

1. The Mass

2. The Office of Vespers

3. Canticles

4. Hymns (full settings with orchestra and congregational settings)

5. Holy Week

6. The Office of the Dead

7. Motets

8. Litanies

9. The Blessing of Bells

10. For the clothing to the religious life

1. THE MASS

It was customary for a Messa di Gloria to be sung, that is, the Kyrie, the Gloria and the Creed, with the emphasis given in length and embellishment to the Gloria. Major feasts included the singing of the Sanctus, Benedictus and Agnus Dei.

a. Complete Settings

b. The Proper of the Mass
    Introits
    Graduals
    Offertories
    Sequences

c. The Common of the Mass
    Kyrie and Christe eleison
    Gloria
      Gloria in excelsis Deo
      Et in terra pax
      Laudamus Te
      Gratias agimus
      Domine Deus

Qui tollis peccata mundi
Qui sedes
Quoniam
Cum Sancto Spirito

d. Credo

e. Sanctus, Benedictus, Agnus Dei

2. THE OFFICE OF VESPERS

a. Domine
    Domine ad adjuvandum
    Gloria Patri
    Sicut erat

b. Psalms
    Afferte Domino (Psalm 29) (In the Book of Common Prayer)
    Miserere (Psalm 50) (See also Office of the Dead)
    Jubilate (Psalm 99)
    Dixit Dominus (Psalm 109)
      Virgam virtutis
      Tecum principium
      Juravit Dominus
      Dominus a dextris
      Judicabit
      De torrente
    Confitebor Tibi (Psalm 110)
    Beatus vir (Psalm 111)
    Laudate pueri (Psalm 112)
    In exitu Israel (Psalm 113)
      Simulacra gentium
      Domus Israel
      Qui timent Dominum
      Dominus memor fuit
      Benedicti
      Non mortui
    Credidi (Psalm 115)
    Laudate Dominum (Psalm 116)
    Levavi oculos (Psalm 120)

Laetatus sum (Psalm 121)
In convertendo (Psalm 125)
Nisi Dominus (Psalm 126)
De profundis (Psalm 129) (See also
Office of the Dead)
Memento Domine David (Psalm 131)
Ecce quam bonum (Psalm 132)
Domine probasti (Psalm 138)
Lauda Jerusalem (Psalm 147)
Miscellaneous a cappella psalms and
canticles.

3. CANTICLES

a. Te Deum

b. Benedictus
   Benedictus Dominus
   Sicut locutus est
   Ad faciendam misericordiam
   Jusjurandum
   Et tu puer
   Per viscera

c. Magnificat

4. HYMNS

a. Full settings with orchestra

b. Hymns and spiritual praises

c. Eucharistic hymns

d. Hymns to Our Lady

e. Stabat Mater
   (Dies irae: see Office of the Dead)

5. MUSIC FOR HOLY WEEK

a. Lamentations

b. Passion Music

c. The Three Hours on the Cross

d. The Way of the Cross

e. The devotion of the Seven Last
   Words of the Saviour

6. THE OFFICE OF THE DEAD

a. Lessons and responsaries

b. The Requiem Mass - complete settings.

c. Requiem aeternam

d. Dies irae
   Dies irae
   Tuba mirum
   Liber scriptus
   Quid sum miser
   Recordare
   Ingemisco
   Oro supplex
   Lacrimosa

e. Libera me

f. Subvenite

g. Miserere (Psalm 50)
   Miserere mei, Deus
   Amplius
   Tibi soli
   Ecce enim
   Asperges me
   Averte faciem
   Cor mundum
   Docebo
   Domine labia mea
   Quoniam si voluisses
   Sacrificium
   Tunc acceptabis

7. MOTETS

8. LITANIES

9. FOR THE BLESSING OF BELLS

10. FOR THE CLOTHING TO THE
    RELIGIOUS LIFE

Appendix III
Music available for performance

INSTRUMENTAL
Ensemble, Solo, Tutors, Solo with orchestra.

ORCHESTRAL
Concert overtures, Opera overtures, Dramatic oratorio overtures, Orchestra with solo instruments.

SOLO VOCAL
Lieder, Arie da camera, Cantatas with orchestra.

CHORAL
Large forces, with chamber orchestra, with instrumental ensemble, Liturgical.

OPERA
Complete operas, excerpts (overtures, arias, duets, trio, quintet).

LIST OF ABBREVIATIONS

C: Mayr + Donizetti Collaboration, 32 Esmond Road, London W4, IJQ, U.K.

M: Musica Aperta, Dr. Pieralberto Cattaneo, Conservatorio Gaetano Donizetti, Via Arena, 24100 Bergamo, Italy

O: Opera Rara; Joseph Weinberger, 12 Mortimer Street, London W1, U.K.

P: C. F. Peters, MUSIKVERLAG, Kennedyallee 101, 6000 Frankfurt 70, West Germany

R: G. Ricordi & Co., Via Berchet 2, 20121 Milano, Italy

S: Spada; Boccaccini e Spada Editori, Via Francesco Duodo 10, 00136 Rome, Italy

T: Teatro Donizetti, 24100 Bergamo, Italy

U.F.A.: Musikverlag, 3 Dreiklang - Dreimasken, Sonnenstraße 19, 8000 Munich 2, West Germany

A = alto, b = baritone, B = bass, B-b = bass-baritone, c-angl = cor anglais, c-bass = corno di bassetto, cb = double bass, fag = bassoon, gc = gran cassa, hp = harp, mS = mezzo-soprano, org = organ, perc = percussion, picc = piccolo, pno = piano, S = soprano, sd = side-drum, serp = serpent (or tuba), str = strings, T = tenor, timp = timpani, tr = treble (boy-soprano), trb = trombone, tri = triangle, trp = trumpet, vl = violin, vla = viola, vlc = cello.

INSTRUMENTAL

INSTRUMENTAL ENSEMBLE

DIVERTIMENTI (8)   for 6 instruments
2 cl, 2 fag, 2 cor.
Duration: average - 4 mins each   Available: M   (Cattaneo)

NOTTURNI (5)
2 cl, 2 fag, 2 cor, (ad lib: + fl, trp, trb)
    Available: M   (Cattaneo)

SERENATA BERGAMASCA
2 cl, c-bass, fag, 2 cor   Available: P   (Bauer)

SERENATA   (7 movements)
ob, 2 cl, 2 fag, 2 cor   Available: M   (Cattaneo)

BASSOON CONCERTINO
fag Solo, Ensemble (0 2 0 0/2 0 0 0/solo strings) [or tutti strings]
Duration: c. 8'00"   Available: S   (Spada)

GOD SAVE THE KING   Piano duet/solo & ensemble [for orch]
pno Duet (or solo), Ensemble (0 2 1 1/2 0 0 0/cl I & II, vla, vlc, cb)
Duration: c. 4'30"   Available: C   (Schofield)

SONATA FOR VIOLIN & PIANO   Available: C

SOLO INSTRUMENTAL

SONATA PICCOLA FOR VIOLIN SOLO   Available: C   (Bauer)

SOLO PER VIOLINO   Available: S   (Spada)

SUITE FOR HARP   Available: P   (Bauer)

PRELUDE & FUGUE FOR ORGAN   Available: C   (L. Jenkins)

INSTRUMENTAL TUTORS

12 PRELUDES FOR ORGAN   Available: C

29 PIECES FOR 2 HORNS   Available: C   (Humphries)

40 CONTRAPPUNTI FOR 2 DOUBLE-BASSES   Available: C

{ PIANO - Solos & Duet   unedited (edited upon request)
                                                Available: C   }

SOLO INSTRUMENTAL WITH ORCHESTRA

PIANO CONCERTO   No 1 in C Major
pno Solo, Orchestra (0 2 0 0/2 0 0 0/str)
Duration: 17'30"   Available: U.F.A.   (Bauer)

PIANO CONCERTO   No 2 in C Major
pno Solo, Orchestra ((0 2 0 0/2 0 0 0/str)
Duration: 20'00"   Available: U.F.A.   (Bauer)

SINFONIA CONCERTANTE   for 3 violins and orchestra   c. 1820
Orchestra (1 0 2 1/2 0 1 0/str)
Duration: c. 10'45"   Available: P   (Bauer)

CONCERTO (Bergamasco)   for picc, fl, cl, c-bass and orchestra
picc/fl/cl/c-bass Soloist(s), Orchestra (1 2 1 1/2 2 1 0/str/timp)
Duration: 31 minutes   Available: P   (Bauer)

ORCHESTRAL

CONCERT OVERTURES

SINFONIA IN D *Pastorale*   c. 1805
Orchestra (1 2 0 1/2 0 0 0/str/timp)
Duration: 5'40"   Available: C   (Facoetti)

SINFONIA IN B FLAT *2 violini obbligati*
2 vl obbli, Orchestra (0 2 0 1/2 0 0 0/str)
Duration: c. 4'10"   Available: C   (Allitt/Caddy)

SINFONIA IN C *Tamburo Militare*
Orchestra (1 2 2 1/2 0 0 0/str/sd)
Duration: 7'00"   Available: 1989 C   (Schofield)

OPERA OVERTURES

SINFONIA PICCOLA (L'INTRIGO DELLA LETTERA)
First performance: San Moisé, *Venice*, 24 September 1797.
Orchestra (2 2 1 1/2 2 0 0/str/timp)
Duration: 7 minutes   Available: P   (Bauer)

ADELAIDE DI GUESCLINO
First performance: Teatro della Fenice, *Venice*, 1 May 1799
                                                           Available: O   (Schmid)

IL CARETTO DEL VENDITORE D'ACETO
First performance: Teatro Sant'Angelo, *Venice*, 28 June 1800
                                                           Available: R

ELISA
Orchestra (1 2 2 2/2 2 0 0/str/timp)
First performance: Teatro San Benedetto, *Venice*, 5 August 1804
Duration: 7'05"   Available: O   (Schmid)

L'AMOR CONIUGALE
Orchestra (1 2 2 1/2 1 0 0/str)
First performance: Teatro Nuovo, *Padua*, 26 July 1805
Duration.: 7'15"   Available: C   (Gazzaniga/Allitt)

LA ROSA BIANCA E LA ROSA ROSSA
First performance: Teatro San Agostino, *Genoa*, 21 February 1813
Duration: 6'30"   Available: T   (Tintori)

MEDEA IN CORINTO
Orchestra (2 2 2 2/4 2 3 1/str/timp/gc/[piatti])
First performance: Teatro San Carlo, *Naples*, 28 Nov 1813
Duration: 8'25"   Available: O and B
                                                                        (Schmid) (Bauer)

FEDRA
First performance: Teatro alla Scala, *Milan*, 26 December 1820
Duration: 8'00"   Available: C   (Bauer)

DRAMATIC ORATORIO OVERTURES

LA PASSIONE
Orchestra (0 2 0 1/2 0 0 0/str)
First performed at Forlì, 1794
Duration: 4'10"   Available: C   (Allitt)

ORCHESTRA WITH SOLO INSTRUMENTS

SINFONIA CONCERTANTE   for 3 violins and orchestra c. 1820
Orchestra (1 0 2 1/2 0 1 0/str)
Duration: c. 10'45"   Available: P   (Bauer)

BASSOON CONCERTINO
fag Solo, Orchestra (0 2 0 0/2 0 0 0/str)
Duration: c. 8'00"   Available: S   (Spada)

PIANO CONCERTO   No 1 in C Major
pno Solo, Orchestra (0 2 0 0/2 0 0 0/str)
Duration: 17'30"   Available: U.F.A.   (Bauer)

PIANO CONCERTO   No 2 in C Major.
pno Solo, Orchestra (0 2 0 0/2 0 0 0/str)
Duration: 20'00"   Available: U.F.A.   (Bauer)

CONCERTO (Bergamasco)   for picc, fl, cl, c-bass and orchestra
picc/fl/cl/c-bass Soloist(s), Orchestra (1 2 1 1/2 2 1 0/str/timp)
Duration: 31 minutes   Available: P   (Bauer)

CHORAL

LARGE FORCES

GRAN MESSA DA REQUIEM   in G Minor
SATB Soli, SATB Choir, Orchestra (2 2 2+2c-bass 2/4 3 2 0/str/timp/org)
Duration: 90 minutes   Available: 1989 C   (Schofield)

TE DEUM   Composed for Napoleon's Coronation
SATTB Soli, SATTB Chorus, Orchestra (1 2 2 2/2 2 1 0/str/timp/org)
Duration: c. 27'00"   Available: C   (Schofield)

CANTATA ON THE DEATH OF BEETHOVEN   1827
SATB Soli, SATB Chorus, Orchestra (2 2 2 2/2 2 1 0/str/timp)
Duration: 15 minutes   Available: P   (Bauer)

SAN LUIGI GONZAGA   Dramatic Oratorio   1822
SAB Soli, SATB Chorus, Large orchestra (1 2 2 1/2 2 1 0/str/sd)
First performed at S. Pancrazio in Città Alta, *Bergamo*
Libretto by Pietro Cominazzi
Duration: c. 100 minutes   Available: P   (Bauer)

WITH CHAMBER ORCHESTRA

STABAT MATER   No 5 in C Minor   circa 1796
SATB Soli, Orchestra (0 2 0 0/2 0 0 0/str/org)
Duration: c. 30'00"   Available: C   (Allitt)

LA PASSIONE   Dramatic Oratorio   1794
SATB Soli, SATB Chorus, Orchestra (0 2 0 1/2 0 0 0/str/org)
Libretto by Metastasio and another hand.
First performed at Forlì:
Duration: c. 135 minutes   Available: C   (Allitt)

WITH INSTRUMENTAL ENSEMBLE

DIXIT DOMINUS   Psalm No 109 (110)
S or tr.TB Soli, Ensemble (0 2 0 0/2 0 0 0/cb/org)
         Available: M   (Cattaneo)

MESSA DA REQUIEM   in E flat Major
SATB Soli, SATB Chorus, Wind ensemble, (1 0 2 1/2 1 1 0/cb/timp/org)
Duration: c. 50 minutes   Available: M (Cattaneo)

LITURGICAL

LIBERA ME
trATB Soli (or chorus), cb, org
Duration: 3'15"   Available: C (Pedemonti)

REQUIEM MASS   in D Minor
trTB Soli (or chorus), cb, org
Duration: 17'45"   Available: C (Pedemonti)

MASS in F (no Gloria)   for Holy Week
S (or A) TB, org or cb
Duration: c. 15 minutes   Available: C (Schäffer)

OPERA & OPERA EXCERPTS

COMPLETE OPERAS

IL CARETTO DEL VENDITORE D'ACETO   Farsa giocosa in 1 or 2 acts: 1800
Libretto by Giuseppe Foppa
First performance: Teatro Sant'Angelo, *Venice*, 28 June 1800
         Available: R

L'AMOR CONIUGALE   Farsa sentimentale in 2 scenes: 1805
S.mS.T.T.B-b.B. Soli, [no chorus] Orchestra (1 2+2c-angl 2 1/2 1 0 0/str)
Libretto by Gaetano Rossi (based on Jean Nicolas Bouilly)
First performance: Teatro Nuovo, *Padua*, 26 July 1805
Duration: c. 150 minutes   Available: C (Gazzaniga/Allitt)

LA ROSA BIANCA E LA ROSA ROSSA.   Opera seria in 2 acts: 1813
Libretto by Felice Romani (based on G. de Pixerecourt)
First performance: Teatro San Agostino, *Genoa*, 21 February 1813
Duration: c. 115 minutes   Available: T (Tintori)

MEDEA IN CORINTO   Opera seria in 3 acts: 1813
S.S.mS.T.T.T.T.B-b. Soli, Chorus, Orchestra (2 2 2 2/4 2 3 serp/str/timp/perc/hp)
Libretto by Felice Romani (based on Euripides' drama)
First performance: Teatro San Carlo, *Naples*, 28 Nov 1813
Duration: c. 145 minutes   Available: O and B
                                                      (Schmid) (Bauer)

FEDRA   Melodramma seria in 2 acts: 1820
S.S.mS.T.[T].B. Soli, Chorus, Orchestra (picc+1 2 2 2/4 2 2 0/str/timp/gc)
Libretto by Luigi Romanelli
First performance: Teatro alla Scala, *Milan*, 26 December 1820
   Currently being edited   Information: C   (Bauer)

                        OPERA EXCERPTS

ADELAIDE DI GUESCLINO   Overture
Libretto by Gaetano Rossi
First performance: Teatro della Fenice, *Venice*, 1 May 1799
                                          Available: O   (Schmid)

ELISA   Overture
Orchestra (1 2 2 2/2 2 0 0/str/timp)
Libretto by Gaetano Rossi
First performance: Teatro San Benedetto, *Venice*, 5 August 1804
Duration: 7'05"   Available: O   (Schmid)

L'AMOR CONIUGALE   Aria: *Rendi il consorte amato*
S Solo, Orchestra (1 2 2 1/2 0 0 0/str)
Libretto by Gaetano Rossi (based on Jean Nicolas Bouilly)
First performance: Teatro Nuovo, *Padua*, 26 July 1805
Duration: 9'10"   Available: O   (Schmid)

ALFREDO IL GRANDE   Aria: *Ov' è la bella vergine*
mS Solo, Orchestra (o c-angl 1 0/1 0 0 0/soli: vl, vlc, cb/hp)
Libretto by Bartolomeo Merelli
First performance: Teatro della Società, *Bergamo*, 26 December 1819
Duration: 7'45"   Available: O   (Schmid)

FEDRA   Aria: *Se fiero, Ippolito*
mS Solo, Orchestra (0 1 0 1/0 0 0 0/str [not violins])
Libretto by Luigi Romanelli
First performance: Teatro alla Scala, *Milan*, 26 December 1820
Duration: 2'20"   Available: O   (Schmid)

CHE ORIGINALI!   Aria: *Che dice mal d'amore*
Libretto by Gaetano Rossi
First performance: Teatro San Benedetto, *Venice*, 18 October 1798
                                              Available: O   (Schmid)

ELENA   Aria: *Ah! se mirar potessi*
b Solo, Orchestra (1 2 2 1/2 0 0 0/str)
Libretto by Andrea Leone Tottola
First performance: Teatro dei Fiorentini, *Naples*, 28 January 1814
Duration: 8'00"   Available: O   (Schmid)

GINEVRA DI SCOZIA   Duet: *Per pietà, deh! non lasciarmi*
                                              Scena ed aria: *Era felice un dì*
S mS Soli, Orchestra (2 2 2 2/2 2 0 0/str)
Libretto by Gaetano Rossi
First performance: Teatro Nuovo, *Trieste*, 21 April 1801
Duration: 6'20" (duet)   Available: O   (Schmid)

LE FINTE RIVALI   Duet: *Il pesciolin guizzando*
mS T Soli, Orchestra (2 0 0 2/2 0 0 0/solo fl/str)
Libretto by Luigi Romanelli
First performance: Teatro alla Scala, *Milan*, 20 August 1803
Duration: 4'00"   Available: O   (Schmid)

ALONSO E CORA   Duet: *Cora mio ben, fuggiamo*
Libretto by Luigi Romanelli after Marmontel's *Les Incas*
First performance: Teatro alla Scala, *Milan*, 26 December 1803
                                              Available: O   (Schmid)

ADELASIA ED ALERAMO   Storm, scena: *Dove salvarmi?*,
                                              Trio: *Ah! ch'io fra voi*
SSS Soli, Orchestra (2 2 2 2/2[+2 on stage] 0 0 0/str/timp)
Libretto by Luigi Romanelli
First performance: Teatro alla Scala, *Milan*, 26 December 1806
Duration: 7'25"   Available: O   (Schmid)

LA ROSA BIANCA E LA ROSA ROSSA   Trio: *Dov'è la destra?*
S mS T Soli, Orchestra (1 2 2 2/2 2 1 0/str)
Libretto by Felice Romani
First performance: Teatro San Agostino, *Genoa*, 21 February 1813.
Duration: 10'25"   Available: O   (Schmid)

CORA   Quintet: *Sempre uniti insiem saremo*
STTTb Soli, Orchestra (2 2 2 2/2 0 0 0/str)
Libretto by Marchese Francesco Berio di Salsa

First performance: Teatro San Carlo, *Naples*, 27 March 1815
Duration: 4'00"   Available: O   (Schmid)

SOLO VOCAL

LIEDER BEIM KLAVIER ZU SINGEN   Pub. 1786 (pno accomp)
                                       Available: O
1) Lied: Ich gieng unter Erlen am kühligen Bach
2) Gute Nacht an mein Mädchen: Vom blauen Himmel hell und fein
3) Der Talisman: Lebt' ich in goldnen Feenzeiten
4) Lied: Ich gieng im Mondenschimmer
5) Lied eines Mädchens: Noch bin ich jung von Jahren
6) Ständchen: Wenn die Nacht in süßer Ruh
7) Zufriedenheit: Ich bin vergnügt
8) Lied eines nordischen Wilden: Mein Weib, mein süßes Weib ist hin!
9) Mädchensitte: Ein hübsches sanftes Knäbchen saß
10) Die Nachtigall: Ich sah ein Mädchen
11) Der Händedruck: Der Geliebten Hand berühren
12) An Laura: Das Schweigen der Liebe: Treu geliebt und still geschwiegen

CANZONI ITALIANE E TEDESCHE   for contralto and pianoforte
                                       Available: C   (Schäffer)

1) da chi naqui il nutrimento
2) Gute nacht
3) La pace de' Santi
4) Die Schwalben ziehn
5) Perchè si mesto, oh Zeffiro
6) Die Wasser ziehn
7) Luci mie belle
8) Still ist die heilge Nacht

PER CARITÀ BETTINA   for mezzo-sop (or ten) and pianoforte
                                       Available: C   (Schäffer)

OH! QUANTO L'ANIMA   Cavatina for mezzo-sop and pianoforte
with ornaments "so admirably introduced by Mme Catalani" (& another!)
                                       Available: C

OPERA RARA has many more songs (some possibly from operas) both printed and in non-autograph manuscript, as well as several opera arias, scenas, duets and ensembles. Write to Opera Rara c/o Weinberger, or to the Mayr + Donizetti Collaboration.

CANTATAS WITH ORCHESTRA

LA MOGLIE DI ASRUBALE   Solo cantata 1816 "No 3"
S Solo, vl obbl, Orchestra (1 1 1 0[2]/2 1 0 0/str)
Words by an unknown poet, written in the style of Metastasio
Duration: c. 12'30"   Available: 1989 C (Caddy)

ANNIBALE   Solo cantata 1816 "No 1"
T Solo, cl obbl, Orchestra (1 1 1 0[2]/2 1 0 0/str)
Words by an unknown poet, written in the style of Metastasio
Duration: c. 9'00"   Available: 1989 C (Caddy)

ANNIBALE A CARTAGO   Solo cantata 1816 "No2"
B Solo, corno obbl, Orchestra (1 1 1 2/2 1 0 0/str)
Words by an unknown poet, written in the style of Metastasio
Duration: c. 12'00"   Available: C (Caddy)

QUAL TERRIBIL VENDETTA   Solo cantata 1794
B Solo, Orchestra (0 2 0 1/2 0 0 0/str)
Words by Metastasio
Duration: 8'10"   Available: C (Allitt)

RODOMONTE   Solo cantata c. 1810
b Solo, Orchestra (1 1 1 0/2 1 0 0/str/timp)
Duration: c. 9'00"   Available: 1989 C (Caddy)

List of Illustrations

A note on the illustrations

I am most grateful to Prof. Giuseppe Angeloni, Ian Caddy, Dr. Norbert Dubowy, Dr. Valerio Marabini, Dr. Giuseppe Paravicini Bagliani and Dr. Gianpiero Tintori for helping me with the illustrative material. I also wish to thank the *Museo Donizettiano* and the *Biblioteca Civica A. Mai*, Bergamo for permission to reproduce photographs of my own. Turner's *The Vision of Medea* is reproduced with the kind permission of the Tate Gallery.

Selected Bibliography

Note:

AASLA = *Atti dell' Ateneo di Scienze, Lettere e Arti*, Bergamo.
JDS   = *Journal of the Donizetti Society.*
NRMI   = *Nuova Rivista Musicale Italiana.*
SD   = *Studi Donzettiani.*

Alborghetti, F. and Galli, G., *Gaetano Donizetti e G. Simone Mayr: notizie e documenti, Bergamo 1875.*

Alighieri, D., *La Divina Commedia*, Milan 1965.

Allitt, J., *Donizetti and the tradition of romantic love*, London 1975.

Allitt, J., *L' amor coniugale,* London 1974 (JDS vol 1).

Allitt, J., *L' importanza di Simone Mayr nella formazione culturale di Donizetti*, Bergamo 1975 (see, *Atti* of the *Convegno Donizettano*).

Allitt, J., Mayr's *La Passione*, London 1975 (JDS vol 2).

Allitt, J., Mayr's *Samuele*, London 1975 (JDS vol 2).

Allitt, J., *The Notebooks of Giovanni Simone Mayr*. London 1974 (JDS vol 1).

Angelini, S., *Santa Maria Maggiore in Bergamo*, Bergamo 1959.

Ashbrook, W., *Donizetti and his operas*, Cambridge 1982.

Bacci, U., *Il libro del massone italiano*, Rome.

Barachetti, G., *La Domus Magna e il Collegio della Misericordia*, Bergamo 1968.

Barblan, G., *L' opera di Donizetti nell' età romantica*, Bergamo 1948.

Barblan, G. and Walker, F., *Contributo all' epistlolario di Gaetano Donizetti*, Bergamo 1962 (SD vol 1).

Barzun, J., *Berlioz and his century - an introduction to the age of romanticism*, New York 1956.

Bauer, H., *Bavaria Antiqua: Simon Mayr (1763 - 1845)*, Munich 1974.

Berengo, M., *La società veneta alla fine del settecento*, Florence 1956.

Berkeley, G. F. H., *Italy in the making 1815 - 1848*, Cambridge 1932.

Blackstone, B., *Byron, a survey*, London 1975.

Blume, F., *Classic and Romantic music*, London 1972.

Boesch, B., (edited), *German Literature*, translated Ronald Taylor, London 1973.

Bellotti, B., *Storia di Bergamo e dei Bergamaschi*, Milan 1940.

Blunt, A., *Nicolas Poussin*, Washington and London 1967.

Bonesi, M., *Note biografiche su Donizetti*, Bergamo 1946.

Bonicelli, G., *Rivoluzione e restaurazione a Bergamo,* Bergamo 1961.

Boschini, M., *Le ricche miniere della pittura*, Venice 1674.

Boschini, M., *La carta del navigar pittoresco*, Venice 1660. Edited by Anna Pallucchini, Venice and Rome 1966.

Burney, C., *Music, men, and manners in France and Italy 1770*, London 1969.

Calvi, G., *Elogio a Giovanni Simone Mayr*, manuscript in the Biblioteca Civica, Bergamo.

Calvi, G., *La musica sacra di Mayr*, Bergamo 1852.

Calvi, G., *Giovanni Simone Mayr*, Milan 1847.

Carner, M., *Simone Mayr and his "L'amor coniugale"*, Music & Letters 52, 1971 p 239-258.

Citati, P., *Goethe*, translated Raymond Rosenthal, New York 1974.

Chailley, J., *La Flute Enchantée: opera maçonnique*, Paris 1968.

Combarieu, J., *La musica e la magia*, Milan 1982.

Commons, J., Text for *Opera Rara's* record volume in "A hundred years of Italian opera" dedicated to Mayr, London 1984.

Commons, J., *The authorship of I piccoli virtuosi ambulanti*, London 1975 (JDS vol 2).

Corbin, H., *Creative Imagination in the Sufism of Ibn "Arabi"*, Princeton 1969.

de Angelis, M., *La musica del Granduca: vita musicale e correnti critiche a Firenze 1800 - 1855*, Florence 1978.

de Bassus, F. T. M., *Esposizione presentata agli illustrissimi Signori Capi della Repubblica de' Grigioni di Loro Ordine da F. T. M. de Bassus riguardo alla Società Segreta chiamata degli Illuminati*, Poschiavo 1787.

De Brosses, C., *Selections from the letters of De Brosses*, translated by Lord Gower, London 1897.

De Filippis, F. and Arnese, R., *Cronache del Teatro di San Carlo*, Naples 1961.

Dean, W., *Simon Mayr* (in the *Age of Beethoven* 1790 - 1830 edited Gerald Abraham), London 1982.

Dionisotti, C., *Manzoni and the Catholic Revival*, London 1973.

Donakowski, C. L., *A muse for the masses - ritual and music in an age of democratic revolution 1770 - 1870*, Chicago and London 1972.

Donati-Petténi, G., *L'arte della musica in Bergamo*, Bergamo 1930.

Donati-Petténi, G., *L'istituto musicale Gaetano Donizetti*, Bergamo 1928.

Donati-Petténi, G., *Donizetti*, Milan 1947.

Dumas, G., *La fin de la République de Venise*, Paris 1964.

Finazzi, G., *Orazione funebre e memorie di Giovanni Simone Mayr*, Bergamo 1852.

Ficino, M., *The letters of Marsilio Ficino Vols I, II and III*, London 1975.

Forcella, P., *Matteo Salvi, musicista bergamasco sul palcoscenico d'Europa*, Sedrina (BG) 1987.

Francovich, C., *Storia della massoneria in Italia dalle origini alla rivoluzione francese*, Florence 1974.

Freedman, J., *Johann Simon Mayr and his "Ifigenia in Aulide"*, Musical Quarterly 57, 1971 p 187-210.

Frost, T., *Secret societies of the European revolution*, London 1876.

Fubini, E., *Gli enciclopedisti e la musica*, Turin 1971.

Fülöp-Miller, R., *The power and secret of the Jesuits*, London 1930.

Gara, E., *Giovan Battista Rubini nel centinario della morte*, Bergamo 1954.

Gazzaniga, A., *Il trattatello sopra gli stromenti ed istromentazione nello zibaldone di Giovanni Simone Mayr*, Bergamo 1971.

Gazzaniga, A., *Il trattatello sopra gli stromenti ed istromentazione di G. Simone Mayr*, Turin 1973 (NRMI).

Gazzaniga, A., *Su l'amor coniugale di Simon Mayr*, Turin 1971 (NRMI).

Gazzaniga, A., *Il Fondo Musicale G. S. Mayr della Biblioteca Civica di Bergamo*, Bergamo 1963.

Geddo, A., *Bergamo e la musica*, Bergamo 1958.

Geddo, A., *Donizetti, L'uomo, le musiche*, Bergamo 1956.

Gervasoni, G., *Angelo Mai*, Bergamo 1954.

Giazotto, R., *Poesia melodrammatica e pensiero critico nel settecento*, preface by Pizetti, Milan 1952.

Giulini, M. F., *Giuditta Pasta e i suoi tempi*, Milan 1935.

Godwin, J., *Robert Fludd*, London 1979.

Goethe, J. W., *The sufferings of the young Werther*, trans. Bayard Quincy Morgan, London 1964.

Goethe, J. W., *Italian Journey 1786 - 1788*, trans. W. H. Auden and Elizabeth Mayer, London 1962.

Goethe, J. W., *Faust* (Parts I and II), trans. Barker Fairley, Toronto and Buffalo 1972.

Goethe, J. W., *Wilhelm Meister, Apprentiship and Travels*, trans. R. D. Moon, London 1974.

Goethe, J. W., *The autobiography*, trans. John Oxenford, London and Chicago 1974.

Goethe, J. W., *Goethe on art*, selected, edited and trans. John Gage, London 1980.

Goethe, J. W., *Goethe: Conversations and encounters*, edited and trans. Davide Luke and Robert Pick, London 1966.

Goethe, J. W., *Wisdom and experence*, selections by Ludwig Curtius, New York 1964.

Goldoni, C., *Collected works*, edited by Giuseppe Ortolani, Milan 1935 - 1956.

Grant, D. J., *A history of western music*, London 1960.

Hales, E. E. Y., *Pio Nono: a study in European politics and religion in the 19th century*, London 1954.

Hales, E. E. Y., *Mazzini and the secret societies*, London 1956.

Hamel, P. M., *Through music to the self*, Tisbury 1978.

Herder, J. G., *On Shakespeare* in *La fortuna di Shakespeare 1393 - 1964*, edited Gabriele Baldini, Milan 1965.

Howard, P., *Gluck and the birth of modern opera*, London 1963.

Hawkins, J., *A general history of the science and practice of music*, London 1853.

Heriot, A., *The castrati in opera*, London 1956.

Hersey, G. L., *Pythagorian palaces: magic and architecture in the Italian Renaissance*, Ithaca and London 1986.

Kelly, M., *Solo recital*, London 1972.

Kohlschmidt, W., *A history of German literature 1760 - 1805*, trans. Ian Hilton, London 1975.

Lang, P. H., *Music in western civilization*, New York 1941.

Lee, V., *Studies of the 18th Century in Italy*, London 1907.

Le Forestier, R., *Les Illuminés de Bavière*, Paris 1913.

Lennhoft, E., *The Freemasons: the history, nature, developement and secret of the Royal Art*, London 1934.

Levy, M., *Painting in 18th century Venice*, London 1959.

Manzoni, A., *Fermo e Lucia*, Bergamo 1984.

Manzoni, A., *I promessi sposi*, Paris 1836.

Manzoni, A., *Inni sacri*, edited Dino Brivio, Lecco 1973.

Marcello, B., *Il teatro alla moda*, Milan 1959.

Mayr, J. S., The Notebooks *(Lo Zibaldone)*, unpublished (except for extracts by John Allitt and Arrigo Gazzaniga), Biblioteca Civica A. Mai Bergamo. Various titles extracted from the Notebooks see also Section V 1 The Notebooks *(Lo Zibaldone)*: *Regolamento delle Lezioni Caritatevoli di musica*, 1812; *Cenni biografici di Antonio Capuzzi*, 1818; *Brevi notizie istoriche* della *vita e delle opere di Giuseppe Haydn*, 1809; *Memoria della storia intorno alla vita di Franchino Gaffurio*, 1820, *Progetto per una cattedra di musica all' università di Pavia*; *Piano del conservatorio di Napoli*; *Questione, Liceo musicale*, Bologna, 1827; *Letteratura musicale* or *Biografie:* essays on: Guido d'Arezzo, Giusquino del Prato, Orlando Lasso, Pier Luigi Palestrina, Ottavio Rinuccini, Giovanni Battista Doni, Astorga, Muzio Clementi, Padre Martini, Corelli; *Metodo di applicatura, ossia per le regolari e più comode posizioni delle dita sul cembalo; Trattato per il pedale; Trattato dell' accompagnamento* (translation of Förster's book); *Dissertazione sul genio e sulla composizione; Trattato sopra gli stromenti ed istromenti; La quarta grande festa musicale di York* (a long and informative essay translated from the German by Mayr - English translation in preparation. J. S. A.); Mayr made manuscript copies of the following publications: Algarotti - *Saggio sopra l' opera in musica*; André - *Dissertation sur le modus, Discours sur le beau musical*; Barca - *Introduzione a una nuova teoria di musica*, Memoria I and II, Benvenuto di San Raffaele - *Dell' arte del suono*; Blainville - *La Liberté de la musique, L' ésprit de l' art musical*; Carli - *Osservazioni sulla musica*; D'Alembert - *Sur l' usage et l' abus de la philosophie en matière de goût*; Riccati - *Saggio sopra le leggi del contrapunto, Esame del sistema musica di Rameau, Dissertazione acustico - matematica, Esame del sistema musico del Sig. Tartini, Riflessioni sopra il libro della scienza teorica e pratica della moderna musica del P. Francesco Vallotti*; Sabatier - *Discours sur la nécessité d' unir la musique au governement*; Venini - *Dell' armonia musicale*. Dispersed titles traced in Milan and Bologna (see section V 1).

Mayr, J. S., *Zibaldone* Vol I, edited by Arrigo Gazzaniga, contains the *Cenni biografici* and the *Cenni confidenziali*, Bergamo 1977.

Mayr, J. S., *Le Lezioni Caritatevoli*, Mayr's *Memoria* translated with notes by John Allitt, London 1971 (JDS vol 2).

Mayr, J. S., *Biografie di scrittori e artisti musicali Bergamaschi nativi od oriundi:* F. Algarotti, A. Barca, G. M. A. Carrara, F. Gaffurio, P. A. Locatelli, L. Marenzio, Domenico e Virgilio fratelli Mazzochi, La famiglia Serassi: Giuseppe il Vecchio, Abbate Pier Andrea Luigi, Maria Caterina, Giovanni Battista, Giuseppe de'Serassi il secondo, Bergamo 1875, reprint Bologna 1969.

Mayr, J. S., *Mayr's thoughts*, trans. by John Allitt, London 1975 (JDS vol 2).

Mayr, J. S., *Letters*, Biblioteca Civica; Bergamo; Ricordi Library; La Scala Museum; Einsieldn Library; Pierpont Morgan Library; Opera Rara Library.

Mayr, J. S., *Cenni biografici intorno al maestro Giovanni Simone Mayr*, Bergamo 1843.

Mayr, J. S., *I sensali del teatro*, published by Schiedermair in Sammelbände der internationalen Musikgesellschaft VI (1904 - 05).

Mayr, J. S., *Osservazioni di un vecchio suonatore di viola*, Bergamo 1852.

Mazzini, G., *Dei doveri dell' uomo*, Milan 1949.

Mazzini, G., *Filosofia della musica*, edited by A. Lualdi, Rome 1954.

Meli, A., *Giovanni Simone Mayr sulla linea musicale Baviera - Bergamo*, Bergamo 1963.

Merelli, B., *Cenni biografici di Donizetti e Mayr raccolti dalle memorie di un vecchio ottogenario dilettante di musica*, Bergamo 1875.

Metastasio, P., *Collected works*, in 12 vols, London 1782.

Meyer-Baer, K., *Music of the spheres and the dance of death*, New Jersey 1970.

Molmenti, P., *Storia di Venezia nella vita privata*, Bergamo 1927.

Noris, F., *La basilica di Santa Maria Maggiore in Bergamo*, Bergamo 1984.

Palisca, C. V., *Humanism in Italian Renaissance musical thought*, New Haven and London 1985.

Perloff, M., *The Futurist movement: avant garde, avant guerre, and the Language of rupture*, Chicago and London 1986.

Portinari, F., *Io la lingua, egli ha il pugnale - storia del melodramma ottocentesco attraverso i suoi libretti*, Turin 1981.

Powell, C., *Turner in the South-Rome, Naples, Florence*, New Haven and London 1987.

Powell, C., *"Infuriate in the Wreck of Hope": Turner's Vision of Medea*, Turner Studies, Vol 2 No 1 pp 12-18.

Raphael, A., *Goethe and the Philosopher's Stone (symbolic patterns in "the Parable" and the second part of "Faust")*, London 1965.

Respighi, O. and Luciani, S. A., *Orpheus, Florence 1925*.

Robbins Landon, H. C., *Mozart and the masons*, London 1982.

Robbins Landon, H. C., *Essays on the Viennese classical style (Gluck, Haydn, Mozart, Beethoven)*, London 1970.

Roncalli, A. (Pope John XXIII), *La Misericordia Maggiore di Bergamo e le altre istituzioni de beneficenza amministrate dalla Congregazione di Carità*, Bergamo 1912.

Ronchi, U. and Birezzi, C. A., *L'Ente Comunale di Assistenza di Bergamo*, Bergamo 1961.

Salvatorelli, L., *Spiriti e figure del Risorgimento*, Florence 1961.

Scherer, W., *A history of German Literature*, trans. Mrs F. C. Conybeare, Oxford 1886.

Schiedermair, L., *Beiträge zur Geschichte der oper . . . Simon Mayr*, Leipzig 1907.

Schneider, M., *Il significato della musica*, Milan 1970.

Scotti, C., *Il pio Istituto Musicale Donizetti in Bergamo*, Bergamo 1901.

Speranza, F., *Giovanni Simone Mayr, bergamasco*, Bergamo 1974 (AASLA vol 38).

Speranza, F., *La Misericordia Maggiore*, Bergamo 1956.

Stendhal, H. B., *Life of Rossini*, trans. Richard N. Coe, London 1956.

Stendhal, H. B., *Rome, Naples and Florence*, trans. Richard N. Coe, London 1959.

Stendhal, H. B., *Lives of Haydn, Mozart and Metastasio*, trans. Richard N. Coe, London 1972.

Tartini, G., *Trattato di musica*, Padua 1973.

Thomson, K., *The masonic thread in Mozart*, London 1977.

Tirroni, L., *Il patrimonio artisco e bibliografico dell'Ateneo: origini e vicende*, Bergamo 1986.

Torri, T., *Dalle antiche accademie all'Ateneo*, Bergamo 1974.

Torri, T., *Giovanni Simone Mayr nei documenti dell'Ateneo di Bergamo*, Bergamo 1965.

Todeschini, G., *Carlo Lenzi*, Azzone 1985.

Various authors, *La cultura illuministica in Italia, edited by Mario Fubini, Turin 1964.*

Various authors, *La civiltà veneziana del settecento*, Florence 1960.

Vassalli, D. C., *Vicenzo Monti nel dramma dei suoi tempi*, Milan 1968.

Webster, N. H., *World Revolution - the plot against civilization*, London 1921.

Webster, N. H., *Secret societies and subversive movements*, London 1924.

Whone, H., *The hidden face of music*, London 1974.

Winternitz, E., *Musical instruments and their symbolism in western art*, London 1967.

Wittkower, R., *Architectural principles in the age of humanism*, London 1962.

Zavadini, G., *Donizetti: vita - musiche - epistolario*, Bergamo 1948.

Zavadini, G., *G. Simone Mayr*, Bergamo 1957.

Zarlino, G., *Dimostrationi harmoniche*, Venice 1571.

Zarlino, G., *Istitutioni harmoniche*, Venice 1573.

Zarlino, G., *Sopplimenti musicali*, Venice 1588.

In addition to the books listed I have found the writings of Titus Burkhardt, Frithjof Schuon and René Guénon useful in interpreting traditional thought. Likewise much was gained through reading Dr Kathleen Raine's *Blake and Tradition* and various books and essays by Edgar Wind. Fundamental to my approach has been the thought of Martin Buber and the insights of Thomas Traherne. It is my opinion that Dante's *Divine Comedy* contains the keys and symbols which help to interpret the essence of the western tradition; and I would therefore consider Dante, read in the light of the spirituality and inner wisdom of his age, as basic reading. I remain convinced that the genius of the inner western tradition is an amalgam between platonic and hebraic thought to which Christianity brought its own insights. (J. S. A).

Index

The Preface, Acknowledgements, Catalogue and Bibliography are excluded from this Index. References to footnotes are in brackets; references to illustrations are in italics.

FERRETTI, Jacopo 76
FERRI, Baldassare 129
FERRONATI, Lodovico 39
FICINO, Marsilio 70, 73, 95, [117], [118]
FIELD, John 81
FINAZZI, Canon Giovanni 24, 71, [71]
FIORAVANTI, Valentino 108
FOPPA, Giuseppe Maria 48, 49, 51, 52
FÖRSTER, Emanuel Aloys 59, [59]
FOSCOLO, Ugo 44
FRANCK (Jesuit priest) 28
FRANKLIN, Benjamin 25
FREDERICK (Friedrich) the Great 132

G

GABBA, Melchiale 87
GABUSSI, Vincenzo 87
GAFFURIO, Franchino 33, 38, [63], 71, 73, [97], *160*
GALILEI, Vincenzo 73
GALUPPI, Baldassare 34, 40, 41, 37, 69
GAMBALE, Luigi 72, 87, 88, 89
GAZZANIGA, Arrigo 78, 80
GEMINIANI, Francesco 130
GENTILI, Serafino 63
GIARDINI, Felice de 130
GIORDANI, Giovanni [58]
GLUCK, Christoph Willibrand 41, [41], 50, 81
GOETHE, Johann Wolfgang v. 24, 26, 31, 32, 34, 35-36, 37, 45-46, 48, 70, 85, 87, 110
GOLDONI, Carlo 40, 43, 46, 69
GONZALES, Antonio 60, 137
GOZZI, Carlo 46
GREGORY, St. the Great 133
GREGORY, St. of Nyssa 99
GROSSI, Gaetano 31
GUADAGNI, Gaetano 129
GUARDI, Francesco 44, 69

H

HAMANN, Johann Georg 33, 37, 84, 85
HANDEL, Georg Frederick 57, [63], 81, 83, 92, [122], 123
HAYDN, Joseph 28, 33, 37, 41, 57, [59], 62, 63, [63], 66, 67, 74, 75, 81, 92, 99, [122], 128
HELVÉTIUS, Claude Adrien 26
HERALEITUS [120]
HERDER, Johann Gottfried 26, 32, 33, 34, 35, 36, 84, 85, 87
HERMES TRISMEGISTRUS [96]
HIPPOLITUS (Bishop of Cortona) 133
HOGARTH, William 27
HOLBACH, Paul-Henri Thiry (Dietrich), Baron d' 26
HORCHIO, Henry [136]

J

JANIN, (journalist) [108]
JOHN, St. of the Cross 98
JOSEPH II, (Emperor of Austria) 47

K

KANT, Emanuel 84
KARL THEODOR (Elector) 28
KNIGGE, Adolf v. 23, 26, 27, 28
KOBRICH, Johann Anton Bernard 21
KREUTZER, Conradin 130
KROMMER, Frantisek 81

L

LALANDE, Joseph-Jérôme Le Français de 25
LAMBERTI, Antonio 41
LAVEZZARI, Giuseppe 60
LEGRENZI, Giovanni 38
LENZI, Carlo 32, 36-37, 38, 39-40, 53
LEO, Leonardo 39, 129

V

VACCAI, Nicola   87
VAERINI, Revd. Barnaba   [71]
VENTURALI, Angiola (Mayr's first
wife)   51
VENTURALI, Lucrezia (Mayr's second
wife)   61, 102
VERDI, Giuseppe   [57], 65, 68, 69, [90]
VERMEER, Johannes   74
VIGANO, Francesco   88
VIGANONI, Giuseppe   134
VINCI, Leonardo   39
VINCI, Pietro   38
VIOTTI, Giovanni Battista   130
VITALI, Filippo   38
VIVALDI, Antonio   46

W

WAGNER, Richard   74
WEBER, Carl Maria v.   81
WEBER (medical doctor)   [129]
WEISHAUPT, Adam   23-29, 32, [37],
39, 72, 84, *141*

Z

ZANETTI, Clemente Alessandro   60
ZARLINO, Gioseffo   33, 73
ZENO, Apostolo   70, 76, 79